Special Education
DESK REFERENCE

Special Education DESK REFERENCE

Mary Buchanan, Ph.D.
Educational Consulting Services
Salt Lake City, Utah

Carol Weller, Ed.D.
Anacortes, Washington

Michelle Buchanan, Ph.D.
Moorhead State University
Moorhead, Minnesota

SINGULAR PUBLISHING GROUP, INC.
SAN DIEGO · LONDON

Singular Publishing Group, Inc.
401 West A Street, Suite 325
San Diego, California 92101-7904

19 Compton Terrace
London N1 2UN, UK

e-mail: singpub©mail.cerfnet.com
Website: http://www.singpub.com

© 1997 by Singular Publishing Group, Inc.

Typeset in 10/12 Palatino by So Cal Graphics
Printed in the United States of America by BookCrafters

Library of Congress Cataloging-in-Publication Data

Educators' desk reference for special populations / editors, Mary
    Buchanan, Carol Weller, Michelle Buchanan.
        p.   cm.
    Includes bibliographical references and index.
    ISBN 1-56593-800-3
    1. Special education—United States—Handbooks, manuals, etc.
2. Exceptional children—Services for—United States—Handbooks,
manuals, etc.   3. Mainstreaming in education—United States-
-Handbooks, manuals, etc.   I. Buchanan, Mary.   II. Weller, Carol.
III. Buchanan, Michelle.
LC3981.E45   1996
371.9—dc20   96-32706
                                                                   CIP

CONTENTS

Preface ix

CHAPTER 1 **Language Methods** 1
Suzanne Shellady, Ph.D., Pamela Pruitt, Ph.D., and
Donna Wandry, Ph.D.

CHAPTER 2 **Early Childhood Interventions** 23
Michelle Buchanan, Ph.D.

CHAPTER 3 **Methods for the Gifted** 49
J. Christine Gould, Ph.D.

CHAPTER 4 **Special Physical Education Programs** 63
Hester L. Henderson, Ph.D., and Ron W. French, Ph.D.

CHAPTER 5 **Behavioral Interventions** 81
Christine Peterson, M.Ed., Ray Bracken, ATR, M.A.,
Ada Mae Crouse RMT-BC, M.A., Sharon Hunter, M.A.,
Lynn Perry, TRS, and Patrick Toomey, ADTR

CHAPTER 6 **Methods for Learners with Hearing or
Visual Impairments** 95
Susan Naidu, Ph.D., Ruby Ryles, M.Ed., and
Michelle Buchanan, Ph.D.

CHAPTER 7 **Mathematics Methods** 109
EvaJean Pickering, Ph.D.

CHAPTER 8 **Reading Methods** 127
EvaJean Pickering, Ph.D., and AvaJane Pickering, Ph.D.

CHAPTER 9 **Written Expression Methods** 173
AvaJane Pickering, Ph.D.

CHAPTER 10 **Study Skills Strategy Instruction** 195
Pamela Pruitt, Ph.D.

CHAPTER 11 **Transition Methods** 211
Donna Wandry, Ph.D.

CHAPTER 12 **Computer Methods** 231
Renet Lovorn Bender, Ph.D.

CHAPTER 13   **Seminal Methods**   **271**
              Carol Weller, Ed.D.

              Index   **301**

CONTRIBUTORS

Dean Becker, M.A.
Henderson, Nevada

Renet Lavorn Bender, Ph.D.
Teacher's Workshop
Bishop, Georgia

Ray Bracken, ATR, M.A.
University of Utah
Neuropsychiatric Institute
Salt Lake City, Utah

Michelle Buchanan, Ph.D.
Moorhead State University
Moorhead, Minnesota

Ada Mae Crouse, RMT-BC, M.A.
University of Utah
Neuropsychiatric Institute
Salt Lake City, Utah

Ron W. French, Ph.D.
Department of Kinesiology
Texas Woman's University
Denton, Texas

J. Christine Gould, Ph.D.
Adjunct Clinical Instructor
University of Utah
Classroom Teacher
Jordan School District
Murray, Utah

Hester L. Henderson, Ph.D.
Department of Exercise and Sport Science
University of Utah
Salt Lake City, Utah

Sharon Hunter, M.A.
Brown Junior High School
Henderson, Nevada

Susan R. Naidu, Ph.D., CCC-A
Program Coordinator
Early Intervention Program for Young
Children with Hearing Loss and Their
Families
Children's Hospital and Medical Center
Seattle, Washington

Lynn Perry, TRS
Woods Cross, Utah

Christine Peterson, M.Ed.
Clark Country School District
Henderson, Nevada

AvaJane Pickering, Ph.D.
Administrative Director
Specialized Educational Programming
Services
Salt Lake City, Utah

AvaJane Pickering, Ph.D.
NeuroEducational Director
Specialized Educational Programming
Services
Salt Lake City, Utah

Pamela Pruitt, Ph.D.
Central Michigan University
Counseling and Special Education
Mount Pleasant, Michigan

Ruby Ryles, M.Ed.
Associate Director
International Braille Research Center
National Center for the Blind
Baltimore, Maryland

Suzanne Shellady, Ph.D.
Central Michigan University
Counseling and Special Education
Mount Pleasant, Michigan

Patrick Toomey, ADTR
University of Utah
Neuropsychiatric Institute
Salt Lake City, Utah

Donna Wandry, Ph.D.
Central Michigan University
Counseling and Special Education
Mount Pleasant, Michigan

Carol Weller, Ed.D.
Anacortes, Washington

PREFACE

The fields of exceptionality have broadened dramatically over the last several years. The Special Education Desk Reference (SEDR) assists educators, psychologists, physicians, students, and others who deliver services to disabled and gifted individuals.

The characteristics of the SEDR allow readers to utilize the accummulated available knowledge from the many disciplines that now serve exceptional populations. Most professionals are now required to assist individuals with diagnosis, education, rehabilitation, and community integration. The SEDR furnishes readers with the tools required to make knowledgeable decisions about appropriate methods to use with specific exceptional individuals based on age, gender, ethnicity, and educational level.

As more institutions require diagnosis for funding and societal demands for various degrees of mainstreaming grow, the SEDR provides usable methods and information based on specific exceptionalities to educate and train these populations. The SEDR provides readers with the best and most current means available to increase quality of life, achieve opportunities, and eliminate barriers for specific exceptional populations.

The SEDR identifies, illustrates, and references major methods, techniques, and strategies designed to benefit exceptional individuals. In addition, those who come in contact with exceptional persons—professionals and paraprofessionals, family, friends, social workers, medical and para-medical professionals, employers, sociologists, psychologists, as well as those in academia—will find the SEDR extremely useful. For the professionals, students, educators, and others who use this book, we know it will serve as a quality reference handbook.

CHAPTER

1

Language Methods

Suzanne Shellady, Ph.D.
Pamela Pruitt, Ph.D.
Donna Wandry, Ph.D.

CONTENTS

▶ Facilitative Play   **2**
▶ Peer-mediated Language Intervention   **3**
▶ Incidental Teaching of Language   **5**
▶ Sociodramatic Script Training   **7**
▶ Teaching Elaboration Skills   **8**
▶ "Wh" Questions   **9**
▶ Parallel Talk   **10**
▶ Storytelling   **11**
▶ Teaching Figurative Language   **12**

▶ Pragmatic Language   **13**
▶ Enhancing Nonsymbolic Communication in Individuals with Severe Disabilities   **15**
▶ Integrating Microcomputers into Language Instruction   **16**
▶ Technology: Hypermedia for Language Intervention   **18**

Language provides the means through which individuals can express their ideas, needs, and beliefs. It represents persons, actions, events, and objects and is arranged through grammatical rules that facilitate understanding of message intent (Polloway & Patton, 1993). Language is comprised of both receptive and expressive communication skills. Receptive language is the ability to understand what is being communicated. Students with disabilities often have deficits in receptive language skills. In the school environment, these students may have difficulty following directions, comprehending the meaning of concepts, perceiving figurative language, grasping multiple meanings of words, and understanding compound and complex sentences (Bos & Vaughn, 1994). Further, students with disabilities may have deficits in expressive language skills. In academic settings, these students may experience problems using appropriate grammar, speaking in compound or complex sentences, recalling the correct word to communicate a message, adapting their communication style to conform to the social context, and providing sufficient information to the listener (Bos & Vaughn, 1994). Therefore, language is comprised of an interplay between words, grammar, and the social rules that govern interactions (Polloway & Patton, 1993).

Educators should be cognizant of how language develops in school-age children and provide multiple opportunities in the classroom to facilitate language development, particularly for students who are experiencing language deficits (Bos & Vaughn, 1994; Wiig & Semel, 1984). A number of general guidelines for providing effective language instruction to students have been developed. Language instruction should occur within the context of the classroom throughout the day. Multiple opportunities exist in this setting to facilitate language development. For example, both receptive and expressive language can be developed through activities such as giving and listening to oral reports, identifying and using new vocabulary, retelling stories, and giving and following directions. The educator also can use self-talk and parallel talk to describe the activities of the class. In addition, educators and peers are in a position to model appropriate expressive and receptive skills for students experiencing language problems. The educator also can employ expansion and elaboration techniques to encourage students to use more complex language (Bos & Vaughn, 1994).

Although the strategies mentioned above are general, many language specialists have developed specific methods and procedures to enhance language acquisition and usage. This chapter presents several methods and models that attempt to reflect the changing philosophy of special education services, wherein the source of language and learning problems is not necessarily found in students, but in other variables that influence student learning. These variables can be addressed through innovative programming. Additional language interventions also can be found in this book in the chapter focusing on early intervention.

FACILITATIVE PLAY

Method: Facilitative Play

Author: Robert D. Hubbell

Source: Hubbell, R. D. (1981). *Children's language disorders: An integrated approach.* Englewood Cliffs, NJ: Prentice-Hall.

Description: Facilitative Play is based on a sociocultural approach to learning. This approach requires educators to adopt and maintain a child-centered focus throughout the intervention process. Two recommendations were made by Hubbell to successfully implement Facilitative Play to increase children's oral language skills. First, age-appropriate toys and activities should be selected to provide the child with a rich and stimulating environment. Second, topics of discussion initiated by the child in this context should receive a minimum of adult direction.

Suggested guidelines for implementing Facilitative Play in a classroom setting include the following:

1. Encourage the child to engage in a play activity of his choice. The educator should observe the child across several play activities to ensure that available free play activities are intrinsically motivating to the child. The educator needs to provide easy access to all materials.

2. The educator may elect to assume a passive role and observe the child's play or may assume a more interactive role. To introduce language usage in the play sessions, the educator may provide a narrative that exposes the child to a verbal description of what is currently occurring or about to take place in the child's play activity (e.g., "You are playing with a bear.").

An additional option for the educator is to engage in more direct interaction with the child by assuming a participative play role in the activity selected by child (e.g., "We are stacking blocks.").

The educator's choice of which option to select is governed by his comfort level and the specific skills and needs of the child. Regardless of the role chosen, the educator should adapt his discourse to match the child's spontaneous language and changes in the child's play.

3. The educator exposes the child to elaborated verbal descriptions of his or her play activities. These descriptions incorporate vocabulary and concepts (e.g., size, position) that are familiar to the child. The educator provides language models that extend the length of the student's original utterances (e.g., The student says, "Bear is fuzzy." The teacher responds, "Yes, the big bear is fuzzy and brown."). Conversely, the educator should also provide a breakdown of the elaborated verbal model he has given

to the child. This breakdown serves to enhance the child's awareness of how she may combine words to describe her play activities (e.g., The teacher says, "Yes, the big bear is fuzzy and brown. The bear is big. The bear is fuzzy. The bear is brown."). This repeated exposure capitalizes on the need for multiple exemplars to demonstrate to the child how language can be used to describe the environment.

Notes: Facilitative Play is an intervention technique that establishes a rich context from which the language of the child may evolve. Furthermore, Facilitative Play provides a safe, nurturing environment in which children are given multiple opportunities to explore, practice, and begin to refine their emerging language skills.

Educators who use Facilitative Play as an intervention technique must be extremely careful to avoid bombarding the child with repeated questions, commands, or prompts aimed at eliciting specific verbal responses. A final caution is that educators must be willing to follow the lead of the child throughout all play activities; however, this should not be interpreted as a free license for the child to engage in inappropriate or destructive behaviors.

PEER-MEDIATED LANGUAGE INTERVENTION

Method: Peer-mediated Language Intervention

Authors: Michaelene M. Ostrosky, Ann P. Kaiser, and Samuel L. Odom

Source: Ostrosky, M. M., Kaiser, A. P., & Odom, S. L. (1993). Facilitating children's social-communicative interactions through the use of peer-mediated interventions. In A. P. Kaiser & D. B. Gray (Eds.), *Enhancing children's communication: Research founda-*

tions for intervention (pp. 159–185). Baltimore: Paul H. Brookes.

Description: Peer-mediated Language Intervention is an approach which presents numerous opportunities for positive receptive/expressive language experiences for all students. Benefits of this approach include exposure of special education students to positive peer models, opportunities to use language within a natural context (e.g., interaction with age-mates versus adults), and generalization of language skills to other environments. This intervention approach incorporates research-based educational techniques, such as direct and individualized instruction and specific programmatic attention on the maintenance and generalization of language skills.

To implement a Peer-mediated Intervention, steps are categorized into four major areas: student selection criteria, preparation of nondisabled peers, specific intervention steps for students with special needs, and maintenance and generalization considerations.

1. *Student Selection Criteria.* To promote initial success of Peer-Mediated Language Interventions, Ostrosky and colleagues recommended that educators implementing this intervention limit the number of nondisabled peers and students with special needs to small groups of students as opposed to the entire class. Nondisabled peers selected to participate as language role-models in this intervention should demonstrate: (a) age-appropriate language skills, (b) willingness to accept adult direction/feedback, and (c) high rates of positive peer interaction during unstructured activities (e.g., free-play, snack-time, circle time). Participating students with special needs should demonstrate the ability to engage in sustained, appropriate free-play activities, and display rudimentary communication skills (e.g., gestures, signs, intelligible one-to two-word responses).

2. *Preparation of Nondisabled Peers.* Educators need to have a strong understanding of the repertoire of the nondisabled peers' communication skills. Prerequisite communication skills which should be demonstrated by these students include: (a) maintaining attention to materials and/or activities of interest to others, (b) identifying activities that could be used as a conversation topic during unstructured play, (c) establishing and maintaining eye contact during interactions with others, (d) providing a descriptive ongoing narrative of the activities, (e) using verbal cues that may prompt responses from the student with special needs, and (f) a willingness to accept varied communicative responses. If the nondisabled peer does not demonstrate the above-mentioned skills, the educator should provide instruction to establish these communicative behaviors prior to proceeding with Peer-mediated Intervention.

3. *Intervention Steps for Students with Special Needs.* Educators should conduct a preliminary assessment to obtain a profile of each student's present level of language competence. Communicative skills essential to the success of the intervention include the students' ability to initiate topics of conversation, respond appropriately to peers' communication prompts, and understand that language can be used to control their environment. If the student does not demonstrate these communication skills, the educator should provide direct individualized instruction. Finally, students should be placed in structured play groups to utilize their newly acquired communication skills.

4. *Maintenance and Generalization.* Educators need to promote the maintenance and generalization of communication skills across contexts. The following considerations should be embodied in Peer-Mediated Language Interventions:

a. require mastery of each communicative skill prior to teaching additional skills and/or increasing the complexity of the environment;

b. provide multiple opportunities to use language in the classroom to reinforce newly acquired skills;

c. systematically reduce the amount of educator support provided to students;

d. incorporate structured play activities into the classroom on a routine basis to encourage and expand communication efficacy of students and to provide opportunities for periodic review and corrective feedback by the teacher;

e. limit the amount of adult involvement, direction, and reinforcement in ongoing play activities and interactions of the students;

f. provide periodic "booster sessions" to review and enhance student awareness of their increased communication skills;

g. provide students with both structured and spontaneous opportunities to interact outside of the initial small group with multiple nondisabled peers who would be supportive of the communicative attempts by the student with special needs;

h. emphasize language skills that serve a functional communicative purpose for all students within the intervention.

Notes: Peer-mediated Language Intervention has utility across a wide range of students with special needs for building communicative skills. This intervention approach also has benefits for both students with and without special needs.

Educators should possess a working knowledge of social skill development and training approaches to avoid making the false assumption that enhancing the communication effectiveness of students with special needs will automatically increase the quality of their social relationships with nondisabled peers. Thus, it is essential that the educator assume full responsibility for the intervention and utilize nondisabled peers only as potential facilitators of language skills for students with special needs.

INCIDENTAL TEACHING OF LANGUAGE

Method: Incidental Teaching of Language

Authors: Betty Hart and Todd R. Risley

Source: Hart, B., & Risley, T. R. (1975). Incidental teaching of language in the preschool. *Journal of Applied Behavior Analysis, 8,* 411–420.

Description: Incidental Teaching of Language is an approach whereby children may acquire expressive language skills of labeling, description, and differentiation through single-word responses and simple sentences. The central context in which incidental teaching approaches are utilized is unstructured free play; however, incidental teaching also has been shown to have applicability in structured learning activities. The most notable benefits of this approach are that children appear to show language growth, as well as maintain and generalize their language responses once intervention is terminated. Incidental teaching incorporates educational strategies such as errorless learning, model-lead-test, and systematic prompting (i.e., most-to-least restrictive prompts).

To implement an incidental teaching approach, the steps in this intervention are organized into four general categories.

1. *Preliminary Assessment of Student Language Skills.* The educator should observe the child in the natural environment to obtain a baseline measure of the child's language skills. Once this assessment is completed, the educator must identify specific types of target behaviors for intervention. Target behaviors may range from replacement of the student's use of gestures with one-word responses to expanding student's one-word responses with complete sentences.

2. *Arranging the Environment.* Educators should provide a variety of age-appropriate

toys and/or activities within the environment to create multiple opportunities for adult-child interaction. The educator then should arrange stimulus materials so the child may see, but not access preferred materials. Thus, even though the incidental teaching situation is child-selected (e.g., the child chooses the free play activity), it is teacher-controlled because the child must request adult assistance to access preferred activities. This creates the opportunity for the educator to begin the incidental learning process.

3. *Prompting and Target Response.* The child may demonstrate a verbal or nonverbal communication attempt to secure the preferred object/activity or request adult assistance. The educator needs to engage in a series of decision-making steps regarding the extensiveness of the prompt he will provide to the child. Specific decisions to be made include:

a. whether to use the child's request as an occasion for incidental teaching;
b. whether the child's response may be shaped to approximate the identified target communicative response;
c. the form of the prompt to be delivered to the child to initiate incidental instruction. Specifically, the educator must decide whether:
  (1) the child's communicative attempt represents a desire for the educator to attend to his or her needs. The educator then demonstrates nonverbal cues such as eye contact or physically approaching the child and giving the child a questioning look. These behaviors focus the child's attention and verify the subject of the interaction for the educator.
  (2) the child's failure to attend to the nonverbal communicative prompts provided by the educator is due to a need for a verbal cue to focus the child's attention on the desired target response. For example, if the child is looking at and pointing to a truck, the educator may specifically ask the child, "Do you want the truck?" In short, the educator sets up an errorless learning situation in which the child is able to gain access to the preferred activity.

d. If the child does not respond to any communicative prompts within a specified amount of time, the educator must decide the degree of prompt to be given and provide contingent positive reinforcement for the desired response. Levels of prompts which may be used are:
  (1) The educator asks the child to imitate the desired target communicative response. For example, the educator prompts, "Do you want the truck? (verbal cue) You need to say, "I want the truck."
  (2) The educator asks the child for a partial imitation of the desired target communicative response. For example, the educator prompts, "Do you want the truck? (verbal cue) You need to say, "I want _____." The educator then waits for the child to produce the statement, "I want the truck."
  (3) The educator directly requests the desired communicative target response. For example, the educator prompts, "Do you want the truck? You need to tell me what you want." The child says, "I want the truck."
  (4) The educator provides no prompts to the child. For example, the educator asks, "What do you want?" If the child does not respond, the educator should immediately provide the least intrusive prompt required to elicit the desired response.

Maintenance and Generalization. It is essential that the educator maintain accurate child data regarding student error patterns, a profile of the level of prompts provided, and the category of communicative response used by the child. This will assist educators in systematically focusing on the child's language use across contexts and guide educational decisions regarding needed changes in the incidental teaching process.

Notes: Incidental teaching, as a language intervention, may be used with children demonstrating a wide range of communicative behaviors. For example, incidental teaching may be used to build basic descriptive language skills (e.g., labeling) to encourage children to employ more advanced communicative structures (e.g., compound sentences). Additional benefits are that parents and other children may be used as intervention agents and that the use of child-selected incidental teaching occasions provides a powerful incentive to motivate children to use language in a functional manner.

SOCIODRAMATIC SCRIPT TRAINING

Method: Sociodramatic Script Training

Authors: Howard Goldstein, Susan Wickstrom, Marilyn Hoyson, Bonnie Jamieson, and Samuel L. Odom

Source: Goldstein, H., Wickstrom, S., Hoyson, M., Jamieson, B., & Odom, S. L. (1988). Effects of sociodramatic script training on social and communicative interaction. *Education and Treatment of Children, 11,* 97–117.

Description: Sociodramatic Script Training, based on a sociocultural approach to learning, provides numerous opportunities to enhance the verbal language skills of young students. In this intervention, students learn to follow a script and act out roles in a variety of social situations. The educator facilitates generalization of the language skills by prompting the students'

verbalizations during free play. Benefits of this approach include (a) students learn daily living and social skills, (b) students exhibit higher levels of sophistication in their sociodramatic play, and (c) students are able to generalize the sociodramatic play and improved social interactions to new environmental contexts.

Suggested guidelines for implementing Sociodramatic Script Training in the classroom include the following:

1. *Structure the Environment.* The educator should create an environment that simulates a community setting that is somewhat familiar to the students (i.e., grocery store, barber shop, or restaurant). A specific area of the classroom may be set up to approximate the environment selected. For example, an area in the classroom created to resemble a barber shop might contain a chair (barber chair), chairs for the customers, magazines, a comb and brush, towels, a shoeshine cloth, a shoeshine brush, a mirror, and play money.

2. *Develop the Script.* The educator should generate a script that includes three roles for the students. For example, in the barber shop scenario, the three roles could include a barber, a shoeshiner, and a customer. The scripted social interactions among the three roles should be representative of the interactions among individuals in the community setting and should incorporate five motor/gestural responses and five verbal responses for each of the three roles. Motor/gestural responses include intentionally touching another child or making a gesture while facing another child (i.e., exchanging money). Verbal responses include talking directly to another child or responding to a question from another child (i.e., "I want a haircut" or "Do you want a shoeshine?").

3. *Developing Groups for Script Training.* The educator should divide the students into groups of three, making sure that the students in the group are as heterogeneous as possible, so that higher functioning students may serve as models. Script training

may be conducted with the triad or the training may be provided to the students individually within the triad.

4. *Script Training.* Script training is presented using direct instruction. Instruction is conducted for 8 to 10 days, with daily lessons lasting approximately 15 minutes. During the training, the educator reads the script and prompts the three children to demonstrate the responses specified for each role. In the initial training sessions, the educator guides the action by telling the students what to do and what to say. For example, the educator might say, "Billy, you are the customer. Say 'I want a haircut'." As training progresses, the educator waits longer for independent student responses and reduces her verbal prompts to "What should you say now?" The educator varies her expectations for student responses based on the ability levels of the students. The educator might prompt the verbalization "Haircut, please," from a student functioning at a low level in expressive language; but prompt a higher functioning student to say, "I would like a haircut, please. I would also like to have my shoes shined." The educator instructs the students to switch roles after they finish the script, giving each child an opportunity to practice two or three roles during the training session.

4. *Free Play.* During structured free play, which occurs each day immediately after the script training, students are encouraged to continue their dramatic play by staying in their roles. The educator's responsibility during free play is to monitor students' behaviors and provide prompts for verbalizations. The educator should gradually withdraw prompting strategies during free play.

Notes: Sociodramatic Script Training is a procedure that effectively promotes social and language interactions of children. However, educators must be aware of the importance of gradually decreasing the amount of their interactions and prompts

provided to the students during free play to increase the likelihood of generalization of the skills to other settings. Further, educators also should be cautioned that young children may quickly tire of participating in this training program, particularly if the same activity is re-enacted on a daily basis. The sociodramatic play training need not occur every day, and the educator has the option of adding new sociodramatic scenarios to provide variety for the students.

This technique was developed specifically for preschool-age children; however, it could be adapted for use with elementary-age students by increasing the level of difficulty of the scripts. The same training procedures used for the preschool setting could be implemented in elementary classrooms.

TEACHING ELABORATION SKILLS

Method: Teaching Elaboration Skills

Authors: Elizabeth Hemmersam Wiig and Eleanor Semel

Source: Wiig, E. H., & Semel, E. (1984). *Language assessment and intervention for the learning disabled.* Columbus, OH: Merrill.

Description: The use of extended verbal elaboration of detail draws on the prior experiences and information possessed by students to enhance precision and flexibility in verbal descriptions. At the onset, the process requires students to describe visual prompts in response to direct questions. During later phases of the intervention, more spontaneous descriptions of abstract events may be requested by the educator. Because the elaboration strategy is dependent on retrieval of prior information, it is essential that a high familiarity with stimuli and related vocabulary are present. A suggested intervention format includes:

1. *Model the elaboration procedure for the student.* The educator presents a familiar object or the picture of a familiar object to the student (i.e., a toy car, a doll, or a ball). The educator then tells the student about the characteristics, qualities, or functions of the object. For example, the educator might say, "This doll is pretty. She has long, curly, blond hair. She has on a bright red dress." The educator also may compare and contrast the attributes of the doll with attributes of other dolls.

2. *Ask the students questions to solicit an elaborated response.* After modeling the elaboration process, the educator asks the student direct questions about the object that requires him or her to focus on its characteristics. For example, the educator might ask the student questions such as: What kind of doll is this? What would you name this doll? What other kinds of dolls can you think of? How does this doll compare with those dolls?

3. *Elicit spontaneous verbal elaborations of details from the students.* The educator presents the students with pictures of one or more familiar objects (i.e., a stove, a tree, a house, a flower, and a bird). The educator asks questions to elicit verbal elaboration and descriptions of the characteristics of the objects. Questions may include the following: Tell me about this object. Can you tell me more about it? What more can you tell me about this object? Are there other things about this object that are important?

4. *Elicit verbal elaboration of details of events from students.* The educator shows the student pictures of familiar events such as fishing, washing dishes, and playing football. The educator may ask specific questions to elicit descriptions of situational relationships, details, and implications of events.

5. *Prompt spontaneous verbal description of familiar pictured events.* The educator shows the student a picture of a familiar event and asks nonspecific questions to elicit the student's description of details and further elaboration.

6. *Request verbal elaboration of details of an event sequence in response to direct questions.* The educator presents a visual stimulus that features a sequence of events. The educator then asks specific questions to elicit descriptions of the sequence details. If necessary, sections of the stimulus may be presented in isolation to facilitate recall.

7. *Promote spontaneous verbal description of an event sequence.* The educator again presents a visual stimulus that features a sequence of events. The educator then asks the student open-ended questions to extract a spontaneous verbal description of the sequence they have observed.

Notes: Retrieval of prior knowledge and its active linkage to current situations is a skill that enhances not only language development, but also the quality of reading comprehension and written expression. However, this link to prior knowledge relies heavily on skills related to the cognitive strategies of memory and categorization, which are often difficult for individuals with cognitive deficits. It is, therefore, essential that the educator adhere to the flow from concrete to abstract prompts and expectations, as necessary for individual students, that are suggested in this intervention model.

"WH" QUESTIONS

Method: "Wh" Questions

Authors: John Yoder, Betty Davies, Kerry Bishop, and Leslie Munson

Source: Yoder, J., Davies, B., Bishop, K., & Munson, L. (1994). Effect of adult continuing wh-questions on conversational participation in children with developmental disabilities. *Journal of Speech and Hearing Research, 37,* 193–204.

Description: As children learn to talk, they also learn to exhibit the functions of language, such as maintaining a topic. Children with developmental disabilities who are in the initial stages of language learning frequently have greater problems continuing an established topic of conversation than their nondisabled peers at the same linguistic level (Rosenberg, 1982). While children who develop normally are quickly able to overcome their initial difficulties in topic maintenance through language maturation, children with developmental disabilities may find this to be a perseverative problem that results in unsatisfying social conversations.

The use of adult topic continuance questions is suggested as a way to elicit child topic continuations for several reasons: (a) questions carry a social obligation for the child to respond, (b) questions allocate speaker turn-taking in conversations, and (c) voice intonations such as those occurring at the end of questions appear to command a child's attention, which sets the stage for further interaction. In the early stages of development, a particularly useful form of adult questions in fostering topic maintenance is wh-questions (who, what, when, where, how).

In research by the authors, the following format for the use of wh-questions was followed:

1. The topic is initiated either by the child or the educator. The child is allowed to speak first. However, if the child does not talk for a set amount of time (15 to 20 seconds), the educator may initiate a conversation. This will be most effective if the topic is one of interest to the child.

2. The educator tries to extend the topic by adding or eliciting new information about the established topic whenever possible. This topic-extending is accomplished by the use of wh-questions such as "what," "what doing," "where going," and "who" inquiries.

3. When the child responds, the educator requests more information about the topic, using wh-questions as needed, until the child ceases to respond or otherwise ends the extension of the topic.

Use of the wh-question process, according to Yoder and his colleagues, results in a greater number, as well as greater length, of responses. Use of topic-continuing wh-questions with children with developmental disabilities, however, is warranted more when assistance is needed to maintain topics. If the desire is to help a child become a more independent conversationalist, the number of wh prompts should be faded as the speaker becomes more proficient in conversing after the previous prompt.

Notes: Organizing verbalizations into a clear, relevant flow of conversation is a skill that appears to emerge with language maturity. However, for individuals who have difficulties categorizing information, retrieving vocabulary, or relating pragmatically to another person, the skill may be an insurmountable challenge. For children with developmental disabilities, techniques that seek responses to direct questions may not foster critical thought. The use of open-ended questions may serve to encourage more mature, critical interactions about a topic. The structured nature of wh-questions is effective as language interactions are developing. However, more open-ended adult topic-continuing prompts may be considered as the speaker matures in his or her ability to critically organize and demonstrate topic maintenance.

PARALLEL TALK

Method: Parallel Talk

Authors: Charles Van Riper and Lon Emerick

Source: Van Riper, C., & Emerick, L. (1990). Speech correction: An introduction to speech pathology and audiology. Englewood Cliffs, NJ: Prentice-Hall.

Description: Suggested as a clinical intervention for individuals with severe deficits in language, Parallel Talk is an example of expanding clinical practices into other settings. Parallel Talk is defined as a technique in which the person who is modeling provides a running commentary on what the individual with oral language difficulties is doing, perceiving, or possibly feeling. The purpose of Parallel Talk is to help the child understand how language can be used to talk about his or her actions and the surrounding environment (Bos & Vaughn, 1994). This practice is a variation on the concept of self-talk, in which the person who is modeling is verbalizing on his or her own actions with the intent of facilitating imitation and subsequent free speech.

In contrast, Parallel Talk demands that the person delivering the intervention (educator, parents, etc.) verbalizes not only his or her own thoughts and actions, but also those of the child. The primary challenge is to time the verbalization in immediate anticipation of or simultaneously to the action being described, so linkages can be more readily recognized by the child.

As with self-talk, the ultimate goal of Parallel Talk is imitation and subsequent free speech. With persons with severe language delays or deficits, the free speech stage may reveal itself first through the vocalization of a word by the client when the educator, parent, or clinician fumbles or postpones an utterance within a phrase. At this point, the person leading the intervention must again time the pause to reflect the exact moment at which a previously modeled word-emotion/action linkage is needed for the appropriate verbalization to fill in the pause.

Notes: Because oral language growth is based primarily on imitation during initial developmental stages, the benefit of using such a structured modeling technique is apparent for persons with severe language delays or deficits. With close cooperation between home, school, and clinic, it is clear that opportunities for constant language modeling are greatly enhanced. It is interesting to note, however, that the use of simple, short, baby-like phrases and sentences ("I cold," "Jimmy fall down") is recommended as a part of this intervention, rather than the modeling of complete and appropriate structures. Also, because of the possible simultaneous use of this strategy by multiple providers, caution may need to be exercised in making sure that vocabularies and word banks are consistently used.

STORYTELLING

Method: Storytelling

Author: Jackie Peck

Source: Peck, J. (1989). Using storytelling to promote language and literacy development. *The Reading Teacher, 42*, 138–141.

Description: Storytelling as an art form has been defined as the oral interpretation of a literary, traditional, or personal experience story according to Peck. The practice has implications for the classroom teacher in facilitating both receptive and expressive oral language development, as well as instructional benefits for language growth through written expression.

The use of Storytelling can take two different perspectives in the classroom, depending on whether the educator or the students are the storytellers. When the teacher functions as storyteller, students build skills in effective and critical listening. They also develop a sense of story, during which they are able to anticipate or predict coming events. Further, students develop evaluative listening skills in discriminating critically between story genres and storytelling styles.

When students perform as storytellers, opportunities for development in oral language and pragmatics, long recognized as an indicator in the effective development of literacy, are provided. Participation in the Storytelling process assists students in developing poise, as well as an understanding of the effects of appropriate voice pitch, volume, and timing. In addition, Storytelling permits the student to perceive the social feedback of listeners through their facial expressions, body language, and oral responses.

Peck suggested a practical format for using Storytelling in the classroom. The format also incorporates the related instructional practice of story mapping and is conducted as follows:

1. Following the telling of a folk story, the teacher assists the students in mapping the action of the story through a visual analysis of the beginning event, the problem, attempts to solve it, and the solution.

2. Students are guided to mentally map their own stories that reflect the topic of the original folk story, paying attention to characters and the components of the story structure (beginning event, problem, etc.) that will assist them in relating their new stories. Mental mapping as opposed to written mapping is encouraged to prevent the memorization of any lines in the telling of the new story.

3. In preparing students to relate their own stories, the educator discusses the effects of different vocalizations, gestures, movement, and eye contact on the impact of Storytelling. A line of dialogue from the original folk tale can be recited in various voices, with students encouraged to echo the different styles. Appropriateness of gestures (e.g., natural versus overdone) is modeled and practiced, as are examples of body movement such as leaning forward for emphasis or recoiling in fear.

4. Students are then grouped in pairs or triads to provide audiences for each other. Stories are told in the groups, and listeners are encouraged to give critical feedback and the tellers make revisions based on that feedback.

Notes: The natural act of Storytelling contains many benefits for the development of the mechanics as well as the pragmatics of oral language. In addition, the framework of stories can provide a structure for enhancing reading comprehension as well as related written expression. Additional benefits that were not mentioned by the author are building word retrieval abilities and "thinking on one's feet." These have been recognized as beneficial by-products of informal drama in the classroom, and are often difficult tasks for students with cognitive disabilities. For these students, however, cognitive strategies such as imagery and mental story mapping may have to be modified to more concrete, visual tasks during the format suggested by Peck.

TEACHING FIGURATIVE LANGUAGE

Method: Teaching Figurative Language

Authors: Elissa L. Fisher, June Miller White, and James H. Fisher

Source: Fisher, E. L., White, J. M., & Fisher, J. H. (1984). Teaching figurative language. *Academic Therapy, 19,* 403–407.

Description: Many adolescents with mild disabilities encounter difficulties recognizing and interpreting figurative language. Figurative language, commonly used in everyday communication, consists of slang, sarcasm, idioms, metaphors, similes, and proverbs. Students with mild disabilities often interpret these types of expressions literally and concretely, resulting in confused or inappropriate actions or responses. Fisher, White, and Fisher stated that educators should provide instruction in the use of figurative language. They recommended the following procedures be employed to facilitate students' recognition and understanding of figurative communication:

1. *Early Work.* The educator should lay the groundwork for figurative language instruction by helping the student to differentiate between literal and figurative statements. The educator must first make sure the student understands literal statements. Fisher, White, and Fisher suggest that the educator provide the student with a literal statement, such as "If I ask you to get up from your seat, go to the window, open the window, and return to your seat, do you know what I mean?" After the student gives the educator a positive or negative response, he or she is asked to demonstrate the series of instructions. Fisher, White, and Fisher recommend that the educator continue instruction with a statement, such as "When I say that you drive me up a wall, do I mean that you and I will get into a car together and we will drive the car up a wall?" Most students realize how ridiculous this translation of the statement would be. The authors suggest that the next step of instruction is to give the students a figurative statement, such as "You drive me up a wall" or "You are pulling my leg," and ask the students to examine the statement and determine its meaning.

Further, Fisher, White, and Fisher recommend that a statement, such as "You drive me up a wall" or "You are pulling my leg," be selected by the students to be used throughout the year as a "special example" to encourage the students to think in a different way about the figurative and literal interpretation of language.

2. *Practice.* After the students have been given instruction on literal and figurative language, the educator should provide multiple opportunities for students to practice figurative and literal interpretations. To implement instruction, the educator may use old sayings, such as "Don't judge a book by its cover" or "Strike while the iron is hot." The students are presented with an old saying, directed to think of their "special example," and together discuss and analyze the saying to determine its meaning. Students also should be encouraged to find examples of figurative language in their written materials and talk with each other about the interpretations. The educator should create and maintain an environment in which students feel comfortable with this type of exploration and know they will not be criticized or humiliated.

3. *Extension.* Understanding figurative language provides a vehicle through which cognitive skills in other subjects can be developed. In the content areas, such as science and social studies, analytical thinking can be examined on three levels: (a) literal—the meaning of communication is very clear; it means what it says; (b) interpretative—the meaning of the communication requires the students' own interpretation of the words; and (c) critical—the meaning of the statement requires discussion or research and calls for agreement or disagreement with the author's statement.

Notes: Throughout the implementation of Teaching Figurative Language, the educator should work slowly and consistently and encourage students to "think differently" about the meanings of words and phrases. An environment should be created in which students are free to explore multiple ways that words and phrases can be used and interpreted and realize there will be no deleterious effects of not immediately understanding the figurative communication. In addition, educators are encouraged to incorporate figurative language instruction throughout the curriculum on a daily basis, rather than as an isolated topic. The educator should be cautioned, however, that instruction in figurative language is most appropriate for older students who typically understand the literal interpretation of communication, but who have difficulty with more abstract meanings.

PRAGMATIC LANGUAGE

Method: Pragmatic Language

Authors: Nancy J. Spekman and Froma P. Roth

Source: Spekman, N., & Roth, F. P. (1988). An intervention framework for learning disabled students with communication disorders. *Learning Disabilities Quarterly, 11,* 248–256.

Description: Individuals with learning disabilities often exhibit difficulties in language and/or communication. Successful communication is predicated not only on the acquisition of semantic and syntactic aspects of language, but also the use of appropriate pragmatic skills, or the rules governing the social use of language. Because social competence is not necessarily linked directly to linguistic proficiency, the area of pragmatics is recognized as an integral component of oral communication that warrants specific intervention.

Spekman and Roth organized their framework of pragmatic skills into three primary components: communicative intentions, presupposition, and social organization of discourse. They also identified social context as the element within which the three components are couched. Within the framework, each of the three primary components carries its own characteristics as well as a shared set of intervention strategies for practitioners.

Communicative Intentions. This component of Pragmatic Language involves the communicative intentions, or message, that the speaker desired to convey. The conveyance may take the form of gestures, voice intonations and pitch, or linguistic structures such as words, phrases, and sentences. The range and subtleties of these "messages" demand varying degrees of inference on the part of both the speaker and the listener. Students with language impairments tend to demonstrate a limited repertoire of communicative intentions.

Presupposition. This component of Spekman and Roth's framework addresses the need for a speaker to formulate a message in relation to the specific informational needs of the listener. That is, the quality of utterances regarding (a) the breadth of information offered and (b) the ability to take the perspective of the listener is key to the concept of presupposition. Information that is both explicit and implicit in the message must be attended to if full understanding between speaker and listener is to occur. An example of inappropriate use of presupposition in social discourse is the overuse of referent pronouns without an established frame of reference for the listener. A simpler example is the choice of degree of formality to be used with particular listeners. Depending on the proximity of the two interlocutors, the availability of feedback regarding understanding of the message changes (e.g., visual and verbal versus verbal alone) and the subsequent opportunities to modify the message are affected. This feedback variable, as well as the possible challenges of some children with learning and language impairments to predict listener needs, appears to warrant instructional intervention.

Social Organization of Discourse. Turn-taking in conversations demands the initiation, maintenance, and termination of dialogue and topic between and among partners. This aspect of dynamic language interaction involves skills in both speaker and listener roles and the ability to move smoothly between the two. It has been posited that individuals with learning and language impairments tend to assume less assertive roles during interactions and, therefore, do not assume control of the conversations in maintaining, altering, or terminating the topic.

Intervention Guidelines and Strategies. Pragmatics difficulties may be due to deficits in any one or more of the component skills or problems related to the integration of those components. Spekman and Roth stressed the importance of basing programming decisions on definite strength and need patterns reflective of the framework's components. Therefore, they suggested several guidelines and principles for the development and implementation of resultant communication intervention programs.

TEACHING IN THE COMMUNICATIVE CONTEXT. The generalization of skills traditionally plagues language interventions with students with disabilities. Spekman and Roth point to two major instructional errors committed in such intervention: (a) the tendency to teach skills in atypical situations or settings and (b) the assumption that generalization will occur automatically. They, therefore, suggest the following guidelines for providing multiple instructional contexts:

1. Provide variation in the physical settings, moving from clinical settings (therapy rooms or classrooms) to relevant nonschool environments in the community.
2. Vary the communication partner, so that experiences with different listening audiences can occur. Peers, younger children, community workers, school personnel, parents, and other persons relevant to the child's individual environments should be included in interventions.
3. Provide interventions in the contexts and settings of most interest to the child. In addition, the teacher or interventionist should remain alert to naturally occurring intervention opportunities.

RESPONDING TO COMMUNICATIVE INTENTIONS. Teachers and others involved in the intervention must learn to make a distinction between the functions of messages and their syntactic quality when offering feedback, because violations of syntax do not necessarily negatively affect successful communication. If the focus of the intervention is on pragmatic skills, the communicative intent should be the basis of feedback, regardless of syntactic accuracy.

ACCEPTING ELLIPTICAL FORMS. Ellipsis refers to the process that reduces or eliminates redundant information during discourse. During normal conversation, it is considered acceptable to give abbreviated sentences or phrases in response to inquiry. The response is no less understandable, and does not require a full sentence structure to relay the crucial information of the message. For example, when asked where a student is going, the acceptable response might be "Principal's office." Demanding a full sentence structure from students, a common practice, may, therefore, be an actual violation of normal discourse. Persons offering language intervention, then, should be cautious to accept and respond to appropriate elliptical forms.

UTILIZING DIRECT INTERVENTION TECHNIQUES. Although the most effective instruction in pragmatic skills occurs in naturalistic environments, Spekman and Roth caution that practitioners should not assume that merely manipulating the environment will be sufficient to teach necessary rules of language. They suggest the incorporation of direct instruction techniques to lend form and structure to skill acquisition in the student's environments. For example, practitioners may make use of modeling, cuing, expansion, and reinforcement to introduce and guide practice in the pragmatic skill being addressed. The exposure to the new skill, then, is guided not only by discovery but by an explicit statement of rules to be learned. Once the rules are familiar, they may themselves serve as a prompt to generalization of a new skill in a different environment. The rules, therefore, are not to be memorized merely for the sake of memorization, but as a basis for generalization and higher order conscious awareness that can guide further new situational demands.

TEACHING FOR REGULARITY OR DIVERSITY. This principle of the framework attends to the frequent changes in the rules and meanings of utterances. Besides the obvious possibility of confusion related to slang vocabulary, there also is an inherent danger in presenting individual sentence forms as being only for one purpose. For example, the use of questions can serve different functions depending on how they are worded and which words are stressed. Questions, therefore, can go beyond the function of information-seeking.

Notes: The Spekman and Roth framework enjoys the benefit of being based on extensive research conducted by the authors and others. It is therefore indicative of best practices in the area of language intervention. However, no specific guidelines are offered regarding how to adapt the components to students functioning at varying linguistic, social, and cognitive skills levels. The method is best used as a framework for teachers and other practitioners to use when considering the precepts on which to base their more specific interventions in pragmatic language skills.

ENHANCING NONSYMBOLIC COMMUNICATION

Method: Enhancing Nonsymbolic Communication in Individuals with Severe Disabilities

Authors: E. Siegel-Causey and D. Guess

Source: Siegel-Causey, E., & Guess, D. (1989). *Enhancing nonsymbolic communication interactions among learners with severe disabilities.* Baltimore: Paul H. Brookes.

Description: This method addresses the needs of learners with severe and profound language delays. Many individuals with severe and multiple disabilities do not use conventional symbolic systems (e.g., verbal or sign language) to communicate. Nonsymbolic means of communication are used instead (e.g., gestures). Expanding nonsymbolic communication repertoires assists learners in developing a means to get their needs met, influence others, and actively participate in social interaction.

This approach emphasizes the reciprocal and interpersonal nature of communication and the need to understand and facilitate the development of functional communication repertoires. Communications may be goal-directed or may give others information about the individual's emotional state, level of arousal, or interest in the environment. Caregivers and service providers must learn to recognize and understand nonsymbolic forms of communication. Some forms may be conventional (e.g., pointing to request) and others unconventional (e.g., banging a cup on the table to request more juice). Forms of nonsymbolic communication include generalized movement and changes in muscle tone, vocalizations, facial expressions, and orientation; pausing, touching, acting on objects; assuming certain bodily positions or going to places in the environment; using depictive actions, withdrawal, aggression, and self-injurious behavior. After learning to recognize and accurately interpret this form of communicative behavior, caregivers and service providers learn to respond appropriately. In doing so, the individual learns that the purposes of the communication and the effect it has on the recipient are the same.

Every effort is made to encourage communicative behavior and to promote a shared understanding between the learner and others. Because intervention emphasizes the reciprocal, shared nature of communicative exchange, it is critical that interaction not be dominated by the adult or the learner. Communicative exchanges are conversations characterized by (a) a joint focus of attention on a topic, (b) balance in leading and responding to the other, (c) development of a topic over time, and (d) as a means for meeting social needs. The individual learns that it is engagement with another through communication that results in predictable and pleasurable outcomes.

Service providers and caregivers learn to respond to the learners' communications in a contingent and personal manner. In addition, they learn to use a repertoire of nonsymbolic communications in interactions with learners. Adults may use auditory, visual, tactile, kinesthetic, or olfactory modalities to communicate in nonsymbolic as well as symbolic ways. Intervention focuses on expanding the repertoire of nonsymbolic communication skills of service providers and caregivers. When a breakdown in communication between adult and learner occurs, intervention consists of strengthening the receptive and expressive language skills of both parties, rather than altering the behavior of the learner.

Communicative interventions take place in natural contexts with nondisabled as well as disabled peers, utilizing materials that are age appropriate, functional, and meaningful. Compensation is made for auditory or visual loss through alternate sensory input. Five instructional guidelines provide a format for applying procedures in a way that promotes trust and active, meaningful, interpersonal communication between service providers, caregivers, and learners. Elements of each of the following guidelines are incorporated in communication interventions: (a) developing nurturance, (b) enhancing sensitivity, (c) increasing opportunities for communication, (d) sequencing experiences, and (e) utilizing movement.

INTEGRATING MICROCOMPUTERS INTO LANGUAGE INSTRUCTION

Method: Integrating Microcomputers into Language Instruction

Authors: Sylvia Steiner and Vicki Lord Larson

Source: Steiner, S., & Larson, V. L. (1991). Integrating microcomputers into language intervention with children. *Topics in Language Disorders, 11,* 18–30.

Description: Computer-based instruction has become an increasingly integral compo-

nent of general and special education during the last decade. The number of computers being used in educational settings has been doubling every year, and computers can be found in well over half of the special education classrooms in this country. Further, the increase in number and use of computers is expected to continue (Hammill & Bartel, 1995). For general guidelines on computer use and software selection, see the chapter titled, Computer Methods.

The computer is a powerful instructional tool for providing language instruction to students with disabilities. However, computer instruction often is underutilized and/or used inappropriately in educational settings. Therefore, educators must become proficient in the areas of computer hardware and software and employing this technology for language instruction. Steiner and Larson provided the following seven guidelines to enhance language instruction through computer technology:

1. *Focus of Intervention.* The educator should focus on the individual needs of students when deciding on whether or not to use computer instruction. Only when instruction would be enhanced through the use of a computer, should this type of instruction be incorporated into a student's educational program.

2. *Embedding Computerized Activities Within the Language Program.* Steiner and Larson recommend that an integrative model be adopted in which the computer is incorporated into a student's educational plan based on its ability to facilitate the achievement of student goals. Computer interventions should be viewed only as one available alternative to increase the variety of activities to promote student learning.

3. *Theoretical Considerations.* The educator should choose computer applications that are based on and consistent with his or her theoretical principles. The educational principles of the educator should not be compromised when integrating the computer into classroom instruction. For example, Steiner and Larson state that drill and practice activities, often featured in computer programs, should not be used if the educator is uncomfortable with and does not use other types of drill and practice materials.

4. *Stimuli, Responses, and Reinforcements.* Computers frequently are recommended for instruction because of their ability to control stimulus and reinforcement delivery. However, the educator should evaluate the software and determine its appropriateness for each student, consider the types of responses required and the appropriateness of the reinforcement given.

5. *Roles of Student and Educator.* Steiner and Larson state that computer instruction is most effective when the student and the educator are both seated at the computer, engaging actively together in the learning activity and verbalizing about the content. The educator should make every effort to assist the student to extract maximum value from the program.

6. *Individualization.* Computer hardware and software generally are not individualized appropriately. Therefore, in purchasing hardware, the educator should consider a color monitor, a printer, and a single-switch input device to be essential. Other features may need to be included based on the individual needs of the students. Computer software is flexible and can be used to meet multiple needs and goals of students. The educator may also consider developing his or her own computer programs.

7. *Designer and Generic Software.* Designer software has been generated specifically to enhance the development of students' language. This type of software, however, is relatively scarce, expensive, and useful for only a limited number of students. Generic programs are less expensive, effective with larger numbers of children, and adaptable to meet individual needs of students. Steiner and Larson point out that educators should be aware that generic software may have the capability of meeting multiple needs of students, regardless of the software developer's description of intended use.

Notes: Computer technology can be used in the educational setting to provide language intervention to both groups and individual students. Computers also can be effectively employed with students from the early preschool age through adolescence. The educator's major responsibility is to match the technology with the individual goals of each student.

Steiner and Larson state that educators often use the computer as reinforcement, promising that students may use the computer as a reward for good work. The authors caution that educators should avoid using a computer in this manner because the power of the computer for instruction is being wasted. Further, the computer is not being integrated into the language intervention program.

In addition, Steiner and Larson state that optimum use of computers only can be achieved only by educators who are knowledgeable about computer technology and are able to integrate this technology into language instruction in the classroom. Therefore, it is essential that educators receive appropriate training in educational technology.

HYPERMEDIA FOR LANGUAGE INSTRUCTION

Method: Technology: Hypermedia for Language Intervention

Author: E. William Clymer

Source: Clymer, E. W. (1991). Using hypermedia to develop and deliver assessment or intervention services. *Topics in Language Disorders, 11,* 50–64.

Description: Hypermedia is the use of data, graphics, video, text, and voice in a hypertext system, wherein information is linked together to facilitate easy movement from one component to another. It makes use of hypercard "stacks," hypertext databases, and interactive systems in preparing intervention tools that allow for proactive participation by the user. This varies from traditional computer-assisted instruction by its focus on a user-activated and -navigated display change rather than a computer-driven format in which the user simply reacts to predetermined linear pathways.

Hypermedia presentations provide innovative ways for individuals to practice both receptive and expressive language skills. They present an opportunity to be flexible in organizing the assembling information to create new formats that meet individual needs of persons receiving language intervention. For example, Clymer described one of the software packages he and his colleagues had been developing. It would allow animated sequences of points of articulation to be used, so practitioners could show accurate visual images of appropriate articulation positions to clients. In addition, the use of videodisc has been indicated for effective instruction in speech-reading and sign language (Sims, 1988; Slike, Chiavacci, & Hobbis, 1989). Hypercard formats that include voice capabilities are one means by which persons with aphasia or other language-production limitations can assemble words and phrases that are then relayed through computer voice synthesis. Hypermedia also can be beneficial in assessing articulation skills through the use of screen displays which allow clients to interface with the program and receive immediate scores from the computer.

Clymer suggested a model for development of hypermedia applications for use in speech and language interventions. The most comprehensive hypermedia presentations can be developed through the efforts of a hypermedia development team consisting of content specialists, an instructional developer, a computer programmer, graphic designer, an evaluation specialist, a writer-editor, and television production support personnel. If all of the desired members are not available to the practitioner, it is possible to create suitable hypermedia tools by following a set of procedures common to most expert developers of software packages. The primary components of the instructional development process around which this model are built are: (a) analysis, (b) design, and (c) implementation.

Analysis. The primary task at this stage is an understanding of the problem being encountered, and the primary factors that influence the student's ability to communicate effectively. Hypermedia may be the most effective approach if the student needs fast access to a large number of graphic images, audio segments, or video segments. Aspects of the analysis stage are (a) instructional goal development, (b) client characteristic identification, and (c) task analysis.

INSTRUCTIONAL GOAL DEVELOPMENT. It is vital that a clear statement be developed at this stage regarding the specific criterion-stated instructional goal for the student. The intended performance or outcome for the student, not the process of the instruction, must be the focus at this point.

CLIENT CHARACTERISTIC IDENTIFICATION. By learning as much as possible about each client/student, it is easier to determine effective motivators for skill training for specific individuals. This allows the formation of an instructional context, such as rock music or poetry, in which to couch the hypermedia presentation content. The presence of an interesting context combined with an exciting interactive tool, serves as a great motivator for performance.

TASK ANALYSIS. A hierarchal list of subordinate and terminal skills within a specific language skill should be developed; this will guide the stepping stones that the client must complete in the presentation's sequence. In addition, the task analysis should determine the different pathways users can travel through a hypermedia presentation, because the computer applications give a certain amount of freedom in reaching given points. Therefore, the task analysis should reflect different levels of users' autonomy.

DESIGN. At this point, the language intervention software program is developed based on accurate performance goals and student/client characteristics. The design phase incorporates (a) objectives, (b) evaluation instruments, (c) instructional strategy, (d) media selection, and (e) lesson writing.

OBJECTIVES. Short-term, measurable objectives (STOs) that address goals developed during the analysis phase are created. These will be very similar to the goals and STOs used in regular types of language skill instruction; only the approach to teaching these skills will vary through the use of computer applications. In the use of hypermedia presentations, the STOs will be directly represented in the sequence of performance paths of the software program.

EVALUATION INSTRUMENTS. As with any intervention, students/clients must be evaluated in their ability to demonstrate the desired skills. Clymer stated that the "evaluation items are particularly important in hypermedia applications because the general instructional format calls for the user to respond to questions and requests for responses in order to take advantage of the branching capabilities of the program" (p. 61). Evaluation should (a) assess prerequisite skills, (b) include practice or embedded questions, (c) evaluate student readiness to move to the next level of instruction, and (d) include items for summative determination of the student's goal acquisition.

INSTRUCTIONAL STRATEGY AND MEDIA SELECTION. A complete instructional strategy for attaining specified objectives include (a) preinstruction activities, (b) instructional presentation, (c) student participation, (d) testing, and (e) follow-up. The most appropriate media selection for incorporating this instructional continuum is then determined. At this point, the developer should question whether specific accommodations to learner styles are necessary and whether the development of a related hypermedia product is the most cost-effective way of meeting specific language deficit needs.

The lesson writing phase then results in a format that reflects task analysis skill hierarchies, response expectations, and feedback responses.

Implementation. At this final phase, a prototype version is implemented with clients and feedback is offered. Any obvious programming and logic errors are then revised.

Notes: As the use of technology increases, it will be necessary for practitioners to educate themselves about new and innovative practices that will benefit their students/clients. The use of hypermedia in language development interventions will allow not only for exciting visual and auditory avenues to increase oral language proficiency, but also increased learner motivation through user-navigated software. This approach has perhaps more obvious implications for the development of phonemics, syntax, and semantics than for the social aspect of language development. Because of the currently limited opportunities for computer programs to provide accurate naturalistic situations relevant to particular individuals, the use of hypermedia is questionable at this time in its effectiveness in the development and generalized use of social language skills.

REFERENCES

Bos, C. S., & Vaughn, S. (1994). *Strategies for teaching students with learning and behavior problems.* Needham Heights, MA: Allyn and Bacon.

Hammill, D. D., & Bartel, N. R. (1995). *Teaching students with learning and behavior problems.* Austin, TX: Pro-Ed.

Polloway, E. A., & Patton, J. R. (1993). *Strategies for teaching learners with special needs* (5th ed.). New York: Macmillan.

Rosenberg, S. (1982). The language of the mentally retarded: Development, processes, and intervention. In S. Rosenberg (Ed.), *Handbook of applied psycholinguistics* (pp. 329–392). Hillsdale, NJ: Lawrence Erlbaum.

Sims, D. G. (1988). Video methods for speechreading instruction. *The Volta Review, 90,* 273–288.

Slike, S. B., Chiavacci, J. P., & Hobbis, D. H. (1989). The efficiency and effectiveness of an interactive videodisc system to teach sign language vocabulary. *American Annals of the Deaf, 134,* 288–290.

Wiig, E. H., & Semel, E. (1984). *Language assessment and intervention for the learning disabled.* Columbus, OH: Merrill.

CHAPTER

2

Early Childhood Interventions

Michelle Buchanan, Ph.D.

CONTENTS

▶ Activity-based Intervention   **25**
▶ Transdisciplinary Play-based
  Intervention   **26**
▶ Systemic Approach to Infant
  Intervention   **27**
▶ Montessori Method: Early Childhood   **28**
▶ Systematic (Direct) Instructional
  Methods   **28**
▶ Environmental Organization   **30**
▶ Milieu Language Intervention   **32**
▶ INclass REActive Language (INREAL)   **33**
▶ Enabling and Empowering Families   **34**
▶ Home Service Delivery Paradigm   **34**
▶ Child Relationship Enhancement
  Family Therapy (CREFT)   **35**

▶ An Interactional Approach to
  Working With Parents and Infants   **37**
▶ Transactional Intervention
  Program (TRIP)   **38**
▶ Enhanced Milieu Language
  Intervention   **39**
▶ Language Interaction Intervention   **40**
▶ Developmentally Based Instruction   **40**
▶ Project Participation   **41**
▶ Encouraging the Use of
  Mastery Behaviors in Play   **42**
▶ Self-management   **43**
▶ Peer-mediated Interventions   **44**
▶ Correspondence Training   **44**
▶ Affection Training   **45**

This chapter describes methods for aiding the development and functioning of infants and young children with special needs. Emphasis is on methods that promote development in everyday contexts. Some methods assist children in using behaviors and patterns of interaction that are identified as important for each child. Other methods support child development by supporting family functioning.

In a review of literature on infant intervention methods, Yoder (1990) speaks of three primary approaches to intervention. This conceptual framework may help the reader make distinctions between the infant, toddler, and preschool intervention methods included in this chapter. Methods for intervention may be characterized by one or a combination of three approaches:

1. direct intervention through nonsocial means;
2. direct intervention through social means;
3. indirect intervention through support to the family.

Yoder refers to the first two approaches as direct interventions because the child experiences the impact of the intervention through direct application of methods. Direct interventions may be **nonsocial** or **social**. An example of a nonsocial intervention is the effective arrangement of materials or space. Social interventions are events or actions mediated by parents or professionals.

Socially mediated direct intervention methods can be conceptualized as lying on a continuum with **responsive interaction** methods on one end and **direct instructional** methods on the other end. **Responsive interaction** methods are based on observations of the naturally occurring interactions between competent caregivers and young children. These methods support the child's highest levels of functioning by responding to the child's focus of attention. Adults seek to maintain balance in interactive exchanges with infants and young children by minimizing adult direction, en-

couraging child initiative and responding to the child's activities and communicative attempts. Variations on these methods include arranging the environment to prompt child engagement and communication or prompting the child to use slightly more advanced developmental behavior to achieve a self-selected goal.

In contrast, socially mediated direct instruction methods are designed to teach specific skills through adult-planned and directed activities. **Direct instruction** methods emphasize the learning and generalized use of cognitive and social behavior in many contexts. Behaviorally oriented direct instruction methods promote generalization by teaching children to apply general response classes to a variety of stimulus classes and by teaching behaviors in the contexts in which they are expected to occur.

Indirect intervention approaches include family-focused intervention methods that give indirect support for infants and young children with special needs by providing support to the family system. These intervention methods are becoming increasingly popular in response to a paradigmatic shift in the field of early childhood special education away from child-centered intervention and toward a family-centered intervention process.

Early intervention methods are used in home, hospital, community, child care, clinical, and preschool settings by a variety of individuals including family members, community caregivers, the child's peers, educators, therapists, social workers, and health care providers. Methods are most effectively applied in the context of the child's daily routines and activities.

The Division of Early Childhood (DEC) of the Council for Exceptional Children recently published a document on recommended practices for early intervention. This document includes recommendations for selecting methods for use with children and their families (DEC, 1993). Practitioners are urged to select methods that (a) support and promote family values and participation, (b) follow the lead of and are responsive to children's behavior, (c) are informed by relevant disciplines, (d) can be applied in various everyday settings, (e) allow for multiple goals to be addressed in a single activity, and (f) provide balance in child and adult-directed learning.

Methods selected for use should promote the acquisition of new behaviors as well as the fluent use of learned behaviors. They should support the maintenance and generalization of behaviors in the whole variety of contexts in which they are expected to occur.

If two methods are deemed to be equally effective, the one that is most normalized (i.e., most similar to that used with typically developing children), least intrusive (i.e., allowing the child and family the most freedom to initiate and make choices), and easiest to use should be selected.

ACTIVITY-BASED INTERVENTION

Method: Activity-based Intervention

Authors: Diane Bricker and Julie W. Cripe

Source: Bricker, D., & Cripe, J. W. (1992). *An Activity-based approach to early intervention.* Baltimore: Paul H. Brookes.

Description: Activity-based Intervention consists of a blend of theoretical orientations and strategies from early childhood education and traditional behavior analytic approaches. The approach was inspired by a desire to model intervention practice on the natural instruction that young children typically receive from caregivers in daily life. Intervention goals and objectives are embedded and targeted in everyday routines and other life experiences of young children with disabilities. According to Bricker and Cripe (1992):

Activity-based intervention is a child-directed, transactional approach that embeds intervention on children's individual goals and objectives in routine planned, or child-initiated activities, and uses logically occurring antecedents and consequences to develop functional and generative skills. (p. 40)

The approach is designed around several principles including (a) targeting multiple objectives from different developmental domains in a single everyday activity; (b) using child-directed activity as a context for teaching skills; (c) teaching functional skills in a variety of everyday settings to promote generalization of learned behavior; and (d) using instructional strategies that are familiar to caregivers and can be easily adopted by them. These principles promote integrated instruction in meaningful contexts. They eliminate the need for artificial reinforcers or supports for behaviors. Instructional strategies are based on common caregiving behavior and can be easily adopted by caregivers without disrupting family child-rearing practices and routines.

Activity-based Intervention sets a broad frame for responding to child and family concerns and interests. Because goals, objectives, and the intervention process are generic in nature, this approach lends itself well for use with families and groups who are culturally diverse.

Interventionists guide children's activities in nonintrusive ways and organize the environment to support development of new and developmentally more advanced behaviors. Bricker and Cripe offer the following guidelines for using Activity-based Intervention:

1. Children are encouraged to initiate activities whenever possible.
2. Interventionists follow the child's lead unless the child's behavior is too repetitive, regressive, or does not lead to progress toward Individualized Educational Plan/Individualized Family Service Plan goals.

3. Interventionists plan activities that hold meaning for children.
4. Children's engagement is sustained by changing and/or rearranging the environment when motivation appears to wane.
5. Interventionists observe child behavior and take advantage of opportunities to enhance problem-solving skills.

Interventionists use a variety of specific strategies to prompt child engagement, action, communication, problem-solving, and other targeted skills. These include introducing novelty into activities and placing desirable objects out of reach. Time delay and other prompting procedures are used to encourage child initiation and responding.

Monitoring the effects of intervention is a critical component of Activity-based Intervention. Child and family outcomes are monitored daily, weekly, quarterly, and annually. All intervention decisions are data-based. Four forms of data collection are recommended: (a) observation, (b) rating scales, (c) permanent products, and (d) anecdotal records.

Activity-based Intervention provides a model for transdisciplinary teamwork. Interventionists function as team members, who work closely with caregivers and other professionals, to provide an integrated and cohesive program for the child and family.

Notes: In many ways, Activity-based Intervention represents current preferred practice by professionals in the field of early childhood special education. The approach is compatible with typical caregiving practices as well as early childhood education practices. It may be used by parents, daycare providers, early childhood educators, and other service providers to assist young children with special needs and their families. The approach provides a process for linking assessment to intervention and to ongoing monitoring of child and family outcomes. Parents and professionals from a va-

riety of disciplines will find this approach useful in bringing structure and coherence to an intervention program.

TRANSDISCIPLINARY PLAY-BASED INTERVENTION

Method: Transdisciplinary Play-based Intervention

Author: Toni W. Linder

Source: Linder, T. W. (1993). *Transdisciplinary play-based intervention: Guidelines for developing a meaningful curriculum for young children.* Baltimore: Paul H. Brookes.

Description: Transdisciplinary Play-based Intervention (TPBI) provides guidelines for strengthening developmental processes and increasing functional behavior of young children with developmental delays from infancy to 6 years of age. Transdisciplinary Play-based Intervention is based on theories related to child development, including the works of Piaget, Vygotsky, Freud, Erickson, Bandura, Fischer, and Lewis and Starr. According to Linder (1993), "These theories contribute to a philosophy of intervention that is child-centered, family-focused, peer-oriented, culturally and developmentally relevant and based on pleasurable play interactions" (p. 13).

Transdisciplinary Play-based Assessment provides information about a child's level of developmental functioning, developmental processes, and patterns of social interaction. This information, along with a knowledge of the child's interests, everyday activities, and family goals, provides the basis for planning interventions. Intervention activities are designed to encourage consistent and qualitatively sound expression of present and emerging skills. Activities also encourage higher functioning levels for children in cognitive, socio-emotional, communicative, linguistic, and sensorimotor development. Goals from all developmental domains are integrated into child play activities. Activities are selected that occur spontaneously or are easily introduced in home, community, daycare, and preschool settings. Linder recommends the use of the TPBI approach with a thematic storybook curriculum.

The TPBI provides a framework for transdisciplinary team building that emphasizes family participation in planning and implementing intervention. The result is ongoing communication and problem solving among parents and professionals providing services for the child and family.

Assessment and intervention are cyclical and dynamic processes. Initial assessment information used to plan intervention and monitoring of outcomes provides a basis for modifying practices in response to child and family needs.

Notes: Linder emphasizes that the TPBI is intended to be used by transdisciplinary teams of parents and professionals who are knowledgeable about sensorimotor, cognitive, socio-emotional, communicative, and linguistic development. The approach is most effective when each member of the team is familiar with developmental issues and child goals in all domains. Intervention must address the needs of the whole child rather than needs in specific areas.

SYSTEMIC APPROACH TO INFANT INTERVENTION

Method: Systemic Approach to Infant Intervention

Source: Dunst, C. J., Lesko, J. J., Holbert, K. A., Wilson, L. L., Sharpe, K. L., & Liles, R. F. (1987). Systemic approach to infant intervention. *Topics in Early Childhood Special Education, 7*(2), 19–37.

Description: A Systemic Approach to Infant Intervention provides a method for planning, implementing, and evaluating intervention services for infants and their families. Dunst and colleagues describe the goal of intervention as facilitating infant interactive competencies that shift the balance of power toward the developing infant. The use of interactive competencies allows the infant to experience control in relation to physical and social environments.

Many special educators are concerned that emphasis on adult-directed strategies over extended periods of time may result in the children becoming more passive. The systemic approach uses responsive interaction techniques and incidental teaching to support infant interactive competence and active learning. Techniques that seek to bring infant behavior under control by prompting and reinforcing select predetermined behaviors are discouraged. Intervention activities are child-initiated. Caregivers and interventionists respond to and encourage the child's ongoing behavior.

The systemic model consists of seven components: (a) a sequence of interactive competencies, (b) a designation of variables influencing the developmental process, (c) a system for categorizing intervention target behaviors, (d) assessment strategies, (e) intervention procedures, (f) a functional contextual framework for intervention, and (g) evaluation procedures.

The approach is based on a developmental model that defines five forms of infant interactive competencies and a process through which competency is achieved. Five levels of competency, from attention to symbolic interaction, are operationally defined and designated as target behaviors. Some curriculum models organize intervention target behaviors by developmental domains. This approach defines intervention targets by behavior functions. These functions assist the infant in using appropriate forms of conventional behavior to gain increasing competence in environmental interactions. Four forms of target behavior contribute to infant interactive competency: initiating, sustaining, regulating, and adapting. Target behaviors are social and/or nonsocial; they may be used for environmental engagement or modulating interactions.

MONTESSORI METHOD: EARLY CHILDHOOD

Method: Montessori Method: Early Childhood

Author: Maria Montessori

Source: Montessori, M. (1965). *The Montessori elementary material.* Cambridge, MA: Robert Bentley.

Description: Maria Montessori's educational philosophy was influenced by Itard, Seguin, and Piaget. From Itard, Montessori learned the value of astute observation of student behavior. From Seguin, she borrowed an educational methodology that he had developed in working with students with disabilities. The physiological method of Seguin focused on the observation and study of individual students, resulting in physiological and psychological data for educational programming. Montessori's practical application of her ideas with normal children between the ages of 3 and 7 helped formulate her educational principles and develop her methods.

Although Piaget was a theorist and Montessori a practitioner, both held similar views (Orem, 1969). Both perceived mental development as an outgrowth of biological factors; thus an individual's thought and behavior were seen as closely linked to biological development. Both were developmentalists who believed that an understanding of normal development is essential to understanding differences in individuals. Orem (1969) summarized the commonalities of the philosophies of Piaget and Montessori.

1. Nature and nurture interact in the development of a child. Nature determines the pattern and time schedule, and nurture fosters the development of the pattern.
2. Capacity influences learning and follows a rate and time pattern.
3. Repetitive behavior is critical to cognitive development.

Montessori advocated student-centered sensory motor teaching with the teacher observing and guiding learning. The environment is organized, but structure that might interfere with learning is not imposed. Language development is an integral part of early learning activities. Students develop abstract thinking through guided interactions with materials, teachers, and others. Rote memorization without physical manipulation of materials is discouraged. This emphasis on the concrete is in harmony with the Piagetian developmental approach; that is, concrete reasoning precedes the development of abstract reasoning. The tactile-kinesthetic experience of manipulating physical materials is expected to enhance interest and increase learning effectiveness.

Notes: This method requires a teacher skilled in questioning and intervening. Frequent assessment of student progress is needed so that incorrect assumptions can be checked. The student needs to possess self-initiated work behaviors or develop them in order to benefit from this method.

SYSTEMATIC (DIRECT) INSTRUCTIONAL METHODS

Method: Systematic (Direct) Instructional Methods

Sources: Barnett, D. W., & Carey, K. T. (1992). *Designing interventions for preschooler learning and behavior problems*. San Francisco: Jossey-Bass; Bailey, D. B., & Wolery, M. (1992). *Teaching infants and preschoolers with disabilities* (2nd ed.). New York: Macmillan; Noonan, M. J., & McCormick, L. (1993). *Early intervention in natural environments: Methods and procedures*. Pacific Grove, CA: Brooks/Cole.

Description: In early intervention practice, Systematic (direct) Instructional methods are often applied in conjunction with incidental teaching in naturalistic contexts. Instruction is adult-planned and directed. Instruction is used to "get a behavior going" and to support and maintain desirable behaviors. The methods are also used to decrease the occurrence of excessive, harmful, or self-injurious behavior.

Current trends in the field of early childhood special education promote learner-oriented instruction, that is, following the child's lead and teaching in response to the child's initiation. Though goals, objectives, and Systematic Instructional methods are adult-planned and directed, intervention often occurs in the context of activities that are initiated by and meaningful to the child.

Interventionists choose from a range of Systematic Instructional methods that provide varying degrees of direction to accommodate child needs. Some systematic instruction strategies are modeled after basic caregiving strategies used by competent caregivers in everyday settings. These strategies include differentially attending to desirable behavior and differentially ignoring undesirable behavior or modeling and prompting desirable behaviors.

Incidental teaching provides a context for use of direct instruction methods. Interventionists take advantage of naturally occurring interactions with children in unstructured situations to teach and reinforce new skills. In such interactions, interventionists respond to the child's focus of attention and elaborate on the child's behavior (Hart & Risley, 1975). Incidental teaching and direct instruction strategies may be used to teach and strengthen behaviors in all developmental domains.

When children have severe deficits or exhibit excesses in their behavioral repertoires, other direct instruction strategies may be used to motivate engagement and encourage expression of desirable behaviors. These strategies include differential reinforcement, prompting, shaping and chaining, and aversive procedures. General case instruction and generalization strategies are used to promote generalized use of acquired skills.

Reinforcement in the form of food, material goods, functional contingencies, or social interaction is used to establish and maintain behavior. Differential reinforcement procedures are used to reinforce some classes of behavior (e.g., communication skills) and reduce others (e.g., aggression). Maladaptive behaviors can be decreased and replaced with more appropriate and functional behaviors through use of these procedures.

Desirable behavior can be encouraged through use of such procedures as modeling and prompting. Prompts may be physical, verbal, or gestural, or they may consist of modeling or time delay procedures. Prompts can be viewed as lying on a continuum of intrusiveness with full physical prompting (e.g., moving the child through a behavioral sequence) being most intrusive. Least intrusive prompts (e.g., time delay) are tried before more intrusive prompts; prompts are faded as soon as possible.

To prompt child behavior, time delay procedures are often used. These procedures have been used widely to teach language. The following is an example of the use of a time delay procedure to teach requesting to young children (Halle, Baer, & Spradlin, 1981):

1. Face the child with an expectant look and display a desired object.

2. Wait a specified time (several seconds) for the child to request or label the desired object.

3. If the child responds correctly, provide the desired object.

4. Provide a verbal prompt or physical prompt if the child does not respond or responds incorrectly.

Shaping and chaining procedures can be used to teach new behaviors or more complex behaviors. In shaping, a desirable behavior is taught by reinforcing successive approximations or small steps toward that behavior. Behaviors may be lengthened or shortened, the frequency or intensity of the behavior may be influenced, or the form of the behavior may be changed. In chaining, a sequence of simple behaviors is taught to produce the expression of more complex behaviors.

Aversive procedures and punishment are sometimes used to reduce and eliminate behaviors involving risk or harm to self or others. **These procedures are used when positive procedures are not effective. They are used only in conjunction with reinforcement for appropriate behavior.** Procedures consist of time out from positive reinforcement, contingent observation (a milder form of time out), response cost, and overcorrection procedures.

Generalization refers to the use of a newly learned behavior in appropriate contexts where instruction does not occur. It also refers to the use of newly acquired behavior in adaptive and variable ways that are not specifically trained. General case instruction consists of teaching general response classes to general stimulus classes concurrently to promote generalization of skills. A number of generalization strategies can be used in general case instruction to further enhance the generalized use of skills.

Notes: The use of Systematic Instruction methods in early childhood special education has been criticized for several reasons.

Instruction that is based on goals and objectives that are of little interest to infants and young learners is likely to lack meaning. Behaviors taught outside of the natural contexts in which they normally occur are not likely to be used in a functional manner in everyday contexts. The use of artificial contingencies to support behavior is not effective in maintaining behavior in the absence of such support.

One concern about the use of these strategies for bringing young learners under stimulus control is that infants and children are reinforced for being responders and for being passive rather than active learners. Systematic (direct) Instruction methods emphasize the shaping and reinforcement of child initiations and the use of child-directed activity as a medium for teaching specific skills. Systematic Instruction, then, is most appropriately applied in naturalistic settings and in the context of everyday routines and activities that are meaningful for the child.

ENVIRONMENTAL ORGANIZATION

Method: Environmental Organization for Promoting Child Development and Functioning in the Classroom

Sources: McEvoy, M. A., Fox, J. J., & Rosenberg, M. S. (1991). Organizing preschool environments: Suggestions for enhancing the development/learning of preschool children with handicaps. *Topics in Early Childhood Special Education,* 11(2), 18–28; McEvoy, M. A. (1990). The organization of caregiving environments: Critical issues and suggestions for future research. *Education and Treatment of Children,* 13(4), 269–273; Nordquist, V. M., & Twardosz, S. (1990). Preventing behavior problems in early childhood special education classrooms through environmental organization. *Education and Treatment of Children,* 13(4), 274–287.

Description: Environmental Organization refers to the physical, social, and programmatic features of early childhood settings. These features influence child engagement in and expression of appropriate behavior. Effective arrangement of space and materials is used to prompt engagement with the social and physical environment, provide cues for appropriate behavior, and encourage higher developmental functioning. McEvoy and colleagues provide the following recommendations for environmental arrangement of the preschool classroom:

I. Divide the classroom into specific, well-defined areas;
2. Allow enough space in each area for activities and movement but keeping spaces small enough to bring children into close proximity to one another to promote social interaction;
3. Arrange compatible areas next to each other;
4. Provide materials and equipment in limited quantities to encourage sharing and increased social interaction and expressive language;
5. Provide materials that will attract engagement and rotate materials regularly to provide greater variety and novelty;
6. Provide toys that promote social coordination and interaction (e.g., dramatic play props, large motor equipment);
7. Structure activities and use social toys to promote social interaction;
8. Include children with special needs in inclusive classrooms;
9. Structure certain activities so that children work in pairs to promote social interaction. Adaptive equipment and positioning should be used to facilitate access to playful activities in the classroom when appropriate.

The classroom schedule also influences child behavior. Time segments should be planned to accommodate children's attention spans and the nature of the activity. Programming activities should be continuous, beginning when the children arrive and continuing throughout the school day. Schedules should include (a) the time each activity will occur, (b) where it will be held, (c) which children will participate, (d) which staff members will be responsible for conducting activities, and (e) how children will make transitions from one activity to another.

Scheduling and staffing patterns are used to minimize the amount of time children need to wait before moving on to the next activity. This reduces the disruption that is likely to occur when children have no activity in place to prompt appropriate engagement. Materials should be ready and accessible from the beginning of the activity. Children should be able to rotate through activities independently rather than being required to move from one activity to another as a group. This independent transitioning requires less waiting and thereby decreases opportunities for disruption. When group transitioning is necessary, moving smoothly from one activity to another is facilitated by use of antecedent events (e.g., cues or instructions) that signal desired behavior.

Activities are purposefully scheduled to encourage the expression of particular behaviors. For example, free play encourages child-child interaction, whereas teacher-directed activities encourage high rates of teacher-child interaction. Arrangement of activities is important also. Transitions from outdoor gross motor activities to indoor rest periods may be eased by inserting a quiet indoor activity between the two.

Notes: McEvoy and co-authors caution that environmental interventions may not be sufficient to influence or manage behavior. Direct teaching and intervention procedures may be necessary as well.

MILIEU LANGUAGE INTERVENTION

Method: Milieu Language Intervention

Authors: Betty Hart and Ann Rogers-Warren

Source: Hart, B., & Rogers-Warren, A. (1978). A milieu approach to teaching language. In R. Schiefelbusch (Ed.), *Language intervention strategies* (pp. 193–235). Baltimore: University Park Press.

Description: Milieu Language Intervention combines a behavioral approach with incidental teaching procedures. The intervention occurs in a naturalistic setting. This method is a hybrid approach (Fey, 1986), consisting of an underlying teaching structure and sequence that is applied in a child's daily activities and routines.

Milieu Language Intervention provides techniques for teaching specific language skills in the context of adult-child communicative exchanges. The adult takes advantage of the child's focus of attention and his or her engagement with the physical and social environment to model, prompt, and selectively reinforce targeted language skills. The approach emphasizes eliciting specific language forms and content; however, it differs from didactic approaches in that the topic of the teaching episode and the reinforcement of communication are defined by the child's immediate interests.

The approach provides frequent opportunities for the child to learn functional language skills in a variety of contexts. In doing so, it supports the child's use of forms and content of language in everyday use. The dispersement of training trials in everyday settings promotes the generalized use of newly acquired language skills. Child progress is monitored through data collection; these data provide a basis for making intervention decisions.

Milieu Language Intervention is particularly appropriate for teaching beginning language learners. It may be used to teach simple request forms, vocabulary, and semantic relations. The method uses direct instructional techniques (e.g., verbal prompting, time delay, systematic commenting) and incidental teaching. In incidental teaching, the adult observes and supports the child's interests and engagement with the environment. The environment may be arranged so that attractive materials or playthings are in sight and out of reach. The child is then prompted to communicate a request for adult assistance in obtaining the object.

Adults may use other means, such as the mand-model, to prompt the child to communicate. The mand-model procedure is a form of verbal prompting applied in milieu teaching. Instead of waiting for the child to initiate interaction, the teacher prompts the child to initiate a communicative interaction. The child may be asked to imitate adult language, or the adult may use mands or other verbal prompts (e.g., questions, choices, instructions) to elicit child language.

Time delay or other nonverbal cues may also be used to elicit communication. Adults may prompt child communication by commenting on objects and events that are the focus of the child's attention. Child language goals are targeted through these prompting procedures. Prompts, selected to provide appropriate levels of support to the child, are faded gradually. Responses to prompts result in consequences, feedback on the correctness of responses, and expansions or extensions of the child's utterance. When a child indicates interest in a toy that is out of reach, for example, the adult prompts the child to communicate, responds to the child's communication and reinforces the child's communicative attempt by providing a functional contingency. For example:

1. When the child approaches the desired object, the teacher provides a

direction or instruction to perform the desired behavior, such as, "Tell me what you want." The direction or instruction given is always related to whatever is maintaining the child's attention at the moment.

2. If the child labels an object, the object may be given to the child. In most cases the child's response is followed by verbal confirmation and expansion, "Okay, I'll get the truck down for you."

3. The adult provides a model of the correct response if the child does not respond or responds incorrectly.

Notes: Milieu Language Intervention is widely used to facilitate language learning of young children with developmental disabilities. It may be particularly effective for use with early language learners whose Mean Length of Utterance is 1.0 to 3.0.

INREAL (*INCLASS REACTIVE LANGUAGE*)

Method: INREAL (*IN*class *REA*ctive Language) Language Intervention for Language Delayed and Bilingual Children

Author: Rita Weiss

Source: Weiss, R. S. (1981). INREAL Intervention for language handicapped and bilingual children. *Journal for Division for Early Childhood. 4*, 40–52.

Description: The INREAL intervention method was originally developed as a component of a federally funded model demonstration project. The INREAL method is based on a pragmatic theory of language development. The method is used to develop language and related skills of preschool and kindergarten children who are language delayed or bilingual. The method

was designed to be used in natural settings and is intended to be nonstigmatizing. IN-REAL is made up of three components that guide implementation: *IN*class delivery of services, *REA*ctive techniques, and Language-focused intervention.

The *IN*class component provides for intervention by placing the speech and language clinician in the classroom. In doing this, the interventionist interacts with the child in the natural setting of the classroom. The child is not pulled aside or singled out for intervention and, therefore, is not stigmatized by the intervention process. The interventionist doesn't manipulate the setting to obtain a predetermined target behavior.

The *REA*ctive component requires the interventionist to observe, listen, and react to the child's communicative behaviors by mirroring the child. The following techniques are used to stimulate language use and support the child's language learning:

1. *Self-Talk.* The interventionist talks aloud about her activity in parallel play with the child.
2. *Parallel Talk.* The interventionist talks aloud about the child's activity in parallel play.
3. *Verbal Monitoring and Reflecting.* The interventionist repeats what the child says or restates what the child said, correcting errors in a nonjudgmental way.
4. *Expansion/Elaboration.* The interventionist expands or elaborates on the child's utterance.
5. *Modeling.* The interventionist converses with the child in order to model appropriate language.

The third component of INREAL is the Language component. This component addresses the child's particular language disorders and the language learning needs of young children who are bilingual.

ENABLING AND EMPOWERING FAMILIES

Method: Enabling and Empowering Families

Authors: Carl J. Dunst, Carol M. Trivette, and Angela G. Deal

Source: Dunst, C. J., Trivette, C. M., & Deal, A. G. (1988). *Enabling and empowering families: principles and guidelines for practice.* Cambridge, MA: Brookline Books.

Description: The method, Enabling and Empowering Families, provides a framework for assessing family strengths, needs, resources, aspirations, functioning styles, and social support networks. Dunst and his colleagues include guidelines for providing services to families with young children with developmental delays and disabilities. The family is the unit of intervention and the method is family-focused. Intervention is based on a social systems' perspective of family functioning. Families are viewed as systems influenced by the social networks in which they are embedded. The intent of assessment and intervention is to "enable and empower families in a way that makes them more competent and better able to mobilize resources" (Dunst, Trivette, & Deal, 1988, p. 3). The intervention process operates in the following way:

1. Family needs and aspirations are identified based on family concerns, desires, and priorities.
2. Ways that the family functions and responds to stressful events are identified as well as aspects of family functioning that are working well.
3. The family's personal social network is "mapped" to identify resources that may be obtained or mobilized to meet desired outcomes.
4. Interventionists work with families to enable them to become more competent and better able to mobilize and access resources for achieving identified family goals.

Notes: This method provides a proactive approach to intervention that focuses on building family strengths and resources rather than correcting or decreasing the risk of problems or deficits. As families begin to access and mobilize available resources, they are better able to meet the needs of all family members, including the special needs of children.

HOME SERVICE DELIVERY PARADIGM

Method: Home Service Delivery Paradigm for Preschool Children with Behavioral Disorders and their Families

Author: Kathryn Paget

Sources: Paget, K. D. (1991). Early intervention and treatment acceptability: Multiple perspectives for improving service delivery in home settings. *Topics in Early Childhood Special Education, 11*(2), 1–17.; Paget, K. D. (1988). Early Intervention: Infants, preschool children and families. In J. C. Witt, S. N. Elliott, & F. M. Gresham (Eds.), *The handbook of behavior therapy in education* (pp. 569–300). New York: Plenum Press.

Description: Paget's Home Service Delivery paradigm provides intervention services for children with behavior disorders and their families. It is based on a presumed relationship between the success of a home program and respect for the priorities and needs of family members. The acceptability of the intervention plan by family members is assumed to be key to the success of intervention efforts.

Vincent, Salisbury, Laten, and Baumgart (1979) proposed the use of a Family Daily

Routine protocol for designing programs. This protocol provides a structure for embedding intervention goals and recommendations into existing family routines. Application of this procedure is enhanced in Paget's paradigm through emphasis on parent-professional collaboration. The developmental status and needs of all family members are taken into consideration. Intervention plans reflect freedom of choice, self-reliance, and respect for beliefs of family members. The home program is based on a family systems' perspective. The paradigm consists of five components:

1. *Assessment of Daily Routines, Structure, and Teaching Resources.* The assessment consists of gathering information about family daily routines. A log, kept by parents, describing these routines provides a basis for identifying opportunities for intervention. Interventionists can suggest opportunities for intervention; then family members choose specific times and opportunities for the intervention activities. During assessment, family teaching and interaction styles between parents and the target child and between siblings and the target child are assessed to determine family members' ability to teach particular objectives.

2. *Selecting Instructional Targets.* Parents and professionals work together to determine priorities for intervention and goals that can be addressed in the course of daily routines. Family beliefs about behavior and its causes, child development, child rearing, and family member roles are some issues given consideration in this stage of the process.

3. *Program Implementation.* Interventionists and parents determine how parents will learn to apply specific techniques. Parents may receive instruction through viewing videotapes, observing interventionists, or through reading. Interventionists observe family members using the techniques and provide ongoing feedback on their quality and effectiveness.

4. *Information and Data Gathering.* Written or verbal methods for data collection that are comfortable and minimally intrusive to family members provide information on child progress toward intervention goals. Both intended and unintended effects of intervention are noted and discussed. Intervention strategies are sustained or modified based on data and discussions with family members.

5. *Program Evaluation.* Program outcomes and success are evaluated along four dimensions: (a) child progress, (b) the family's ability to carry out the program, (c) the ease with which the program is embedded in family life and (d) the family's willingness to undertake another program.

CHILD RELATIONSHIP ENHANCEMENT FAMILY THERAPY (CREFT)

Method: Child Relationship Enhancement Family Therapy (CREFT)

Authors: L. F. Guerney and B. Guerney

Sources: Guerney, L. F., & Guerney, B. (1985). The relationship enhancement family of family therapies. In L. L'Abate & M. Milan (Eds.), *Handbook of social skills training and research* (pp. 506–524). New York: John Wiley; Guerney, L. (1988). *Parenting: A skills training manual* (3rd ed.). State College, PA: I.D.E.A.L.S; Guerney, L. (1991). Parents as partners in treating behavior problems in early childhood settings. *Topics in Early Childhood Special Education, 11*(2), 74–89.

Description: Child Relationship Enhancement Family Therapy (CREFT), a child-centered play therapy, teaches parents to improve behavior in their preschool children at home. The method requires the instruction and supervision of a trained CREFT provider. CREFT offers a proactive approach to behavioral change by focusing on the positive potential of both child and parents. Unlike behavioral therapies that focus on specific behaviors, play therapy is generic. It is aimed at improving self-esteem and feelings underlying inappropriate behavior such as anger and frustration, fears, and performance or social anxiety. Behavioral change occurs as underlying feelings are addressed in child-centered therapy with a warm, responsive adult.

The CREFT process begins with an assessment of child and family interaction patterns. Data also are gathered on child functioning in daycare and preschool settings.

1. A CREFT trainer observes family members with the target child in a free play situation to see how the child functions in his or her family.
2. After the observation, parents are asked to give their account of what happened during the observation period. They tell how the behavior of the child and family members resembled or differed from behavior at home. Parents also provide information about child behavior, parental attitudes, and family interaction patterns via checklists and questionnaires.
3. While parents are interviewed, an adult interacts with the target child and his or her siblings to observe how the children act when the parents are absent. The observer may lead the child and siblings through specific activities to evoke behaviors of interest or to screen for possible neurological or psychological assessment or speech and hearing evaluation.
4. The child is observed in daycare and/or school settings to see how he or she functions in those settings.
5. Cross-contextual information on the child's functioning in major contexts is compiled and analyzed to reveal patterns and antecedent conditions associated with inappropriate behavior.

6. Parents and the CREFT provider discuss observations. The CREFT approach is explained to parents so that parents can decide whether they would like to participate.

Once CREFT is determined to be an appropriate and acceptable approach for a child and family, the family begins participation in a four-stage training process. The training format consists of a weekly "families" group meeting with six to eight parents (couples and single parents), target children, and siblings of target children in attendance. If group meetings are not feasible, the training can take place with individual parents or couples. The training process occurs in the following stages:

Instruction. Parents of target children observe the CREFT trainer playing with all children in the group and applying principles of child-centered play therapy. Play therapy principles include responding to the child at play in empathetic ways and setting clear and rational limits on child behavior when necessary. Parents discuss the goals of therapy and the child's responses to specific techniques used by the trainer. Parents then practice the techniques they observed in role play while the trainer provides positive feedback and encouragement.

Practice. Parents play with their children (all children, including the target child) using therapy techniques. The CREFT trainer observes and discusses the session with parents. The discussion focuses on how parents feel about relating to their children in this new way and on the effective application of play therapy techniques.

Home Sessions. Parents are instructed to play at home with their children (the target child and siblings) once a week for 30–40 minutes. The play sessions are planned and carefully structured for each family. The home play continues over a 12-week period. Home play is supplemented by the play sessions in weekly families' group meetings with the CREFT trainer. Parents learn and master new play therapy techniques in these weekly meetings.

Transfer and Generalization. After parents note improvement in their children's behavior and are able to demonstrate competence in applying therapy techniques in play sessions, they are encouraged to begin using principles such as empathetic responding and limit-setting in other contexts. Parents are assisted in using play therapy techniques in other settings through Guerney's parent education program, *Parenting: A Skills Training Program*. The ultimate goal of CREFT is positive behavioral change within the family system and with the target child.

Notes: Parents are particularly powerful CREFT providers. However, the method is an educational intervention that can be learned and used by educators and daycare providers as well.

AN INTERACTIONAL APPROACH TO WORKING WITH PARENTS AND INFANTS

Method: An Interactional Approach to Working with Parents and Infants

Author: Rita Bromwich

Source: Bromwich, R. (1981). *Working with parents and infants: An interactional approach.* Baltimore: University Park Press.

Description: Bromwich's Interactional Approach to Working with Parents and Infants provides intervention services for parents and young children with special needs. It is an outgrowth of the Infant Studies Project at the University of California at Los Angeles. This approach is based on research indicating that stimulating and contingent adult responding in interaction with infants is associated with positive child developmental outcomes. Parents are considered primary change agents in the lives of infants and young children. The program incorporates the following principles:

1. Strengthening parental responsiveness, sensitivity, and skills results in a parent-child relationship in which the parent experiences success and pleasure in caregiving;
2. Infant-parent relationships are reciprocal and are a result of complex and delicate transactions between infant and parent;
3. Parental feelings of competence as a primary change agent in the child's life will have long-term positive consequences for the child's development.

The intervention process is a collaborative effort between service providers and parents. Parents define goals and priorities for their infants. Then they determine how the goals and concerns will be addressed in intervention. Emphasis in intervention is on responding to a parent's expressed concerns and his or her priorities for the child. It focuses on building on parent strengths and respecting individual parenting styles. Interventionists explain why and how parental behaviors facilitate child development. They ask parents to choose or reject suggestions offered and contribute suggestions of their own. The intervention approach focuses on social-affective behavior, cognitive-motivational behavior, and language. Parents and interventionists work together to promote parent interactional behaviors including:

1. reading and responding to infant cues;
2. initiating and responding to playful interactions;
3. determining infant interests, preferences and skills;
4. promoting stimulation with appropriate materials and activities;
5. interacting in a manner that doesn't intrude on infant goals and activities;

6. acknowledging and responding to infant sounds;
7. talking in a focused manner;
8. realizing infants understand more than they can say.

When stress on the family or parent precludes focus on the parent-infant interaction, interventionists provide support for the parent and the family by helping the parent find quality child care, access community resources, or resolve financial, legal, or housing problems. Care is taken to attend to siblings during home visits. The purpose is to preserve good feelings between siblings and the infant and to help the parent understand needs of older children in relation to the infant.

The frequency and length of home visits are determined by the parent and service provider. Formative evaluation of intervention outcomes is accomplished using (a) the Parent Behavior Progression for assessment of parent behavior and (b) the Play Interaction Measure for assessment of parent-child interaction. In her book, Bromwich provides examples of successful, partially successful, and unsuccessful cases as well as a guide for addressing specific problems that may arise in intervention.

TRANSACTIONAL INTERVENTION PROGRAM (TRIP)

Method: Transactional Intervention Program (TRIP)

Authors: Gerald Mahoney and A. Powell

Source: Mahoney, G., & Powell, A. (1988). Modifying parent-child interaction: Enhancing the development of handicapped children. *The Journal of Special Education, 22*(1), 82–96.

Description: The Transactional Intervention Program (TRIP) addresses patterns of interaction between parents and their young children with developmental disabilities. TRIP was developed in response to research indicating that parents of young children with disabilities tend to be more directive and less responsive in interactions with their children than parents of nondisabled children. The approach is designed to help parents become more responsive and child-oriented in interactions with their infants and toddlers. The approach utilizes responsive interaction intervention methods including **turn-taking** strategies and **interactive matching** strategies. Parents are taught to become increasingly aware of the balance of turn-taking in interactions. They learn to minimize directiveness while focusing on responding to their child's initiations. Interactive matching strategies involve (a) modulating interactive behavior in response to the child's pace and tempo and (b) engaging in activities that are within the child's current (rather than potential) range of development. Parents are encouraged to:

1. match activities with a child's interests and level of functioning;
2. achieve a balance of turns in activities;
3. prolong turn-taking sequences by imitating the child, waiting for or signaling and prompting the child to take a turn.

The TRIP program is home-based and consists of weekly visits from a teacher consultant trained in TRIP philosophy and procedures. During home visits, teacher consultants model turn-taking and interactive matching strategies. They assist parents in planning activities that allow for frequent incorporation of those strategies in daily interactions with their child.

Notes: Didactic teaching of specific skills is discouraged. Parents are taught that engaging in a balanced interaction that focuses on the child's interests and developmental level will provide optimal conditions for infant learning and development.

ENHANCED MILIEU LANGUAGE INTERVENTION

Method: Enhanced Milieu Language Intervention: Parent Implementation

Author: Ann P. Kaiser

Sources: Kaiser, A. (1993). Parent-implemented language intervention: An environmental system perspective. In A. Kaiser & D. B. Gray (Eds.), *Enhancing children's communication: Research foundations* (Vol. 2, pp. 63–84). Baltimore: Paul H. Brookes.; Hemmeter, M. L., & Kaiser, A. P. (1994). Enhanced milieu teaching: Effects of parent-implemented language intervention. *Journal of Early Intervention, 18*(3) 269–289.

Description. Enhanced Milieu Language Intervention is a naturalistic approach that combines milieu teaching and responsive interaction approaches. This hybrid method focuses on the language development of young children with developmental delays. The intervention model may be implemented by parents. The model consists of three components: environmental arrangement, responsive interaction, and milieu teaching strategies.

1. Environmental arrangement consists of strategically arranging the physical setting to increase child engagement and parent-child communication. This is done by introducing toys and activities of interest to the child. Parent and child engage in play activities of the child's choosing. The parents support the child's engagement by imitating and elaborating on the child's play. Parent and child engagement in play provides opportunities for the parent to teach, prompt, and reinforce child communicative attempts in a meaningful context. Parents "charge" the social environment with positive affect when responding to their child's communications. They learn to modulate their input in communicative exchanges to provide an optimal affective environment for engagement.

2. Responsive interaction intervention principles include responding to the child's lead, seeking balance in adult-child turn-taking, and communicative exchange, mirroring, modeling, extending, and expanding on child utterances. These strategies support child initiative and provide language learning in functional and social communicative contexts.

3. Milieu teaching is a naturalistic language intervention method. The method takes advantage of the child's interest in and engagement with the environment to elicit and teach specific language skills. Parents are taught to use incidental teaching techniques, child-cued modeling, the mand-model, and time delay procedures for teaching new language forms to their children.

Notes: This hybrid intervention model uses interaction patterns normally used by parents interacting with their young children. The approach encourages an environmental arrangement and social interaction that supports parent teaching of language skills and child responsiveness to that teaching. The model is flexible so that different components can be emphasized to accommodate a child's developing skills and needs. Responsive interaction strategies support social communicative exchange; milieu teaching strategies facilitate the teaching of specific language skills.

LANGUAGE INTERACTION INTERVENTION PROGRAM

Method: Language Interaction Intervention Program

Authors: Lucille Weistuch, Michael Lewis, and B. Byers-Brown

Sources: Weistuch, L., Lewis, M., & Sullivan, M. W. (1991). Project profile: Use of a language interaction intervention in the preschool. *Journal of Early Intervention, 15*(3), 278–287; Weistuch, L., & Byers-Brown, B. (1987). Motherese as therapy: A program and its dissemination. *Child Language Teaching and Therapy, 3*(1), 57–71.; Weistuch, L., & Lewis, M. (1986, April). *Effect of maternal language intervention strategies on the language abilities of delayed two to four-year-olds.* Paper presented at the meeting of the Eastern Psychological Association, New York.; Weistuch, L., & Lewis, M. (1986). The language interaction intervention project. *Analysis and Intervention in Developmental Disabilities, 5,* 97–108.

Description: The Language Interaction Intervention program is designed to teach parents to facilitate language use with their language-delayed preschoolers. The method is used by parents in natural play settings with their children. Intervention is based on the rationale that parents contribute to their child's language development by expanding, imitating, modeling, and commenting on their child's speech.

The model is to be used with children between the ages of 2 and 5 years of age who have language delays and who are in the early phases of language learning (Mean Length of Utterance is 1.0–3.0). The model consists of several key components.

1. Workshops designed to teach parents about forms, sequences, and content of child language development are offered to parents. Parents are also given infor-

mation about ways that adults can support child language development. They learn strategies like commenting on ongoing events, expanding on children's utterances, and extending child utterances by elaborating on meaning. Workshops provide parents with the opportunity to talk about how the information presented is relevant in their daily lives.

2. While parents participate in workshops, their children participate in group language stimulation activities with a speech and language clinician or special educator.

3. After the workshop, parents and children are reunited, and the facilitator demonstrates techniques for supporting child language development. Parents then practice these techniques with their children while facilitators observe and comment on their use.

The model is designed to change parent language interaction patterns by increasing the amount of parallel talk or context-related speech they use with their children. Parents are encouraged to provide their children with semantic information and expansions and extensions.

Notes: The authors emphasize that this approach is intended for children who are in the early stages of language development; that is, they are able to symbolize, represent, and manipulate words when supported in doing so. Children who have not gained these skills may require a more structured, direct instructional approach.

DEVELOPMENTALLY BASED INSTRUCTION

Method: Developmentally Based Instruction for Young Children with Autism and other Disorders of Behavior and Development

Authors: S. J. Rogers, J. Herbison, H. Lewis, J. Pantone, and K. Reis

Sources: Rogers, S. J., Herbison, J., Lewis, H., Pantone, J., & Reis, K. (1986). An approach for enhancing the symbolic, communicative, and interpersonal functioning of young children with autism and severe emotional handicaps. *Journal of the Division for Early Childhood, 11*, 180–188.; Rogers, S., & DiLalla, D. L. (1991). A comparative study of the effects of a developmentally-based instructional model on young children with autism and other disorders of behavior and development. *Topics in Early Childhood Special Education, 11*(2), 29–47.

Description: The Developmentally Based Instructional method is based on the theoretical work of Piaget and Mahler and the pragmatics theory of language development. The method was originally designed to address the needs of preschool children with severe emotional and behavioral disorders (e.g., autism). Specifically, it targets children who exhibit deficits in symbolic thought, communication, dramatic play, impulse control, and social competence in interaction with family members and peers.

The method is play-based; that is, objectives for social-emotional, communicative, and cognitive development are targeted in adult-child play. Adult participation in play and the purpose of the play activity vary as a function of the relevant learning objectives. Other features of the method include the following:

1. *Emphasis on the Role of Positive Affect in Learning.* Strong affect is believed to influence attention, motivation, the strength of interpersonal relationships, and short- and long-term memory.
2. *Emphasis on Communicative Intent.* Child-directed activities in natural environments are a basis for verbal and nonverbal communication. The child is integrator and organizer of language learning.
3. *Emphasis on Social Relationships.* At this stage, the emphasis is on developing positive relationships including that between a "primary teacher" and each

child. Children are brought together with other children and required to interact in order to get their needs and desires met. Adults facilitate this process by helping children get what they need and desire from peers. Adults model and prompt social interaction and skills. They highlight the effect of one child's behavior on another to help the children learn about other peoples' emotions, behavior, and perspectives.

4. *Managing Undesirable Behavior.* Behavior is managed by increasing the number, variety, and complexity of children's behavioral repertoires rather than reducing already deficient repertoires. Brief removal from the group may be necessary to control injurious or destructive behavior.
5. *Classroom Structure and Routines.* Precise planning sets the structure and daily routine that is, in turn, communicated clearly to the children.

Notes: This approach may be supplemented with speech and language therapy or psychotherapy using play techniques.

PROJECT PARTICIPATION

Method: Project Participation: Facilitating Active Learner Participation

Authors: S. Rosenberg, M. Clark, J. Filer, S. Hupp, and D. Finkler

Source: Rosenberg, S., Clark, M., Filer, J., Hupp, S., & Finkler, D. (1992). Active learner participation for young children with severe motor disabilities. *Journal of Early Intervention, 16*(3), 262–274.

Description: This approach is designed to enhance the participation of children with severe motor impairments in educational programs. The method was first developed and implemented in Project Participate, a federally funded model program. The goal of the project was to make program activities and learning environments accessible for children with motor impairments. The aim was to achieve a match between individual child characteristics and environments.

In the decision-making process, teachers examine reasons for a child's limited participation. Then they develop intervention plans that result in the child becoming more actively involved in home and school activities.

The decision process begins with an assessment of the levels of child participation in everyday activities at home and in the classroom. Barriers to participation are identified as well as child strengths and needs. Child strengths provide the basis for choosing an appropriate intervention strategy. Four intervention strategies are used to assist children in overcoming barriers to participation.

1. Strengthening and increasing the use of specific skills that are underdeveloped will assist the child in becoming more competent and independent. If the development of specific skills is precluded because of the nature of the child's impairment or the excessive amount of time it will take the child to learn the skill, another intervention strategy is chosen.
2. The child is taught to use alternative skills already present in his or her repertoire. Alternative behaviors must be functionally similar to the original target behaviors. If possible, they are eventually replaced with the target behavior.
3. Environmental modifications are called for when the environment is unsuitable for the activity or for accommodating the unique characteristics of the child. Modifications may include using adaptive equipment or adjusting seating or child positioning so the child can participate.
4. Adapting the activity may be necessary when the child's skill level is too discrepant from the demands of the activity.

Adaptations may involve changing the rules, the materials, or the task. Adaptations should be used only when other alternatives are unavailable. They should not be used if they stigmatize the child or reduce his or her motivation to participate. Adaptations may be permanent or temporary. After implementation of the intervention approach is underway, changes in levels and quality of child participation are monitored. In addition, child performance is tracked relative to his or her Individualized Education Plan/Individualized Family Service Plan.

ENCOURAGING THE USE OF MASTERY BEHAVIORS IN PLAY

Method: Encouraging the Use of Mastery Behaviors in Play

Authors: J. Jaeger, D. Meidl, and S. Hupp

Sources: Jaeger, J., Meidl, D., & Hupp, S. (1989) *Exploring the world through play.* Department of Educational Psychology, Minneapolis: University of Minnesota; Hupp, S., & Abbeduto, L. (1991). Persistence as an indicator of mastery motivation in young children with cognitive delays. *Journal of Early Intervention, 15*(3), 219–225.

Description: Several strategies are offered to encourage the use of mastery behaviors in young children with cognitive delays. Mastery behavior is goal-directed; that is, the child persists in an activity to create or experience an effect. In engaging in such behavior, infants and young children learn that their actions can reproduce the same effects repeatedly. Also, they learn to act purposefully to produce new effects. Toys that can be manipulated, using behaviors at the child's level of competence, are provided. Reactive toys are especially effective in encouraging exploration and practice of skills. Aspects of toy reactivity that seem to be especially engaging include noise, malleability, reflection, and movable parts. Adults aid children's use of mastery behavior by encouraging the child to reengage in the behavior when they are distracted or when they persist in trial-and-error activity during play.

SELF-MANAGEMENT

Method: Self-management

Source: Barnett, D., & Carey, K. (1992). *Designing interventions for preschool learning and behavior problems.* San Francisco: Jossey-Bass.

Description: Self-management is used to teach young children to gradually assume control over their own behavior. Self-control can be thought of as a global intervention goal. Self-management promotes independence by reducing the child's need for adult direction and monitoring of behavior. Child-initiated use of appropriate behavior, in response to the demands or expectations of a particular setting, is inherent in the generalization of skills. Self-management is more attractive than adult-directed methods of managing child behavior. It is less stigmatizing than forms of external control, and it places responsibility for control of behavior on the child instead of an adult. The following training sequence is an example of a general procedure for teaching Self-management to preschool children:

1. The child is taught to observe and self-monitor his or her own behavior;
2. The child learns expectations and rules for a task or situation;
3. The child learns skills to perform according to expectations;
4. The child is given the opportunity to perform learned skills in appropriate situations;

5. The child is asked to evaluate his own performance by recording and rewarding his or her successful performance.

DeHaas-Warner (1991) used a self-monitoring technique drawn from the theoretical work of Vygotsky (1978) who observed that young children use self-talk (i.e., talking aloud to self) to direct their own behavior. Self-monitoring training consists of the teaching of three skills: (a) self-talk, (b) self-appraisal, and (c) self-recording of performance.

To introduce the idea of self-monitoring and behavior control, the target child hears a story about another preschool child who has a hard time sticking with one thing. In the story, the boy gets up and moves around the classroom, talks to others, and doesn't finish what he started. The story includes drawings illustrating on-task and off-task behavior. It describes a self-monitoring procedure that the preschool boy used to learn to stay on-task. In the story, an adult models the procedure for the boy; the boy practices it until he achieves mastery of the behavior; the adult praises the boy as he practices and masters the procedure. The procedure in the story is then replicated with the target child in the classroom. A self-recording sheet is taped to the child's table before the child is given a task. The sheet contains three rows of 10 boxes each that are to be marked by the child over a 10-minute period. A tape recorder is placed near the child with a tape that emits a low frequency tone every 20 seconds that only the child and an observer can hear. When the child hears the tone, he or she is instructed to quietly verbalize, "Am I doing what I am supposed to be doing?" The child then colors a box on the self-recording sheet for on-task behavior or draws a line through a box for off-task behavior. After marking the box in the appropriate manner, the child returns to the task until the next tone is heard. After a 15-minute period, the adult observer, who has also been recording the child's performance, takes the child, the self-monitoring sheets, and the child's work to another room. Then the observer asks the child for his or her opinion about performance during the work period. In this way, the child learns to record and evaluate his or her own performance accurately and receives praise for on-task behavior. Once the child learns the procedure, self-monitoring may be used by the child in the classroom when independent work is required.

Notes: Preschool children who develop the ability to control their own attending are more likely to have an easier time transitioning into kindergarten where they are often required to work independently and stay on-task. Self-management may be used to teach preschool children to sustain attention to a task through self-monitoring.

PEER-MEDIATED INTERVENTIONS

Method: Peer-mediated Interventions for Promoting Social Competence

Source: McEvoy, M. A., Odom, S. L., & McConnell, S. R. (1992). Peer social competence intervention for young children with disabilities. In S. L. Odom, S. R. McConnell, & M. A. McEvoy (Eds.), *Social competence of young children with disabilities: Issues and strategies for intervention* (pp. 113–133). Baltimore: Paul H. Brookes.

Description: Peer-mediated Intervention strategies use peers to prompt and support desirable social behavior in young children with disabilities. McEvoy and her co-authors describe procedures that may be used to increase social interaction between children with disabilities and their peers. Peers are trained to initiate interactions, to persist in initiating if the target child fails to respond, and to prompt and support the target child in maintaining social interaction.

In contrast to teacher-directed social interaction strategies, teachers do not directly intervene in the child-child interaction; however, they play a critical role in training peers to use initiation strategies and in prompting and reinforcing peers for use of these strategies. A variety of strategies is offered for encouraging reciprocal exchanges between children with disabilities and their peers and for promoting generalization of social interaction skills outside of training settings.

Notes: Procedures have been used successfully with children with cognitive disabilities and those with social and behavior disorders including autism and social withdrawal. McEvoy and colleagues state that generalization of social interaction skills appears to be related to the child's level of social competence at the time of training. Children with limited social behavioral repertoires may need more extensive intervention. Intervention may be enhanced by use of teacher- and peer-mediated strategies. Peer-mediated strategies may place excessive demands on teacher time. Other methods may be more appropriate for use in the classroom (e.g., Affection Training or Social Script Training).

CORRESPONDENCE TRAINING

Method: Correspondence Training

Authors: Betty Hart and Todd Risley

Sources: Risley, T., & Hart, B. (1968). Developing correspondence between nonverbal and verbal behavior of preschool children. *Journal of Applied Behavior Analysis, 1*, 267–281; Baer, R. (1990). Correspondence training: Review and current issues. *Research in Developmental Disabilities, 2*, 379-393; McEvoy, M. A., Odom, S. L., & McConnell, S. R. (1992). Peer social competence intervention for young children with disabilities. In S. L. Odom, S. R. McConnell, & M. A. McEvoy, (Eds.), *Social competence of young children with disabilities* (pp. 113–133). Baltimore: Paul H. Brookes.

Description: Correspondence training is similar to self-management methods in that a primary goal of the intervention is to teach young children to control their own behavior by verbally cuing themselves to act appropriately. The method is used for teaching correspondence between verbal and nonverbal behavior, that is, teaching the child to do what he or she says he will do. The child is reinforced for doing what he says he will do or for accurately reporting on past behaviors (Baer, Williams, Osnes, & Stokes, 1985). In this process, the child's verbalizations mediate desired behaviors. Correspondence training is based on the premise that reinforcement of appropriate verbal behavior, related to desirable nonverbal behavior (i.e., statement of intention to engage in desirable behavior), will lead to increased occurrences of desirable behavior. Training procedures often involve the reinforcement of statements of intention or reports about past behavior. Reinforcement is contingent on a correspondence between a verbalization and a related behavior. For example, when a child is trained and then prompted to state before free play, "I am going to play with John" and subsequently plays with John, the child is reinforced.

One goal of intervention is assisting the child in developing verbal control over his or her behavior. If the child is cued to verbalize an intention to engage in appropriate behaviors, and the correspondence training is effective, the statement of intent alone may prompt desirable behavior that can then be reinforced. The method may also be used to promote maintenance and generalization of desirable behaviors. Correspondence training has been used to increase social interaction among preschool children with disabilities in classroom settings.

Children are asked to name a child in the classroom with whom they are going to play with during free play. They receive reinforcement after free play for playing with the child that they named. This procedure has been effective in increasing social interactive behavior in young children with disabilities who were socially isolated.

A variation on this procedure involves the addition of self-evaluation in relation to the stated intention as a final step in the process. After being given the opportunity to act on their intentions, children are asked to evaluate their performance and reward themselves for successful performance. Correspondence training procedures, applied to social interaction, are less intrusive than teacher-directed or -dependent procedures that require high levels of teacher prompting and reinforcement. The following is a generic procedure for correspondence training:

1. child is asked to state an intention to engage in some functional and desirable behavior;
2. child enters a context/activity where there is opportunity to act as intended;
3. child is asked to report whether behavior occurred or is given feedback on his or her behavior;
4. if behavior occurs, child receives reinforcement.

AFFECTION TRAINING

Method: Affection Training

Authors: Mary A. McEvoy, S. Twardosz, and N. Bishop

Sources: McEvoy, M. A., Twardosz, S., & Bishop, N. (1990). Affection activities: Procedures for encouraging young children with handicaps to interact with their peers. *Education and Treatment of Children, 13*(2),

159–167; Twardosz, S., Nordquist, V. M., Simon, R., & Botkin, D. (1983). The effect of group affection activities on the interaction of socially isolate children. *Analysis and Intervention in Developmental Disabilities, 13,* 311-338.

Description: Affection training is used to increase social interaction between preschool children with disabilities and their peers. The method is easily applied in preschool classrooms. It is effective in promoting social interaction in specific affection activities and in free play.

Affection activities are typical preschool activities that are modified to incorporate exchanges of affection among participating children. Activities involve large or small groups of children with and without disabilities. They include games and songs such as "Duck, Duck, Goose" or "Ring Around the Roses." The teacher introduces the activity to a group of children by talking about the importance of friendship and expressions of friendliness. Then they discuss the purpose of the affection activity. The teacher introduces the activities by asking two children to exchange an expression of affection (e.g., hold hands, smile at one another, give high fives) or by suggesting a group expression of affection (e.g., give each other "warm fuzzies"). The teacher then leads the activity and modifies it to include expressions of affection. For example, in playing "The Farmer in the Dell," the teacher sings, "The farmer hugs his wife" or "The wife pats the child." The teacher reinforces children's affectionate expressions whether they are prompted or they occur spontaneously during the activity.

Activities are conducted regularly each day for 10–15 minutes. Activities are most appropriate for preschool and kindergarten children. For the activities to be effective, the majority of children in the groups should be typically developing socially. Group size varies depending on the number and severity of disabling conditions of children in the group. Children with serious social deficits may require more teacher attention during activities. They may need more prompting and opportunities to participate than other children. Observation of children exchanging affection in the activity may serve as a prompt for other children to do likewise. If physical expression is overwhelming for a child, the teacher may choose to begin by prompting verbal or facial expressions and gradually introducing physical expressions. Teachers encourage children's enthusiasm and active participation by taking advantage of activities that are particularly effective in inspiring participation.

Notes: Affection training has been used effectively with children with autism, behavior disorders, and cognitive delays. Increases in social interaction have been found to generalize to free play periods after initiation of affection training activities in preschool classrooms. The intervention procedure is easily learned and applied by teachers. In addition, it can be conducted in the context of daily classroom routines and activities. This method may be supplemented with individual treatment strategies. For example, to encourage social interaction, teachers may use prompting and reinforcement, structured social activities, modified spatial density in the classroom environment, and toys that prompt social play.

REFERENCES

Baer, R. A., Williams, J. A., Osnes, P. G., & Stokes, T. F. (1985). Generalized verbal control and correspondance training. *Behavior Modification, 9,* 477–489.

Bricker, D., & Cripes, J. (1992). *An activity-based approach to early intervention.* Baltimore: Paul H. Brookes.

DEC Recommended Practices: Indicators of quality in programs for infants and young children with special needs and their families. (1993). Reston, VA: The Division for Early Childhood, Council for Exceptional Children.

DeHaas-Warner, J. (1991). Effects of self-monitoring on preschoolers on-task behavior: A pilot study. *Topics in Early Childhood Special Education, 11*(2), 59–73.

Fey, M. E. (1986). *Language intervention with young children.* San Diego, CA: College-Hill Press.

Halle, J. W., Baer, D., & Spradlin, J. E. (1981). Teachers' generalized use of delay as a stimulus control procedure to increase language use in handicapped children. *Journal of Applied Behavior Analysis, 14,* 389–411.

Hart, B, & Risley, T. R. (1975). Incidental teaching of language in the preschool. *Journal of Applied Behavior Analysis, 8,* 411–420.

Linder T. (1993). *Transdisciplinary play-based intervention: Guidelines for developing a meaningful curriculum for young children.* Baltimore: Paul H. Brookes.

Orem, J. C. (1969). *Montessori and the special child.* New York: G. P. Putman's Sons.

Rainforth, B., & Salisbury, C. L. (1988). Functional home programs: A model for therapists. *Topics in Early Childhood Special Education, 7*(4), 33–45.

Vincent, L. J., Salisbury, C., Laten, S., & Baumgart, D. (1979). *Designing home programs for families with handicapped children.* Unpublished manuscript. University of Wisconsin. Department of Rehabilitation Psychology and Special Education, Madison.

Vygotsky, L. (1978). *Mind in society: The development of higher psychological processes.* Cambridge, MA: Harvard University Press.

Yoder, P. J. (1990). The theoretical and empirical basis of early amelioration of developmental disabilities: Implications for research. *Journal of Early Intervention, 14,* 27–42.

CHAPTER

3

Methods for the Gifted

J. Christine Gould, Ph.D.

CONTENTS

▶ Academic Acceleration   **51**
    Administrative Acceleration   **51**
    Classroom Acceleration   **52**
    Beyond Traditional Schooling   **52**
▶ Autonomous Learner Model   **53**
▶ Integrative Education Model   **54**
▶ Individualized Teaching of the
    Gifted in Regular Classrooms   **54**
▶ The Purdue Three-Stage
    Enrichment Model   **55**
▶ The Purdue Secondary Model   **56**

▶ The Grid   **56**
▶ The Enrichment Triad/
    Revolving Door Model   **57**
▶ Multiple Talent Approach/
    Talents Unlimited   **58**
▶ Individualized Programming
    Planning Model   **59**
▶ Academic Competitions   **59**
▶ Future Problem Solving Program   **60**
▶ International Baccalaureate   **61**
▶ Talent Searches   **62**

Gifted learners exhibit unusual complexity and depth in thinking processes. They think abstractly at early ages in ways not seen in chronological peers and demonstrate exceptional sensitivity to the world around them (Silverman, 1993a; Silverman, 1994). These characteristics typically are seen in the upper 3 to 5% of ability ranges. To meet their needs, these learners require differential education that alters the complexity and depth of the curriculum. Failure to differentiate means some of the highest ability students are the least intellectually challenged.

Optimal learning conditions are created when a match occurs between student ability and curriculum complexity. In some school programs, a one-size-fits-all approach is used; the same curriculum is employed for all ability ranges. Unfortunately, this often means that gifted learners are exposed to high rates of repetition of material they already know and understand. Consequently, because of lack of time and resources, opportunities to pursue areas of high interest are limited.

The methods reviewed in this chapter match student ability to curriculum complexity in integrated models. Ability and interest levels are addressed so unnecessary repetition of previously learned material is minimized. Curricular time and support are focused on in-depth, advanced learning. Additionally, affective needs are considered.

Methods for teaching gifted learners traditionally have fallen into two categories: (a) methods that accelerate student progress and (b) methods that provide enrichment beyond traditional programming. Acceleration and enrichment do not need to be used independently of each other. In a well-designed program, they are used in a complementary manner.

Acceleration refers to school placement ahead of chronological peers. Some forms of acceleration are unobtrusive while others are radical. Methods of acceleration include (a) early school entrance, (b) grade level skipping, and (c) advanced class placement.

Some administrators, teachers, and parents have expressed two major concerns about possible negative effects of acceleration. First, the emotional well-being of gifted students may be damaged by altering the peer group. However, gifted students frequently relate to older students or adults more effectively than their chronological peers (Silverman, 1993b). Second, students will miss activities designed for specific age groups. While participation in activities may be very important for some students, others may express little or no interest.

Although there is reluctance in the educational community to utilize acceleration, research has been generally positive (Brody & Benbow, 1987; Clark, 1992; Kulik & Kulik, 1984; Silverman, 1993b). In spite of these findings, acceleration remains controversial and is infrequently used. However, for the student who is significantly advanced, it may be an important option.

To mitigate possible negative effects of acceleration, methods and programs have been developed that involve students in extracurricular activities and community service projects (International Baccalaureate, Future Problem Solving, Integrative Education). This creates situations in which students' emotional well-being is fostered by balancing intellectual stimulation with social involvement and personal interaction.

Enrichment refers to comprehensive alteration of the complexity or depth of the curriculum. Clark (1992) suggested that curricular enrichment can be achieved by "adding disciplines or areas of learning not normally found in the regular classroom . . . using more difficult or in-depth material" (p. 186). In this way, more complex curriculum can be provided that challenges the higher level thinking processes exhibited by gifted learners.

Educators sometimes misunderstand the concept of enrichment. This is seen in programs that simply require gifted learners to complete more of the same work, such as requiring an 8-page report instead of a 6-page one. While extra work keeps gifted learners busy for longer periods of time, it does not alter the complexity or depth of curriculum. Other programs have added extra art projects or field trips to an otherwise traditional program. These adaptations are appropriate for all students and do nothing to alter curriculum complexity.

In addition to acceleration and enrichment, comprehensive thinking models have been developed for use with any content-based curriculum. Thinking models address gifted learners' tendencies to explore concepts more deeply. Some methods for gifted learners place more emphasis on the process of learning than subject content. Mastery of subject content is emphasized.

Several programs are also discussed in this chapter (Academic Competitions, Future Problem Solving, International Baccalaureate, Talent Searches). These programs have become so closely identified with gifted learners that any discussion of differentiated curriculum would be remiss without their inclusion. In fact, in some schools, implementation of these programs is the full extent of programming for gifted learners.

The methods and programs reviewed in this chapter represent a departure from traditional education methods. They are highly student-centered, -managed, and -evaluated. Therefore, the traditional relationship between teacher and student is altered; the student takes a more active role in designing and evaluating his or her own work. By utilizing these methods in a comprehensive program, the unique needs of the gifted learner can be met.

ACADEMIC ACCELERATION

Method: Academic Acceleration

Source: Southern, W. T., & Jones, E. D. (1991). *The academic acceleration of gifted children.* New York: Teacher's College Press.

Description: Academic Acceleration consists of several practices in which gifted learners are placed ahead of their chronological peers to establish a more appropriate curricular match. One advantage of acceleration is that almost any school can accelerate individual students without implementing extensive programs. This allows the rare student who is profoundly gifted to be served in a general school setting.

Acceleration can be implemented for specific subjects or entire school days. The major types of acceleration are described in three categories: (a) acceleration facilitated through schoolwide administrative practices, (b) acceleration facilitated through classroom practices, and (c) acceleration facilitated beyond traditional schooling.

Administrative Acceleration

EARLY ENTRANCE. Students are allowed to enter elementary, junior high, high school, or college ahead of chronological peers. Early entrance can often provide intellectual stimulation for gifted learners through exposure to advanced curriculum and interaction with older students. It can also provide classes for students who have completed sequences in traditional programming. For example, a junior high student who has completed the required program can enter high school early to begin the high school curriculum.

SKIPPING GRADE LEVELS. Students are allowed to skip grades (such as from fourth to sixth) because of their ability to function ahead of chronological peers. There are two major reasons a student may be advised to skip a grade: (a) to obtain more intellectual stimulation and (b) to obtain a different social climate. One potential problem rising from grade skipping is that the content of the skipped grade will be missed. For example, a fourth to sixth grade skip may provide extra challenge in reading or math, but the fifth grade social studies content will be missed. However, opportunities to fill in knowledge gaps can be created through independent study or individual tutoring.

COMBINED CLASSES. Students from two grade levels are combined into a single class, such as a third and fourth grade class. This is often referred to as a "split" class because they have the ability to work independently. This allows the teacher to accommodate two grade levels in the same classroom. This setting often will provide more stimulation for students in the lower grade as they interact with older students.

CONCURRENT ENROLLMENT. Students are allowed to enroll at two schools at the same time. For example, a high school student may be allowed to enroll in college for advanced science classes while maintaining most of the day at high school. Concurrent enrollment allows for more advanced training while not moving the student from the primary setting. In this way, the chronological peer group is maintained for most of the day.

CREDIT BY EXAMINATION. Students are allowed to take examinations that indicate subject mastery. Appropriate credit is then awarded. For example, through examination, a high school student may demonstrate mastery of college level English and be awarded credit.

Classroom Acceleration

CURRICULUM COMPACTING. Students who need less drill and practice than their classmates are allowed to pre- and posttest through curriculum units. When the class requirements are met, the student is allowed to move to other studies (e.g., advanced exploration of subjects, individual or group projects, presentation of seminars). For example, a student who can demonstrate an understanding of pronouns may be provided opportunities for creative writing while the rest of the class continues studying pronouns.

TELESCOPING. The time sequence allotted to courses is condensed. For example, the requirements for junior high may be finished in two, rather than three, years. This allows time for students to pursue other academic interests which may not be in the traditional curriculum. For example, astronomy may not be a junior high science

offering; however, if the general program is telescoped, time for the study of astronomy can be created.

SELF-PACED INSTRUCTION. Students determine their own pace for a specific course. This allows gifted students to finish the curriculum more rapidly than typical students. In addition, it eliminates unnecessary drill and practice. For example, a student who learns rapidly may complete an algebra sequence in 5 months while the rest of the class completes the sequence in a 9 month period.

CONTINUOUS PROGRESS. Students are allowed to progress at their own rates without regard for schedules. As teachers determine that students are ready for more advanced subject matter, they are allowed to proceed. This individualized curriculum management allows students to continue studying until they have mastered skills instead of ending practice at prearranged times. For example, students quit studying long division when they have mastered it, not when the unit ends.

SUBJECT-MATTER ACCELERATION. Students are placed partially with their chronological peers and partially with more advanced students. However, students remain in their original grades. For example, a seventh grade music student may be placed with a ninth grade performing group. This type of acceleration is frequently used for advanced study of a single subject.

ADVANCED PLACEMENT. Advanced placement classes are college level courses taught in high schools by specially trained teachers. Students are evaluated through a system of national examinations. Students scoring at high enough levels receive college credit. English, history, math, and science are commonly taught AP subjects in large high schools.

Beyond Traditional Schooling

MENTORSHIPS. Students are teamed with community- based mentors who are expert in specific content areas. The mentor provides advanced, specialized study for individual students. For example, a student with a serious interest in marine biology might be teamed with a working marine biologist. Mentorships are used almost entirely at the secondary school level and can be difficult to monitor. The personal relationship and highly individualized educational experience are the most important features of mentorship.

EXTRACURRICULAR PROGRAMS. In-depth or fast-paced learning is provided through summer programs or outside coursework. These programs are often provided by school districts or universities in the local area. For example, a summer program might focus on a performing skill (music or drama) or a specific interest (space travel).

CORRESPONDENCE COURSES. Students are allowed to take correspondence courses which provide more advanced learning. Credit is given at the discretion of the school district or university. Through correspondence, a student might study calculus when it is not offered at his/her school.

Notes: Criticism of Academic Acceleration has centered around two issues: (a) the emotional well-being of gifted students and (b) gifted students participation in age-appropriate activities. Sometimes gifted learners are stereotyped as emotionally underdeveloped and socially lacking. However, research indicates that gifted students are often well-adjusted and popular; they also possess positive self-concepts. What may be seen in the gifted student actually is dissonance between intellectual, motor, and social development (Silverman, 1993a). Age-appropriate activities (e.g., participation on athletic teams, learning to drive, and attending school activities and dances) may or may not be important for individual students.

In addition, it must be remembered that acceleration refers to a variety of options, some more radical than others. For example, if a student is accelerated for music only, the rest of the school day is not altered. In terms of peer association, this is vastly different from a program in which a younger student attends a different level class for the full day.

Finally, it must be noted that teachers and parents are critical components of successful acceleration. Teachers of complex subject matter may not be skilled in working with younger students and may have to find ways of adapting. Parents become critical in helping students adjust to new, unfamiliar situations. When teachers and parents provide critical support, acceleration can be a highly successful option for gifted learners.

AUTONOMOUS LEARNER MODEL

Method: Autonomous Learner Model

Author: George T. Betts

Sources: Betts, G. T. (1985). *Autonomous learner model for the gifted and talented.* Greeley, CO: Autonomous Learner Publications and Specialists; Betts, G. T. (1986). The autonomous learner model for the gifted and talented. In J. S. Renzulli (Ed.), *Systems and models for developing programs for the gifted and talented* (pp. 27–56). Mansfield Center, CT: Creative Learning Press; Betts, G. (1995). The autonomous learner model. In C. J. Maker & A. B. Nielson, (Eds.), Teaching models in education of the gifted (2nd ed., pp. 21–52). Austin, TX: Pro-Ed.

Description: The Autonomous Learner Model (ALM) is a method specifically designed for secondary gifted students that focuses on helping them develop, implement, and evaluate their own courses of study. It is designed to help students improve their skills in cognitive, emotional, and social areas. It also allows a student to pursue an area of strong interest.

The ALM is divided into five dimensions: (a) orientation, (b) individual development, (c) enrichment, (d) seminars, and (e) in-depth study. The orientation dimension introduces students to concepts of giftedness and the ALM. The individual development dimension introduces students to the concept of autonomous learning. The enrichment activities dimension allows students to study subject content too complex or specific to be included in the traditional curriculum. The seminar dimension guides students in researching and presenting information to small groups. Evaluation of each seminar is made through student-developed criteria. The in-depth study dimension provides for individual or small group in-depth study over lengthy periods of time.

When utilized together, the five dimensions are designed to provide an integrated and student-centered curriculum. In addition, students are allowed increased autonomy through control over their program of study.

The ALM is designed as a one-period class that extends over 3 years. For example, it may extend from grades 7–9 (encompassing junior high) or grades 9–12 (encompassing senior high). In schools where it is not offered as a separate program, extra class time to implement the ALM can be created through the use of curriculum compacting.

Notes: Maker and Nielson (1995) reported that little empirical research has been completed on the ALM. Although it is designed with the needs of gifted learners in mind, data to support its effectiveness are not currently available.

INTEGRATIVE EDUCATION MODEL

Method: Integrative Education Model

Author: Barbara Clark

Source: Clark, B. (1992). *Growing up gifted.* New York: Merrill; Clark, B. (1986). The integrative education model. In J. S. Renzulli (Ed.), *Systems and models for developing programs for the gifted and talented* (pp. 57–91). Mansfield Center, CT: Creative Learning Press.

Description: The Integrative Education Model (IEM) is unique from other models in that it utilizes research on brain function to enhance knowledge acquisition among gifted learners. Clark suggested that brain function and cognition should be treated as interrelated issues in teaching gifted learners. The IEM was designed for gifted learners and utilizes the concept of holistic teaching to address their needs.

The IEM is composed of four functions: (a) thinking, (b) feeling, (c) physical, and (d) intuitive. The thinking function consists of cognitive abilities used analytically. The feeling function consists of emotion and affect. The physical function consists of movement and physical senses. The intuitive function consists of creativity and the ability to know something outside of the rational realm.

Beyond the four functions, there are seven components. They are: (a) responsive learning environment; (b) relaxation and tension reduction; (c) movement and physical encoding; (d) empowering language and behavior; (e) choice and perceived control; (f) complex and challenging cognitive activities; and (g) intuition and integration.

The IEM functions as an organizing framework with any other program content. By implementing the four functions and seven components, a teacher should be able to facilitate a holistic experience for gifted learners. Connectedness and wholeness of the learning process are underlying concepts for this model.

Notes: In addition to the focus on cognitive brain function, the IEM makes a serious attempt to attend to the affective needs of the gifted learner. Emphasis is placed on altering the traditional environment so that the gifted learner can flourish.

INDIVIDUALIZED TEACHING

Method: Individualized Teaching of the Gifted in Regular Classrooms

Author: Hazel J. Feldhusen

Sources: Feldhusen, H. J. (1993). Individualized teaching of the gifted in regular classrooms. In C. J. Maker (Ed.), *Critical issues in gifted education: Programs for the gifted in regular classrooms* (pp. 263-273). Austin, TX: Pro-Ed; Kitano, M. K. (1993). Critique of Feldhusen's individualized teaching of the gifted in regular classrooms. In C. J. Maker (Ed.), *Critical issues in gifted education: Programs for the gifted in regular classrooms* (pp. 274–281). Austin, TX: Pro-Ed.

Description: Individualized Teaching of the Gifted in Regular Classrooms is a method designed to challenge gifted learners who are placed in heterogeneous settings. The program has five basic goals: (a) mastery of basic skills at appropriate ability levels, (b) development of enthusiasm for reading, (c) development of independence and self-direction, (d) development of cooperative work skills, and (e) development of positive self-concepts.

The core subjects (typically language arts, math, science, and history) are taught during the first part of the school day. During the second part of the school day, students plan their own courses with guidance from teachers. Large varieties of instructional materials on varied ability levels are provided for students in learning centers. Students are taught to schedule their time and record activities. Weekly class meetings are held to brainstorm ideas and address problems.

Notes: When curriculum is individualized in a heterogeneous setting, effective classroom management becomes critical. As the year progresses and students mature, theoretically they transition from a teacher- to a student-directed program. However, even as students make this transition, teachers must monitor them daily and track individual progress. The complex classroom managment required for this program may be too difficult for beginning teachers.

THE PURDUE THREE-STAGE ENRICHMENT MODEL

Method: The Purdue Three-Stage Enrichment Model for Gifted Education at the Elementary Level

Authors: John Feldhusen and Penny Kolloff

Source: Feldhusen, J., & Kolloff, P. (1986). The Purdue three-stage enrichment model for gifted education at the elementary level. In J. Renzulli (Ed.), *Systems and models for developing programs for the gifted and talented* (pp. 126–152). Mansfield Center, CT: Creative Learning Press.

Description: The Purdue Three-Stage Enrichment Model (PEM) is designed to meet the needs of gifted learners by providing an enriched program for elementary students through a pull-out service delivery method. Each gifted learner has an instructional program determined by an Individualized Educational Plan.

The PEM is divided into three distinct areas: (a) Divergent and Convergent Thinking, (b) Development of Creative Problem-Solving Abilities, and (c) Development of Independent Learning Abilities. All three areas must be utilized to create a comprehensive program.

Feldhusen and Kolloff explained the concepts of divergent and convergent thinking as development of fluency, flexibility, originality, elaboration, decision making, and forecasting. As these skills are developed, Creative Problem-Solving Abilities and Independent Learning Abilities are designed to foster skill application, extension, and creativity

Notes: Because of the recent nationwide move from homogeneous to heterogeneous classrooms, pull-out programs may not receive administrative support. Without adequate administrative support, it is not possible to implement this service delivery method.

THE PURDUE SECONDARY MODEL

Method: The Purdue Secondary Model for Gifted and Talented Youth

Authors: John Feldhusen and Anne Robinson

Source: Feldhusen, J., & Robinson, A. (1986). Purdue secondary model for gifted and talented youth. In J. Renzulli (Ed.), *Systems and models for developing programs for the gifted and talented* (pp. 153–179). Mansfield Center, CT: Creative Learning Press.

Description: The Purdue Secondary Model (PSM) is a comprehensive program that addresses the interests and learning styles of gifted learners. Initially, gifted learners are identified for the program. After identification, they are counseled and guided toward an array of educational options designed to promote the growth of their abilities.

Counseling services are utilized extensively in this program. Counseling services provide identification information, placement options, and career exploration. As a result of these services, gifted learners may be placed in advanced placement classes, honors classes, cultural enrichment experiences, Saturday enrichment classes, correspondence courses, summer programs, or some combination of these options. Placement is based on individual need, desire, and learning style. Another important component is participation in seminars. Seminars are designed to provide individual learning opportunities.

The PSM utilizes the concepts of enrichment and acceleration to meet the needs of gifted learners. The comprehensiveness of the PSM is unusual among secondary programs.

Notes: Most large, urban secondary schools utilize many of the features suggested in the PSM. However, the comprehensive nature of the program is generally not implemented, and the counseling provision is frequently overlooked. Secondary programs implemented in a comprehensive manner as described in the PSM are rare.

THE GRID

Method: The Grid

Author: Sandra Kaplan

Source: Kaplan, S. (1986). The grid: A model to construct differentiated curriculum for the gifted. In J. Renzulli (Ed.), *Systems and models for developing programs for the gifted and talented* (pp. 182–193). Mansfield Center, CT: Creative Learning Press.

Description: The Grid is a model designed specifically for gifted learners which differentiates curriculum in an integrated way to provide challenging learning opportunities. Kaplan proposed that curriculum for gifted learners should be (a) differentiated, (b) intentionally designed, (c) well-defined, and (d) planned. To achieve these goals, unit planning is organized by themes.

In traditional planning, units usually are organized by topics. The Grid organizes study units by themes, which are defined as umbrella conceptualizations under which several topics may be subsumed. Kaplan suggested that themes more closely mirror the way gifted students think and learn.

Kaplan proposed three elements of curriculum: (a) content, (b) process, and (c) product. The content consists of relevant information for gifted learners. Kaplan defined content as "knowledge and information defined as useful, important, timely and interesting for gifted students" (p. 185). The process consists of sets of skills or competencies students are expected to learn. Kaplan suggested that competencies should be chosen on the basis of student developmental readiness. The product consists of a form of communication that demonstrates the understanding of content and process. Products might take several forms (e.g., oral, written, or graphic).

Differentiation of curriculum for the gifted learner is a major component of curricular planning utilizing the Grid. It attempts to create a curricular match between the abilities and interests of the gifted learner and the educational program. Differentiation is seen as the key to addressing the needs of gifted students.

Notes: An important distinction made by Kaplan is that individualization and differentiation are not the same thing. She indicated that individualization follows differentiation and that both need to occur for the needs of gifted learners to be adequately addressed.

THE ENRICHMENT TRIAD/ REVOLVING DOOR MODEL

Method: The Enrichment Triad/Revolving Door Model

Author: Joseph Renzulli

Sources: Maker, C. J., & Nielson, A. B. (1995). *Teaching models in education of the gifted* (2nd ed., pp. 163-198). Austin, TX: Pro-Ed; Renzulli, J. S., & Reis, S. M. (1985). *The schoolwide enrichment model: A comprehensive plan for educational excellence.* Mansfield Center, CT: Creative Learning Press; Renzulli, J. S., & Reis, S. M. (1986). The enrichment triad/revolving door model: A schoolwide plan for the development of creative productivity. In J. S. Renzulli (Ed.), *Systems and models for developing programs for the gifted and talented* (pp. 216–266). Mansfield Center, CT: Creative Learning Press.

Description: Renzulli developed two models which are used separately or in conjunction with each other. The Revolving Door Model is a broad-based enrichment

model that was later supplemented by the Enrichment Triad Model. Both models are designed around a broadened definition of giftedness that is behaviorally based.

In a departure from models that identify gifted learners through ability levels, Renzulli defined giftedness as the interaction among three traits: (a) above-average ability, (b) task commitment, and (c) creativity. He suggested that these behaviors are not always present in students. In addition, he suggested that these behaviors can be developed through stimulating experiences.

The Revolving Door Model. The Revolving Door Model utilizes both pull-out and resource room designs to provide enrichment experiences for a larger group of students than traditional gifted programs serve. Each school forms a talent pool of approximately 15-20% of its students. From this talent pool students revolve into advanced experiences based on their needs as illustrated through classroom performance assessment.

The Enrichment Triad Model. The Enrichment Triad Model divides enrichment experiences into three types: (a) Type I, General Exploratory Activities; (b) Type II, Group Training Activities; and (c) Type III, Individual and Small Group Investigations of Real Problems. Type I and Type II enrichment activities are designed for all students and are implemented in the general classroom by classroom teachers. Only Type III enrichment is suggested specifically for gifted students. Type III enrichment should be provided by a teacher with special training in the area of giftedness.

Notes: One reason for the development of the Enrichment Triad and the Revolving Door models was to counteract charges of elitism of gifted programs among some parents and members of the educational community. By forming the talent pool with 15-20% of the students and making services available only when necessary, a greater number of students can participate in enriching experiences.

MULTIPLE TALENT APPROACH/ TALENTS UNLIMITED

Method: Multiple Talent Approach/Talents Unlimited

Authors: Calvin Taylor and Carolyn Schlicter

Sources: Guilford, J. P. (1967). *The nature of human intelligence.* New York: McGraw-Hill; Taylor, C. (1995). Multiple talent approach. In C. J. Maker & A. B. Nielson, (Eds.), *Teaching models in education of the gifted* (2nd ed., pp. 283–321). Austin, TX: Pro-Ed; Schlicter, C. (1986). Talents unlimited: Applying the multiple talent approach in mainstream and gifted programs. In J. S. Renzulli (Ed.), *Systems and models for developing programs for the gifted and talented* (pp. 352–390). Mansfield Center, CT: Creative Learning Press; Taylor, C. (1986). Cultivating simultaneous student growth in both multiple creative talents and knowledge. In J. S. Renzulli (Ed.), *Systems and models for developing programs for the gifted and talented* (pp. 306–350). Mansfield Center, CT: Creative Learning Press.

Description: The Multiple Talent Approach (MTA) is designed to provide a framework that teaches thinking skills. Taylor formulated the MTA on a broadened concept of giftedness based on the "Structure of Intellect" model developed by Guilford. Taylor suggested that all students are potentially gifted in at least one area. The purpose of the MTA is to help students develop talent in many areas. Taylor referred to the MTA as a "simultaneous double curriculum which involves developing both innate talent processes and adding knowledge to one's existing knowledge base" (p. 307).

Taylor identified six talent areas: academic, productive thinking, planning, communicating, forecasting, and decision making. Since its initial development, this list has been expanded to include implementation, human relations, and discerning opportunities. Because academic talent has been frequently used as a marker of giftedness in schools, the MTA effectively broadens the concept by illustrating talent across several areas. Taylor suggested that all students function at different levels of talent development.

A "totem pole" chart is used to identify the strength of each talent for each student. By utilizing this approach, students are able to see varied profiles. This is intended to help them understand that they may be advanced in one area, but not another.

The talents (MTA terminology for what appear to be skills) are explained to students. Extensive practice is then completed with each talent. For example, once they learn the productive thinking talent, students are taught to apply this talent to content-based information. The talent training is said to increase depth of knowledge and level of creativity expressed through thinking processes.

Talents Unlimited (TU) is the practical application of the MTA in a school setting. It contains (a) skill components, (b) instructional materials, (c) an in-service training program, and (d) an evaluation system. The TU has been used with heterogeneous groups and gifted groups. It may be of most use for gifted students in the area skill development for in-depth investigations.

Notes: Maker and Nielson (1995) suggested that, because the MTA broadens the concept of giftedness, it is possible that approximately 50% of the students in any school would be identified as gifted. This is in direct contrast to a definition of giftedness which indicates that only 3–5% of students need differential programming. Therefore, the MTA may not be an appropriate model for a categorically funded gifted program.

INDIVIDUALIZED PROGRAMMING PLANNING MODEL

Method: Individualized Programming Planning Model

Author: Donald Treffinger

Sources: Treffinger, D. J. (1995). Self-directed learning. In C. J. Maker & A. B. Nielson (Eds.), Teaching models in education of the gifted (2nd ed., pp. 323–355). Austin, TX: Pro-Ed; Treffinger, D. J. (1986). Fostering effective, independent learning through individualized programming. In J. S. Renzulli (Ed.), *Systems and models for developing programs for the gifted and talented* (pp. 430–460). Mansfield Center, CT: Creative Learning Press.

Description: The Individualized Programming Planning Model (IPPM) is designed to promote "effective, independent learning based on the strengths and talents of the student" (Treffinger, 1986, p. 431). Treffinger identified four components of independent learning: (a) characteristics and identification, (b) process development, (c) content competence, and (d) management and environment.

The characteristics and identification component introduces students to three elements. First, the IPPM model is inclusive rather than exclusive. Treffinger suggested that much of the identification of giftedness excludes students through arbitrary cut-off points. He indicated that student needs should determine educational services. Second, information should serve an instructional diagnostic purpose. This means identification would connect to instruction, making identification purposeful. Third, an operational conceptualization of giftedness would be based on the individual talents and needs of students.

The process development component focuses on abilities that help improve process development and intellectual skills. In ad-

dition to learning to think creatively and critically, students learn to combine these skills with specific content. Once process development has been mastered, students move to more complex skills, such as problem solving.

The content competence component is designed to ensure that students do not focus on the process of learning to the exclusion of content. Because gifted learners tend to make generalizations easily, they may learn content in a superficial manner. The IPPM is designed to place emphasis on learning content; however, independent learning is not deferred until content is mastered. The two concepts are taught in conjunction.

The management and environment component regulates the learning situation. Students and teachers are taught to create and maintain an environment that fosters independent learning. Treffinger indicated that self-directedness is a skill that must be learned gradually. Gifted students are often expected to know how to self-direct learning. However, gifted and typical learners must be taught to develop this skill. The IPPM puts an emphasis on acquisition and practice of self-directed learning.

Notes: Maker and Nielson (1995) reported that self-directed learning may be best utilized as a program that enhances the effectiveness of other programs, such as the ALM and the Enrichment Triad Model. When used exclusively, self-directed learning may not provide enough of a framework to form a complete program for gifted learners.

ACADEMIC COMPETITIONS

Method: Academic Competitions

Source: Tallent-Runnels, M. K., & Candler-Lotven, A. C. (1996). *Academic competitions* *for gifted students.* Thousand Oaks, CA: Corwin Press.

Description: Academic competitions provide enrichment and intellectual stimulation for high achieving students in general and specific areas. Competitions are usually divided into elementary and secondary age groups.

Several constructive effects are gained from participating in academic competitions. First, the positive aspects of intellectual achievment are emphasized. Second, students are provided contact with similarly achieving peers. This type of contact validates student interest and achievment and may be missing in some schools. Third, students are allowed to pursue specific areas of interest. This may satisfy individual desires that are otherwise unmet.

Participation in competitions may also help students realistically assess their own capabilities. For example, a student may be the most advanced math student in his or her school but, when compared with a larger group, may be only above average. Also, competitions are usually evaluated by independent judges, rather than the student's teacher. This may give the student an alternate and somewhat more objective assessment of his or her achievment.

Some competitions are individual, while others require partners, small groups, or larger teams. However, many competitions use team organization. Team participation requires the learning and utilization of cooperative group skills. For students who have not participated on athletic teams, this method gives them an opportunity to fulfill a role as a team member.

Notes: Because curricular time and resources are limited, it is important to select competitions carefully. Teachers and students should research each competition to establish the level of commitment required.

FUTURE PROBLEM SOLVING PROGRAM

Method: Future Problem Solving Program

Author: E. Paul Torrance

Sources: *Training manual and coach's handbook.* (1993). Ann Arbor, MI: The Future Problem Solving Program; Schewach, D. L. (1994). *Scenarios: A guide to writing futuristic short stories* (rev. ed.). Ann Arbor, MI: The Future Problem Solving Program; *Community problem solving: Preparing students to become active problem solvers.* (1993). Ann Arbor, MI: The Future Problem Solving Program.

Description: The Future Problem Solving Program is designed to increase creative thinking among gifted students. The emphasis is to improve thinking processes over the school year.

The program consists of three parts: (a) a problem-solving competition, (b) a scenario-writing competition, and (c) local community problem solving. The three parts may be used independently or in combination. The level of use is individual with each school and program.

Future Problem Solving Competition. Students compete in groups of four that are organized by age: the Junior Division (grades 4–6), the Intermediate Division (grades 7–9), and the Senior Division (grades 10–12). In addition, there is a noncompetitive division for students in kindergarten through grade 3. Each team is coached by an adult who is registered with the program, frequently the classroom teacher. Many parents also fulfill this function.

During the participating year, students are given three problems to solve. For example, a recent problem set was Cities, Homelessness, and Kids and Violence. Students are presented with a stimulus, known as a "fuzzy." They identify problems, brainstorm solutions, and evaluate solutions to the problem. They then prepare booklets containing their ideas and submit them for evaluation. Booklets are prepared in a 2-hour time frame, although students complete research prior to beginning the problem-solving process.

Only the third problem is submitted for competition. Students are invited to participate in a State Bowl based on the results of the third problem. In addition, there is an International Conference to which students are invited based on the results from the problem. Evaluation is based on two elements: (a) applied research and (b) creative strength. Participating in the problem-solving process enhances the following skills: thinking, creativity, futures, research, teamwork, oral and written communication, self-direction, and contending with ambiguity.

Scenario-writing Competition. An additional scenario-writing competition is conducted. Students project 20 years into the future and develop scenarios of daily life based on their ideas of how the world will be at that time. The format used for scenario writing is the "short short" story (1,000–2,000 words). The scenario topics are based on the Future Problem Solving competition topics.

Local Community Problem Solving. Local Community Problem Solving allows students to focus their talents and creative ideas toward solving a real-life problem instead of a theoretical one. Teams may be of any size. Students follow the same problem solving process. They identify a problem, brainstorm solutions, and evaluate their solutions. Once this has been completed, students implement their solutions. The teams follow organizational plans which require them to formulate budgets, meet deadlines, work with members of the community (e.g., business partners), and prepare media presentations. The projects are then submitted for competition.

Notes: Dr. E. Paul Torrance began The Future Problem Solving Program in the 1970s. Since then, it has grown to international proportions. It provides an excellent opportunity for students to utilize higher level thinking skills and creativity.

The program requires significant amounts of preparation time for both students and coach. To make this method effective in a classroom, the coach must devote substantial time and energy in support of the students.

INTERNATIONAL BACCALAUREATE

Method: International Baccalaureate

Source: International Baccalaureate North America, 200 Madison Avenue, New York, NY 10016; (212) 696-4464.

Description: The International Baccalaureate is a rigorous, classical curriculum program in which students earn credits in six academic categories (mathematics, native language, foreign language, experimental sciences, humanities, and electives). Courses are designed to be taught over 2-year periods. Essay examinations are given in each subject area, usually encompassing 20–25 hours of evaluation per year. Students who score high enough are awarded a diploma. In addition, students must complete a Theory of Knowledge course and participate in a minimum of 150 hours of extracurricular activities. All curricula and final examinations are supervised by the International Baccalaureate Organization.

Notes: The implementation of the International Baccalaureate requires a school-wide or program-wide commitment that extends over several years. Examination procedures must be followed explicitly and are monitored by the international organization.

Many colleges and universities (both American and European) will grant credit to a student possessing this diploma. Some schools will admit a student as a sophomore.

TALENT SEARCHES

Method: Talent Searches

Sources: Benbow, C. P. (1986). SMPY's model for teaching mathematically precocious students. In J. S. Renzulli (Ed.), *Systems and models for developing programs for the gifted and talented* (pp. 3–25). Mansfield Center, CT: Creative Learning Press; Center for Talented Youth, The Johns Hopkins University, Baltimore, Maryland; Center for Talent Development, Northwestern University, Evanston, Illinois; Duke University Talent Identification Program, Durham, North Carolina; Rocky Mountain Talent Search, University of Denver, Denver, Colorado; Utah Talent Search, Utah State Office of Education, Salt Lake City, Utah.

Description: Talent searches are yearly programs that identify high-achieving junior high school students by scores on college entrance examinations. Students who score at the 95th percentile or above on standardized tests in their own schools are invited to a local or regional university to take out-of-level standardized tests (ACT, SAT). The scores from the out-of-level tests are used to identify mathematically and verbally talented adolescents.

Once identified, students receive score interpretations that compare them to chronological peers and high school seniors who are applying for college admission. Additionally, students are linked with enrichment programs that are designed to provide intellectual stimulation. Individual schools and school districts also receive information that helps them respond to the needs of their academically talented students.

REFERENCES

Clark, B. (1992). *Growing up gifted.* New York: Merrill.

Brody, L., & Benbow, C. (1987). Accelerative strategies: How effective are they for the gifted? *Gifted Child Quarterly, 3*(3), 105–110.

Kulik, C-L. C., & Kulik, J. A. (1982). Effects of ability grouping on secondary school students: A meta-analysis of evaluation findings. *American Educational Research Journal, 19*, 415–428.

Maker, & Neilson. (1995). *Teaching models in education of the gifted* (2 ed.), Austin, TX: Pro-Ed.

Silverman, L. K. (1993a). Counseling families. In L. K. Silverman (Ed.), *Counseling the gifted and talented* (pp. 151–178). Denver, CO: Love.

Silverman, L. K. (1993b). Social development, leadership, and gender issues. In L. K. Silverman (Ed.), *Counseling the gifted and talented* (pp. 291–237). Denver, CO: Love.

Silverman, L. K. (1994). Affective curriculum for the gifted. In J. VanTassel-Baska (Ed.), *Comprehensive curriculum for gifted learners* (pp. 325–346). Boston: Allyn and Bacon.

CHAPTER

4

Special Physical Education Programs

Hester L. Henderson, Ph.D.
Ron W. French, Ph.D.

CONTENTS

▶ Preschool Recreation Enrichment
  Program (PREP)   65
▶ Aquatics for Individuals
  with Disabilities   65
▶ Peer Tutors: Physical Education
  Opportunity Program for
  Exceptional Learners (PEOPEL)   66
▶ The Achievement-based Curriculum
  (ABC) and Project I CAN   67
▶ Physical Management   67
▶ Sports, Play, and Active Recreation
  for Kids (SPARK)   68
▶ Every Child A Winner With
  Physical Education   69

▶ New Games   69
▶ Project Transition   70
▶ Project C.R.E.O.L.E.   70
▶ Halliwick Method of Swimming   71
▶ Project ACTIVE   71
▶ Special Olympics   72
▶ Data Based Gymnasium   72
▶ Body Skills: A Motor Development
  Curriculum for Children   73
▶ Project Explore   73
▶ Physical Best and Individuals
  with Disabilities   74
▶ Perceptual Motor Activities   74

Special Physical Education is a term used to define programs that provide instruction in physical education to students with disabilities. In 1975, with the enactment of The Education for All Handicapped Children Act (1977), otherwise referred to as PL 94–142, all students who were classified as requiring special education services were to be provided services in physical education. In the law, the definition of special education is as follows:

> The term "special education" means specially designed instruction, at no cost to parents or guardians, to meet the unique needs of a handicapped child, including classroom instruction, instruction in physical education, home instruction, and instruction in hospitals and institutions.

The intent of this law was to provide students with disabilities educational programs in the least restrictive environment that would best meet their individual needs safely and successfully. To integrate students with disabilities as much as possible with their nondisabled peers, the law states that all special education students should go to regular physical education with two exceptions: (a) if they are in a special school and there is no regular physical education or (b) if, based on the student's evaluation in physical education, it is determined that his or her needs cannot best be met in a regular physical education class. Students in a special school must be provided instruction in physical education at that school. Those whose needs cannot be met in regular physical education will be placed in the least restrictive placement that will best meet their individual needs. There are a number of placement options on the continuum of services in physical education as can be seen in Figure 4–1.

Approximately 93% of special education students are placed in regular physical education classes. These students are not required to have goals and objectives in physical education written on their Individualized Educational Programs (IEPs). However, if a special education student does require specialized services in physical education, beyond the regular physical education class, then goals and objectives must be written on the IEP.

The goal of the special physical educator is to provide students with the skills and knowledge necessary to be able to successfully function in the regular physical education class.

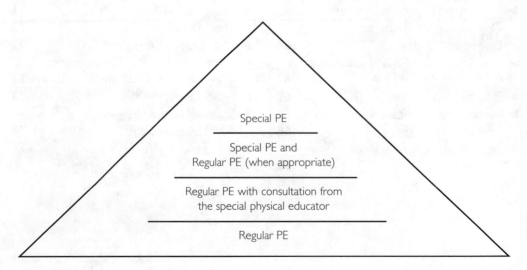

Figure 4–1. Continuum of physical education services.

With this goal in mind, the special physical educator will plan instructional activities using the core curriculum in physical education as well as input from the regular physical educator as to what skills are necessary to function successfully in his or her class.

PL 94–142 defines physical education as instruction in (a) physical and motor fitness, (b) fundamental motor skills, (c) aquatics, (d) dance, and (e) individual and group games. Goals must be defined in at least one of these five areas.

A number of programs and teaching methods have been designed to provide instruction in physical education to students with disabilities. Some of these programs are described in this chapter.

PRESCHOOL RECREATION ENRICHMENT PROGRAM (PREP)

Method: Preschool Recreation Enrichment Program (PREP)

Authors: Karen Littman and Lin Leslie

Source: Littman, K., & Leslie, L. (1978). Preschool Recreation Enrichment Program (PREP). Washington, DC: Hawkins & Associates.

Description: PREP is a model recreation program based on motor and associative learning. It uses a life experience approach emphasizing motor, language, social, and emotional development of preschool children with disabilities. The target population for the PREP Program is children ages 3 through 5 with developmental delays not severe enough to preclude independent functioning. PREP is a workable, flexible system that aids recreation professionals in initiating programs for preschool children with delays in motor and associative skill areas.

PREP focuses on (a) developing and improving basic fine and gross motor skills essential to daily living, (b) developing receptive and expressive language skills, (c) developing a healthy self-concept, (d) maximizing socialization skills through play, and (e) establishing a recreation value through the provision of successful experiences in play activities. The PREP program includes the following components: (a) long and short term program planning; (b) program planning based on the assessed needs of the target group; (c) planning and implementation based on goals and objectives; (d) implementation based on an approach that utilizes small groups to introduce skills and large groups to practice these skills; (e) continuous evaluation of the total program; and (f) regular staff involvement for problem solving, program planning, evaluation, and modification.

The PREP Implementation and Resource Guide is designed to assist recreation professionals in planning and implementing preschool recreation programs based on the PREP Model. The PREP manual is designed to assist recreation personnel in establishing the content of programs addressing the motor and associative learning needs of preschool children. Included in the manual are task analyses of 27 fine and gross motor skills. Illustrations are provided to describe existing behavior as well as the behavior to be achieved. Also included are suggested life experience activities, games, reinforcement activities, language activities, and recommended equipment.

Notes: The Preschool Recreation Enrichment Program received funding from the Bureau of Education for the Handicapped in 1975. The Implementation and Resource Guide and the manual can be obtained from Hawkins & Associates, Inc. 804 D Street N.E., Washington, DC 20002-6186.

AQUATICS FOR INDIVIDUALS WITH DISABILITIES

Method: Aquatics for Individuals with Disabilities

Author: American Red Cross

Source: American Red Cross. (1992). Disabilities and other conditions. In *Swimming and diving* (Chap. 9, pp. 204–221). St. Louis: Mosby Lifeline.

Description: This chapter discusses a number of issues related to aquatics programs for individuals with disabilities. The physiological, psychological, and social benefits to be derived from an aquatics program are discussed highlighting the specific benefits to people with disabilities.

The following disabilities are discussed: hearing impairment, visual impairment, tactile impairment, intellectual impairment, learning disability, autism, behavior disorders, amputations, paralysis, cerebral palsy, multiple sclerosis, muscular dystrophy, aging, arthritis, asthma, allergies, cardiac and blood conditions, cystic fibrosis, diabetes, fragile bones, obesity, and seizures. The specific needs of people with particular disabilities relative to an aquatics program are clearly defined and special emphasis is given to teaching suggestions and safety precautions for each disability.

The modifications necessary to make a swimming facility accessible to individuals with disabilities are discussed. Modifications are described for the building structure, the locker rooms, and the pool. In addition, there is a brief discussion of the federal laws that ensure accessible facilities for individuals with disabilities.

In the discussion on programming, the concept of mainstreaming is discussed. The rights and responsibilities of people with disabilities when applying for an aquatics program are clearly described. Advantages and disadvantages of mainstreamed and nonmainstreamed programs are delineated.

Finally the chapter discusses mainstreamed and nonmainstreamed competitive aquatics programs and describes other leisure activities involving aquatics that are available to individuals with disabilities. A list of organizations that promote participation in aquatic activities, including fitness, competition, and leisure activities for people with disabilities is included in Appendix A of the text.

Notes: This is a chapter in the book, *Swimming and Diving*. It is available through the American Red Cross.

PEER TUTORS

Method: Peer Tutors: Physical Education Opportunity Program for Exceptional Learners (PEOPEL)

Authors: Larry Irmer, Benita Odenkirk, and Gary Glasenapp

Source: Irmer, L. D., Odenkirk, B., & Glasenapp, G. (1970). *Physical education opportunity program for exceptional learners (PEOPEL): An administrative guide for secondary schools.* Phoenix: Arizona Department of Education.

Description: The goal of the PEOPEL Project is to offer exceptional learners at the junior high and secondary levels the opportunity for individualized physical education learning by concentrating on abilities and potentials. Exceptional learners are those with some physical, mental, social, or emotional disabilities who would benefit more from an individualized and developmental physical education program than from general physical education. Individualized learning is made possible through trained student peer tutors who work with exceptional peers under the guidance and direction of the PEOPEL teacher. PEOPEL provides the opportunity for students to improve at their own pace through peer teaching.

Notes: The PEOPEL Project received Federal funding initially through ESEA Title IV-C and the Arizona Department of Education in 1974. In 1979, PEOPEL was granted National Validation from the Joint Dissemination and Review Panel, Washington, DC. PEOPEL is now part of the National Diffusion Network.

THE ACHIEVEMENT-BASED CURRICULUM (ABC) AND PROJECT I CAN

Method: The Achievement-based Curriculum (ABC) and Project I CAN

Authors: Janet Wessell and Luke Kelly

Source: Wessell, J., & Kelly, J. (1986). *Achievement-based curriculum development in physical education.* Philadelphia: Lea & Febiger.

Description: The I CAN Achievement-based Curriculum Project was designed to train regular and special educators and regular physical educators to implement individualized, assessment-based instruction of the physical and motor needs of the students with disabilities in their classes. The ABC is a process model for training teachers how to plan, assess, implement, and evaluate instruction. Teachers first learn the ABC model in order to effectively use the I CAN resource materials. The I CAN resource materials are designed to cover the scope (preprimary through secondary) and essential content typically addressed in physical education, with accommodations made for students functioning at a wide range of levels (zero competency to advanced). The program is competency-based for both the teachers and their students. The curriculum materials represent a bank of over 200 student performance objectives for qualitative assessment, prescriptive instruction, evaluation, student reports, and a computer management system for the school program. Certified trainers conduct workshops on assessing students' performance levels, prescribing instructional activities, teaching individualized instruction in group settings, and evaluating student change and program effectiveness. Teachers are subsequently monitored on their implementation competencies and receive feedback. The program's performance objectives cover such areas of motor development as aquatics, locomotor skills, body awareness, physical fitness, dance, team sports, individual/dual sports, and outdoor activities.

Notes: The Achievement-based Curriculum (ABC)-Project I CAN was approved by the Joint Dissemination and Review Panel for Teachers (special education, physical education, special physical education, and/or combinations) of children with disabilities in special and/or regular educational programs in 1981 and was recertified in 1985. This project is now part of the National Diffusion Network.

For more information on this project contact: Luke Kelly, Ph.D., Project Center, Curry School of Education, Ruffner Hall, 405 Street, Charlottesville, VA 22903.

PHYSICAL MANAGEMENT

Method: Physical Management

Author: Eileen Solberg

Source: *Educational programs that work: The catalogue of the National Diffusion Network* (21st ed.). (1995). Boston: Sopris West.

Description: The Physical Management program was developed to give overweight students, grades 10–12, the knowledge and opportunity to interrupt the cycle of obesity and inactivity that prevents a fully healthy and effective lifestyle. The curriculum includes:

1. Behavior change—to replace inappropriate eating and exercise habits which have led to obesity and poor physical condition.

2. Physical conditioning—to enable students to evaluate their fitness and body composition, and design a conditioning program based on principles of exercise prescription.
3. Nutrition education—to provide practical nutrition education by teaching food group selection, portion control, and caloric density of foods.
4. Positive image building—to set the stage for positive change through goal setting, social skills, and assertiveness training.

Enrollees may earn either required or elective physical education credit.

Notes: Physical Management can be implemented in schools of any size with minimal cost and adaptation. No new staff or special facilities are required. A complimentary awareness packet is available.

The Physical Management Project received Federal funding initially through ESEA Title IV-C. In 1983 it was granted National Validation from the Joint Dissemination and Review Panel and is now part of the National Diffusion Network.

For more information on this project contact: Eileen Solberg, Director of Physical Management, P.O. Box 891, Billings, MT 59103.

SPORTS, PLAY, AND ACTIVE RECREATION FOR KIDS (SPARK)

Method: Sports, Play, and Active Recreation for Kids (SPARK)

Authors: Thom McKenzie and Paul Rosengard

Source: *Educational programs that work: The catalogue of the National Diffusion Network* (21st ed.). (1995). Boston: Sopris West.

Description: SPARK is a curriculum and staff development program designed to help elementary teachers provide quality physical education. Primary goals are to provide students with substantial amounts of physical activity through a program that can be implemented by trained specialists and classroom teachers. SPARK activities encourage maximum student participation during class time, as well as promote regular physical activity outside of school.

The Physical Education Program promotes individual improvement, and students are encouraged to monitor their own progress. The curriculum calls for classes to be taught a minimum of 3 days a week throughout the school year. The yearly plan is divided into instructional units that are typically 4 weeks (12 lessons) in length. A standard 30-minute lesson has two parts: Part I activities focus on developing health-related fitness and locomotor skills; Part II activities focus on developing generalizable motor skills. The Self-management Program is a classroom curriculum that teaches behavioral skills that are important for maintaining physical activity. Its emphasis is on behavior change skills rather than knowledge alone. The Teacher Training Program is designed to develop teachers' commitment to health-related physical education, help them understand SPARK curricular units and activities, and develop management and instructional skills for effective implementation.

Notes: SPARK is the product of a 5-year National Institutes of Health grant. In 1994 it was granted National Validation from the Joint Dissemination and Review Panel and is now part of the National Diffusion Network.

Based on the results of the evaluation of this project, students in the SPARK Program made significant improvements in cardio-respiratory fitness, muscular strength and endurance measures, and sport skills. Teachers implementing the program provided significantly improved quantity and quality of physical education, as evidenced by increased frequency and length of classes, fitness activities, skill drills, and the minutes children engaged in moderate to vigorous physical activity.

For more information on this project contact: Dr. Thom McKenzie, Director, or Paul Rosengard, Coordinator, SPARK, San Diego State University, 6363 Alvarado Court, Suite 225, San Diego, CA 92120.

EVERY CHILD A WINNER

Method: Every Child a Winner with Physical Education

Authors: Martha Owens and Susan Rockett

Source: *Educational programs that work: The catalogue of the National Diffusion Network* (21st ed.). (1995). Boston: Sopris West.

Description: The Every Child A Winner with Physical Education (ECAW) program is a developmentally appropriate physical education program which improves fitness, motor skills, and contributes to improved self-esteem and academic success for all children, regardless of physical or mental ability. This program uses the concepts of space awareness, body awareness, qualities of movement, and relationships as the basis for child-designed games, gymnastics sequences, and dance. The discovery learning or indirect teaching method is used to encourage critical thinking, one of the National Goals for Education. Children are given movement tasks that can be solved individually or in a group. Cooperation and competition are handled developmentally through educational games, educational dance, and educational gymnastics. Children are encouraged to reach their personal potentials and winning occurs when each child does his or her best. A variety of solutions successfully answers each task posed by the teacher so children will not feel pressured or become embarrassed in this program. Inclusion has been a major focus of the program since its inception. Teacher implementers rate the program as highly successful in physical education to meet special needs.

Notes: The Every Child a Winner Project received Federal funding initially through ESEA Title III. In 1974 it was granted National Validation from the Joint Dissemination and Review Panel for Grades K–6 and was recertified in 1985 and 1991 for Grades 1–3. It is part of the National Diffusion Network. For more information on this project contact: Martha Owens or Susan Rockett, Every Child A Winner, Educational Excellence, Inc., P.O. Box 141, Ocilla, GA 31774.

NEW GAMES

Method: New Games

Author: Andrew Fluegelman

Sources: Fluegelman, A. (1976). *The new games book.* New York: Doubleday; Fluegelman, A. (1981). More new games. New York: Doubleday.

Description: New Games is a collection of games that can be played competitively with opportunity to display skill and strategy or with no goal beyond getting people together to play and enjoy each other's company. Neither sex, age, nor size determines a person's ability to have fun. People are the most important part of the game. The point is for everyone to play hard and have fun. There are games for one player, two players, up to a hundred players. Rules can be changed to be whatever the players want them to be. The games are easy to learn and require very little equipment. All that is needed are a few friends and the desire to celebrate the day with play. There are no spectators in New Games; everyone plays.

Notes: The first book is a collection of 60 New Games. Also included is a commentary on how and why New Games were invented, how to playfully referee them, and how to create your own New Games Tournament. The second book is a collection of 60 more New Games. Included in this edition are new approaches to participation and winning, essays on game inventing and adaptation, and a description of a New Games Training.

PROJECT TRANSITION

Method: Project Transition

Authors: Paul Jansma, Jeff McCubbin, Sue Combs, Jim Decker, and Walter Ersing

Source: Jansma, P., McCubbin, J., Combs, S., Decker, J., & Ersing, W. (1987). *Fitness and hygiene programming for the severely handicapped: A curriculum-embedded assessment guide.* Worthington, OH: Moody's Printers.

Description: Project Transition is a program designed to train institutionalized adults with moderate to profound mental retardation to prepare them for transition into community living environments. The curriculum materials in this program include a series of task-analyzed, curriculum-embedded tests in personal hygiene and physical fitness. The five hygiene-related tests are: hand washing, face washing, toothbrushing, deodorant use, and personal appearance. The five physical fitness tests are: cardiorespiratory endurance, upper body strength and endurance, lower back and hamstring flexibility, abdominal endurance, and grip strength.

Notes: The tests are actually curriculum materials used to teach the selected skills; the program is therefore referred to as a curriculum-embedded system. All 10 of the skills in the main part of the curriculum were selected on the basis of their functional value. This was determined by surveying the fitness and hygiene needs of institutionalized adults with severe retardation prior to implementing the project.

PROJECT C.R.E.O.L.E.

Method: Project C.R.E.O.L.E.

Authors: Jennifer Wright, Susan Dark, and Bruce Theuerkauf.

Sources: Wright, J., Dark, S., & Theuerkauf, B. (1988). *Leisure/recreation curriculum for secondary aged students with disabilities.* Special Education Department, Jefferson Parish Public School System, 501 Manhattan Boulevard, Harvey, LA; Theuerkauf, B. (n.d.). *Project CREOLE: Wheelchair sports and mobility curriculum.* Special Education Department, Jefferson Parish, Public Schools, 501 Manhattan Boulevard, Harvey, LA.

Description: Project CREOLE (Community *Recreation Education* on *Leisure Education*) includes both curriculum and assessment materials for students with various disabilities (i.e., mental, physical, and multiple disabilities). Although these materials were developed for secondary-age students with disabilities, the material can be applied to various settings and curriculum areas. Many of the functional skills can be adapted easily for younger students and students with mild disabilities. The focus of the model is based on the instruction of functional, lifetime leisure skills by special educators; however, it can also be used by parents, case managers, and staff at residential alternatives, community agencies, and vocational programs.

Notes: This curriculum guide was not designed to include all appropriate leisure/

recreation activities for the targeted population, but instead provides several samples of possible activities. The selection of activities included in this curriculum guide should only serve as a resource in structuring appropriate leisure/recreation training. Individual and family interests and local opportunities should guide activity selection rather than a set curriculum which mandates instruction in specific skill areas. All activities are designed to reflect the ultimate goal, which is the self-initiated use of leisure time with functional skills. There is also a wheelchair sports and mobility curriculum component of Project CREOLE.

HALLIWICK METHOD OF SWIMMING

Method: Halliwick Method of Swimming

Author: James Martin

Source: Martin, J. (1981). The Halliwick method. *Physiotherapy, 67*, 288–292.

Description: This method is based on known scientific principles of hydrodynamics and body mechanics. The program teaches students about water orientation, water safety, how to stand up in the pool from a horizontal position, how to move independently in the water, and how to roll over from a prone to a supine position and back to a prone position, how to float, how to do a prone glide, ways to swim underwater and explore with the eyes open, how to scull, and finally how to do a basic backstroke. It has been found to be safe for people of all ages with many types of disabilities as well as for the able-bodied.

Notes: In the development of the teaching technique, consideration was given to the various needs and abilities of individuals who are disabled to enable them to control the movement of their asymmetrical body shapes and densities. In this regard, no two people are alike so the basic principles of hydrodynamics are used to teach each person individually.

PROJECT ACTIVE

Method: Project ACTIVE

Author: Joe Karp

Source: Karp, J., & Adler, A. (1992). *ACTIVE*. 20214 103rd Place N.E., Bothell, WA 98011-2455.

Description: Project ACTIVE is a validated teaching model kit for inservice programs for special education, physical education and recreation teachers so that they can individualize and personalize physical activity programs for their students who are disabled; specifically those with mental retardation, learning disabilities, orthopedic impairments, sensory impairments, eating disorders, and breathing disorders. This program includes both norm-referenced and criterion-referenced tests in the areas of physical fitness, motor ability, posture, and nutrition. There are also instruction programs in these areas with activities to practice skills.

Notes: In 1974, Project ACTIVE was granted National Validation from the Joint Dissemination and Review Panel and is now part of the National Diffusion Network. Project ACTIVE was revised and updated in 1992 by Karp and Adler.

The teaching model kit consists of eight manuals: Teacher Training, Low Motor Ability, Low Physical Vitality, Postural Abnormalities, Nutritional Deficiencies, Breathing Problems, Motor Disabilities or Limitations, and Communication Disorders.

SPECIAL OLYMPICS

Method: Special Olympics

Author: Special Olympics Incorporated

Source: International Special Olympics. *Fact Sheets*. (1992). Joseph P. Kennedy Jr. Foundation for the Benefit of Citizens with Mental Retardation. 1350 New York Ave N.W. Suite 500, Washington DC 20005.

Description: Special Olympics was created in 1968 by Eunice Kennedy Shriver and the Joseph P. Kennedy, Jr. Foundation. It is an international program of year-round sports training and competition open to individuals with mental retardation ages 8 and older regardless of ability. The following are official Special Olympic sports: alpine skiing, aquatics, badminton, basketball, bowling, cross-country skiing, cycling, equestrian sports, figure skating, floor and polo hockey, golf, gymnastics, powerlifting, rollerskating, sailing, soccer, softball, speed skating, table tennis, team handball, tennis, and volleyball.

The benefits of participation in Special Olympics for persons with mental retardation include improved physical fitness and motor skills, greater self-confidence, a more positive self-image, friendships, and increased family support.

Notes: Special Olympics has recently developed three programs. The intent of these programs is to integrate Special Olympic athletes into after school and community sports programs with nondisabled athletes. First, Unified Sports combines approximately equal numbers of athletes with and without mental retardation, of similar ages and abilities, on teams that compete against other Unified Sports teams. Unified Sports is an important program because it expands sports opportunities for all athletes seeking new challenges and dramatically increases inclusion of persons with mental retardation in the community.

The second program is the Sports Partnership Program in which students who are mentally retarded train and compete alongside nondisabled athletes who serve as peer coaches, scrimmage teammates, or boosters. In individual events like track and field, the Special Olympic competition would be run with the varsity meet (i.e., the varsity shot put event would be followed by the Special Olympic shot put event). In team sports the Special Olympic team would play either before or after the varsity team at the same site.

The third program is the Partners Club in which students from the high school or college serve as partners to Special Olympians and train and compete with them in sporting events as well other social and community activities. This school program should get club status with a faculty advisor, scheduling facilities, and other privileges.

Another Special Olympics Program is the Motor Activities Training Program (MATP). It provides comprehensive motor activity and recreation training for people with severe mental retardation or multiple disabilities, with emphasis on training and participation rather than competition.

DATA BASED GYMNASIUM

Method: Data Based Gymnasium

Authors: John Dunn, Jim Morehouse, and Bud Fredericks

Source: Dunn, J. M., Morehouse, J. W., & Fredericks, H. (1986). *Physical education for the severely handicapped: A systematic approach to a data-based gymnasium.* Austin, TX: Pro-Ed.

Description: The Data Based Gymnasium was designed to assist teachers in developing, implementing, and maintaining individualized physical education programs for students with severe disabilities. The curriculum consists of individual skills and behaviors considered essential for the severely disabled. There are four major sections of skills: (a) movement concepts including moving in the child's own personal space as well as moving in general space; (b) skills found in popular games such as throwing, kicking, catching, dribbling, and so on; (c) physical fitness skills such as rope skipping, bench stepping, curl ups, toe touches; and (d) leisure skills such as tricycle riding, bicycle riding, scooter board riding, roller skating, and swinging. There is also a section on swimming skills.

All skills and behaviors are presented in a task analysis format. The criterion for each behavior or skill in the curriculum can be used as a criterion- referenced test to determine the student's level of performance. Once that is determined, the physical educator can plan for educational programming.

Notes: The Data Based Gymnasium instructional model emphasizes placement tests, baselines, cues, consequences, posttests, probes, and maintenance procedures.

BODY SKILLS: A MOTOR DEVELOPMENT CURRICULUM FOR CHILDREN

Method: Body Skills: A Motor Development Curriculum for Children

Authors: Judy Werder and Robert Bruininks

Sources: Werder, J. K., & Bruininks, R. H. (1988). *Body skills: A motor development curriculum for children.* Circle Pines, MN: American Guidance Service; Bruininks, R. H. (1978). *Bruininks-Oseretsky Test of Motor Proficiency.* Circle Pines, MN: American Guidance Service.

Description: This is a comprehensive motor skill curriculum designed for children 2

to 12 years of age. The Body Skills curriculum provides a systematic approach for assessing, planning, and teaching gross motor skills. The program has task analyzed 31 skills in the areas of body management, locomotion, body fitness, object movement, and fine motor development. The program contains the Motor Skills Inventory which is a criterion-referenced assessment of all the skills taught in the program. The scores on the Motor Skills Inventory can be related to a more standardized test, the *Bruininks-Oseretsky Test of Motor Proficiency* for comparison for placement, programming, and developing goals for the IEP. The motor skills curriculum activities then are all related to the components of the subtests of the motor proficiency test.

Notes: In the curriculum, there is a folder for each area in the modules. The folder contains an illustration of the developmental sequence of the skills at the rudimentary, functional, and mature levels; the characteristics of each level; and background information about the skills and modifications for students who are disabled. This curriculum has been designed for early childhood, classroom and special education teachers, special physical educators, occupational therapists, and other developmental specialists.

PROJECT EXPLORE

Method: Project EXPLORE

Author: Steve Brannan

Source: Brannan, S. A. (Ed.). (1979). *Project EXPLORE: Expanding programs and learning in outdoor recreation and education.* Washington DC: Hawkins & Associates.

Description: Project EXPLORE is a competency-based program designed to teach outdoor recreation skills to individuals who are disabled. It is a skill-oriented curriculum. Materials have been developed to serve as a resource to develop various types of outdoor programs.

Notes: The Project EXPLORE program includes a user's manual, a number of helpful teaching suggestions, and a comprehensive set of task cards that address five major content areas related to outdoor recreation and education: Nature Study and Development, Camping and Self-maintenance, Safety and Survival, Arts and Crafts, and Sports, Games, and Physical Development. Within each of the areas, subject matter is organized according to appropriate sub-content topics and related goals and objectives (tasks).

PHYSICAL BEST AND INDIVIDUALS WITH DISABILITIES

Method: Physical Best and Individuals with Disabilities

Authors: J. Seaman, C. Houston-Wilson, L. Kalinowski, B. Lavay, W. Liemohn, and J. Winnick

Source: American Alliance for Health, Physical Education, Recreation, and Dance. (l995). *Physical best and individuals with disabilities: A handbook for inclusion in fitness programs.* Available from AAHPERD, 1900 Association Drive, Reston, VA 22091.

Description: This instruction manual was designed to help teachers develop fitness programs that include individuals with disabilities. The four basic components of physical fitness; aerobic capacity, body composition, flexibility, and muscular strength and endurance are defined and ways to evaluate each component are discussed in detail, including modifications for individuals with disabilities. Techniques for developing physical fitness profiles for the nondisabled population are described, then ways to personalize fitness programs for individuals with all types of disabilities are discussed. Also included are safety considerations for testing and programming as well as fitness activities that may be contraindicated for individuals with disabilities.

The authors encourage the use of the Prudential FITNESSGRAM test as the assessment component of the comprehensive fitness program. Ways to modify test items or suggested alternative items are discussed in detail. Standards are given for each of the test items for a variety of disabilities so some comparisons can be made. Ways to measure quality of movement instead of quantity of movement are presented which may provide a more descriptive fitness profile for individuals with disabilities. The manual also includes suggestions for prescribing and developing group and individual physical fitness programs and ideas for giving recognition and awards. A resource list that includes fitness tests, books, periodicals, and organizations that address specific disabilities is provided.

PERCEPTUAL-MOTOR ACTIVITIES

Method: Perceptual-Motor Activities

Sources: Charlesworth, R., & Radilof, D. (1978). *Experiences in math for young children.* Albany, NY: Delmar; Croft, D., & Hess, R. (1972). An activities handbook for teachers of young children. Dallas: Houghton Mifflin; *Elementary teacher's handbook of indoor and outdoor games.* (1985). West Nyack, NY: Parker; Ferretti, F. (1975). *The great American book of sidewalk, stoop, dirt, curb, and alley games.* New York: Workman;

Foster, D., & Overhol, J. L. (1989). *Indoor action games for children.* West Nyack, NY: Parker; Humphrey, J., & Sullivan, J. (1970). *Teaching slow learners through active games.* Springfield, IL: Charles C. Thomas; Jackson, A., & Randall, J. (1971). *Activities for elementary physical education.* West Nyack, NY: Parker; Mulac, M. (1971). *Educational games for fun.* Evanston, NY: Harper & Row; *The reader's digest book of 1000 family games.* (1971). Pleasantville, NY: The Reader's Digest Association; Vecchione, G. (1989). *The world's best street and yard games.* New York: Sterling.

Description: If a special educator is looking for a different medium to teach preacademic or academic skills, gross motor activities could be one medium. Using gross motor activities can be highly motivating for children and youth; they, in turn, will learn preacademic or academic concepts. This is the same idea as using computer activities as a medium to teach preacademic and academic concepts.

The following are just a few examples of gross motor activities that include preacademic or academic components.

Geography

Let's Make Africa and How to Get to Africa

In this game, the class discusses Africa. The teacher tells the children to make a group map of Africa. The teacher helps the children to stretch out on the floor in the shape of Africa. Then the children name different ways to get to Africa. (Children move as cars, trains, and airplanes.) The teacher would then ask how they would cross the ocean. (Children move as boats and airplanes.) How would they travel into the jungle? (Children move through trees and wade and swim through rivers.) Different circumstances are presented to the children, and they re-enact the movements as they are discussing Africa.

Map Toss

Divide students into squads of four or five, facing the map (on the ground). The first person in each squad stands behind a marker with a Frisbee in hand. When the teacher signals, she throws her Frisbee toward the map. Then the student stands in the state where her Frisbee landed. The player must correctly give the name of the state (or capital) in which she is standing, then go to the end of her squad.

Around the World

Prepare posters of different countries with facts about each country and posters with drawings of exercises or words describing the exercises. Place the posters around a large circle resembling the "world." Each group starts at one poster. On the teacher's signal, groups change stations by jogging once around the "world," and stopping at the station to their right. The game continues until the groups have traveled to all stations. Stations should contain activities appropriate for each age level.

Community Match Race

Divide the class into two groups, people and places. Members of the people group are each assigned an occupation in the community; members of the places group are assigned places where people work. Examples are below. At the start signal the children gallop around the room and find their partner.

People	Places
fireman	station
police officer	police station
teacher	school
nurse	hospital
mayor	city hall
librarian	library
minister	church
mailcarrier	post office
grocer	grocery store
waiter	restaurant
doctor	emergency room

Steal the Globe

This game is a variation of Steal the Bacon. There are five players on each team. Each player on both teams is given the name of a continent. The teams stand behind a line facing each other. Between the two lines (which are about 20 feet apart) is a bean bag that looks like a globe. The teacher calls out the name of a country. The player from each team who was assigned the continent where the named country is located runs to the bean bag, tries to grab it, and get back to the team's line before being tagged.

DESCRIPTION: Divide the students into two teams. Ask continental questions (e.g., Where do you find kangaroos? Where were you born?). One player from each team races to reach the large map of the world poster or a wall painted map on the playground. You repeat the process for all of the students.

Transportation

Students scatter throughout the play area. They will act out the movements of a car. When the teacher says "out of gas," students do sit-ups to fill up tanks; for "car with a wheel off," students move on two hands and one foot; for "flat tire," students do push-ups to pump the air. The teacher is a police officer who can give a speeding ticket if someone is moving too fast. If there are many players, other situations can be added. Award 5, 3, and 1 points for finishing 1st, 2nd, and 3rd, and deduct 1 point for each runner who fails to follow instructions.

Language Arts

Word Action Board or Mat

A full sheet of one-quarter inch plywood or vinyl material is cut into a large mat. The surface contains a block grid of different words and dividing lines are painted on the board; the edges are protected with tape. The board blocks contain such words as Easter, Valentine's Day, hearts, bunny, flag, Fourth of July, pilgrims, and tree. Several students spread out on a board, with each student standing on an individual word block. The students read the holiday name or word having to do with the particular holiday they are standing on and act out its meaning using their bodies, in their own creative ways. After a short time, which gives the teacher a chance to make sure students can read and understand the individual words, students switch to another word. The process continues in this manner.

Astronomy

Planets

In "I declare war on . . ," a large circle is marked off on the floor and divided into pie-shaped wedges. The name of a planet is written in each section. Each player stands in one section. One player stands in the center of the circle, tosses the ball straight up in the air, and shouts "I declare war on— Mars." All the players scatter. The student standing on Mars must catch the ball. As soon as "Mars" catches the ball, he or she screams "Freeze." The catcher may take three giant steps toward any player. If "Mars" touches another player with the ball, that player goes to the center of the circle. If he or she cannot touch another player, the thrower remains in the center of the circle and throws the ball again, naming another planet.

Community

Grocery Shopping

"Grocery Shopping Relay" is played with teams of six. On the starting signal, one player from each team puts on a hat and coat and gets a grocery bag. The player runs to a box filled with empty food containers, then places the containers in a sack one at a time. The player then runs to a cone and back to the box. After emptying the bag into the box, the player runs back to the team, and the next player takes a turn. Play continues until all players take a turn. The first team to finish is the winner.

History

Categories

Mark off a court with several categories (eight gives a good variety). Categories such as Presidents, States, Rivers, Famous Dates, Famous Historical People, Famous Historical Places, Colonies, and Territories might be used. The first player stands about 4 feet from the court and rolls the ball into one of the first squares. Then she runs to catch the ball before it rolls into a neighboring square. If the ball is not stopped in time, her turn is over, and the next player gets to roll the ball. If she stops the ball in time, she steps into the next square, bounces the ball once, and calls out a fact learned from that category. The player then steps into the third square, bounces the ball, and gives a fact from that category. The step, the bounce, and the fact must all be done together. No player is allowed to linger in a square and no fact may be used twice. If the player stumbles or if she cannot give a fact, she must leave the court and start at the beginning square on the next turn.

Nutrition

Smiley Face Food

This game can be played with any size group or groups. Each group has two large faces, one with a smile and one with a frown. Pictures of different kinds of food are scattered around the room. The players race around the room collecting the pictures and placing them on the appropriate faces. If the food is nutritional, it is placed on a smile face. If the food is not nutritional, it is placed on a frown face. The teacher determines the correctness of the matches and can use the matches as "teachable moments." If more than one team is playing, the first team that is most correct is the winner. If playing with a single team, race for times.

Vitamin Toss

Create a grid with the names of vitamins in each square. Have one person from each group throw a bean bag onto the grid. The player's team must then list as many foods containing that vitamin as they can. The team with the most correctly named foods wins.

Feed the Monster

On large pieces of tagboard, draw and color five monsters. Cut out large mouths on each monster. Label each monster as a food group, for example, Dairy, Fruit and Vegetables, Meat, Bread, and Other. Label 20 to 30 beanbags, pingpong balls, or cards with "food" items for the monsters to eat (e.g., milk, oranges, coke, candy, and pasta). List the correct foods on the back of each monster. Make a box in which to store the "food." (The distance between the line and the monsters will vary according to age of players.)

The manager explains that the object of the game is to "feed" monsters the correct kinds of food (match food items to food group). For example, the "Dairy" monster eats milk, ice cream, and yogurt. Players take turns closing their eyes and picking 10 pieces of food. They toss the food to the appropriate monsters, scoring 5 points for each correct "feed." A player with no correct "feeds" gets 5 consolation points. At the end of each player's turn, the leader returns the food to the food box. The player with the highest score wins.

Animal, Vegetable, Mineral

One player stands in the center of a circle. The player in the center tosses the ball to another player, calling out "Animal," "Vegetable," or "Mineral." The player who catches the ball must name something belonging to that group before the player in the center counts to five. If a player cannot name something from that group, he or she must go to the center of the circle.

Hygiene

Germs and the Toothbrush

This activity can be used to reinforce a unit on dental care. Select one student to be the toothbrush and several students to be the germs. The rest of the students are teeth. All of the teeth hook arms to form a line. The germs run around and around the teeth. The toothbrush tries to catch the germs as they run. If a germ is caught, the player becomes another part of the line of teeth. The toothbrush is allowed to run under the arms of the teeth to catch the germs. This will help to remind students that a proper brushing has to take place between the teeth too. When all the germs have been caught by the toothbrush, another game can be started by selecting new players to be the toothbrush and germs.

Reading

Match the Meaning

The children are divided into several teams. The teams stand in rows 10 to 15 feet from the blackboard. Groups of definitions of words are written on the blackboard for each team. Each child is given a card with a word that matches a definition on the board. A few extra definitions are included in each list on board. On the teacher's signal, the first child of each group runs to the board and erases the definition that defines his or her word. The child may seek the help of his team before going to the board. The teacher checks each child's choice before a definition is erased. If the child has selected a definition that is incorrect, he must run back to his team so they can determine the correct definition. Each child proceeds in the same manner until every child has identified the definition of his or her word and returned to the team. The first team finished wins.

Alphabet Relay

Provide a large space in the front of the room or push desks aside. Students form groups of 10 to 16 players then scatter around the play area. The leader should be elevated to better detect the winner. The leader calls a letter, such as the letter T, and each group quickly forms the letter. The

group forming the correct letter first scores a point for their team. Modifications include: (a) using numbers instead of letters and (b) having younger students form letters by contorting their bodies to represent letters or numbers.

Body Alphabet

Divide the children into groups of three or more. Make sure the groups have open floor space. The teacher writes a letter on the blackboard. Using their bodies, the children form the letters on the floor. Words or numbers can also be used.

Sentence Relay

Divide the class into equal groups. The teacher writes five letters on the blackboard. On the teacher's signal, the first player in each group walks quickly to the blackboard, makes a word with one of the letters, and returns to the end of the line. The first team that makes a real sentence wins.

Math

Count and Go

Children line up on the long side of a rectangular hard surfaced court on which parallel lines have been drawn in chalk. The teacher stands across from the children with number cards. The teacher holds up any card at random (numbers on the cards are from one to the total number of lines on the court). The children must count the lines as they run, skip, hop, and so on toward the teacher. When the children get to the line that corresponds to the number on the card, they stop and stand still. If they do not stop on the correct line, they return to the starting line. The child who reaches the far side first is the winner.

Numbers

Set up a flannel board with many felt shapes or a magnet board with many magnet shapes. Put up two groups of shapes and ask students: Are there as many circles as squares? (red circles as blue circles? bunnies as chickens?) Which set has more? How many circles are there? How many squares? The children can point, tell with words, and move the pieces around to show that they understand the idea.

Have the children form a circle. Have all the girls stand up. Then ask: Are there more boys or girls here today? Have the children sit down. Tell all children with long hair to stand up and ask: Are there more children with long hair or short hair? Continue to ask questions requiring a response involving numbers.

Red Light

Mark off two lines 30 feet apart in a play area. Designate one child to be "It." The child who is "It" stands on one line. The remaining children are grouped at the other line. "It" turns his back to the children and counts loudly "10, 20, 30, ... 100, Red Light!" The other children advance toward him as he counts, but they must stop when he calls "Red Light." When he calls "Red Light," he turns around and sends anyone still moving back to the starting line. The object of the game is to see which child can reach the goal line first.

Maze

Set up a maze using any or all of the following: big wooden blocks (for walking around, jumping over, hopping onto and off of), four chairs, two or more yardsticks (use with chairs or blocks for going over or under), a walking board, a mattress, big boxes, barrels, auto or bicycle tires (for hopping into, running through, walking on), chalk for drawing guidelines through the maze, a rope at least 9" in length, or footprint patterns.

Allow the children to go through the maze any way they want to the first time as long as they follow the guidelines. Keep the children spaced 15 feet apart. The second time they go through the maze ask them to do something specific at one point (e.g., hop off the blocks). Each time change the point at which they are to do something specific.

Find the Answer

The teacher places a numbered grid on the floor and has the children sit around it while she explains the game to them. The teacher writes a math problem on the blackboard, such as $2 + 2 = ?$. The teacher then asks one child to look for, run to, and stand on the correct answer. Older children can be given problems that require two grids for the answer (example: $6 \times 6 = 36$).

Spelling

Spelling Baseball

Draw a baseball diamond on the blackboard and below it a score card showing five innings. Then divide the group into two teams. One team is "at bat," the second is "in the field." Using a graded spelling list, give a word to the first player, who will attempt to spell it. If he spells it correctly, he scores a hit and goes to first base. (The player stays in his place, but a marker is placed on first base on the diagram.) A misspelled word is an "out," but only if the team in the field recognized it as misspelled. If no protest is made by the fielding team, the player goes to first on an error, advancing the first "runner" to second. At the end of three outs (recognized misspelled words), the teams change sides, and the runs scored in that inning are shown on the score card. At the end of three or five innings, depending on how much time you have, the winner is declared.

There are numerous variations to this game. Chairs can be placed at the front of the room and designated as first, second, and third base. As a player makes a "hit," he moves from his seat to first base. He advances when his teammates make a "hit." A runner moves from third base to his own seat to score a run.

Slam Dunk Spelling

Divide the group into two equal teams. The first player from one team goes to the chalkboard. The leader gives the child a word to spell, and if she spells the word correctly, a point is scored for her team. The same player then shoots a foam rubber ball into a trash can from a predetermined distance. If the player makes the basket, she scores another point for her team. Thus, a player can score zero, one, or two points for her team on a given turn. The first player from the other team repeats the process, and the game continues until each player has had a turn or a predetermined point total is reached.

There are numerous variations. Players from both teams can play at the same time. In this version, after the players have spelled their words, a signal is given, and both players pick up a ball and shoot. The first one to make a basket from the line scores the additional point for his or her team. In another variation, a "slam dunk" round can be played in which players use their fanciest dunk shot instead of shooting from the line.

Spelling with a Twist

Have players line up in two equal teams. Compile a spelling list that includes as many vowels as possible. The two players in front of the lines walk, hop, skip, or run to the front of the room. Each player is given a word to spell. Players score one point for their team each time a word is spelled correctly. When spelling the words, players pronounce all of the letters in the word except the vowels. For the vowels, the following are required:

A = Five push-ups

E = Run in place 10 steps

I = Point to eye

O = Point to mouth

U = Point at the leader

The team with the most points at the end of a predetermined time period wins.

Variations include changing the requirements for vowels and changing the task for players making their way to the front of the room.

REFERENCES

Education for All Handicapped Children Act of 1975, Pl 94–142. (1977). Title 20, U.S.C. 1401 et seq. *U.S. Statutes at Large, 89,* 773–796.

CHAPTER
5

Behavioral Interventions

Christine Peterson, M.Ed.
Dean Becker, M.A.
Ray Bracken, ATR, M.A.
Ada Mae Crouse, RMT-BC, M.A.
Sharon Hunter, M.A.
Lynn Perry, TRS
Patrick Toomey, ADTR

CONTENTS

▶ Assertive Discipline	82	
▶ Skillstreaming (Structured Learning)	82	
▶ Behavior Modification in the Classroom	83	
▶ Contingency Contracting	85	
▶ Token Economy	86	
▶ Self-behavior Management	87	
▶ Social Competence	88	
▶ Bibliotherapy	89	
▶ Creative Arts Therapy	89	
▶ Recreation and Leisure Interventions	91	
▶ Biofeedback	92	

Efforts to predict, control, and understand human behavior have their genesis in science, philosophy, and psychological theories. With experience, the classroom teacher gains collective knowledge from these disciplines and the technical expertise for managing and responding to a wide variety of student behavior in the classroom. This knowledge and expertise serve the teacher in establishing a climate for learning in the classroom. Teachers know that, while one intervention may be effective with a student, the same intervention may fail with another student. Classroom teachers need a repertoire of methods that are based on theory and provide options for dealing with challenging students. A classroom management system provides a structure for establishing expectations for learning and social behavior.

Most schools rely on the classroom teacher to design and implement an effective classroom management system. Creative teachers develop effective classroom management techniques through daily interaction with their students, collaboration with other teachers, practicing ideas presented at workshops, and applying techniques based on research.

This chapter describes selected methods for behavioral and therapeutic intervention. Methods include (a) behavioral management techniques, (b) creative arts interventions, and (c) recreational interventions. Behavioral management techniques can help a teacher develop valid, effective interventions for an identified problem. Creative arts interventions may prove useful for students who have not responded to more traditional approaches. Recreational interventions may be used to meet the difficult-to-reach students who do not respond to interventions generally carried out within the confines of a classroom.

Author: Lee Canter

Source: Canter, L. (1980). *Assertive discipline.* Santa Monica, CA: Canter and Associates.

Description: Assertive Discipline is a method of behavioral management that trains teachers to take charge of students' misbehavior. Teachers are instructed to assert their authority and develop a systematic plan to take charge of their students.

An Assertive Discipline plan consists of a series of steps. Teachers determine what they want students to do, communicate their goals to students, back up unmet demands with disciplinary action, and provide reinforcement when demands are met. Students' manipulations, promises without action, belligerence, whining, and noncaring behaviors are not accepted. Teachers arrange contingencies to modify students' behavior toward teacher compliance.

Assertive Discipline is based on the principles of behavior modification. It is used in special and regular education classrooms. Teachers establish their authority by applying the techniques of Assertive Discipline to manage noncompliant and nonparticipatory behavior. This approach neither oppresses students nor imposes unrealistic behavioral demands. It teaches respect for authority and maintains differentiation of teacher-student roles.

Notes: Assertive Discipline is not a teaching strategy, but a management system. No attempt is made to teach students alternative behaviors or learning strategies. If used without methods that teach appropriate responding skills, students may not acquire sufficient prosocial behaviors.

ASSERTIVE DISCIPLINE

Method: Assertive Discipline

SKILLSTREAMING

Method: Skillstreaming (Structured Learning)

Author: Arnold Goldstein

Source: Goldstein, A. P., Sprafkin, R. P., Greshaw, N. J., & Klein, P. (1980). *Skillstreaming the adolescent.* Champaign, IL: Research Press.

Description: Skillstreaming is a method for teaching prosocial skills to children and adolescents with behavioral disabilities. The method consists of psychological and educational techniques that provide a structured learning environment for dealing with stress, feelings, and aggression. Students learn to cope with their feelings and control their behavior by learning new social competencies.

Skillstreaming instruction is conducted in structured learning groups. The optimal size for a group is five to eight students and two teachers. Grouped by skill deficits whenever possible, students participate in role-playing situations that address basic social skills. The method is comprised of 50 learning skills, which include:

1. beginning social skills (listening, conversing, introducing, asking questions, and giving compliments);
2. advanced social skills (asking for help, joining in, apologizing, and giving and following instructions);
3. skills for dealing with feelings (expressing affection, expressing feelings, dealing with fears, and dealing with feelings of others);
4. skill alternatives to aggression (asking permission, sharing, helping, negotiating, avoiding trouble, and using self-control);
5. skills for dealing with stress (making and answering complaints, dealing with embarrassment, responding to failure, and dealing with accusation, contradictory messages, and group pressure);
6. planning skills (gathering information, setting goals, making decisions, and consent rating on tasks).

Each skill is outlined in behavioral steps with notes to teachers about techniques that facilitate training. Teachers model appropriate skills that students should master and provide feedback to students when they display the skills in their own behavioral repertoires.

Skillstreaming is a learning and behavioral strategies approach that can be used with special students whose language skills are sufficient to participate in group discussion and role play. This method teaches students how to learn rather than what to learn and teaches behavior strategies in conjunction with learning strategies.

Notes: Because Skillstreaming was designed for students with behavior disabilities in resource room settings, it may not be appropriate for students with severe disabilities. The authors purport that Skillstreaming may be useful for behavioral change among students with cognitive disabilities.

BEHAVIOR MODIFICATION

Method: Behavior Modification in the Classroom

Author: B. F. Skinner

Source: Rosenberg, M. S., Wilson, R., Maheady, L., & Sindelar, P. (1992). *Educating students with behavior disorders.* Boston: Allyn & Bacon.

Description: Behavior modification is based on a set of principles drawn from research in operant conditioning with animals and applied to the study of human behavior. These principles have been translated into classroom techniques by many researchers and educators. Behavior modification is an effective and efficient approach to behavior management in the classroom. When incorporated into teaching experiences, behavioral principles provide opportunities for educational achievement to occur.

Behavior modification is a method for changing the form, frequency, duration, or intensity of behavior. Behavior changes are a result of the modification of antecedent stimuli that precede behavior and/or consequences that follow behavior. The following is an overview of techniques designed to modify specific behaviors by managing antecedent events and consequences for those behaviors.

Modifying Behavior by Managing Antecedent Events. Behavior, including academic behavior, occurs in response to some stimuli. Changes in specific events that precede behavior can result in changes in behavior. Books, worksheets, questions asked by the teacher, directions given, and the arrangement of the physical environment of the classroom are stimuli that elicit behaviors from students. Stimuli are modified by (a) selecting materials that are on the student's level of current performance; (b) breaking materials into small steps; (c) presenting materials in sequential order; (d) limiting the number of stimuli that are presented at any given time; (e) arranging the physical environment (e.g., one portion of the room used for working independently, another for working in groups).

Modifying Behavior by Managing Consequences. Certain consequences that follow behavior modify behavior. Four types of consequences are positive reinforcement, negative reinforcement, extinction, and punishment. Positive reinforcers may take the form of (a) edibles or tangibles (e.g., candies, small toys), (b) privileges (e.g., free time), (c) secondary reinforcers (e.g., token which may be traded for other desirable reinforcers), (d) social praise (e.g., "excellent work,"), and (e) self-reinforcements (e.g., student self-rewards).

Teachers determine which forms of reinforcement are effective and readily deliverable. They use a variety of reinforcers to prevent boredom and satiation and gradu-ally withdraw or reduce the number of reinforcements given over time. Reinforcers of all types should be selected because people need all forms of positive reinforcement in their daily lives.

Negative reinforcers involve the removal of a specific stimulus that results in the desired behavior. A teacher does not remove the aversive condition unless and until the desired response is produced (e.g., student remains in class after a dismissal bell until the work area is clean). Negative reinforcement also occurs when a student behaves in a way to avoid a particularly aversive stimulus (e.g., a student refuses to comply with directions so a favorite toy is removed until compliance occurs, at which time the toy is replaced).

Extinction and punishment techniques are both applied to decrease the rates of a specific behavior. In the classroom, these may include ignoring certain student behaviors, withdrawal of reinforcers (e.g., response-cost techniques), and application of undesirable consequences (e.g., time out, phone calls home). Such interventions must be meaningful to the students, deliverable, and directly related to the undesirable behaviors.

Schedules of Reinforcement. The time and manner in which reinforcements are delivered are called the schedule of reinforcement. Use of these schedules has direct bearing on the success or failure of a behavior modification program. Reinforcement schedules are either continuous, wherein a reinforcement follows every specified behavior that occurs, or intermittent, wherein several behaviors must be made before reinforcement occurs.

Intermittent schedules can be arranged so that a certain number of behaviors must occur before a reinforcer is given. They can also be arranged so that a certain number of minutes must pass before a behavior can be reinforced. Each of the schedules has differing effects on behavior. Continuous schedules tend either to increase or decrease behaviors very rapidly. Intermittent schedules tend to maintain behaviors with some increase over time being noted.

Teachers who plan to use schedules of reinforcement in a consistent manner to modify behavior should always deliver aversive reinforcers on continuous schedule of reinforcement. That is, each undesirable behavior should immediately be met with an appropriate consequence. Positive reinforcers should begin on continuous schedules of reinforcement and gradually change to intermittent schedules over time. Teachers should remember that behavior that is maintained on an intermittent schedule of reinforcement will decrease much more slowly than behavior that is maintained on a continuous schedule of reinforcement. The most effective schedules of reinforcement are those in which a student cannot be sure when a reinforcement will be delivered. The most ineffective schedules of reinforcement are those that require a student to produce a certain number of behaviors in a given length of time. For example, an assignment due in 2 weeks will show little movement towards completion at first and increased movement as the 2-week period comes to a close. This schedule, therefore, is not appropriate for a classroom promoting continuous learning experiences.

Notes: Prior to using behavior modification in a classroom, a teacher must become familiar with behavioral principles. Application of these principles provides powerful motivation for the modification of behavior, and therefore, principles need to be applied in a conscientious manner to avoid misuse of this method. They are powerful motivators in the modification of behavior and should be studied with both their uses and misuses in mind.

Behavior modification is substantiated by years of research in operant conditioning and applied psychology. It would be difficult to find any facet of teaching or learning with more documentation to attest to its success.

CONTINGENCY CONTRACTING

Method: Contingency Contracting

Source: Homme, L., Csanyi, A., Gonzales, M., & Rechs, J. (1970). *How to use contingency contracting in the classroom.* Champaign, IL: Research Press.

Description: A contract is an agreement between two or more persons that stipulates the responsibilities one has to the other. A *contingency contract* is a contract between teacher and student that stipulates the learning or behavior responsibilities of a student. In addition, it stipulates the conditions under which the teacher will respond in a specified manner. In a contingency contract, if one desirable activity is performed, another item or activity stipulated in the contract is delivered.

Contingency contracts clearly articulate the goals of a behavior management program or token economy. Although contracts may be verbal, written documents are most effective. Teachers and students discuss the behaviors, conditions, criterion, and reinforcers to be designated in the contract, prepare and sign the contract, and hold each other accountable to the contract terms. Dates for an interim and final review should appear in the contract to monitor progress and allow renegotiation, if necessary. Setting the final date specifies the student's time limit. If contracts are breached by teachers or students, the contingencies specified in the contract are delivered. If contract agreements are upheld, reinforcers are delivered as stated.

Contingency contracts are positive documents. Students take part in their preparation and play an active role in deciding their terms. Teachers and students review the contract at frequent intervals to reestablish responsibilities and accountability. Contingency contracts have been utilized in numerous token economy classrooms and in classrooms that utilize only minimal behavioral management systems.

Notes: When contingency contracting is initiated, small tasks and small reinforcers are used frequently. As tasks become larger, so must reinforcers. Reward should focus on accomplishment rather than obedience and should be provided after the performance occurs. The language of the contract must be positive (I will do _____ if you do _____). The value of the task and the value of the reinforcer must be equivalent. If these guidelines are breached, the effectiveness of the contract is compromised.

TOKEN ECONOMY

Method: Token Economy

Sources: Stainback, W. C., & Stainback, S. B. (1975). A few basic elements of token reinforcement. *Journal for Special Educators of the Mentally Retarded, 11*, 152–155; Kazdin, A. E. (1977). *The token economy: A review and evaluation.* New York: Plenum Press.

Description: Token Economy is a method for systematically reinforcing desirable behavior in the classroom. Reinforcement is contingent on appropriate behavior and is delivered immediately after the behavior occurs. Reinforcers that are delivered too long after a behavior has occurred either lose their meaning or reinforce another behavior that has occurred in the meantime. A token economy allows for the immediate reinforcement of behavior.

The use of tokens is analogous to the use of money in general society. Students are rewarded for their efforts through tokens, just as workers are rewarded with a paycheck for their skills. Individual student token reinforcers accumulate and are then exchanged for a wide variety of attractive items. A variety of token reinforcers can be used in the classroom. The items may include play money, funny money, check marks on a sheet, or gold stars on a board. Tokens are often traded for events (talking to a friend, free time, watching a movie, or playing with classroom toys) or tangible reinforcers (candies, puzzles, small toys, or pencils). The type of event or tangible reinforcer does not matter provided (a) it appeals to the student, (b) is affordable, and (c) is paid for by tokens the student has earned.

Tokens are earned in many ways. Often, compliance with classroom rules is rewarded. Compliance may include raising one's hand before speaking, being seated when the starting bell rings, helping others, or having the necessary materials for class. Academic work may also earn tokens. Completion of work, number of correct answers, decreasing errors, or following directions are often reinforced with tokens. Prosocial skills such as admitting one's mistakes, waiting turns to speak, and showing kindness to one's peers are further examples of how tokens may reinforce appropriate skills.

Teachers need to clearly define behaviors to be rewarded with tokens. Each occurrence of a desired behavior need not be reinforced with a token. However, enough behavior should be reinforced to keep the behavior accelerating or maintaining. During the initial phases of the Token Economy, earning tokens for appropriate behaviors should not be a difficult task. Tokens should be delivered often and traded regularly. Besides defining behaviors that earn tokens, a teacher should also provide students with knowledge of what their tokens will buy and the cost of each back-up reinforcer. Also, teachers should explain when items will be available for trade. After the Token Economy has been established, the frequency of delivery of tokens and trades is diminished. Tokens may also be withheld or removed as a form of response cost if the desired behavior is not forthcoming.

The use of token systems necessitates precautions to guard against counterfeiting.

A system of marking each token to validate its source or confirm its ownership is needed to ensure the integrity of the Token Economy. One solution is to have students write their initials on the back of their paper money token and not accept tokens from students whose money shows evidence of erasures or other tampering.

Many special variations of Token Economy have been devised to maintain student and teacher interest. Some classrooms operate a store where students may purchase school supplies or edible reinforcers at particular times. Other classrooms hold auctions where students are allowed to bid as high as they wish for the desired reinforcer, up to the number of tokens they have earned. When used properly and thinned appropriately, Token Economy can be a valuable addition to a behavior management program.

Notes: It is debatable whether or not, once begun, token economies should be continued. Proponents of discontinuation suggest thinning token delivery until the economy can be withdrawn without affecting behavior. Opponents of discontinuance point to the world of work and its monetary system as a model. Opponents contend that few, if any, of us would continue to work without payment (monetary tokens) that buys the tangibles and activities we desire or need. Because this debate may not be resolved through empirical investigation, careful consideration of the pros and cons of token economies is necessary.

SELF-BEHAVIOR MANAGEMENT

Method: Self-behavior Management

Sources: Kanfer, F. (1975). Self-management methods. In F. Kanfer & A. Goldstein (Eds.), *Helping people change: A textbook of*

methods (pp. 309–355). New York: Pergamon Press; Meichenbaum, D. H. (1977). *Cognitive-behavior modification: An integrative approach.* New York: Plenum Press.

Description: Behavior modification techniques of observation, record keeping, and reinforcement were originally conceived by educators as a means of managing student behavior. Self-behavior Management uses these techniques to encourage self-management. Students are taught self-management by instructing them to monitor their behavior through self-data recording, evaluating their own behavior, and providing their own consequences through self-reinforcement and self-punishment. Students can also learn to manipulate behavioral stimuli by using self-instruction. Teachers are available to assist students with goal setting, delivery of reinforcement, and monitoring behaviors of self-control.

Self-behavior Management begins with observation. Students become aware of the behaviors they produce and select target behaviors they want to change. After students have observed the target behaviors for a week, they create reinforcement plans and set their goals. Students count the target behaviors as they occur, chart their frequency of occurrence, analyze the data, and deliver self-reinforcements. The teacher's role is to assist students in selecting target behaviors, setting realistic goals and reinforcers, and analyzing the charted data. Teachers do not interfere with student management plans, nor do they deliver reinforcers.

A variety of techniques are used to self-manage behavior, with combinations of behavior management procedures combined into one. Frequently, self-recording is conducted in conjunction with self-reinforcement, or self-instruction with self-reinforcement. Students write contracts with themselves, set up private token economies, or modify the classroom environment to enhance their plans. Although teachers may suggest behaviors to be targeted, they do not interfere if students select other behaviors.

A major criticism of behavior modification is that the majority of control is external to the student. Through the use of Self-behavior Management, some of these problems are alleviated. Rather than the teacher providing an external locus of control, the student becomes responsible for determining which behaviors to change, the consequences of the behaviors, and the measurement of progress toward a predetermined goal.

Notes: Teachers who choose to implement Self-behavior Modification in the classroom must be well versed in the principles of behavior modification and willing to teach these principles to students. Inadequate training, inappropriate application of the principles, and inadequate preparation for using this method can result in confusion, chaos, and an increase in undesirable behaviors.

SOCIAL COMPETENCE

Method: Social Competence

Author: Oliver Kolstoe

Source: Kolstoe, O. P. (1976). *Teaching educable mentally retarded children* (2nd ed.). New York: Holt, Rinehart & Winston.

Description: Social Competence addresses skills that are critical for adjustment of a handicapped student into all facets of school, home, and community life. Emphasis is placed on skills needed to work, obtain a job, and hold that job. According to the author, teaching social competencies begins in preschool. Skills include a continuum ranging from none or minimal competence to complete and constant competence. Students are taught to adapt to a middle range of this continuum in order to achieve social adequacy. For adequate life

functioning, a happy medium, and an understanding of the flexible deviations from it, must be achieved.

The method of Social Competence designed by Kolstoe is based on characteristics deemed desirable by employers: trustworthiness, loyalty, friendliness, courtesy, kindness, obedience, thriftiness, valor, cleanliness, and respect. The development of these traits is contingent on a person's self-image as well as his or her spiritual and cultural background. If students with disabilities are to enter the world of work, they must be trained to accept and emulate these traits.

Social Competence is considered a supplementary method to be used with academic training and vocational preparation. Rather than setting aside a specific time for teaching these skills, they are incorporated into a variety of other subjects. If specific instruction is needed, techniques of role playing or sociodrama are used. When the skills have been mastered in the classroom, they are generalized to life situations.

The first step of Social Competence is the development of self-image. Teachers provide opportunities for students to experience both success and failure. Failure experiences are carefully planned and monitored, with particular attention given to the selection of failures that will enhance, not inhibit, the development of self-image.

The development of self-image is accompanied at each level by the development of social competencies in the school, home, neighborhood, and community. Various competencies to enhance independence are taught at preschool, primary, intermediate, prevocational, and vocational levels.

Although designed for persons with mental retardation, Social Competence is applicable for educational planning for persons with mild-to-moderate as well as severe-to-profound disabilities. The activities proposed in this method are sequential, logical, and comprehensive. Teaching this or related methods in early elementary grades may diminish transition problems experienced by students as they pass from one level of instruction to another, or from school to the world of work.

Notes: Although Social Competence was written as a supplemental method for academic-based training, it should be considered the focus of total transition and career education programming rather than an add-on. The skills taught by the method may be better taught in community rather than classroom settings.

BIBLIOTHERAPY

Method: Bibliotherapy

Authors: Arleen McCarty Hynes and Mary Hynes-Berry

Source: Hynes, A. M., & Hynes-Berry, M. (1986). *Bibliotherapy: The interaction process. A handbook.* Boulder, CO: Westview Press.

Description: Bibliotherapy is a technique that uses reading materials to help students understand their handicaps, emotional problems, or difficulties coping with life. This, in turn, leads to improved self-esteem and morale. Teachers can develop an awareness of students' problems, offer students books and reading materials that deal with their problems, and discuss the content of the material with them after it has been read. During this time, bibliotherapists maintain sensitivity to students' reading levels, disabling conditions, and the degree of understanding students have of their particular problems. Materials are never forced on students, and choices of literary styles are provided.

Although short stories are often the quickest, most natural, and efficient literary style for Bibliotherapy, poetry, nonfiction, science fiction, romances, and self-help books also can be used. The content of these materials should not be moralistic, but rather descriptive of how young persons deal with situations such as death, divorce, drug addiction, alcoholism, sexual abuse, illness, or single-parent families. Bibliotherapists plan interventions with these materials carefully, making sure a story will provide growth toward psychological maturity rather than excessive anxiety or pain.

Bibliotherapy was developed in the 1940s for maladjusted students. As a cathartic therapy, Bibliotherapy allows students emotional release through neutral media. Books and stories my be read by or read to students. They may also be played from video tapes, talking books, or compact disks.

Notes: Teachers, therapists, and librarians who engage in Bibliotherapy must carefully evaluate the content of therapeutic materials. All materials must be previewed and selected according to individual student needs. Bibliotherapy must be used over extended periods of time. It should not be considered a panacea for solving all emotional problems. Thus it may need to be accompanied by other therapeutic interventions.

CREATIVE ARTS THERAPY

Method: Creative Arts Therapy

Sources: Davis, W., Gfeller, K., & Thaut, M. (1992). *An introduction to music therapy, theory and practice.* St. Louis: MMB Music, Inc.; Kramer, E. (1984). *Art as therapy with children.* New York: Shocken Books.; North, M. (1975). *Personality assessment through movement.* Boston: Plays, Inc.

Description: Creative art therapy is the use of art, dance, or music to accomplish therapeutic goals. The use of creative arts therapies in an educational setting can aid the integration of cognitive and emotional processes to enhance development, behavior, motivation, and learning. Art, dance, and music therapy techniques can be used to explore the unconscious world. In addition, it provides a structure in which one's inner reality can find concrete expression in the external world. Emphasis on self-exploration through creative expression and intuitive processes can provide students and teachers with new understandings of behavior and motivation.

Music, art, and dance are expressions that have an inherent form and structure. Music therapy interventions involve the appropriate selection of music in terms of pitch, rhythm, form, timbre, style, and variability. Dance therapy utilizes a focus on movement, rhythm, spatial relationships, body awareness, and kinesthetic response. The basic visual tools of the artist are lines, shapes, colors, values, space, texture, and patterns. The value of creative arts becomes apparent when a student has the opportunity to manipulate the media for self-actualization. The experiential approach of creative arts therapies can be improvised or planned because they involve a reflective reaction to the art or an active role in creation.

Creative arts therapies provide an outlet for self-expression. This can result in reducing inappropriate behaviors. Participants experience an opportunity to assess their thoughts, feelings, and images. With minimal boundaries to guide them, students may explore self-expressive ideas which lead to an improved sense of self-mastery, productivity, and success.

Students involved with music, art, or dance may experience an improved ability to concentrate and recall information. Their ability to learn sequences, make associations, and conceptualize also may improve. Sensory motor awareness might be enhanced also. Repetitive patterns in rhythm, motion, and/or design, paired with verbal expression, can enhance reading comprehension, self-concept, intrinsic motivation, and creative thinking.

Creative arts in schools can be used to improve cognitive and emotional responses to learning. Such approaches are particularly effective when included in the curriculum for students with specific learning disabilities, physical impairments, emotional disturbances, behavior disorders, autism, traumatic brain injuries, and sensory impairments. Creative arts therapies provide an effective media for affective education in the classroom. Through creative personal expression, a student's sense of self-mastery, self-esteem, and social development may become enhanced, resulting in successful peer and teacher-student relationships.

Notes: Properly designed creative arts programs rely on assessments of physical, emotional, and cognitive factors prior to engaging students in these activities. Such assessments are necessary to create programs appropriate for students' limitations and gifts. The following professional associations and catalogues are available to assist educators in developing creative arts programs:

American Dance Therapy Association
2000 Century Plaza, Suite 108
Columbia, MD 21044-3263

National Association for Music
Therapy, Inc.
505 Eleventh St., S.E.
Washington, DC 20910
(202) 543-6864

American Association for Music
Therapy
P.O. Box 27177
Philadelphia, PA 19118
(215) 242-4450

The American Art Therapy
Association
1202 Allanson Road
Mundelein, IL 60060

Creative Arts Therapy and General
Music Education Catalogue
MMB Music, Inc.
Contemporary Arts Building
3526 Washington Avenue
St. Louis, MO 63103-1019

RECREATION AND LEISURE INTERVENTIONS

Method: Recreation and Leisure Interventions

Source: Bigge, J. L. (1976). *Teaching individuals with physical and multiple disabilities.* Columbus, OH: Merrill.

Description: Recreation and leisure interventions comprise a major part of an individual's growth and development. Recreation provides exercise, tension release, and identification of personal responsibilities, and heightens feelings of success and accomplishment. Through recreation and leisure activities, students develop appropriate socialization and communication skills in addition to interpersonal conflict management. Rigorous physical activity also increases productivity by providing a release for nervous energy and stimulating the mind and body when fatigued.

A key component of recreational and leisure interventions occurs during the **processing**, or discussion, of the event which immediately follows conclusion of the event. Such teacher-directed discussions are intended to stimulate a connection between physical experiences and personal growth. Similarities between recreational performance and related problems in living are discussed and analyzed so participants can develop insight into personal approaches with daily living problems. Through processing, students becomes aware of problem-solving techniques that may be ineffective and learn how communication skills can be improved. They learn more effective social skills, develop assertiveness, and become aware of how their ability to be responsible for their own behaviors as manifested through personal actions. New behavioral insights may then be used to alter their approach to intra- or interpersonal problems. Several types of activities may be considered.

1. *Noncompetitive Games.* Unlike competitive games, noncompetitive games consist of one team working to accomplish a mutual goal. Noncompetitive games are effective in developing teamwork, communication, and interpersonal skills. These games provide students with opportunities to learn appropriate ways to socialize and interact with others. Personal productivity and concentration are increased. In addition, structured games provide a setting in which nervous energy is released. Fluegelman (1976, 1981) explores these ideas in a compilation of specific games designed to address intra- and interpersonal issues.

2. *Experiential Education.* Experiential education dates from the early 1960s when the British Navy developed the original Outward Bound program to teach sailors survival skills and teamwork. Through experiential education, students learn about their inner selves as well as new skills that may be useful in interpersonal relationships and daily living. Through what appear to be ordinary games, individuals explore preconceived notions of self and beliefs that can impede their psychosocial development. Objectives of experiential education include (a) increasing self-confidence and self-esteem, (b) goal setting, (c) identifying new ways to achieve goals, (d) developing and implementing new behaviors, and (e) promoting trust, responsibility, and teamwork. Rohnke (1989a, 1989b) explores these ideas through problem-solving games which may be played by persons with any disability.

3. *Creative Expression.* Creative expression is the use of art to express oneself through color, movement, and design. With prompting and processing, a student may be more inclined to talk about his or her art rather than feelings, but because each person perceives the world in a uniquely different way, students' use of color and design may give more insight into psychosocial feelings than they can express verbally. Examples of creative expression include making face masks with casting gauze which are then painted and decorated individually, constructing scrap art collages, and using fingers and toes to paint an array of emotions.

Notes: Recreational and leisure interventions are appropriate for students with all disabilities, at all levels of severity, provided the teacher accommodates students' ability levels and ensures their safety. For noncompetitive games interventions, contact the New Games Foundation, P.O. Box 7901, San Francisco, CA 94120. For specific experiential interventions, contact Kendall-Hunt Publishing Company, P.O. Box 1840, 4050 Westmark Drive, Dubuque, IA 52004-1840.

BIOFEEDBACK

Method: Biofeedback

Author: John Basmajian, M.D.

Source: Basmajian, J. F. (1989). *Biofeedback: Principles and practice for clinicians* (3rd ed.). Baltimore: Williams & Wilkins.

Description: Biofeedback involves the use of electronic equipment to alert human beings to internal psychological events. It manipulates visual and auditory signals to develop awareness of events. Through biofeedback, individuals monitor involuntary responses and modify those responses via voluntary control. Unlike conditioned responses, the person involved must want to change his or her physiological signals to meet some personal goal.

Microelectronic devices are the heart of the biofeedback system. Tiny sensors (electrodes) are placed on an individual's skin at various points on the body to pick up internal electrical activity. As a nerve cell is activated by a stimulus, the outside of the cell becomes negatively charged with respect to the inside of the cell. As the cell regains a resting state, the inside of the cell becomes negative with respect to the outside of the cell. This changing difference from inside to outside and outside to inside produces a voltage wave pattern that can be detected by sensors. Biofeedback equipment uses these voltage waves by converting their energy into either an auditory sound such as a hum, bleep, or buzz or a visual image such as a blink, moving dot, or curving-spiking line.

Therapeutic use of biofeedback involves several steps. First, the therapist prepares the individual for biofeedback and the procedures used. The therapist explains that the instruments are safe and will not produce shocks; that falling asleep is a positive sign of relaxation; that sensations such as rushes of warmth, tingling, floating, or heaviness may be experienced; and that the individual will "come out" of these sensations because they are only normal sensations of drowsiness. In addition, the therapist makes sure the individual knows the specific reasons for the use of the method, whether they are general relaxation, relaxation of specific muscle spasticity, counteracting psychological stress, or reduction of stress-related tension and/or migraine headaches.

A physical setting that enhances relaxation is provided. This setting is quiet, relatively stimulus free, and undisturbed by extraneous noise or visual distractions. Within this setting, the therapist trains the participant to monitor external sensors and change internal behaviors through changing the visual or auditory signals. The following steps are suggested for biofeedback training:

1. Help individuals become aware of the signals and what they are reporting about inner behaviors.
2. Help them read the baseline data of muscle tension levels as they are recorded. Clarify that baseline data are collected to evaluate the future effectiveness of the method.

3. Cultivate the muscle sense by having individuals tense and relax muscles. This procedure demonstrates muscle tension and provides changes in the visual or auditory display for observation.

4. Begin relaxation training with the forearm. Have participants practice letting the tone or visual cue subside. Point out sensations of warmth, heaviness, or lightness that occur. After 20 minutes of training, discuss the sensations.

5. Train them to use biofeedback for relaxation of portions of the body that need modification.

6. Have individuals visualize stressful situations while maintaining a relaxed state through biofeedback monitoring.

This training involves at least three sessions in which the participant sequentially images stress building from low to high levels and, at the same time, maintains a relaxed level of internal activity. Following these procedures, individuals are encouraged to carry this relaxed state into the home, classroom, and everyday environment. Sometimes visual cues such as words to repeat in stressful situations are used as relaxation signals.

Biofeedback is a means of increasing an individual's sensitivity and self-awareness by rendering the individual more attuned to the inner working of the central nervous system and physiological systems. Carried out in a therapeutic situation, biofeedback may provide the necessary relaxation and self-control to help students function more appropriately in the classroom.

Notes: Biofeedback training may be too stimuli specific and nongeneralizable to the environment. Although tension relaxation appears to be more rapid with biofeedback than with other forms of relaxation therapies, the effects do not appear to last as long. The more sensitive the biofeedback instrument, the more likely the individual's physiological changes will be monitored. The less sensitive the equipment, the more likely that distortions of the signal will occur. Power changes, improper placement of sensors, or normal wear and tear on the biofeedback equipment can cause distortions that inhibit the potential benefit of biofeedback therapy.

REFERENCES

Fluegelman, A. (1976). *The new game book.* Garden City, NJ: Dolphin Books/Doubleday.

Fluegelman, A. (1981). *More new games.* Garden City, NJ: Dolphin Books/Doubleday.

Rohnke, K. (1989a). *Cowstails and cobras*, II. Dubuque, IA: Kendall-Hunt.

Rohnke, K. (1989b). *Silverbullets.* Dubuque, IA: Kendall-Hunt.

CHAPTER

6

Methods for Learners with Hearing or Visual Impairments

Susan R. Naidu, Ph.D, CCC-A[1]
Ruby Ryles, M.Ed.
Michelle Buchanan, Ph.D.[2]

CONTENTS

Methods for Learners with Hearing Impairments 96
▶ Prelinguistic Communication 96
▶ Oralism 97
▶ Auditory-verbal 97
▶ Cued Speech 98
▶ Total Communication 98
▶ American Sign Language 98
▶ Ling Speech Program 99
▶ Diagnostic Early Intervention Program 100
▶ Ski*Hi Program 101

Methods for Learners with Visual Impairments 101
▶ Cognitive and Communicative Development in Infancy and Early Childhood 102
▶ Orientation and Mobility Skills 103
▶ Daily Living Skills for Young Children and Adolescents 104
▶ Social Competence Skills for Young Children and Adolescents 104
▶ Braille 105
▶ Alternative Modes of Reading 107

[1] Author, Methods for Learners with Hearing Impairments
[2] Co-authors, Methods for Learners with Visual Impairments

This chapter consists of instructional methods designed for individuals with hearing or vision loss. These methods are intended to be incorporated into everyday routines, activities, and educational programs. Methods may be used best in conjunction with methods from other chapters in this book (e.g., Early Childhood Intervention methods), particularly if the learner is at risk for or has disabling conditions in addition to hearing or vision impairments. The first section of this chapter presents methods for those with hearing impairments; the second section contains methods for those with vision impairments.

communication skills through an exclusively oral approach or (b) methods that incorporate sign language or use sign language as a primary means for teaching language. If a family chooses an exclusively oral approach, three kinds of methods may be used: (a) Oralism, (b) Auditory-verbal (A-V), and (c) Cued Speech. For families who choose to use sign language, two methods are available: (a) Total Communication (TC), and (b) American Sign Language (ASL). The following section also includes description of programs that use a combination of methods to meet child and family needs.

METHODS FOR LEARNERS WITH HEARING IMPAIRMENTS

Hearing impairment interferes with the young child's development of an effective communication system. Lack of ability to communicate impacts a child's social relationships (especially relationships with family members) as well as his or her conceptual development and acquisition of literacy skills. Early identification of hearing loss and early intervention is thought to enhance child-family relationships and child functioning in everyday environments. Early intervention efforts are likely to focus on finding ways to assist children in understanding and communicating with family members and others in their daily lives.

A primary issue facing parents of young children with hearing impairment is choosing a method of communication and language instruction that is most appropriate for their child and family. This choice is not always based on preference. Availability of instructional services in the community in which the family resides becomes a major consideration.

Methods of communication instruction can be classified under two general approaches: (a) methods that teach the child

PRELINGUISTIC COMMUNICATION

Method: Prelinguistic Communication

Sources: Spencer, P. E., Bodner-Johnson, B. A., & Gutfreund, M. K.. (1992). Interacting with infants with a hearing loss: What can we learn from mothers who are deaf? *Journal of Early Intervention, 16*(1), 64–78; Jamieson, J. R. (1995). Interactions between mothers and children who are deaf. *Journal of Early Intervention, 19*(2), 108–117.

Description: Infants and young children communicate using eye contact, vocalization, facial expression, movement, and gestures long before they begin to use words or signs to convey thoughts and desires. This prelinguistic communication provides a foundation for later language development, regardless of the approach or methods for language instruction chosen by the family of the young hearing-impaired child.

Caregivers of infants and young children with hearing loss are encouraged to recognize, interpret, and respond to the child's idiosyncratic and conventional forms of prelinguistic communication. In this way, the child learns that his or her communicative behavior is meaningful to others. Caregiver responsiveness to child communicative behavior is one way that adults support communicative development.

Another way that caregivers support children's communicative development is by using strategies to prompt and mediate communication with infants and young children with hearing loss. These strategies include using eye contact and other visual input for establishing and maintaining joint attention and joint action routines with young children in everyday contexts. Caregivers can also encourage child communication by following the child's attentional lead and responding to the "topic" or focus of communication. Use of these strategies and others contributes to active communication and balanced interactions between the child and his or her caregivers. In these exchanges, infants and young children learn the basic structure of language and practical uses for communication.

ORALISM

Method: Oralism

Source: Alexander Graham Bell Association. 3417 Volta Place NW, Washington, DC 20007 (202) 337-5220.

Description: Oralism is sometimes referred to as the Aural/Oral method. It focuses on teaching speechreading, coupled with using residual hearing and auditory cues, for learning speech and language skills. Critical to the success of oralism is the fitting of appropriate amplification (i.e., hearing aids) so that maximum auditory benefit may be achieved. Auditory training is an integral component of oralism. It includes teaching the child how to make sense out of sound, attach meaning, and eventually understand speech auditorily.

The speech training models most often used are Daniel Ling's speech program, discussed later in this chapter, or a model similar to Ling's. Auditory skills are critical to the development of speech skills and ultimately to the oral expression of language; therefore, they are taught simultaneously with speechreading and speech production.

AUDITORY-VERBAL

Method: Auditory-verbal

Sources: Alexander Graham Bell Association. 3417 Volta Place NW, Washington, DC 20007 (202) 337–5220 (VTTY); Estabrooks, W. (1994). *Auditory-verbal therapy for parents and professionals.* Washington, DC: Alexander Graham Bell Association.

Description: The Auditory-verbal method allows the child to use his or her residual hearing to listen to and understand spoken language and to acquire spoken communication skills. Critical to the success of Auditory-verbal therapy is ongoing hearing evaluation, appropriate fitting of hearing aids and continuous monitoring of the hearing aid settings.

Unlike the oralism method, auditory-verbal therapy does not emphasize the use of visual cues (e.g., speechreading) for understanding language. The child learns to listen to his or her own voice, the voices of others, and environmental sounds in order to develop and understand spoken language.

The family is an integral part of the auditory-verbal team. Parents actively participate in the therapy sessions and learn how to incorporate the listening activities into everyday routines at home. The auditory-verbal therapist is a trained professional in the area of audiology, speech pathology, and/or education of the hearing impaired. The therapist receives additional training specifically in auditory-verbal therapy.

CUED SPEECH

Method: Cued Speech

Sources: Cornett, R. O., & Daisey, M. E. (1992). *The cued speech resource book: For parents of deaf children.* Raleigh, NC: National Cued Speech Association; Cued Speech National Center, National Cued Speech Association (NCSA). P.O. Box 31345, Raleigh, NC 27622 (919) 828–1218 (V/TTY); Gallaudet University Cued Speech Team, Department of Audiology, Speech and Language Pathology, 800 Florida Ave. N.E., Washington, DC 20002–3695 (202) 653–5330 (V/TTY)

Description: The Cued Speech method is a multisensory approach for teaching communication and language skills to children with hearing loss. The method emphasizes the child's use of the visual and auditory senses. The goal of cued speech is for the child to receive spoken language clearly both visually (i.e., through speechreading) and auditorily (i.e., through appropriate amplification). In addition, the child is cued with handshapes that accompany and assist in clarifying speech. A trained professional working with the child uses eight handshapes in four different locations around the mouth to supplement what the child sees on the mouth when speechreading. These handshapes clarify vowels and consonants being used in the speech the child is reading. The purposes of the method are to (a) assist the child in accurately perceiving phonemes in speechreading, (b) allow the child to internalize a model of spoken language, and (c) ultimately enable the child with hearing impairment to develop good literacy skills.

TOTAL COMMUNICATION

Method: Total Communication

Sources: Roush, J., & Matkin, N. D. (1994). *Infants and toddlers with hearing loss: Family centered assessment and intervention.* Baltimore: York Press; Modern Signs Press, Inc., P.O. Box 1181, Los Alamitos, CA 90720. Toll free: (800) 572–SEE2 (V/TTY); Information: (310) 596–9548 (Voice) or (310) 493–4168 (V/TTY); Gallaudet University, Seventh & Florida Ave. N.E., Washington, DC 20002-3695.

Description: Total Communication utilizes all means of communication for teaching children with hearing impairments. This includes (a) appropriate fitting of hearing aids, (b) maximizing hearing aid wearing with consistent auditory training, (c) speechreading and speech production training, and (d) the use of sign language. Children are consistently provided spoken and signed language so that they have the opportunity to improve auditory skills while being given clear language input. The sign language system most often used in Total Communication programs is one that is referred to as "manual English" or the use of signs and fingerspelling that represents spoken English manually. This may include Signing Exact English (SEE I or II), Signed English, or Pidgin English.

Notes: The Total Communication method seeks to assist children in making use of all senses to learn communication skills from a very young age. The goal is to facilitate caregiver-child communication, child social competence, and the development of language and literacy skills.

AMERICAN SIGN LANGUAGE

Method: American Sign Language

Source: Gallaudet University, Seventh & Florida Ave. N.E., Washington, DC 20002–3695; National Association of the Deaf, 914 Thayer Ave., Silver Springs, MD 20910.

Description: American Sign Language (ASL) has been a primary mode of communication for the deaf for centuries. American Sign Language is a manual form of language that has a defined and complete structure that is different from English or other forms of spoken language. In ASL concepts are conveyed through signs and gestures. Those who choose this method of communication for instructing young children with hearing impairments emphasize the learning of American Sign Language from infancy as a primary mode of communication. Although ASL is the primary language for the child, this does not mean that the understanding and use of speech is precluded. ASL programs may include a speech and auditory component in addition to sign language.

LING SPEECH PROGRAM

Method: Ling Speech Program

Author: Daniel Ling

Sources: Ling, D. (1976). *Speech and the hearing-impaired child: Theory and practice.* Washington, DC: Alexander Graham Bell Association; Ling, D. (1989). *Foundations of spoken language for hearing-impaired children.* Washington, DC: Alexander Graham Bell Association; Stoker, R. D., & Ling, D. (Eds.). (1992). Speech production in hearing-impaired children and youth: Theory and practice. *The Volta Review, 94*(5); John Tracy Clinic, 806 West Adams Blvd., Los Angeles, CA 90007.

Description: The speech program developed by Daniel Ling is the most commonly used method for teaching vocal and speech production skills to children with hearing loss. Early writings and discussions of the Ling model focused on children older than 3 years of age; however, the model can be adapted and modified for use with children from birth to 3 years of age. The model is based on the typical sequence of speech development for hearing children beginning at birth. This model is applied in instructing young children with hearing impairments.

The Ling program may be used by the following individuals:

1. early interventionists working with children with hearing impairments from birth to 3 years of age;
2. preschool teachers and speech/language pathologists in programs for the hearing impaired beginning at 3 years of age;
3. parents who are taught to implement speech objectives through informal vocal and speech activities.

The Ling program is commonly used in the following programs:

1. oral programs that focus on teaching and developing a child's communication system through amplification of hearing, effective use of the auditory system, and the development of speech and speech-reading skills;
2. auditory-verbal programs that focus on teaching and developing a child's communication system primarily through the use of the auditory system and through acquisition of speech skills;
3. total communication programs that incorporate the use of sign language for teaching receptive and expressive language skills along with developing the use of the auditory system and speech skills.

The Ling speech program, with its accompanying workbooks, specifies a sequence of seven stages of speech acquisition including phonetic and phonologic levels of acquisition occurring at each stage. The seven stages begin at the level of spontaneous vocalizations and proceed through the stages of speech development including vowel and consonant development. The seven stages consist of:

1. vocalization of a variety of sounds, spontaneously and in imitation;
2. acquisition of and use of the suprasegmental patterns of duration, intensity, and pitch, spontaneously and in imitation;
3. production of vowels and diphthongs and the use of word approximations;
4. production of consonants by manner and increased intelligibility of a few words along with good voice patterns;
5. production of consonants by manner and placement and continued increase in word intelligibility with good voice patterns;
6. production of consonants by manner, placement, and voicing with regular production of intelligible words with good voice patterns;
7. production of initial and final blends with intelligible speech and natural voice patterns.

The child's rate of progress through each stage of speech production is dependent on appropriate amplification, the child's use of residual hearing, and the child's individual rate of learning and acquisition of speech production skills.

DIAGNOSTIC EARLY INTERVENTION PROGRAM

Method: Diagnostic Early Intervention Program (DEIP)

Sources: Moeller, M. P., Coufal, D., & Hixson, P. (1990). The efficacy of speech-language intervention: Hearing impaired children. *Seminars in Speech and Language,* 11(4), 227–241; Moeller, M. P., & Condon, M. (1994). D.E.I.P.: A collaborative problem-solving approach to early intervention. In J.

Rousch & N. D. Matkin (Eds.), *Infants and toddlers with hearing loss* (pp. 163–192). Baltimore: York Press.

Description: The Diagnostic Early Intervention Program (DEIP) is based on the premise that families require time to make decisions regarding the best early intervention approach for their child and family. Following the diagnosis of their child's hearing loss, a family enters the DEIP project at Boys Town National Research Hospital in Nebraska for a least 6 months. A DEIP advocate is assigned to the family, provides intervention services twice a week, and coordinates the other team members' assessment activities. Family members are able to participate in parent support groups, obtain resource material regarding deafness, and explore the various options available to them for long-term intervention services. A series of assessments are conducted in areas of family support, parent-child interaction, communication/language development, developmental status, phonological development, and auditory development.

The specific objectives of DEIP are to:

1. support the parents and family in understanding and coping with a child's hearing impairment;
2. guide the family in the stimulation of their child's language, auditory, and speech development, while helping them understand and cope with the impact of hearing impairment;
3. assist the family in developing an objective information base to support the decision-making and goal-selection process;
4. gain a comprehensive understanding of the family's and child's needs through diagnostic teaching/discovery and transdisciplinary evaluation of the child and family;
5. provide a mechanism within the school district for longitudinal monitoring of the family/professional decision-making process and the efficacy of intervention.

SKI*HI PROGRAM

Method: Ski*Hi Program

Sources: Clark, R., & Watkins, S. (1985). *The Ski*Hi model-programming for hearing impaired infants through home intervention: Home visit curriculum* (4th ed.). Logan, UT: HOPE; Watkins, S. (1979). *The Ski*Hi language development scale: Assessment of language skills for hearing impaired children from infancy to five years of age.* Logan: Utah State University.

Description: Ski*Hi is a program for children with hearing impairments and their families that was developed in 1972 in Utah. Since that time, it has served as a model program for approximately 250 agencies in the United States. The Ski*Hi program is a home-based program serving families of children with hearing impairments in rural and urban settings. "Parent advisors" work directly with families in their homes providing support, modeling, and education regarding child hearing loss and the development of auditory, speech, and language skills. The program consists of the following components and resources.

1. The hearing aid program is a tutorial which is designed to teach families about proper fitting, maintaining, and wearing of hearing aids.
2. The auditory program is designed to teach the family about maximizing the child's residual hearing to enhance speech development.
3. Families choose one of four methods for communication/language development with which they feel most comfortable. The choices are (a) Total Communication/Manually Coded English, (b) Cued Speech, (c) Aural/Oral, or (d) American Sign Language.
4. HOPE, Inc., is a publication available through Ski*Hi. It is distributed nationwide and includes books and videotapes for purchase.

The Ski*Hi Language Development Scale (LDS) was designed for use in early intervention programs for the hearing impaired. The LDS is based on the language development of hearing children, but is adapted for use with the hearing impaired. Specifically, the LDS credits children for using word or sign language. The LDS is a checklist that is administered directly to the parent through a semistructured interview. Child language is assessed through this parent report. The LDS provides a developmental profile that can be used as a framework for designing a program for the child. The LDS can be used in total communication programs, oral programs, and auditory-verbal programs. It encourages a family-focused approach to early intervention and active family participation in the evaluation of child language skills and the writing of intervention goals.

METHODS FOR LEARNERS WITH VISUAL IMPAIRMENTS

The methods included in this section are drawn primarily from the *Handbook for Itinerant and Resource Teachers of Blind and Visually Impaired Students* (1989) by Doris Willoughby and Sharon Duffy. The handbook was developed under the sponsorship of the National Federation of the Blind.

Duffy states in her introduction to the text that positive attitudes about blindness are as essential to the optimal development of individuals with visual impairments as appropriate instruction methods. Furthermore, visual impairments or blindness may be reduced to a physical nuisance if learners are exposed to and adopt positive attitudes about their capabilities while receiving appropriate instruction in alternative techniques.

The instruction methods for the visually impaired included in this section address development in motor, cognitive, communicative, and social-emotional domains from infancy. Orientation and mobility, adaptive living, and literacy skills for young children and older learners are also included. Willoughby and Duffy emphasize that methods should be applied with a thorough understanding of various optional approaches and philosophies about blindness. The National Federation of the Blind is a rich source of such information (1800 Johnson Street, Baltimore, MD, 21230; (410) 659–9323).

COGNITIVE AND COMMUNICATIVE DEVELOPMENT

Method: Cognitive and Communicative Development in Infancy and Early Childhood

Source: Willoughby, D. M., & Duffy, S. L. (1989). Early childhood. In D. M. Willoughby & S. L. Duffy (Eds.), *Handbook for itinerant teachers of blind and visually impaired students* (pp. 15–26). Baltimore: National Federation of the Blind.

Description: Sighted infants and young children acquire an understanding of their environment through self-directed exploration and play. Parents encourage this activity and further support the child's understanding by providing the child with information that he or she may not acquire incidentally. Like sighted children, infants and young children with visual impairments need to actively engage in interaction with the environment to develop cognitive ability. The first step in facilitating active infant engagement is to encourage child-initiated exploration of the environment using a variety of flexible exploration and play behaviors.

Infants and young children with visual impairments learn to explore and observe their surroundings and tactually investigate objects in their everyday environments. They learn new behavior from adults as they are taught to imitate adult models after tactile observation of adult behavior. These young children learn about the world by being exposed to real objects and by being encouraged to explore those objects tactually. In addition to tactile exploration, children are encouraged to learn about the properties and functions of real objects through play with those objects.

Adults support conceptual development by commenting on the child's ongoing activity, labeling objects that the child is exploring or playing with, and conversing about events in the social and physical environment. Providing verbal descriptions of spatial concepts as children explore and play with objects facilitates an understanding of object orientation in space.

Children with visual impairments grow in their conceptual ability as they continue to use auditory and tactile information to make associations. Hands-on experiences provide the ideal basis for concept development. However, when it is not possible to provide the child with a real-life object to explore, models may provide essential information that cannot be actively experienced. Like sighted children, children with vision loss also benefit from participating in everyday activities (e.g., cooking) where they gain a concrete understanding of the components and sequence of actions in those activities. To promote optimal development during early childhood, tactile defensiveness and fears and aversions to exploration need to be alleviated so that the child is not self-imposing limits on his exposure to a variety of experiences.

Willoughby and Duffy discuss the development of communication skills during early childhood. The development of communication skills for young children with visual impairments proceeds in a typical manner if children have acquired the social and cognitive skills that provide a foundation for communication.

To develop receptive language skills, infants and toddlers with vision loss need to be assisted in interpreting sounds and words associated with objects and events in the environment. With encouragement, they will learn to read affect in the inflection and voice tone of others. Encouraged to do so, they will learn to monitor and modulate their own tone and volume of voice in speaking to others. During infancy, communication begins with joint attention and joint action routines that occur in child-caregiver interactions. Through these routines, infants learn about turn-taking in communicative exchanges. Expressive language becomes a primary means for communicating during toddlerhood. Adults support the communicative development of young children with visual impairments by responding to the child's communications and by providing meaningful language input (e.g., commenting on the child's ongoing activity), labeling objects that the child is attending to, and elaborating on what the child says. Adults may model more mature language for the child during the early stages of language development.

For all children, cognitive and communicative development during early childhood provides a foundation for independent functioning and the development of skills associated with social and scholastic success.

ORIENTATION AND MOBILITY SKILLS

Method: Orientation and Mobility Skills

Sources: Willoughby, D. M., & Duffy, S. L. (1989). Orientation and mobility for children eight and under, and those with special problems. In D. M. Willoughby & S. L. Duffy (Eds.), *Handbook for itinerant teachers of blind and visually impaired students* (pp. 175–184). Baltimore: National Federation of the Blind; Willoughby, D. M., & Duffy, S. L. (1989). A cane travel curriculum for those eight and under, and those with special

problems. In D. M. Willoughby & S. L. Duffy (Eds.), *Handbook for itinerant teachers of blind and visually impaired students* (pp. 187–196). Baltimore: National Federation of the Blind; Duffy, S. L. (1989). Travel with the long white cane. In D. M. Willoughby & S. L. Duffy (Eds.), *Handbook for itinerant teachers of blind and visually impaired students* (pp. 157–168). Baltimore: National Federation of the Blind; Duffy, S. L. (1989). Planning a cane travel curriculum. In D. M. Willoughby & S. L. Duffy (Eds.), *Handbook for itinerant teachers of blind and visually impaired students* (pp. 169–174). Baltimore: National Federation of the Blind.

Description: Infants and toddlers learn to move about the environment by creeping, crawling, and walking. At this time, the very young child is forming a body image and learning about parts of the body and how those parts can be utilized in movement. Children with vision loss can be expected to develop motor skills on the same developmental timeline as normally sighted children if given the proper support and encouragement to do so. This includes minimizing adult overprotectiveness, alleviating the child's fear of moving about the environment, and providing the child with incentive for movement (e.g., an interesting environment to explore). Mobility skills are especially critical for infants and young children with vision loss because they provide a basis for early cognitive and communicative development.

Willoughby recommends that children be introduced to the use of the cane for orientation and mobility during their toddler years. The toddler will first use the cane to explore the environment and experiment with the uses and effects of the cane. By age four, the child should be learning to use the cane as a functional tool. Willoughby discusses the advantages of teaching children with vision impairments to use a cane, and she discusses the consequence of noncane use. Acquiring caning skills is a developmental process that begins with the introduction of the cane to the very young child (or the newly blinded). Young children are then taught the proper use of the cane and quickly come to understand its value. Willoughby and Duffy provide a cane travel curriculum for children under 8 years of age and for older children and adults.

DAILY LIVING SKILLS

Method: Daily Living Skills for Young Children and Adolescents

Sources: Willoughby, D. M., & Duffy, S. L. (1989). Early childhood. In D. M. Willoughby & S. L. Duffy (Eds.), *Handbook for itinerant teachers of blind and visually impaired students* (pp. 15–26). Baltimore: National Federation of the Blind; Willoughby, D. M., & Duffy, S. L. (1989). Home economics and daily living skills. In D. M. Willoughby & S. L. Duffy (Eds.), *Handbook for itinerant teachers of blind and visually impaired students* (pp. 285–296). Baltimore: National Federation of the Blind.

Description: Infants and young children need to learn functional and independent daily living skills. Infants with visual impairments can be prompted to begin learning daily routines so that they can participate in those routines and assume responsibility for independent functioning. For example, the infant can learn sounds associated with food preparation and learn to interpret other cues that indicate that it is dinner time. In this way, the infant can coordinate her actions with those of her caregiver. Young children should also learn routines associated with sleeping, dressing, bathing, toileting, riding in the car, and so forth. Active participation in these routines helps young children with visual impairments make the associations they need to function independently.

Important independent living skills include (a) learning to organize belongings;

(b) managing time, money, and clothing; and (c) engaging in housekeeping, cooking, shopping, and other everyday activities. Maintaining an appropriate appearance and adhering to table etiquette are also essential daily living skills that contribute to social competence. Willoughby and Duffy provide a list of basic daily living skills for children, adolescents, and adults that can be incorporated into any educational program.

SOCIAL COMPETENCE SKILLS

Method: Social Competence Skills for Young Children and Adolescents

Sources: Willoughby, D. M., & Duffy, S. L. (1989). Early childhood. In D. M. Willoughby & S. L. Duffy (Eds.), *Handbook for itinerant teachers of blind and visually impaired students* (pp. 15–26). Baltimore: National Federation of the Blind; Willoughby, D. M., & Duffy, S. L. (1989). Fitting in socially. In D. M. Willoughby & S. L. Duffy (Eds.), *Handbook for itinerant teachers of blind and visually impaired students* (pp. 343–354). Baltimore: National Federation of the Blind; Willoughby, D. M., & Duffy, S. L. (1989). Dating marriage and family. In D. M. Willoughby & S. L. Duffy (Eds.), *Handbook for itinerant teachers of blind and visually impaired students* (pp. 355–362). Baltimore: National Federation of the Blind; Erwin, E. J. (1994). Social competence in young children with visual impairments. *Infants and Young Children, 6*(3), 26–33.

Description: Willoughby and Duffy offer suggestions for teaching appropriate social behavior to infants and young children with visual impairments. Appropriate social behavior is founded on the child's ability to interact comfortably and flexibly in the physical and social environment. Active engagement is important because perseverative and self-stimulating behaviors may occur as a result of lack of stimulation or experiences that leave the child feeling unconnected to the world. Keeping the child engaged in meaningful activity is the key to minimizing socially inappropriate mannerisms.

Modeling, prompting, reinforcement, and other behavioral strategies should be used to encourage the young child to use conventional social behaviors and to discourage use of inappropriate mannerisms (e.g., eye pressing). For behavioral strategies to be successful in reducing the occurrence of undesirable mannerisms, the child needs to learn to respond to auditory and tactile prompts that cue him or her to cease the undesirable mannerism and substitute appropriate behavior.

During the preschool years, young children with vision loss need to learn peer play and other social skills. This instruction includes learning how to (a) share with others, (b) play with others, (c) play with toys appropriately, and (d) enter and leave the play of others. In her discussion of the literature on social competence instruction for young children with visual impairments, Erwin (1994) recommends several strategies for helping children form and maintain social interactions.

1. Teach specific strategies for repairing communicative breakdowns that may occur in exchanges with others (e.g., "I'm not sure what you meant."). Teach children to "officially" withdraw from an exchange (e.g., "I'm finished.") so that they experience and convey a sense of closure in the interaction.
2. Assist the child in participating in a variety of topical discussions. Children with poor social skills may tend to discuss self-centered topics or limit references to the immediate context. Strategies should assist children in broadening the scope of discussion and extending it out of immediate context.
3. Teach children to use a variety of strategies for initiating social exchanges. These

strategies can include gaining the attention of another, collaborating toward a goal, directing a play scheme, or complimenting others.

Young children need to learn skills for social discourse. Children need to (a) learn the proper distance for discourse, (b) face people when talking to them, (c) be polite, and (d) avoid interrupting others. It is important to encourage age-appropriate interaction between children with vision loss and their peers. Sighted children should be cautioned not to be overly protective or overly directive in relationships.

During adolescence, social competence applies to free time with peers. Social competence for sighted teens and teens with visual impairments includes holding a job and maintaining close personal relationships successfully. The ability to travel independently within and outside the home community provides the age-appropriate freedom necessary to use these social skills. Teens with visual impairments should be able to use public transportation and other services, explain their visual impairments to others, be assertive when dealing with the public, and comfortably use self-advocacy skills.

BRAILLE

Method: Braille

Sources: Duffy, S. L., & Willoughby, D. M. (1989). A braillewriter in my pocket. In D. M. Willoughby & S. L. Duffy (Eds.), *Handbook for itinerant teachers of blind and visually impaired students* (pp. 135–140). Baltimore: National Federation of the Blind; National Federation of the Blind (1989). Braille: What is it? What does it mean to the blind? In D. M. Willoughby & S. L. Duffy (Eds.), *Handbook for itinerant teachers of blind and visually impaired students* (pp. 95–98). Baltimore: National Federation of the Blind;

National Federation of the Blind. (nd). *That the blind may read.* {Videotape}. Baltimore: National Federation of the Blind; Willoughby, D. M., & Duffy, S. L. (1989). Teaching Braille to young children. In D. M. Willoughby & S. L. Duffy (Eds.), *Handbook for itinerant teachers of blind and visually impaired students* (pp. 107–124). Baltimore: National Federation of the Blind; Willoughby, D. M., & Duffy, S. L. (1989). Braille reading and writing. In D. M. Willoughby & S. L. Duffy (Eds.), *Handbook for itinerant teachers of blind and visually impaired students* (pp. 125–134). Baltimore: National Federation of the Blind; Willoughby, D. M., & Duffy, S. L. (1989). Mathematics. In D. M. Willoughby & S. L. Duffy (Eds.), *Handbook for itinerant teachers of blind and visually impaired students* (pp. 307–312). Baltimore: National Federation of the Blind; Willoughby, D. M., & Duffy, S. L. (1989). Books and supplies. In D. M. Willoughby & S. L. Duffy (Eds.), *Handbook for itinerant teachers of blind and visually impaired students* (pp. 151-156). Baltimore: National Federation of the Blind.

Description: Braille is a system of reading and writing by touch. In an article entitled, Braille: What Is It? What Does It Mean to the Blind?, published by the National Federation of the Blind, the development of Braille is identified as the single most important contribution to the education of learners who are blind or visually impaired. Braille is the most efficient means of reading and writing for blind and low vision readers.

Louis Braille developed the Braille code in 1820. The use of the Braille code by individuals who are visually impaired greatly facilitates speed in reading and writing. Experienced Braille readers read at a speed comparable to print readers, about 200-400 words per minute. With proper instruction, Braille is learned in a similar manner and rate as print reading.

Braille symbols consist of arrangements or "cells" of raised dots on paper which make up letters, numbers, and punctuation marks. These symbols are read tactually. Braille materials prepared for mathematics and science use the Nemeth Code (American Association of Workers for the Blind, et al., 1972). The Nemeth Code provides correspondence between scientific and mathematical print symbols and Braille equivalents.

There are two basic modes for Braille writing just as there are for print writing. Braille may be produced manually with a slate and stylus. The stylus is used to push dots down through paper with the slate as a guide. This method of writing is as efficient as writing with a pencil or pen. Braillewriters are similar to typewriters. The writer has six keys and a space bar. The braillist pushes different combinations of keys to produce letters and other Braille symbols.

The earlier Braille is learned in life the more likely the student is to become a fluent reader. As with normally sighted children, young children with visual impairments should be introduced to Braille from infancy. Families and early childhood educators can provide the child with many opportunities for incidental learning by providing a literacy rich Braille environment. In this way, young children with visual impairments gain the same foundation of early literacy skills as young normally sighted children. Children are encouraged to feel the Braille in "Twin Vision" storybooks (i.e., books with both print and Braille symbols) as stories are read. Children are encouraged to feel the Braille in these books. Thus they come to understand that Braille symbols convey ideas. Braille labels can be attached to common household items, furniture, and playthings (e.g., alphabet blocks) so that children become familiar with their future reading medium at an early age.

When children understand that Braille represents concepts/words expressed on paper, they begin learning basic Braille keys. They learn to identify features of and distinctions between Braille symbols, learn Braille letters, associate sounds with Braille letters and words, and learn dot numbers in Braille cells.

Young children with visual impairments should be expected to acquire basic Braille skills on the same developmental timeline as young sighted children learn basic print skills. However, the sequence of skill acquisition may be different. Willoughby recommends *Patterns: The Primary Braille Reading Program* (Caton, Pester, & Bradley, 1980–1983), a basal reading series for young Braille readers. The series introduces Braille signs and format in a carefully controlled sequence. Instruction in the use of the stylus and slate for Braille writing should be introduced during the primary grades. Writing activities can then be used to reinforce newly acquired reading skills. As with Braille reading, speed and fluency in Braille writing should be emphasized so that writing becomes an efficient and effective process. The Braillewriter may be used by young learners but is not recommended as a substitute for learning the more practical basic writing skills with the slate and stylus. Willoughby also recommends *Just Enough to Know Better: A Basal Primer* (Curran, 1988) as a resource for parents who wish to assist their young children in developing early Braille reading skills.

Duffy and Willoughby provide suggestions for helping children move through the *First Reader* of the Patterns series while acquiring good Braille reading habits and emphasizing the importance of speed in reading. Though Braille readers benefit from using the Patterns *Primer* and *First Reader* in kindergarten and first grade classrooms, they should make the transition into classroom reading groups and into the classroom reading curriculum prior to or during the second grade. Suggestions are offered for preparing the child, family, and classroom teacher for this transition.

Notes: The opportunity to learn Braille is not often available. In an effort to "normal-

ize" low vision readers, educators often encourage them to use print. These ideas are becoming outmoded, and the National Federation of the Blind has recently launched a literacy campaign to educate the public about the effectiveness and efficiency of Braille reading for blind and low vision readers.

ALTERNATIVE MODES OF READING

Method: Alternative Modes of Reading

Source: Duffy, S. L., & Willoughby, D. M. (1989). Other modes of reading. In D. M. Willoughby & S. L. Duffy (Eds.), *Handbook for itinerant teachers of blind and visually impaired students* (pp. 141–150). Baltimore: National Federation of the Blind.

Description: Duffy and Willoughby state that visually impaired individuals should be skilled in using a variety of media to access written material when Braille is not available or is not a practical medium for obtaining information. Alternative modes of reading include large print reading materials, magnification, and closed circuit TV (CCTV) for those with functional vision. Although these modes are not appropriate for individuals who are legally blind or those who have degenerative eye conditions, they can be helpful for visually impaired learners who can make use of print. Duffy and Willoughby emphasize that these modes are relatively inefficient and should be used to supplement, not substitute for, Braille reading.

For older students, advances in technology make electronic modes of accessing print available. For example, the Kurzweil Reading Machine (KRM) reads printed pages with an optical scanner as the text is spoken aloud with a speech synthesizer. These and other electronic devices make print accessible, but costs are often prohibitive. Although young children need to learn basic Braille before they benefit from the use of technology, rapid advances in the field of technology are a boon to older experienced Braille readers.

Tape-recorded materials are a valuable resource for individuals with visual impairments. Popular books and college textbooks on tape are available from many libraries including libraries for the blind. Willoughby recommends equipment and guidelines for the use of taped materials for study. Live readers (i.e., those who read text aloud) offer several advantages over taped reading materials. Live readers can be directed to focus on certain aspects of the reading material or to skip around and among books. Live readers also can be taped for later reference. However, it is important to note that early or overreliance on taped materials is detrimental to the young

visually impaired child's emerging literacy development.

REFERENCES

American Association of Workers for the Blind, et al. (1972). *The Nemeth Braille code for mathematics and science notation* (rev. ed.). Baltimore: American Printing House for the Blind.

Caton, H., Pester, E., & Bradley, E. J. (1980–83). *Patterns: The primary Braille reading program.* Baltimore: American Printing House for the Blind.

Curran, E. P. (1988). *Just enough to know better: A Braille primer.* Boston: National Braille Press.

Erwin, E. J. (1994). Infants and young children with visual impairments. *Infants and Young Children, 6*(3), 26–33.

Willoughby, D. M., & Duffy, S. L. (Eds.). (1989). *Handbook for itinerant teachers of blind and visually impaired students.* Baltimore: National Federation of the Blind.

CHAPTER 7

Mathematics Methods

EvaJean Pickering, Ph.D.

CONTENTS

▶ Chisanbop   **110**
▶ Cuisenaire Rods   **111**
▶ Direct Instruction: Arithmetic   **112**
▶ Laboratory Method   **114**
▶ Montessori Arithmetic   **116**
▶ Piagetian Mathematics   **116**
▶ Problem Solving and Conceptual
    Math Development   **118**

▶ Structural Arithmetic   **119**
▶ Strategic Math Series Approach   **120**
▶ Kumon Math   **121**
▶ MATHFACT   **122**
▶ Math Problem-Solving Strategy   **123**
▶ Saxon Mathematics   **124**
▶ Touch Math   **124**
▶ Mathematics as Communication: IU   **125**

Mathematics is a symbolic language that theoretically facilitates reasoning. Its practical application is to express quantitative and spatial relationships (e.g., time, form, order, distance, space, and number or quantity). Levine (1994) describes mathematics as having a logical structure that is highly cumulative and convergent. Algorithmic sequences of mathematics integrate many developmental functions. They require continual alternation between symbolic notation, practical application, and implication (Levine, 1994).

Several cognitive processes are required to do mathematics: visual processing, language processing, attention, conceptualization, problem solving, and memory (active working, declarative, and procedural). Automaticity—the rate with which an individual can retrieve declarative or factual information—and selective attention to detail are intrinsic characteristics of mathematics (Bender, 1995; Levine, 1994).

Mathematics instruction occurs in any of three stages, concrete/ manipulative, representational/pictorial, and abstract/symbolic. Additionally, there are four areas in mathematics instruction: the number-fact mastery, computation (solving algorithms), concept learning, and problem solving. Some methods of instruction emphasize one of these areas, while other methods include all three areas. Methods are reviewed in the following chapter.

CHISANBOP

Method: Chisanbop

Author: Sung Jin Pai

Source: Lieberthal, E. (1978). *Chisanbop: Finger calculation method*. New York. Van Nostrand Reinhold. Chisanbop Enterprises.

Description: Sung Jin Pai, a Korean mathematician, first conceived Chisanbop, a

method of calculating basic math operations using one's fingers. Hong Young Pai, a son of Sung Jin, refined the method and introduced it to the United States. The Chisanbop method is commonly called finger math.

Chisanbop is useful with all age groups and ability levels, but it is most successful with preschoolers who are beginning to acquire number concepts. Their previous mathematical learning is not likely to be an interfering variable. For remedial purposes, Chisanbop may be taught to older students, adolescents, and adults. Chisanbop does not emphasize memorization and, unlike electronic calculation, allows students to learn the meaning of numbers and to understand the structure of mathematics. It is important to keep in mind that this method is designed to be used to supplement other mathematics programs.

The fingers are the calculation system, and the hands represent numbers at a 10 to 1 ratio. Chisanbop consists of a sequence of skills that must be monitored by the instructor to ensure that students master every step. However, the sequence need not be rigidly followed if a student is showing evidence of rapid advancement or achievement.

It is crucial for students to learn how to manipulate their fingers on an automatic level, a skill that may take weeks to master. To learn number representations for their fingers and hands, students must know the numbers 1 through 10. Then, the numerical value of the fingers and decimal value of the hands must be understood. The right hand represents a total value of 9; each finger is 1 and the thumb is 5. The left hand has a total value of 90; 10 for each finger and 50 for the thumb. The hands are kept in a relaxed position similar to the positioning of hands on the keyboard of a piano. At the command, PRESS, a student strikes the appropriate finger against the desk or table. In this way, students are taught number representations 1 through 9 using the right hand and 10 through 99 using the left and right hands concurrently.

Before advancing to calculations, finger values are practiced and overlearned so that responses are automatic. This factor cannot be emphasized too strongly.

PRESS and CLEAR shortcuts are included in the Chisanbop method. This shortcut allows students who have mastered basic operations to phase out counting with their fingers.

Notes: The Chisanbop method is designed to build speed, comprehension, and accuracy. Unlike a hand calculator, mechanical problems are eliminated. Chisanbop becomes an acceptable use of fingers as a mathematics aid or tool. In addition, Chisanbop creates a multisensory experience for the student and requires active involvement on the student's part to learn. Further, Chisanbop remains with the student always and cannot be lost or misplaced.

Chisanbop is an effective way to teach students with visual impairments. Teachers who use this method with any special population should monitor students' progress carefully. Teachers need to be trained in the use of the Chisanbop method.

CUISENAIRE RODS

Method: Cuisenaire Rods

Author: George Cuisenaire

Sources: *An introduction to Cuisenaire rods.* (n.d.). New Rochelle, New York: Cuisenaire Co. of America; Baroody, A. J. (1993). Introducing number and arithmetic concepts with number sticks. *Teaching Exceptional Children,* 26(1), 7–11.

Description: A Belgian schoolmaster, George Cuisenaire, invented the Cuisenaire Rods method—commonly called colored rods— about 40 years ago. His purpose was to provide an alternate method of learning for his students who were having difficulty grasping mathematical principles. Dr. Gattegno, an international educator, learned of Cuisenaire Rods and offered to promote the method. He translated Cuisenaire's booklet, *Nombres en Couleurs,* into English with his own augmentations. The colored rods method gained acceptance in the 1960s.

With Cuisenaire Rods, rote memorization is perceived as a stifling and ineffective method of learning. Instead, students have the opportunity to observe, discover, and describe mathematics through directed exploration. This discovery approach to teaching encourages student motivation and student-teacher dialogue. Developers and practitioners of the method believe the visual exploration component of the Cuisenaire Rods method allows students to "see" mathematical relationships, then progress to comprehend mathematical abstractions.

The colored rods used in instruction are rectangular solids that have two identifying attributes, color and length. Each rod is one of 10 colors, and each color represents a given length. The color range from shortest to longest is white, red, light green, purple, yellow, dark green, black, brown, blue, then orange. The numerical value of the rods is arbitrary. For example, if the orange rod has a value of one (1), the smaller rods are fractions of one. If the white rod is one, the larger rods are multiples of one.

Cuisenaire Rods serve as a mathematical tool for students ranging in ability from the preschool to high school levels. This method has the capacity, in simpler applications, to represent whole numbers and, in more complex applications, to represent exponents. Colored rods are used to teach counting, one-to-one correspondence, spatial relationships, and symmetry. Colored rods may also provide a system for defining and understanding the vocabulary of mathematics that enables students to progress to solving addition, multiplication, and division sentences. In addition, this method may help the student to (a) understand the relationships between the customary and metric systems, (b) conceptualize volume and area problems, and (c) understand or create problem solving techniques.

In using colored rods in math instruction, the following sequence may be followed:

1. Each student is allowed to experiment with the rods, independently of other students and the teacher.

2. Independent and directed activities are combined; the teacher guides the student through a series of mathematical relationships, then discusses the student's questions. Mathematical notation is not included in this step.

3. Next, mathematical notation is the directed activity. Students are still provided an opportunity for independent exploration, but the rods are not yet assigned numerical values.

4. Finally, numerical values are assigned to the rods, and the use of mathematical notation is expanded. Independent activities are encouraged.

Notes: Colored rods provide an alternate method of presenting mathematical concepts, besides motivating students to learn. Teachers should use colored rods as a supplement to the curriculum, not as a comprehensive teaching method. The rods are recommended for use in beginning instruction in seriation, conservation, and reversibility exercises. In addition, the method may be used when specific concepts need to be emphasized or trouble concepts need to be clarified. Students may use the rods independently or collaboratively.

Cuisenaire Rods may be used by students with visual impairments, auditory impairments, cognitive deficits, and with gifted students or students with behavior disorders. This method is most effective when students are in the manipulative or pictorial level of learning.

DIRECT INSTRUCTION: ARITHMETIC

Method: Direct Instruction: Arithmetic

Author: Siegfried Engelmann

Source: Engelmann, S. (1970). *Preventing failure in the primary grades.* Chicago: Science Research Associates.

Description: Direct Instruction Arithmetic is a language-based approach to teaching mathematics concepts. For teaching any concept, the language used may be verbal or nonverbal, responsive or demonstrative, but must clearly convey that specific concept. Reciprocally, responses from students must indicate their understanding of the concept.

Four factors make this method different from other methods of arithmetic instruction: One, the level of each student's knowledge is not assumed. Once a teacher has determined an entry level, every skill at that level is taught. Two, the order of skills taught is definite and detailed. Three, instruction of skills traditionally considered to be simple, such as multiplication and fractions, is accelerated. Teaching is as rapid as student mastery of each step allows. And four, all skills to be taught are necessary for future problem-solving.

The structure of arithmetic is emphasized in direct instruction. Students are instructed in the importance of understanding arithmetic rules and the role they play in solving simple and complex arithmetic problems. For example, students must be able to count to enter the beginning arithmetic level.

The process of learning mathematical skills begins with the concept of zero. Lines drawn on the chalkboard, as well as objects students can touch or hold, are used to demonstrate the zero concept. During instruction, verbal interaction, between students and between the teacher and students, is continual.

Adding is introduced as "plussing." For example, "If I have two lines and I plus one line, I will have _____ lines." Students progress in their counting skills, moving from manipulating objects to finger counting to abstract thinking in addition problems.

After number symbols are taught, students learn to read and interpret arithmetic statements. For example, students read aloud the arithmetic statement, "4 + 3 = a" as "Four plus three equals a." The equal sign (=) is emphasized in discussion and by drawing a thick vertical line beneath it. In the same way, by emphasizing it in discussion and in written exercises, the meaning of the plus sign (+) is taught. Lines that correspond to numbers (three lines would represent 3) are used in place of each number in an addition equation.

The equation rule is then introduced. Pointing to vertical lines drawn to the left of an equal sign, the teacher might say, "Count the number of lines on this side (indicating the left side) of the equal sign." When the students have counted the lines correctly, the teacher might respond, "That is how many lines need to be on this side (indicating the right side) of the equal sign." Students read the statements together, mastering the equation rule. The goal of this technique is not for students to memorize facts but to become familiar with the language and meaning of operational statements.

Moving away from reliance on fingers and lines, students are introduced to abstract, verbal problem solving. In beginning arithmetic, a sequence is presented for teaching addition algebra, initially as an extension of counting and then in problem format (i.e., 3 + a = 4). In addition, algebraic word problems are taught, and students learn subtraction, subtraction algebra, and multiplication.

Advanced arithmetic builds on the basic principles taught in beginning arithmetic. Often students instructed by other methods possess arithmetic proficiency in some areas and so may start at the advanced level in those areas. However, these students must be taught the operations of beginning arithmetic that they have not yet mastered.

In advanced arithmetic, column addition and "carrying," column subtraction and "borrowing," and fractions are taught. The instructor first teaches zero (0), then 10, 20, 30, and so forth. To learn "carrying," students are taught a new rule: "When you see a 1 on this side of the line (indicating the left

side of a vertical line, or "1|"), it is not a 1; it is a 10. When you see a 2... (or "2| "), it is not a two; it is a twenty", and so forth. The instructor teaches zero (0) by placing a zero (0) in position on the other side of the vertical line (i.e., the right side, or "|0"). Thus, "1|0" represents 10; "2|0" represents 20, "3|0" represents 30, and so forth. To continue with the double-digit numbers concept, the teacher can teach 11, 21, 31, and so forth, by substituting 1 for 0 in the above schema. Therefore, "1|1" represents 11; "2|1" represents 21; "3|1" represents 31, and so forth. By extending this technique, students learn to "carry." "Borrowing" is instructed in a similar manner, but as the reverse operation of "carrying."

Fractions are taught using advanced addition and subtraction concepts. The sequence of teaching concepts is definite, and rules are learned before students progress. Equation rules are employed to solve problems. Addition of fractions, factoring, and other fraction operations are also taught in advanced arithmetic. Students learn concepts more quickly at this level, and the pace can be accelerated. The program may be completed within 2 years' time.

Notes: The method requires minimal preparation after the teacher's initial training. The instruction is sequenced and mastery learning is demanded. Student response rate is rapid, and teacher-engaged time is extensive. The instruction material, DISTAR Arithmetic, was developed by Englemann and Carnine (1976).

A language-based approach, like direct instruction, which may prove advantageous to some students, may create problems for others. Verbal methods, in general, are less appropriate for teaching the earlier stages of math. These methods use pictorial rather than concrete techniques for illustrating mathematical concepts. For example, in direct instruction, concrete manipulatives are not provided for students. Therefore, young students may not have the knowledge that would help them grasp more complex mathematical concepts. However, verbal methods, like direct instruction, are more efficient approaches than inductive approaches if students have the prerequisite knowledge. In addition, the demand in direct instruction classrooms for students to respond in unison may overwhelm some students.

Direct instruction is not an effective method for teaching gifted students because it makes little use of investigative elements. However, direct instruction has been used successfully with preschoolers and students in elementary grades. Although this method may seem less appropriate, it is often successful in teaching students with math disabilities. It tends to level the playing field in classrooms with students from culturally and socio-economically diverse backgrounds. Direct instruction arithmetic has consistently resulted in significant academic gains for students with learning disabilities. Particularly, students with Attention Deficit Disorder are better able to focus when taught with direct instruction.

LABORATORY METHOD

Method: Laboratory Method

Authors: K. Kidd, S. Myers, and D. Cilley

Source: Kidd, K., Myers, S., & Cilley, D. (1970). *The laboratory approach to mathematics.* Chicago: Science Research Associates.

Description: The laboratory method allows students to discover the structure of mathematics through practical application and exploration. This method is based on the premise that students involved in meaningful learning—learning that is relevant to their "real" lives—develop positive attitudes toward the subject they are studying and thus learn more successfully.

In this method, students are provided objects to manipulate. With manipulatives,

students construct ideas and gain insight into practical applications of mathematics. As a result, students interest in and enthusiasm for learning mathematics increases. Additionally, experiential learning allows students to link their knowledge and experiences with new concepts. This, in turn, facilitates clarity and order in learning.

Mathematical problems are presented as open-ended opportunities to explore. The results of particular mathematics problems are not emphasized in this instruction method, but rather the process of discovery. The teacher guides students with questions and directives. Students progress at their own rates. Furthermore, the techniques for motivating students are nonthreatening and noncompetitive.

Instructional goals cover six areas: (a) readiness, (b) concept development and synthesis, (c) recall, (d) application and planning, (e) evaluation, and (f) remediation. Classroom activities are designed to enhance problem-solving skills and reduce demands on students' verbal abilities.

To develop effective and independent problem solving skills, students must understand the problem- solving process. This process is relatively simple. Abstractions are presented to the students or are generated by the students. Students learn to identify the problem and state it in mathematical terms. Students then plan a course of action, collect relevant data, and begin to solve the problem. Finally, by comparing and contrasting results, the students draw conclusions from the data.

Laboratory lessons may be conducted in the classroom in the following ways: as a whole class with teacher demonstration; as small groups working collaboratively on one experiment; or as small groups working on different experiments that are specific to the abilities and interests of the students in each group. Success in all three situations is contingent on the presence of suitable materials, teacher preparedness, and student interest and involvement.

Demonstrations made by the teacher and visible to all students are useful for all phases of any problem-solving process. Large-scale models, overhead projectors, familiar materials, and properly functioning instruments are prerequisites for success. Several techniques are suggested to encourage student involvement, including written outlines of key questions, designated question and answer time, and student involvement in demonstrations.

Depending on the availability of materials and the purpose of the lesson, all students can work on the same experiment in small groups. In this case, each group is assigned a station where materials are provided in a small kit. The teacher still gives general instructions and raises questions. In addition, the teacher may circulate from group to group observing, evaluating student responses, and directing and encouraging further exploration.

Small groups may work independently on lessons that reflect the needs and interests of students in each group. However, the teacher must consider practical aspects of the lesson before it is assigned, such as (a) the type of activity, (b) availability of materials, and (c) the capacity of students to work independently.

Organization is an important component of the laboratory method of mathematics instruction. Procedures need to be in place that enable the class to move smoothly from one activity to another. In addition, guide sheets should be created for each group to provide students with direction independent of teacher supervision. Also, kits of materials should be assembled to be used with the guide sheets.

Once groups are prepared to work together, the teacher moves from group to group. The teacher evaluates assignments, observes group productivity, directs or redirects the course of lessons, and motivates students. For tracking class progress, it is recommended that the teacher describe assignments and chart the progress of each group. All students keep daily logs of their individual progress in relation to their group. Teacher monitoring is crucial to assess progress accurately, evaluate strengths and weaknesses of individual students, and provide feedback.

Notes: The laboratory method requires extensive student involvement and encourages diverse thinking among students. If teachers use the laboratory approach, they must be creative in generating ideas for laboratory investigations. These investigations should (a) fit their mathematics instruction goals, (b) meet the needs and interests of students, and (c) not exceed the scope of the teacher's time and resources. Classroom furniture and equipment must be arranged for both small and large group activities, individual investigations, and teacher demonstrations. Space for free movement is necessary; and equipment, materials, and storage areas are vital to effective teaching.

The laboratory method may prove useful for students with learning disabilities, especially those who combine strong quantitative thinking skills with a related disorder (e.g., visual, spatial). Moreover, students with attention and behavioral disorders may be able to maintain their focus on mathematics using this method, because their direct involvement is required.

Some students with disabilities may have difficulty learning abstract concepts in the informal setting created by the laboratory method. In many applications, the laboratory method requires students to use materials independently and to discover and generalize basic mathematics concepts. For any classroom, this method requires skill, time, and organizational abilities on the part of the teacher. When the laboratory method is used with students with disabilities, the teacher must devote additional time to guiding and supervising the students. The needs of students with disabilities are individualized, thus continuous assessment is necessary. When teachers select this method, they will need to plan extensively to ensure that activities are appropriate to the experiences of students with disabilities.

MONTESSORI ARITHMETIC

Method: Montessori Arithmetic

Author: Maria Montessori

Source: Montessori, M. (1965). *The Montessori elementary material*. Cambridge, MA: Robert Bentley.

Description: The Montessori arithmetic method provides very specific guidelines for the use of materials and presentation. Rods, beads, and counting frames, for example, are used extensively to teach mathematical concepts.

Sets of rods, graduated in length, are used to represent quantities, for example, 1 through 10. The rods are a specified length and color and represent relative quantity (i.e., 2 is twice as long as 1; 4 is twice as long as 2, and so on). By placing rods end to end, students discover the principles of addition and subtraction. Students are also taught sequencing and counting by manipulating the rods.

At about 5 ½ years of age, students are introduced to beads. These beads are strung on wires to represent quantitative concepts. Each set of beads is a different color. In addition, numbers can be used with the "bead wires" in activities that aid the conceptual development of computation skills. Because beads depict the aspect of quantity, concepts of place value are also taught using "bead wires." Wires hold 10 beads or 100 beads, from which "100 chains" and "1,000 chains" may be constructed. Once mental computation becomes automatic, beads are no longer counted.

Counting frames are a more sophisticated version of the bead wires. The first wire in the frame holds 1 bead; the second, 10; the third, 100; and the fourth, 1,000. The counting frame simplifies more advanced addition and subtraction, including concepts of place value and regrouping. An advanced counting frame has seven horizontal wires to accommodate computations beyond 1,000.

Quadrille paper is designed for recording mathematical computations. This paper, which is ruled in various colors, piques interest. Similarly, special paper is provided for other activities as needs dictate.

An arithmetic board and 100 loose beads are provided to teach multiplication and division. While manipulating the arithmetic board, students write the answers to problems on prepared work papers. Through practice, multiplication tables are learned. Division is taught using the same materials with different work papers. A counting frame is used to teach advanced operations of multiplication involving several figures. Procedures are also provided for long division, multiples, prime numbers, factoring, squaring and cubing numbers, and plane geometry.

Notes: This method is a developmental approach with sensorimotor roots combined with a discovery approach. It stresses the process of learning. Although this method stresses discovery learning, teacher presentation, guidance, and input are crucial. Guidance is critical for students with disabilities who have problems learning intuitively or through self-initiated activities. Verbal interactions initiated by the teacher may be necessary to introduce and develop mathematical concepts. For example, an activity may need to be provided by the teacher to demonstrate the concept of zero.

PIAGETIAN MATHEMATICS

Method: Piagetian Mathematics

Author: Richard Copeland

Source: Copeland, R. (1979). *Math activities for children: A diagnostic and developmental approach*. Columbus, OH: Merrill.

Description: Logical and mathematical thinking skills are taught through a developmentally sequenced approach based on the work of Piaget. According to Piaget, the highest form of reasoning is logico-mathematical, developed from interactions between physical experiences and logical processes. The development of mental structures is necessary to acquire logico-mathematical knowledge. The mathematics activities in this approach are designed to elicit responses at three of the four levels of intellectual development described by Piaget: **preoperational, concrete operational,** and **formal operational**. The **preoperational** level is considered premathematical; students at this level (ages 2 to 7 years) respond perceptually rather than logically. At the **concrete operational** level, logical reasoning emerges with the aid of physical objects. Abstract thinking characterizes the **formal operational** level.

Each activity in this mathematical approach provides response categories for Piagetian levels. Stage I responses are **preoperational**; Stage II responses are transitional, ranging between the **preoperational** and **concrete operational**; Stage III responses are **concrete operational**.

The teacher's role in the Piagetian mathematics approach is fourfold. First, students must be provided the opportunity to explore their physical world. Second, the teacher must question students rather than supply them with information. Third, students must be encouraged to interact with their peers and others in solving problems. Fourth, the teacher must become a skillful diagnostician who can determine the developmental levels of students through interviews.

Copeland divides Piagetian mathematics activities into seven areas:

1. *Logical Classification:* the prenumerical period.
2. *Number:* conservation, seriation, and class inclusion.
3. *Space Orientation:* geometric activities including topological, Euclidean, and projective concepts.
4. *Measurement:* length, volume, area, time, and motion.
5. *Knowing versus Performing:* understanding the concept underlying a mathematics operation rather than simply performing the operation.
7. *Mathematical Memory:* reconstruction of previously introduced concept.
8. *Chance and Probability:* "Why" questions are answered when a logical explanation exists as well as when one does not, as with chance occurrences.

Each of Copeland's seven areas has several activities that function as the basis for instructional planning. These activities are arranged sequentially from simple to complex. They are accompanied by charts that link activities with various age levels. Moreover, each activity has a purpose statement followed by a materials and procedures section. The materials and procedures section is followed by a level of performance section, which contains three stages and teaching implications. Students solve problems by trial and error. In Stage II (transitional), they revisit Stage I (preoperational) to verify answers whenever necessary. Stage III responses, however, are at the concrete operational level and do not require the trial and error approach of Stage II. Other higher level activities, such as map-making, conservation, and measurement of volume include formal operational, or Stage IV, thinking for students who formulate rules abstractly.

Notes: This method offers students sensorimotor experiences in addition to opportunities for social interaction. Students function and explore at their own developmental levels. The method is designed for students who are developmentally between the ages of 4 and 12 years. It provides a natural setting in which developmental abilities may be assessed. This method adequately provides for the placement of students who are developmentally diverse.

Teachers who use this method need good organizational skills and adequate time. They must also have a basic understanding of Piagetian principles. For example, students must be allowed to interact freely in an informal classroom atmosphere. Because of the need to assess students' logico-mathematical development for appropriate placement, teachers must become skilled interviewers.

PROBLEM SOLVING AND CONCEPTUAL MATH

Method: Problem Solving and Conceptual Math Development

Authors: John Cawley, Anne M. Fitzmaurice-Hayes, and Robert A. Shaw

Source: Cawley, J. F., Fitzmaurice-Hayes, A. M., & Shaw R. A. (1988) *Mathematics for the mildly handicapped: A guide to curriculum and instruction*. Boston: Allyn & Bacon.

Description: This approach focuses on teaching mathematics to students with mild disabilities. The curriculum is designed to expose students to a variety of learning experiences. Inability in mathematics or inadequate skill development are minimized in this approach. Instead, mathematics experiences are aimed at enriching the affective and cognitive domains of students.

Mathematics for the mildly handicapped is a developmental and remedial program, an outgrowth of Cawley's Project Math (Cawley et al., 1976). This problem-solving curriculum and instructional guide covers skills normally taught from preschool through the eighth grade. It reflects the philosophy of Jerome Bruner (1960), in that it is language-based and input for instruction may be concrete, pictorial, or symbolic. At the concrete level, students manipulate physical objects to encourage the formation of mental images. Pictures of physical ob-

jects are used at the pictorial level, and symbolic representations are used at the third and final level. Here, abstract thinking replaces the mental images of the previous two levels. Bruner maintains that adequate mathematical language and general language concepts must be present for students to grasp the basic mathematical concepts at all three levels of instruction and to achieve intellectual growth.

Interactive teaching units are designed specifically for students with mild disabilities. The first chapter details individual and developmental characteristics of these disabilities. A full chapter is devoted to assessment for placement and diagnostic considerations.

Interactive teaching units include the mode of presentation and the response of students to the learning process. Two hundred activities are organized to monitor the teacher's and the students' actions in an attempt to maximize the students' potential for learning math. Many materials are used to accomplish the program goals, such as geometric models, clocks, tape recorders, and calculators.

Notes: Mathematics for the mildly handicapped may be used with students with mild handicaps or other students at risk for academic difficulties (e.g., slow learners and the socially or economically disadvantaged). The program may be administered by regular or special education teachers, and tutors or aides, because no specialized training is required. This program provides educators with a conceptual understanding of math. Its format helps instructors teach problem solving and concept development in a practical and efficient manner. Furthermore, the program is individualized. Small group and one-to-one instruction are preferred, so immediate feedback can be provided to the student and careful observations can be conducted by the instructor. The program is criteria-referenced and self-paced. Mastery learning is stressed and successful experiences are built in.

STRUCTURAL ARITHMETIC

Method: Structural Arithmetic

Authors: Catherine Stern, Margaret Stern, and Toni S. Gould

Source: Stern, C., Stern, M., & Gould, T. S. (1971). *Children discover arithmetic: An introduction to structural arithmetic.* (rev. ed.). New York: Harper & Row.

Description: Stern, Stern, and Gould describe Structural Arithmetic as a laboratory approach. Number concepts are presented sequentially, using concrete materials, so that students can focus on and understand the structure of mathematics. From the beginning of the teaching process, students use specialized materials to illustrate the relationship between numbers and the number system. Stern, Stern, and Gould contend that students do not develop number concepts by counting elements of unstructured groups. Students are instructed using cats, dogs, and balls, for example, or other random pictorial and object groups. This approach introduces irrelevant clues that interfere with the students' ability to see mathematical structures. For example, students may count 10 marbles but will not necessarily understand the relationship of 2 marbles to 10 marbles. Or students may count 5 cats and 3 cats in a picture task but fail to see them as a Gestalt representation of "eightness," and therefore, according to authors, fail to see the relationship among any of the numbers.

To teach structure using Structural Arithmetic, blocks of different dimensions and colors are introduced. A block of 10 units is 10 times as long as a block of 1 unit; therefore, the units function as a system of measurement. As a result, a three-unit block plus a two-unit block is equal to a five-unit block. Because the blocks are different colors, students can see the relationships more readily.

Structural Arithmetic may be used for children as young as preschool age. Kindergartners, for example, focus on understanding the number system through the structured use of concrete materials. Initially, students are involved in "number games without number names" to develop a number sense. This development of number sense occurs prior to learning number names and enumeration.

At this point, "number games with number names" are introduced. Students learn number names, one-to-one correspondence, and oral addition and subtraction. Importantly, they also learn to express themselves using the language of arithmetic. The next step introduces "number games and number names and symbols." Students learn the symbols 1 to 10 and associate them with number names and ordinal placement in a series. They also associate the equivalent number of concrete objects representing a relationship of size. Students also learn the plus sign (+), equal sign (=), and zero (0). Addition and subtraction problems are now written by students who solve them using concrete materials. In these activities, sums do not exceed 10, and missing addends, remainders, and difference are introduced.

Subsequent activities expose students to two- and three-place numbers, more advanced addition and subtraction skills, oral computation, and problem-solving activities. Multiplication, division, and fractional parts are studied as well as problem solving in preparation for later work in algebra.

In Structural Arithmetic, students learn important mathematical concepts in a programmed sequence. Computational drills are forbidden. Instead, oral computation activities are provided. Reading problems are minimized by providing vocabulary words that do not exceed the second grade level. Students learn to think mathematically through the extensive use of concrete materials before moving to abstract activities. In addition, students engage in experiments that are self-correcting, so feedback is immediate. The mastery of one concept is verified before proceeding to a new one.

Notes: This method provides an opportunity to acquire basic mathematics concepts using concrete objects. It provides visual pictures for students with semantic language difficulty and may be useful for students who have difficulty visualizing mathematics structures.

THE STRATEGIC MATH SERIES APPROACH

Method: The Strategic Math Series Approach

Authors: Cecil D. Mercer and Susan Peterson Miller

Sources: Mercer, C. D., & Miller, S. P. (1993). *Strategic math series: Division facts 0 to 81.* Lawrence, KS: Edge Enterprises; Mercer, C. D., & Miller, S. P. (1992). Teaching students with learning problems in math to acquire, understand, and apply basic math facts. *Remedial and Special Education, 13*(3), 19–35.

Description: The Strategic Math Series approach uses a concrete-representational-abstract (C-R-A) teaching sequence. This approach was developed to provide a systematic means of using C-R-A math instruction. Specifically, this series contains levels of instruction designed for students who lack knowledge of basic math facts and operations, such as addition, subtraction, multiplication, and division (Level 1). Students who possess this knowledge are already prepared, therefore, to learn more complex computation and word problem skills (Level 2).

The C-R-A method divides instruction sequentially. At the **concrete** level students manipulate three-dimensional objects to solve computation problems. At the **representational** level, students employ two-dimensional drawings to solve problems. And at the **abstract** level, students work computational problems and attempt to

solve them without using objects or drawings. Additionally, in the C-R-A method, students understand concepts before they memorize facts.

The Strategic Math Series divides teaching and learning manuals into 22 basic lessons that comprise seven fundamental phases. It is vital that all 22 lessons be completed; first, because lessons are carefully sequenced and build in complexity; and second, even when skills are achieved, practice must continue to increase fluency and ensure further skill development.

The Strategic Math Series follows a seven-phase instructional sequence:

1. *Pretest.* This diagnostic assessment places students at appropriate learning levels. Assessment scores are compared against a mastery criterion; scores and the need for instruction are thoroughly discussed with students individually.

2. *Teach Concrete Application.* At this level of instruction, students manipulate objects to learn basic computational skills. This level prepares students for the representational and abstract levels.

3. *Teach Representational Application.* At this level of instruction, students substitute drawings and tallies for objects to learn computational skills.

4. *Introduce the "DRAW" Strategy.* This strategy is introduced to promote independent learning techniques, because students with learning difficulties often do better when using cognitive strategies. The acronym, DRAW, represents the four steps of this strategy. These steps are: Discover the sign; Read the problem; Answer, or draw and check; Write the answer.

5. *Teach Abstract Application.* At this level of instruction, students solve computational problems without the aid of manipulatives or representational drawings. However, if they have difficulty, students may use the DRAW strategy.

6. *Posttest.* A posttest is administered to evaluate how well students have learned basic computational skills. Instruction in this phase is designed to increase computational fluency and further develop skills. When the posttest has determined they need additional practice, students may repeat skills.

7. *Provide Practice to Fluency.* At this phase of instruction, students solve increasingly more complicated word problems. They increase the rate at which they compute facts, and they discriminate between various computational problems (e.g., addition, subtraction, multiplication, and division). Furthermore, students learn a strategy designed to ease the computation of more complicated word problems. This strategy, "FAST," helps students perform a process that sets word problems up in a numerical format. The acronym "FAST" represents the following strategy: **F**ind what you're solving for; **A**sk yourself, "What are the parts of the problem?"; **S**et up the numbers; and **T**ie down the sign.

In addition to the seven-phase C-R-A instructional method, the Strategic Math Series approach provides instructors and students with further guidelines and procedures that facilitate the process of learning basic math skills. These guidelines include procedures to review skills and promote individual work and advancement. Feedback components and practices to establish strategy mastery and mastery of computational skills are also included.

Notes: The Strategic Math Series is one of the few methods that implicitly systematizes the teacher's instruction of mathematics concepts. This method allows students to learn number facts through concept development. It also allows them to progress in their learning by mastering each stage, moving from concrete to representational to abstract.

KUMON MATH

Method: Kumon Math

Author: Toru Kumon

Source: Kumon, T. (1995). *Introducing Kumon math*. Fort Lee, NJ: Kumon USA.

Description: Kumon Math provides supplementary mathematical instruction applicable to all learning levels. It emphasizes individualized self-instruction that promotes speed and accuracy in the learning of basic math concepts.

Developed by Toru Kumon, Kumon Math uses 4,000 worksheets formatted sequentially, with problems ranging from preschool to college levels. The basis of Kumon Math is repetition; students engage in drill and practice. This approach promotes overlearning mathematical concepts; concepts are assimilated through constant practice and review. Overlearning, or assimilating, in this manner seems to enhance the learning process.

In Kumon Math, students spend 20 to 30 minutes a day timing themselves as they work on 5 to 10 small worksheets. The students record their elapsed time on each worksheet and correct each previously completed worksheet. They also confer with a teacher after checking their speed and accuracy. Students must meet required standards before advancing to the next learning level. Students are required to practice and rework their worksheets until they achieve a score of 100%. No other score is acceptable. If students do not achieve scores of 100%, they must repeat prior worksheets to improve their speed and accuracy. By repeating the same problems, it is thought that students can achieve mastery of these problems.

Notes: The strength of Kumon Math is that is aids students with automaticity, or recall of facts and information. Thus, the Kumon Math method works effectively with students who learn best by repetition and overlearning. It is useful for basic classroom activities like completing worksheets. Students at risk of academic difficulty (due to underprivileged socioeconomic or culturally diverse backgrounds) are receptive to this method. However, teachers should exercise caution when using this method of instruction for students with disabilities. This method may have limited benefit for students who have problems with the speed at which they write, difficulties with visual perception abilities, or simply prefer auditory learning approaches.

MATHFACT

Method: MATHFACT

Authors: Carol A. Thornton and Margaret A. Toohey

Sources: Thornton, C. A., & Toohey, M. A. (1982–1985). *MATHFACT: An alternative program for children with special needs.* Brisbane, Australia: Queensland Division of Special Education; Thornton, C. A., & Toohey, M. A. (1985). Basic Math Facts: Guidelines for Teaching and Learning. *Learning Disabilities Focus, 1*(1), 44–57.

Description: MATHFACT is an alternative basic fact program designed for students with learning disabilities. This program combines a metacognitive focus on learning strategies for fact recall with multisensory approaches. Vital to this program are options for adjusting core activities to match the learning strengths and weaknesses of students and for developing self-monitoring skills.

MATHFACT isolates 10 factors that function as a basic program guideline for teaching students. Teachers should give the following factors equal attention:

1. *Prerequisite Learnings.* Concepts prerequisite to learning basic facts (i.e., counting on, recognizing the greater of two numbers, visual and auditory patterning)

should be consolidated and taught before introducing fact learning.

2. *Ongoing Diagnosis and Assessment.* Accurate diagnostic information for students should be obtained before introducing fact learning. In addition, ongoing assessment is crucial.

3. *Modify the Sequence of Presented Facts.* The traditional sequence of facts presentation—usually arranged according to the size of sums—should be adjusted to meet the needs of individual students.

4. *Teach Strategies for Learning Facts.* Students should be taught strategies or patterns prior to drill that can be generalized to new experiences and promote learning unknown facts.

5. *Modify the Presentation.* Activities should be adjusted to match the unique styles of auditory, visual, and kinesthetic/tactile learners.

6. *Control the Pace.* Instruction should be accelerated or slowed down to match students' needs.

7. *Help Students to Discriminate When to Use a Strategy.* Students should be aided in learning the appropriate strategy to be applied to a situation.

8. *Provide Verbal Prompts.* Students should be provided with specific verbal prompts to assist them in establishing learning strategies.

9. *Help Students Develop Self-Monitoring Skills.* Students with learning disabilities should be taught learning techniques in addition to facts.

10. *Provide for Overlearning.* Once a strategy has been mastered, focus should be shifted to the memorization of facts, particularly to placing them in long-term memory.

Again, MATHFACT suggests giving equal attention to these various program factors.

Notes: MATHFACT's specific strategies for fact recall benefit students with math disabilities. Several factors help these students achieve mastery of basic math facts. These include (a) sequencing facts strategically for recall, (b) presenting facts to match the unique learning styles, and (c) helping students to develop self-monitoring skills.

MATH PROBLEM-SOLVING STRATEGY

Method: Math Problem-Solving Strategy

Authors: Marjorie Montague and Candice S. Bos

Source: Montague, M., & Bos, C. S.(1986). The effect of cognitive strategy training on verbal math problem solving performance of learning disabled adolescents. *Journal of Learning Disabilities, 19*, 26-33.

Description: The Math Problem-Solving Strategy enables adolescent students with disabilities to understand, complete, and check verbal math problems encountered in a secondary level, general math curricula. This approach provides students with cognitive strategies to solve math problems.

Cognitive strategy training emphasizes (a) processing of information, (b) organizational skills, (c) the application of information, and (d) problem- solving techniques. This teaching approach increases the likelihood of success when the strategies are used appropriately, maintained, and generalized to similar situations and settings.

The Math Problem-Solving Strategy is an eight-step approach developed to improve the abilities of adolescent students in solving story problems.

1. *Read the Problem Aloud.* The teacher helps students by defining unknown words. The pronunciations and meanings of unfamiliar words can be clarified at this step.

2. *Paraphrase the Problem Aloud.* Students restate the problem aloud, clarify the question that is being asked, and identify the material required to solve the problem.

3. *Visualize.* Students draw a picture of the problem or otherwise represent it graphically.

4. *State the Problem.* Students identify and state the significant information in a problem and complete the sentences aloud: "I have . . . I want to find . . ." Additionally, students underline the relevant information in the text of the problem.

5. *Hypothesize.* Students complete the following sentence aloud: "If . . ., then . . ." For example, "If 10 people each have 12 books, then I need to multiply to determine the total number of books." Students recognize the specific operational quality of the problem and write it using operational signs.

6. *Estimate.* Students round the numbers involved in the problem and approximate the answer.

7. *Calculate.* Students calculate and label the answer.

8. *Self-check.* Students review the problem in story form, verify their computations, and ask whether their answer makes sense.

Notes: The Math Problem-Solving Strategy attempts to modify the approach of students to math problem-solving. It provides students with a cognitive strategy; instructs them in the use of this strategy; allows them to apply and practice the strategy; cues them to their own use of the strategy; and provides them with corrective feedback on their performances.

In time, some students who use this cognitive strategy select only certain facets of it. Teachers, therefore, need to be aware that there are aspects of this cognitive strategy that must be tailored to accommodate individual needs. Students' metacognitive awareness of strategy use indicates their awareness of the problem solving process.

This results in increased attention to the process and a more focused, systematic approach to solving math problems.

SAXON MATHEMATICS

Method: Saxon Mathematics

Authors: Stephen Hake and John Saxon

Source: Hake, S., & Saxon, J. (1995). *Math 65: An incremental development.* Norman, OK: Saxon.

Description: The Saxon approach to mathematics is designed to teach the abstractions of math by assimilating mathematical concepts through praxis. Basic math tools are taught, including concept identification and computational skills.

In this approach, students are taught to work math problems. They will later learn to understand the concepts themselves. The abstractions of mathematics are introduced in problems incrementally; concepts, or even facets of concepts, are assimilated before another concept or facet is introduced. The primary task of instruction is to ensure that students complete all the steps of every problem in every designated problem set. Concepts are never eliminated from problem sets or dropped from the curriculum. Instead, they are continuously reviewed and applied to new problems. This kind of repetition and continuous review provides adequate time and opportunity for the concepts to become familiar. In turn, this kind of familiarity allows students to recognize "old" concepts in new and unfamiliar problem sets. Consequently, students can apply an understanding of concepts to problems and concentrate on their solutions. In the Saxon approach, students concentrate on 24 or 25 review problems during the year; at the same time only four to six new problems are introduced.

Notes: The main focus of the Saxon method is on concepts rather than computation. Because the method uses story problems as its main vehicle for instructing math, students learn life skills relating to math.

If students need work, particularly on computational skills, then practice outside the Saxon method is appropriate before continuing with the Saxon method. Students can learn the language of mathematics if the teacher is (a) sensitive, (b) willing to work one-on-one or in small groups, and (c) prepared to make modifications for students with problems in reading, language or visual memory abilities.

TOUCH MATH

Method: Touch Math

Authors: J. Bullock and N. Walentas

Sources: Bullock, J., & Walentas, N. (1989). *Touch math instructional manual.* Colorado Springs: Innovative Learning Concepts; Bullock, J. (1992). *Touch math: The touchpoint approach for teaching basic math computation.* Colorado Springs: Innovative Learning Concepts; Scott, K. S. (1993). Reflections on "Multisensory mathematics for children with mild disabilities." *Exceptionality: A Research Journal, 4*(2), 125-129.

Description: Touch Math is a multisensory approach to basic computational and mathematical skills. It is meant to supplement regular math or to be used in remedial instruction. The method is also an effective approach in teaching students who have difficulty memorizing math facts.

This method uses several steps to teach the basic procedures of addition, subtraction, multiplication, and division. These steps range from simple to complex. Students are taught to count, for example, using numbers with Touchpoints, or large dark circles. Each of the numbers 1 through 9 has Touchpoints that correspond to the numerical units they represent. For example, the number 1 has one Touchpoint; the number 2, two; the number 3, three; and so on. Students touch these Touchpoints while verbally rehearsing their actions.

This method uses the kinesthetic mode. "Touching," combined with the routine verbalization of simple procedures, reinforces learning the sequences of counting and, later, of computation. Touch Math encourages the development of verbal rehearsal. It makes use of visual cues and other aids that increase the learners' retention of computational procedures.

Notes: Touch Math is particularly effective with students who will always need to count manually. Touch Math is a counting strategy students may use without embarrassment. In addition, Touch Math is developmentally precise and appropriate for students with nearly any disability. It is a multisensory approach to teaching that combines visual, verbal, and kinesthetic aspects for effective learning. Teachers may include as many multisensory aspects as students need; however, verbal and visual aspects may be diminished until only kinesthetic movement is used.

MATHEMATICS AS COMMUNICATION

Method: Mathematics as Communication: IU

Authors: John F. Cawley and Rae Reines

Source: Cawley, J. F., & Reines, R. (1996). Mathematics as communication: using the interactive unit. *Teaching Exceptional Children,* *28*(2), 29–34.

Description: This method is a systematic approach to communication that is applicable to most elementary school mathematics classrooms. It seeks to compensate for a lack of the systematic application of alternative representation in classroom mathematics instruction. That is, it provides students with ways of examining the interrelationships among and correspondences between physical representations and various written, oral, and visual forms. In addition, it provides students with activities for expressing their ideas using all modalities.

Mathematics as Communication is based on an instructional model called the Interactive Unit (IU). The theories on which the IU is based emerged from the need to provide alternative representations of math principles and practice in the classrooms. This approach is intended to better meet the needs of students of varying abilities and students with special needs. The foundations of the IU developed from work with students with aphasia and other symbolic-processing disabilities.

The IU provides the teacher with four means of presenting concepts, principles, or problems to students—**manipulate, display, say,** and **write**. Furthermore, students are provided with four means of responding to their teacher or instructor—**write, say, identify,** and **manipulate**. The teacher, for example, can present problems on a practice sheet. Students respond by using blocks, chips, or other materials to make corresponding representations of each problem. Or in response, for example, to the teacher's cue, "Show me a representation of three times two," students can **manipulate** materials that correspond to the problem; they can **identify** a correct representation of the problem from among several possibilities; they can **say** the problem back to the teacher; or they can **write** out the problem out, i.e., "2 × 3."

Students can be organized into groups that use different response modalities, and they can move from one group to another. Teachers can use the IU in a direct instruction approach by (a) modeling a sequence of steps, (b) having students repeat the sequence, (c) providing students with practice sufficient to effect transfer, and (d) providing further practice of dissimilar items, to effect generalization. Teachers can also use the IU in a constructivist approach, wherein a situation is devised and students work to resolve it. Teachers then engage students in an analysis of their approaches and efforts to solve problems.

Notes: This method is a systematic approach to communication that may be used with nearly every concept taught in kindergarten through sixth grade mathematics. This method is systematic and integrates assessment and instruction. Both teachers and students are able to use alternative representations of mathematic meanings and procedures.

REFERENCES

Bender, W. N. (1995). *Learning disabilities: Characteristics, identification, and teaching strategies.* Needham Heights: MA: Allyn & Bacon.

Bruner, J. S. (1960). *The process of education.* Cambridge, MA: Harvard University Press.

Cawley, J., Fitzmaurice, A. Goodstein, H., Lepore, A., Sedlak, R., & Althaus, V. (1976, 1977). *Project Math.* Tulsa, OK: Educational Progress Corporation.

Engelmann, S., & Carnine, D. (1976). *Distar arithmetic* (Levels I, II, III). Chicago, IL: Science Research Associates.

Levine, M. (1994). *Educational care: A system for understanding and helping children with learning problems at home and in school.* Cambridge, MA: Educators Publishing Services.

CHAPTER 8

Reading Methods

EvaJean Pickering, Ph.D.
AvaJane Pickering, Ph.D.

CONTENTS

▶ ABDs of Reading · **128**
▶ Auditory Conceptual Function · **129**
▶ Ball-Stick-Bird · **130**
▶ Basic Language Skills Program · **131**
▶ Carden Method · **132**
▶ Clinical Teaching: Reading · **133**
▶ Cloze Procedure · **134**
▶ ColorSounds · **136**
▶ Direct Instruction: Corrective Reading · **136**
▶ Direct Instruction: Reading · **137**
▶ Edmark Reading · **138**
▶ Fernald Method · **139**
▶ Gillingham and Stillman: Reading · **140**
▶ Glass Analysis · **142**
▶ Herman Method · **143**
▶ Individualized Reading · **144**
▶ Initial Teaching Alphabet (ITA) · **145**
▶ Language Experience · **146**
▶ Laubach Method · **147**

▶ Let's Read: A Linguistic Approach · **149**
▶ Modality Blocking · **150**
▶ Montessori Reading · **151**
▶ Neurological Impress · **152**
▶ Organic Reading · **153**
▶ Reading Recovery · **154**
▶ Rebus Reading · **155**
▶ Remedial Reading Drills · **157**
▶ Repeated Reading · **158**
▶ Semantography (Blissymbols) · **159**
▶ Slingerland Multi-Sensory Approach · **160**
▶ Structural Reading · **162**
▶ Success for All · **164**
▶ Taped Books/Audio Books · **165**
▶ Traub Systematic Wholistic Method · **166**
▶ Unifon · **167**
▶ Whole Language Method · **167**
▶ Words in Color · **168**
▶ Writing Road to Reading · **170**

Reading is cognitively and emotionally interpreting printed material. Reading is a basic skill that directly impacts academic and life functioning. Levine (1994) postulates that reading acquisition is a merging of numerous neurodevelopmental functions, including phonological awareness, memory (active working and paired association), visual processing (perception, pattern recognition), semantic knowledge, and comprehension (both sentence and discourse). Proficient reading requires automaticity, or the simultaneous and instantaneous integration of the above-mentioned factors with a minimal expenditure of mental effort. Other factors are preacademic and academic opportunities and the match of neurodevelopmental functions with the reading curriculum.

The development of reading skills follows one of three models—bottom-up, top-down, and interaction. Each of these models is distinct from the others in its approach to reading comprehension and reading mechanics (Chall & Stahl, 1982). The reading mechanics stage develops from prereading and decoding to fluency. The reading comprehension stages are initiated with the acquisition of information generally. Comprehension moves progressively from comparing and evaluating information from multiple sources to the synthesis of information.

Some reading methods focus on one of the three models such as decoding; other reading methods emphasize more interactive instruction. This chapter presents a variety of reading methods. Some historical methods are included because these methods, or elements of these programs, are in current use. These methods also may add to the readers' perspective on the development of reading methods over time.

ABDs OF READING

Method: ABDs of Reading

Author: Joanna Williams

Source: Williams, J. (1980). Teaching decoding with an emphasis on phoneme analysis and phoneme blending. *Journal of Educational Psychology, 72*, 1–15.

Description: The ABDs of Reading is a supplemental method designed to teach decoding skills to students with reading disabilities. The name ABD refers to **Analysis, Blending,** and **Decoding**. This method provides structured, sequential learning tasks, explicit instructional scripts to be used by teachers, extended practice, immediate feedback, built-in success, and a motivating, comfortable environment.

The ABDs of Reading method is an outgrowth of research indicating that segmenting phonemes and blending them into words are important reading skills, but skills that are often difficult to master. The difficulty associated with learning these skills arises from the inability of some students to distinguish between phonemes when they are pronounced orally. The process of recognizing phonemic cues in words is both simultaneous and sequential. Analysis, therefore, requires an awareness that speech can be segmented into phonemic units. This process of recognition is variously called linguistic insight, phoneme awareness, and linguistic awareness.

The ABDs of Reading begins with a brief introduction to the analysis of the phonic qualities of words. Students first identify the syllables in the initial, medial, and final positions of a word and then represent and delineate them by drawing small squares around each syllable. This procedure is repeated as students move to phoneme analysis, which requires students to identify the number and order of sounds in various two- and three-letter combinations. Only seven consonants and three vowels are taught throughout the process of analysis.

Students are then introduced to blending two- and three-letter phoneme combinations (of consonant-vowel-consonant, or "CVC"), which are presented with various breaking points. For example, the last phoneme may be separated from the first two (_ _ _); the first phoneme from the last two (_ _ _); or all three can be separated (_ _ _). Next, students learn the letter names of these phonemes using wooden squares with the letters written on them to decode other two- and three-letter combinations. Five additional consonants and one more vowel are introduced to form CVC combinations that students read. Gradually, students are introduced to more word patterns in sequence.

This method is divided into 12 units; each has specific objectives and begins with a short story that the teacher reads to students. This method describes procedures and provides teachers with instructional scripts. In addition, its format includes teacher demonstrations, individual student responses, other possible examples, student imitation, and further examples that are followed by additional independent student responses. Student errors are corrected by the teacher, who provides correct responses and asks students to repeat them. This method provides its own comprehension activities; and extensive practice comes through playing games and completing worksheets.

Notes: The ABDs of Reading is a supplemental method for students with severe reading disabilities who have difficulty with segmenting and blending of syllables and phonemes. Pretesting is necessary to identify disabled readers who would benefit the most from this method. Students who benefit from this method are able to decode unfamiliar nonsense letter clusters as well as one-syllable and multisyllabic words that are spelled regularly, skills which will allow them to enter a regular reading program. This method is inexpensive. Furthermore, it can be used in a regular school setting, for small group instruction, and without a teacher's aide. Special teacher training is not required, nor is special preparation in advance of lessons.

AUDITORY CONCEPTUAL FUNCTION

Method: Auditory Conceptual Function: Key to Reading and Spelling Problems

Authors: Phyllis Lindamood, Patricia C. Lindamood, and Nancy Bell

Source: Lindamood, P. C., Bell, N., & Lindamood, P. (1992). Issues in Phonological Awareness Assessment. *Annals of Dyslexia, 42*, 242–259.

Description: Auditory Conceptual Function provides intensive intervention for individuals with reading, spelling, and language comprehension difficulties. It utilizes diagnostic evaluations to determine the cause of these difficulties, their severity, and subsequent plans for treating them. The goal of the Lindamood-Bell learning processes is to assist individuals in becoming autonomous, self-correcting learners who are able to continue their own development through cognitive awareness and command of the learning process.

The authors believe that a primary cause of difficulties with reading and spelling is incomplete development of auditory conceptual function. This disorder is typified by the inability to register phoneme segmentation or to compare the sequence of sounds in spoken words. It is a neurophysiological disorder that negatively affects cognitive judgment. Its secondary symptoms include adding, omitting, substituting, and reversing sounds and letters in reading and spelling. These are symptoms commonly associated with the general term "dyslexia" when it is used in its broadest context.

This approach introduces students with this disorder to another modality, **tactility**, which allows them to discern speech sounds and to verify sound-symbol relationships. Students are taught ways to feel the action and shape of the tongue, lips, and mouth in forming various speech sounds. They learn to integrate this knowledge with information derived from other modalities (e.g., visual, auditory, and motor) to become self-correcting readers and spellers. This approach also helps students become cognizant of the processes of reading and spelling.

The Lindamood-Bell learning processes identifies difficulties in imaging language as the rudimentary cause of difficulties in structuring Gestalt forms and extracting coherent meaning from textual passages. This disorder may not affect decoding, but it can disrupt comprehension skills in such a way that students may manifest severe difficulties in extrapolating, evaluating, generalizing, and synthesizing information. Moreover, it typically prohibits individuals from understanding the mechanisms of causality, which can negatively impact higher cognition. This inability to image language and, therefore, to structure forms can affect oral language comprehension and expression and reading comprehension.

This method teaches students a Visualizing and Verbalizing program that develops imagery with words and extends it to sentences, paragraphs, and entire text passages. Students are gradually able to recognize themes, extrapolate and evaluate information, and express the images they employ by using "structure words," or words that detail size, color, number, and so forth.

The Visualizing and Verbalizing program requires specific steps and intensive interaction between students and teachers; however, it is easily implemented. Furthermore, once they are able to image automatically, students make significant achievements in reading comprehension, oral language comprehension, oral language expression, and paragraph writing.

Notes: This method prevents incorrect practices by teaching students skills for self-correction. However, this method also requires intensive intervention to provide the most effective remediation.

The Lindamood-Bell approach has preventative, developmental, and remedial modules that are available for all ages through school districts and corporations. In addition, it has multimedia products ranging from video discs to CD-ROM's.

BALL-STICK-BIRD

Method: Ball-Stick-Bird

Author: Renee Fuller

Source: Fuller, R. (1974). Breaking down the IQ walls: Severely retarded people can learn to read. *Psychology Today, 8*(5), 96–100, 102.

Description: The Ball-Stick-Ball method is an outgrowth of Fuller's efforts to teach reading to children born with phenylketonuria, a metabolic disorder typically manifesting severe intellectual deficits. This method uses a circle, a line, and an angle— called "a ball," "a stick," and "a bird"—as mnemonic devices used to teach letter morphology. To identify the three forms further, Fuller uses the color red for large balls and yellow for small ones, black for sticks, and blue for birds.

With this method, all capital letters are formed by employing the ball, stick, and bird. Students sound out letters as they build their upper case forms. Initially, the names of letters are not taught. When students are able to form a letter, using the colored and structural mnemonic devices, and give its common sound, that letter is subsequently introduced in black type. Words are introduced only after the first two capital letters—"I" and "T"—have been learned. The print of reading exercises is in black. After 10 books have been read using upper case letters, lower case letters are introduced.

Some parts of the Ball-Stick-Bird method are unusual. For example, complete mastery is not required of students before they are allowed to advance. Students may move from the first lesson to the second once they know as few as seven letter sounds. The teacher is seeking code approximation; therefore, exact pronunciation is not necessary. In addition, Fuller instructs teachers *not* to establish eye contact with students when giving them positive feedback. She also maintains that students should not be subjected to drill exercises; instead, their practice comes through reading stories.

Like many other methods, the Ball-Stick-Bird method is multisensory and letters are not introduced in sequence. Instead, teachers first introduce letters that are easy to distinguish and can form common, simple words. Moreover, teachers receive specific instructions for presenting lessons to students.

This method also provides stories that are designed to motivate students. Associative cues are used to promote interest in learning letter sounds. For example, the letter "V" is called a "bird flying down," and students are told that "it makes the sound of /v/ as in 'vanishing vampire.'" The associative cues introduced at this stage are used to develop the stories for reading.

Notes: The motivating factors and the mnemonic devices used in the Ball-Stick-Ball method may have positive implications for higher functioning individuals with severe reading disabilities. Fuller recommends some procedures that challenge certain teaching principles, such as not requiring exact pronunciation and mastery and encouraging a lack of eye contact when giving students feedback.

BASIC LANGUAGE SKILLS PROGRAM

Method: Basic Language Skills Program

Authors: Byron Chapman and Louis Schulz

Source: Aukerman, R. C. (1984). *Approaches to beginning reading*. New York: John Wiley & Sons.

Description: The Basic Language Skills Program is an outgrowth of a need recognized by Chapman, Schulz, and others to address the problem of adult illiteracy in the United States. As a result, the Basic Language Skills Program, originally called the Mott Basic Language Skills program, was developed especially for adult non-readers or readers functioning at low levels of competency. This method was developed after years of study and discussion about the needs of adult learners.

The Basic Language Skills Program is semi-programmed and begins by introducing the alphabet, even though some adults may already be able to recognize and write some letters. Using notebooks with models of letters, the adults practice writing both upper and lower case letters in cursive. To facilitate this, paper in the notebooks is marked off in squares. The goal is to produce legible writing.

Next, the adults are introduced to consonants that are reproduced in bold type and as large capital letters with smaller lower case letters. Each letter is accompanied by a familiar photograph representing a key word corresponding to it. As adults drill the consonants using these key words, they print the appropriate letters. Teachers use only whole words, not isolated sounds.

Students learn short vowel sounds after the consonants have been mastered. After the vowel "a" has been learned, for example, the adults begin reading monosyllabic words in their books. The vocabulary is controlled, and the words are learned as whole words. Other short vowels are presented in the same manner. Gradually more consonant sounds and consonant digraphs are introduced. Consonant blends are also taught using key word pictures.

After the first two series (300 A and B) are completed, adult learners should have acquired reading, writing, and spelling skills equivalent to those of a student completing third grade. The series is estimated to take about 4 hours a week for 30 weeks, which is roughly equivalent to an academic year.

Notes: The Basic Language Skills Program seems to be successful when used by instructors without training in the teaching of reading. This is particularly useful with adult populations, who often seek reading remediation through volunteer agencies. This method is semi-programmed so that adults can study with minimal guidance. Moreover, little time is required to prepare for each lesson. Given the elementary level of the reading, materials are designed to be as interesting to adult learners as possible. Also, in spite of criticism about its brisk teaching pace and some gaps in its presentation of skills, this method represents a serious effort to address the problem of adult illiteracy.

CARDEN METHOD

Method: Carden Method

Author: Mae Carden

Sources: Aukerman, R. C. (1984). *Approaches to beginning reading.* New York: John Wiley & Sons; Terman, S., & Walcutt, C. (1958). *Reading: Chaos and cure.* New York: McGraw Hill.

Description: The Carden Method is an outgrowth of Mae Carden's reaction to the "progressive" movement of her time. It was developed as a total language arts method for grades 1 through 8. Mae Carden did not support the use of readiness materials initially, but she later added them to her curricula. In teaching reading, her method begins immediately with phonics. The program introduces students to speech and sentence rhythms and to identifying key words, summarizing, outlining, and grammar. The Carden Method stresses mastery at each step so that students can experience success.

Beginning in first grade, students learn the alphabet. Consonants are introduced, and students learn them by sound and name. Each consonant is associated with an object, person, or action that resembles that letter's morphology. Students first learn the letters that are formed using the letter "c" as their foundation. Other consonants are taught in pairs: "l/h," "n/m," "k/f," and "r/t." The so called "bent legs" letters—"v," "w," "y," "u," and "z"—follow. The letters "b" and "p" are taught carefully to avoid confusion between them. After students have mastered consonants, they learn vowels. Students learn the "two-vowel rule" and follow this with further practice.

The Carden Method uses books without pictures to generate mental images of words. Under the teacher's direction, students read letter names and sounds in unison. The purpose is to generate images of letters and words themselves, rather than representative images. Students move on to learn digraphs and words. In addition, comprehension checks are provided in the Carden materials to monitor students' progress.

The second book of the Carden Method continues to build phonetic skills while introducing more difficult words and longer stories. Oral readings are required to correct any problematic reading habits that students may develop. Phrasing and rhythmic reading is also taught so that students develop complete thought units. In addition, spelling materials and sentence analysis activities are incorporated from the beginning. At this point students are ready for the primer book in any basal series. By the end of first grade they are reading children's classics. Students read fables, myths, Grimm's fairy tales, the Bible, classics, and world history.

For their first writing activities, students form letters by making a series of dots and then use the dots as guides to write the letters. By the time students complete the second book, they are already writing original stories. The Carden Method emphasizes enunciation, intonation, and reading content, all of which it espouses as marks of a cultivated individual.

Notes: The Carden Method is a highly structured, total language arts method that applies phoneme analysis for spelling and decoding regular words. The mental imagery and rhythmic phrasing stressed by this method may be useful strategies for disabled readers with memory deficits. Comprehension is introduced very early in the program. Students are introduced and encouraged to read a variety of materials from an early age, which can spark their interest and motivate reluctant readers.

Although this method was not developed for individuals with reading disabilities, the Carden Method may be appropriate for some students. The method is rigid, but all students are not expected to proceed at the same pace. Indeed, this method stresses that individualized attention must be given to students. However, the self-selected reading materials do not control vocabulary enough for many students with disabilities. They may have difficulty decoding the irregular words. Moreover, materials are available only to teachers who have taken the Carden course.

CLINICAL TEACHING

Method: Clinical Teaching: Reading

Authors: Doris Johnson and Helmer Myklebust

Source: Johnson, D., & Myklebust, H. (1967). *Learning disabilities: Educational principles and practices.* New York: Grune & Stratton.

Description: Clinical Teaching: Reading was developed to teach reading disabled students who manifest characteristics of either visual or auditory dyslexia. These characteristics include memory impairments, sequencing difficulties, left-right disorientation, time disorientation, poor body image, topographic disorders, dis-

turbed motor patterns, and spelling and writing problems.

Visual Dyslexia. Students with "visual dyslexia" may have difficulty discriminating between letters and retaining the visual sequence of letters. They may demonstrate a slow rate of perception, reverse words, and invert letters. In addition, they typically have poor visual memories, produce inferior drawings, and are unable to analyze and synthesize visual information. auditory activities.

This reading method uses an alphabetic or phonetic approach unless students are unable to acquire blending skills. In this case, a whole word, multisensory approach is recommended. Generally Clinical Teaching: Reading begins with the introduction of two or three dissimilar consonants, using flashcards with large, lower case letters printed in bold black ink. Letter names are not taught initially, only letter sounds. The teacher models these sounds carefully and students repeat them. Students then name words that begin with these sounds. As reinforcement, students are shown the three consonants again and asked to point to the letter that represents a phonetic sound that the teacher gives them.

Multisensory input is used if students have difficulty with the task. Unlike some other alphabetic methods, key words (e.g., "b" for "ball") are not used, because the authors believe that key words can confuse some students with visual deficits. However, an exception to this general rule is made for students who need the word association with the phonetic sound to assist recall.

When students have mastered a few consonant sounds, one or two vowel sounds are introduced. For some students, it is easier to discriminate between long vowel sounds; therefore, it is more appropriate to begin with long vowels. However, for other students with auditory strengths it may be more appropriate to begin with short vowels, because these may be easier to recall than many two-letter, long vowel combinations. In either case, in order to control the vocabulary, only one sound for each letter or letter combination is taught initially.

As soon as they learn a few consonants and vowels, students can use words from their spoken vocabularies to learn blending. In this sequence a word is pronounced; students give its meaning and use it in a sentence to reinforce their comprehension of it. Once several words have been mastered in this way, word families are introduced so that students can see how words are formed and recognize similarities between them. Students continue to expand their reading vocabularies. Consonant blends in initial and final positions are introduced, as well as vowel and consonant combinations.

Clinical Teaching: Reading does not recommend teaching rules. Instead, it integrates writing and spelling with reading from the beginning. Students write simple sentences, paragraphs, stories, and several sight words using their reading vocabularies. They are introduced to books when their reading vocabularies and story readings are adequate enough to assure them of successful experiences.

Auditory Dyslexia. Learners with auditory dyslexia frequently demonstrate difficulty in auditory discrimination and perceptual disabilities, inability to analyze and synthesize auditory information or to reauditorize sounds and words. Impairments in auditory sequencing and a preference for visual activities may also be present. For these students, a whole-part educational approach is recommended.

In this approach, students are taught what words are and how spoken words can be represented by printed words. For the purpose of teaching these students, sight words that are dissimilar in sound and configuration are selected from their spoken vocabularies. Nouns are taught by relating them to familiar objects. For example, various objects in the room are labeled in manuscript form with the words that signify them. Students are taught to see these words, hear them, and say them. In this sequence, students name an object; students match the object with the word that signifies it; and students read the word. Verbs are taught in the same way. Many strategies are used to acquire a sight word vocabulary.

Furthermore, Clinical Teaching: Reading uses simple phrases and sentences that are meaningful to students to introduce other parts of speech. This method also uses a controlled vocabulary adaptation of language experience stories. In this adaptation, pictures accompany words in stories to enhance the retention of sight words. This method provides many other activities to improve auditory deficits in discrimination, sequencing, blending, and analysis and synthesis.

This method does not overlook the importance of comprehension. The authors believed that, for most students with dyslexia, decoding is the most significant obstacle to acquiring and developing adequate reading skills. This method provides a means for clinically evaluating the comprehension proficiency of students with various types of reading disabilities. For students who have problems with both decoding and comprehension, this method employs techniques such as scanning, skimming, reading main headings, reading for main ideas, reading in thought units, outlining main ideas, and supporting details on paper or in mental activities.

Notes: Clinical Teaching: Reading is similar to many other alphabetic-phonetic approaches to teaching reading to students with disabilities. This method was designed specifically for students with particular reading disabilities and is based on assumptions about training certain auditory and visual process dysfunctions. Teachers will need to develop, adapt, or purchase materials, because this methodology is described in books but does not have curricula of its own.

CLOZE PROCEDURE

Method: Cloze Procedure

Authors: Wilson L. Taylor and Florence G. Schoenfeld

Sources: Taylor, W. L. (1953). Cloze procedure: A new tool for measuring readability. *Journalism Quarterly, 30,* 414–438; Schoenfeld, F. (1980). Instructional uses of the cloze procedure. *Reading Teacher, 34,* 147–151; Marlow, L., & Reese, D. (1992). Strategies for using literature with at-risk readers. *Reading Improvement, 29*(2), 130–132.

Description: The Cloze Procedure is an outgrowth of research into the readability of language. Taylor first conceived the cloze test procedure as a means of measuring the readability of written materials. The term, "cloze," is derived from the Gestalt concept of closure or the tendency of sophisticated readers to fill in the missing parts of a written structure.

In the Cloze Procedure, students are asked to restore a passage from which words have been systematically deleted to its original condition. The extent to which students can perform this task accurately determines the degree of their comprehension of a passage. This procedure can also be used in place of readability formulas to determine whether materials are appropriate for students' instructional levels. In addition, it can be used to measure the language competency of individual students, including those with limited English proficiency.

The Cloze Procedure may be used as a teaching technique for reading comprehension. Cloze procedures focus on three categories of deletions: (a) grapheme deletions may include deleting phonic units (e.g., consonant blends or dipthongs) and morphological units (prefixes and suffixes); (b) semantic deletions are contextual in nature and include verbs, nouns, and descriptor words (e.g., adjectives and adverbs); (c) syntactical deletions include pronouns and pronominal referents, specific parts of speech, relationships among concepts, and organizational patterns.

Teachers can design their own cloze exercises by (a) selecting passages long enough to allow for approximately 50 deletions; (b) deleting words systematically throughout a passage, not to exceed more that 20 words out of every 100; or (c) indicating missing words by inserting blanks of the same length as the deleted words. Traditionally, deleting every fifth word has functioned effectively in the Cloze Procedure; however, if the passage is extremely long, modifications such as deleting every tenth or twelfth word may be more appropriate. Cloze exercises may be designed that delete every so many words, words at random, or words of any given type. An example of a cloze passage follows:

> This is the first _____ of winter. The snow _____ falling heavily and resting _____ the green pine trees. _____ love the first snowfall _____ the season. They bring _____ their sleds and coast _____ the rolling hills.

Notes: In order to select the correct word in a cloze exercise, students must have knowledge of word meanings. In addition, they must be able to understand the main idea of a passage and attend to its details; they must also possess word recognition skills, make inferences, and draw conclusions. Moreover, students with word recognition difficulties are likely to find the cloze exercises too difficult; therefore, this technique should not be utilized until students have mastered basic decoding. Students' background knowledge relating to the content of any particular passage can greatly affect performance.

The Cloze Procedure may be an effective approach to teaching reading comprehension to normal populations, at-risk students, and students with reading disabilities. It has been used for students in first grade through college. It is also useful in guiding teachers in the selection of appropriate levels of reading materials.

COLORSOUNDS

Method: ColorSounds

Author: John Bell

Source: Aukerman, R. C. (1984). *Approaches to beginning reading*. New York: John Wiley & Sons.

Description: ColorSounds is a method that was developed for students with limited English proficiency or with learning disabilities. A unique feature of this method is its use of color and popular music to teach language and reading skills. Songs are selected that are familiar to young students; contain no references to sex, violence, or deviant behavior; and use correct diction, grammar, and vocabulary. In addition, this method utilizes 16 different colors representing 16 vowel sounds; these color names are as closely associated with vowel sound as possible (e.g., the color "gray" represents the letter "a"). This method emphasizes vowel sounds using a dynamic format of see, say, read, mark, write, repeat, colors, and music.

ColorSounds features songs with human interest stories about the songs' composers and singers. The song lyrics are printed in a monthly periodical, *The ColorSounds Monthly*, along with several reading activities, such as writing the silent "e" words or filling in missing vowel sounds. In addition, students are provided with worksheets that have the lyrics written on them. Using crayons that represent the 16 vowel sounds with their different colors, students draw or

fill in each word with the color that corresponds to its vowel sound. For example, the long "i" words, such as "by," "fly," or "night," are all colored in violet. Spelling lists are comprised of words taken from the song lyrics, and tests are given weekly.

ColorSounds attempts to provide a variety of role models of both sexes and from different ethnic backgrounds among its selected singers and composers. The monthly periodical provides focal points for teaching vowel sounds. This method can also be used to teach reading comprehension.

Notes: This method applies motivational devices to a phonetic pedagogy. It provides visual cuing with high interest materials in an attempt to teach reading to students with limited English proficiency and reading-related disabilities. The lessons that teach vowel sounds provide students with positive role models with whom they can identify. Because of its motivational aspects, the ColorSounds method can be used with reluctant readers or readers who have previously experienced repeated failure and have not yet acquired basic vowel phonic skills. The ColorSounds method is limited to a small but significant segment of the general reading community.

DIRECT INSTRUCTION: CORRECTIVE READING

Method: Direct Instruction: Corrective Reading

Authors: Siegfried Engelmann and Wesley Becker

Source: Engelmann, S., Becker, W., Hanner, S., & Johnson, G. (1978). *Corrective reading*. [series guide]. Chicago: Science Research Associates.

Description: Direct Instruction: Corrective Reading is a highly structured, direct instruction reading program that includes decoding and comprehension components. Each component includes three levels.

The lowest decoding level is for nonreaders. The second level teaches the common phonetic sounds of letter combinations, the decoding of VCE words, derivatives, and two- and three-syllable words with prefixes or suffixes. The third level of the decoding component teaches structural analysis skills and more multisyllabic words. In addition, to practice their skills, students are provided with stories that have controlled vocabularies.

The first level of the comprehension component contains few written items. The material is presented orally, and written exercises are increased in subsequent levels as students acquire more decoding skills. For independent reading, books that are of high interest and have limited vocabularies are used.

This method is designed for students who have been exposed to a relatively large vocabulary, but have not mastered decoding skills. It is not a developmental program, but rather one designed to correct inappropriate reading behavior and to develop decoding strategies. It is intended for use by students between the fourth and twelfth grades, although it can also be used with slightly younger students. Ideally, students are taught in groups of four to eight; and the daily lessons comprise a 1-year program, each lesson requiring about 50 to 60 minutes to complete. Furthermore, because the program is adaptable to other materials and content areas, it is useful for adult education and regular classroom teachers.

Notes: Direct Instruction: Corrective Reading is designed for individuals who lack decoding skills. It has the advantages of other direct instruction methods. Like other highly structured methods based on direct instruction, this method has been criticized as being too rigid and inappropriate for some students with learning disabilities. There is research, however, that verifies this method's effectiveness.

DIRECT INSTRUCTION: READING

Method: Direct Instruction: Reading

Author: Siegfried Engelmann

Sources: Engelmann, S. (1970). *Preventing failure in the primary grades*. Chicago: Science Research Associates; Carnine, D., & Silbert, J. (1979). *Direct instruction reading*. Columbus, OH: Charles Merrill; Baumann, J. F. (1988). Direct instruction reconsidered. *Journal of Reading, 31*(8), 712–718.

Description: Engelmann, author of Direct Instruction: Reading, found that students who fail in reading lack any number of reading subskills. These include knowledge of sound-symbol relationships and the ability to telescope a series of blended sounds or segment words into their phonetic sounds. These and other prerequisite skills must be acquired before students begin to read successfully. In this method, students must first learn that words are separate entities that can be counted. They must also be able to rhyme words, understand alliteration, and say words rapidly as well as slowly. Direct Instruction: Reading details instructional parameters for both beginning and primary reading.

In **beginning reading**, once students have mastered the prerequisite skills, they begin systematic reading instruction. Students are introduced to letter sounds, but not their names. Four tactics can be used to introduce the letters: (a) letters can be introduced using only the most common sounds of the letters; (b) the most useful letters can be introduced first; (c) lower case letters can be introduced first to be followed by upper case letters; and (c) letters that are phonically or morphologically similar should not be introduced in close proximity to one another.

Furthermore, words to be presented should be comprised only of letters the students have previously learned. Other factors to consider in presenting words are the familiarity of the words, their length, and the locations of stop sounds and consonant blends within the words. Words with continuous sounds are easier to decode that those with stop sounds, and final consonant blends are easier to decode than initial blends.

Students are introduced to sight word reading of regular words as soon as they have learned several VC and CVC words. The procedure for teaching sight words is explained in detail in other direct instruction materials. For example, this procedure introduces irregular words only after proficiency has been reached in reading regular CVC words.

To prepare students to sound out reading passages, they sound out words in lists and then in phrases. Passage reading begins after students can sound CVC words proficiently. The transition from reading word lists to reading passages is monitored carefully.

Vocabulary and language teaching accompany initial reading instruction, particularly for students who are disadvantaged or who have disabilities in language areas. Vocabulary can be taught by modeling, using synonyms familiar to students, and definition. Students also are taught such basic language skills as repetition (repeating sentences); sentence comprehension involving who, what, when, where, and why questions; and comparisons (understanding the concepts of same and different).

In **primary reading**, students are taught that words are made up of letter units. They are introduced to the most common sounds of letter combinations, less common sounds of letters and letter combinations, and the means to decode VCe words such as "use." Students are also taught structural analysis skills, including the functions of prefixes, suffixes, and root, or base, words. They are instructed in contextual analysis skills, including decoding irregular words and passage reading. Irregular words are defined as those containing letter-sound relationships unfamiliar to students. Learning these words requires that the teacher en-

courage students to use contextual and decoding strategies to decipher them.

Once students are able to read passages fluently, written comprehension activities become an integral part of their direct instruction activities. All levels of comprehension questions are taught; nevertheless, some students will require more direct teaching of these skills than others.

In addition, there are procedures for teaching direct instruction at the intermediate level where vocabulary development, comprehension, and decoding continue to be stressed. Furthermore, Direct Instruction: Reading can also be used to teach content area reading and study skills.

Notes: There are advantages to using Direct Instruction: Reading; for example, this method is well researched, and numerous studies support the use of this method with many disadvantaged students or students with reading disabilities.

EDMARK READING

Method: Edmark Reading

Author: Edmark Associates

Source: Edmark. (1990). *Edmark reading program, teacher's guide*. Redmond, WA: Edmark Associates.

Description: Edmark is a reading method based on repeated reading programmed intervention and behavior modification. This method teaches whole sight words which allows students who lack phonological awareness (i.e., an awareness of the segmentation of speech into syllable and phonemic units) an opportunity to be more functional. The only prerequisites are language receptivity, the ability to repeat or sign a word, and the ability to point.

The Edmark teaching procedure was developed on a stimulus-response-reinforcement model. The teacher presents a skill to be learned and then cues the students. This method recommends a four-step sequence to cue students: (a) students respond without help; (b) students are prompted with verbal cues; (c) students are given demonstration cues; and (d) students receive physical prompts. If students respond incorrectly, cues can be repeated in greater detail. If responses are correct, however, students are reinforced, preferably with social praise.

After students have learned five words, they begin comprehension activities. Words are repeated several times in this method to ensure long-term retention. The number of repetitions is determined by longitudinal testing. This procedure consists of prereading activities, a discrimination test, word recognition lessons, including word endings, direction lessons, and phrase and storybook reading.

The Edmark method features a vinyl display mask with a window that displays only the material being learned. This mask covers information on the page that might otherwise distract learners. Moreover, the Edmark method requires no special training of teachers. According to the publisher, parents, students, aides, and volunteers can teach Edmark Reading.

In addition, this method has two software programs. One is designed to teach beginning reading and language development to nonreaders, and the other is designed to teach independent living skills. Both programs employ multisensory techniques. A goal is to develop a positive self-concept in students who have previously had difficulty with other reading methods. These programs generate student success by utilizing short learning steps, repetition, and constant positive reinforcement.

Notes: The Edmark method is most appropriate for individuals with reading disabilities who need a purely visual method rather than a phonetic-linguistic method. This method provides a signing manual for use with students who are nonverbal and

for individuals with communication disorders, hearing impairments, autism, behavior disorders, or learning disabilities. In addition, it is appropriate for individuals from preschool age to adulthood.

FERNALD METHOD

Method: Fernald Method

Author: Grace Fernald

Sources: Fernald, G. (1943). *Remedial techniques in basic school subjects.* New York: McGraw-Hill; Fernald, G. (1988). *Remedial techniques in basic school subjects.* Austin, TX: Pro-Ed.

Description: The Fernald Method is a multisensory approach developed for young students and adults who have had difficulty learning with traditional visual and auditory methods. With the Fernald Method, students write the words they use in their oral language. They are allowed to select any word they want to learn, regardless of its length. Reading materials are comprised of stories that the students compose. Initially, these stories may be only a sentence or two in length, but they increase in length as students learn more written words. Stories are kept on file and reviewed frequently. As soon as students have learned the words in a basal reader, they are introduced to books.

Few materials are needed for this method. Only a black grease pencil, strips of oak tag or manila folders cut into 5" × 10" sections, and scratch paper are required. The sequence of Fernald's visual, auditory, kinesthetic, and tactile (VAKT) method follows:

In stage I, the teacher writes a word selected by students in large cursive or manuscript writing. Students trace this word with a finger in direct contact with their paper, pronouncing the word aloud syllable by syllable and then as a whole word. The word is then covered and students write it from memory, as a single word and later in a story. Students read the story containing the word, and the word itself is filed in a word box and reviewed periodically.

In stage II, tracing is no longer necessary. Students simply look at a word, repeat it while looking at it, and then write it from memory. The word is repeated aloud as students read and write it. These words are also filed and reviewed as often as necessary.

In stage III, students select four- and five-syllable words, study them, and write them from memory. Students are allowed to read from books and are told the meaning of any unknown words. New words are studied, written, and filed by students for future review.

In stage IV, students are encouraged to read and recognize words based on their similarity to known words. New words can be written and filed as necessary. Comprehension is stressed in reading. In the final stage, stage V, fluency and comprehension are stressed. Pacing is improved by using such devices as tachistoscopes and metronomes.

This method can also be used if a spelling disorder is accompanied by a reading disability. If spelling is an isolated disorder, however, the following adaptation may be tried:

1. The teacher writes a selected word.
2. The teacher pronounces the word; students look at the word as they pronounce it themselves.
3. Students examine the word in order to establish a distinct visual image. This step can be adjusted to accommodate the individual needs of students with different learning orientations: auditory students through vocalization, kinesthetic students through tracing.
4. Only when students indicate that they know the selected word is it erased and then students write it from memory.

5. As students write the word correctly, they are required to turn over their papers and write the word again from memory.
6. Students are encouraged to continue to use these words in various writing assignments.

This adaptation, designed as a remedial approach, attempts to develop in students a perceptual approach to spelling that will gradually facilitate the reproduction of words from memory.

Notes: The VAKT method is recommended to teach disabled readers with average or above average intelligence who have failed to learn to spell using less intense methods. Students who have both visual and auditory deficits may benefit from a multisensory approach.

Because this method is a whole word rather than a phonic approach, it does not capitalize on the auditory aspects of reading and spelling. This method may not benefit students with tactile disorders or those who react adversely to overstimulation.

GILLINGHAM AND STILLMAN: READING

Method: Gillingham and Stillman: Reading

Authors: Ann Gillingham and Bessie Stillman

Source: Gillingham, A., & Stillman, B. (1973). *Remedial training for children with specific disability in reading, spelling and penmanship.* Cambridge, MA: Educators Publishing.

Description: Gillingham and Stillman: Reading is an alphabetic-phonetic approach for teaching students with reading disabilities in grades 3 through 6. (Adaptations are necessary for teaching other grade levels.) This method incorporates reading, handwriting, and spelling. It bases its reading instruction on the belief that phonics cannot merely be a supplement to sight word reading; indeed, this method asserts that phonics and sight word reading are mutually exclusive.

In the Gillingham and Stillman: Reading method, students learn letter sounds that are built into words. This technique is based on a "language triangle," which stresses linkages between the visual, auditory and kinesthetic modalities. All phonograms are taught by these linkages, which are referred to as phonetic associations.

In Association I (V-A, A-K), the visual symbol is associated with the letter name. To make this association the teacher exposes a drill card, says the letter's name, and the students repeat it. When this has been mastered, the teacher exposes the card again, says the letter sound, and students repeat it. Careful attention is given to student responses to ensure that correct phonetic sounds are made. This associative technique forms the basis of oral reading.

In the next step, Association II (A-A), the teacher makes a letter sound, and without visual cues, students name the letter. This step forms the basis for oral spelling.

In the final step, Association III, (V-K, K-V), the teacher writes a letter, discusses its shape, direction, and so on. Students then trace over the letter, copy it, and write it from memory. The A-K association, which is the basis of spelling, is formed by the teacher giving letter sounds and students writing the corresponding letters. The Gillingham and Stillman: Reading method recommends fixing these associations firmly through a regimen of drill and exercise.

Students read or spell only with the teacher who teaches them this method. Students are not allowed, for example, to listen to classmates "stumble read." Consequently, to keep up in content area classes,

students need readers (e.g., their parents). The authors of this method assert that all students must start at the beginning of the program and follow its "logical sequence" without deviation.

This method's logical sequence contains the following major steps:

1. *Letters.* All phonograms have key words. When students are shown a drill card, they must give the key word and the sound of the letter it signifies (e.g., "apple," /a/). Consonant sounds are printed on white drill cards and vowel sounds on salmon-colored cards.

2. *Writing Procedure.* Writing is incorporated into the association procedures. Students are taught correct body position; double-ruled paper is used to stress the relative height of letters. Visual cues are placed prominently in the classroom for students to refer to as needed.

3. *Words.* Students learn to blend after they have mastered 10 letter names and sounds and know how to write them. The first two letters of a word are pronounced together to avoid the incorrect pronunciation of initial consonant sounds. For example, the word "bat" is sounded /ba/ and /t/ to avoid the initial /buh/ sound. The words are put on word cards and placed in the student's word box as they are learned. These words are used to teach reading and spelling which are taught simultaneously.

4. *Story Reading.* After students learn one-syllable, phonetically regular words, they begin to read sentences and short stories. Stories are read both silently and aloud for the teacher.

Before advancing to more difficult stories, students learn consonant blends, long vowel sounds, and dipthongs. Students learn to give both the long and short vowel sounds with the key words on their drill cards. Many extended reading activities are provided.

Notes: Gillingham and Stillman: Reading contains information on how to teach reading integrated with spelling and handwriting. The method is highly structured and focuses on the mechanics of reading rather than on comprehension. Students are restricted to the use of particular materials until their basic reading skills are well established. This method has been criticized for lacking interesting activities. Caution should be used when integrating reading with spelling and writing, particularly with students whose writing skills lag far behind their reading skills. Nevertheless, this multisensory method has been effective with students who have severe and pervasive reading disabilities. Furthermore, this method can be adapted for older students who have not learned to read.

GLASS ANALYSIS

Method: Glass Analysis

Author: Gerald Glass

Sources: Glass, G. (1976). *Glass-Analysis for decoding only teacher guide*. Garden City, New York: Easier to Learn; Miccinati, J. (1981). Teaching reading-disabled students to perceive distinctive features in words. *Journal of Learning Disabilities, 14*(3), 140–142.

Description: Glass Analysis is a method for teaching decoding skills to children and adults using auditory and visual input. Students are "perceptually conditioned" to learn letter clusters within whole words. This method was developed on the premise that reading disabilities are decoding disabilities. It stresses that reading is decoding, obtaining meaning from words, and utilizing the meanings learned from words to enhance personal growth. Furthermore, Glass asserts that learning to decode typically does not require, nor does it allow, creativity or imagination. Only one response is

ever acceptable or correct.

Several principles underlie Glass Analysis:

1. Decoding should be taught separately from the teaching of reading, because it is viewed as a prereading skill.
2. Students should not decode words that they have not heard and whose meanings are unclear to them.
3. Picture and context cues inhibit the development of decoding skills and should be avoided. The only tasks of decoding are to learn the letters and their placement and sounds within words.
4. Syllabication and rigid rules and principles are not taught in decoding. Students are introduced to whole words or clusters of letters that result in familiar and meaningful words.
5. Students are conditioned to see three- and four-letter clusters within words as easily as single letter sounds. Students respond to whole words or structural parts of words in decoding.
6. Auditory and visual discrimination are important in the decoding process so that students hear the sounds and see the letter clusters.

A 15- or 20-minute teaching session is required each day to teach decoding. Whole words are printed on the blackboard, overhead, or on flashcards. Students see only whole words; and they look directly at these words. They must be able to cluster appropriate letters visually and to give correct oral response when shown letters. The teacher pronounces a word, for example, "play." The teacher directs the learning of each word by asking students which letters make which sounds and which sounds specific letters make. For example, a teacher might ask, in teaching the word "play," what letters make the /pl/ sound? What letters make the /ay/ sound? What sound does "pl" make? And what sound does "ay" make?

Students progress through a controlled list of l0 to l5 words that focus on particular vowel clusters. Students learn single consonants, blends, and consonant digraphs through the repetition of words that contain these vowel clusters. A list of common vowel clusters found in basal readers is included in the program. Students are required to read daily from a basal reader at their instructional levels for about 12 minutes. Comprehension is not stressed.

Notes: Glass Analysis is an alternative method to teaching decoding skills. The only materials necessary are word lists and basal readers at students' instructional levels. Teacher training is minimal, and easy tests are provided to determine whether or not students are in need of remedial help in reading. Some students may benefit by augmenting this method with the Traub Systematic Holistic Method (Traub & Bloom, 1990) which emphasizes individual letter sounds in a multisensory framework.

In Glass Analysis, the teacher is cautioned against augmenting the program in any way, because this can cause "conditioning leakage." This method's redundancy can be alleviated only by the teacher's enthusiastic involvement. Although this method is described as a structured approach to decoding, its reading books and vocabulary are not controlled as they are, for example, in linguistic methods. Nevertheless, Glass believes that vowel clusters appear often enough in basal texts to be a dependable means of teaching decoding.

HERMAN METHOD

Method: Herman Method

Authors: Renee Herman and Carlos P. DeAntonio

Source: Antonio, C. P. (1995). *Overview of Herman method*. Sherman Oaks, CA: ROMAR Publishing.

Description: The Herman Method for Reversing Reading Failure is an approach designed specifically for remedial reading students who are typically diagnosed as having learning disabilities or being dyslexic. It evolved from the Orton/Gillingham instructional philosophy that (a) dyslexic students can become proficient readers if their instructional needs are met and (b) language skills should be taught systematically by integrating visual, oral, tactile, kinesthetic, and auditory learning modalities. Therefore, the Herman Method is a multisensory reading method that is sequenced to progress incrementally from students' levels of deficit through each level of skill mastery to reading proficiency.

This method teaches students a wide range of reading skills, including decoding, sight words, use of contextual clues, structural analysis, and dictionary use. In addition, it continually focuses on both fluency and reading comprehension. The Herman Method meets the challenge of ensuring skills retention and avoiding boredom among students by providing numerous diverse review possiblities. It employs a multimedia approach that includes phrase lists, sentence cards, stories with follow-up exercises, word wheels, reading games, software programs, workbooks, and reading film strips. Furthermore, this method is self-contained; all materials needed to teach this controlled reading program and lesson plans are included. There are 20 instructional levels with mastery tests that assess learning progress.

Notes: The Herman Method integrates visual, auditory, tactile, and kinesthetic modalities to assist remedial reading students in overcoming their deficits. Teachers use spelling, writing, and reading curricula. Students achieve an independent reading ability by the time they complete this program.

INDIVIDUALIZED READING

Method: Individualized Reading

Author: Jeanette Veatch

Source: Veatch, J. (1959). *Individualizing your reading program.* New York: Putnam's & Sons.

Description: Individualized Reading was developed to meet the needs of individual students in regular classroom settings. By individualizing reading programs, the teacher can help each student have a meaningful reading experience. This method has three characteristics: (a) materials are self-selected by the students; (b) conferences are necessary between teachers and students; and (c) students are not grouped according to ability.

To determine the instructional needs of each student, the teacher uses diagnostic tests, observes silent reading patterns, listens to each student read orally, conferences with students, and keeps concise records. The role of the teacher is to provide a daily reading period during which students read at their own pace. The strength of this approach is the increased motivation that comes from self-selection. In addition, instruction is continuous, because the teacher is free to move about the room and provide instruction as needed. When students do experience difficulty with skills, teachers can directly intervene. Remediation is integrated with other classroom activities. Students work independently, rather than in large groups.

The most important part of Individualized Reading is the student-teacher conference. Conferences are held once or twice a week to monitor students' progress. Strengths and weaknesses may be noted and discussed at conference time. Both teachers and students keep records. The conference is intended to be a motivational mechanism, as motivating students to read is the function of all of this method's activities. Indeed, this method seeks to make reading an intrinsically rewarding experience.

To start an effective individualized reading program, teachers must have adequate supplies of books, magazines, newspapers, and other reading materials. A minimum of three to five books per student is recommended. Teachers should have read as many of these books as possible. The teacher selects students who have enough word recognition skills to read independently. If students read less than 60 words a minute orally with two errors or less, they may find independent reading unsatisfying and unprofitable. It may be best to begin with students who show the most interest in books, and then broaden the program to include other students.

Preparation to manage the classroom activities is also necessary. Teachers need to determine the interests of students so that appropriate materials can be provided. In addition, a system is needed to track student assignments and monitor students' progress and materials; and a schedule needs to be designed for conferencing with students. Student files, for example, should contain records of skills deficits and strengths so that teachers have a basis for planning instructional activities.

Notes: The most apparent advantage of Individualized Reading is the motivational factor of self-selecting materials. In addition, students working independently are not compared to other students, so that slower readers are not stigmatized. Personal contact between teacher and students, through private conferences, can be rewarding to students. This method is intended for regular classroom use, but skillful teachers may adapt it for use with some mild to moderately disabled learners.

Lack of sequential instruction may make this method less appropriate for students with reading disabilities. However, if students have acquired appropriate reading skills, but lack motivation, as may be the case with some at-risk or behaviorally disturbed students, this method may be appropriate. Reading materials can be comprised of a selection of interesting books with limited vocabularies, sports and auto magazines, and trade books of interest to particular age groups. The ability to convey to students that reading can be an enjoyable activity should not be overlooked as a teaching skill.

INITIAL TEACHING ALPHABET (i.t.a.)

Method: Initial Teaching Alphabet (i.t.a.)

Author: John Downing

Sources: Downing, J. (1979). *Reading and reasoning*. New York: Springer-Verlag; Downing, J. (1965). *The initial teaching alphabet reading experiment*. Chicago: Scott Foresman; Aukerman, R. C. (1984). *Approaches to beginning reading*. New York: John Wiley & Sons.

Description: The i.t.a. is a regularized writing system designed to provide beginning readers with a consistent medium. It is designed to be used with any number of various teaching methodologies. When using the i.t.a., students learn by relating their spoken language to written symbols. To do this they employ the 45 i.t.a. characters that correspond to phonemic counterparts in American English. Teachers must know the i.t.a. phonemic key and need to follow these rules:

1. The i.t.a. uses majuscules (enlarged letters) rather than capital letters,
2. The i.t.a. retains the double spelling of consonants,
3. The teacher needs to learn to print the i.t.a. characters to resemble the published materials as closely as possible,
4. Punctuation is unchanged in the i.t.a.

Students must understand two concepts, the function and the features of written language, to use the i.t.a. successfully. Teachers demonstrate to students that writing is a way of communicating with others and a way of recording personal ideas and feelings. "Language Experience" (Van Allen, Venezky, & Hahn, 1975) can be used effectively to teach students the communicative function of written language.

Students must also understand the features of written language. They need to understand, for example, that it is nonphonetic as well as phonetic. The use of the i.t.a., in conjunction with the Language Experience method, provides beginning readers with a regularized system and a methodology that accommodates this duality of written language. If students are exposed only to the rigidly controlled vocabulary typically found in formal phonics, they do not see the co-existing phonemic and nonphonemic features of written language. They learn to read only contrived, nonfunctional texts.

The i.t.a. is designed to retain the teaching of the function of language and maintain cognitive clarity. By combining the Language Experience approach with the i.t.a. in the initial reading phase, students can learn the communicative function of uncontrived language while learning the underlying linguistic concepts of the phonemic code. Students are instructed in traditional orthography later.

Notes: The i.t.a. regularizes written English. Combined with Language Experience, the i.t.a. develops reading skills based on students' experiences and language. There are practical concerns to consider in employing the i.t.a. Its materials are not easily available, nor are they diverse. For example, more sophisticated nonreaders may find the material to be juvenile in content. Teachers may need to adapt materials to maintain the interest of students. Students transferring in the middle of i.t.a. instruction to traditional orthography may experience confusion, which can inhibit their reading progress. Switching from one orthography to another constitutes considerable obstacles for students with reading disabilities.

LANGUAGE EXPERIENCE

Method: Language Experience

Author: Roach Van Allen

Sources: Lee, D., & Van Allen, R. (1963). *Learning to read through experience*. New York: Appleton-Century-Crofts; Van Allen, R., Venezky, R., & Hahn, H. (1975). *Language experiences in reading, Level III: Teachers Resource Guide*. Chicago: Encyclopedia Britannica Educational Corp.; Van Allen, R. (1976). *Language experiences in communication*. Boston: Houghton Mifflin.

Description: The Language Experience method uses students' spoken language to develop their reading content. The method uses oral language skills and personal experiences. Moreover, it is an integrated language arts and reading approach.

The Language Experience method stresses the need for readiness reading, including personal and experience readiness, as well as related abilities readiness. Readiness activities such as trips and excursions, group activities, discussions, story telling, dramatization, and visual aids are suggested to extend experiential learning.

With the Language Experience approach there are basic concepts that lead to reading success:

1. Experience and imagination are the foundations of thinking and communication.

2. What students talk about they can think about.
3. Students are able to express in some form what they are able to talk about.
4. What students write can be retrieved through speaking and reading.
5. Students can read what they write for themselves, or they can read what others write for them.
6. Some words are used repeatedly in speaking and writing.
7. Words and word clusters are used to express meanings in writing and speech.
8. Writing the speech sounds involves the same letters again and again.
9. Each alphabet letter represents one or more speech sounds.
10. Reading for content meaning involves studying carefully what has been written.

The Language Experience method is based on the premise that students can read many things when they start school. For example, many of them can read about color, size, shape, weather, texture and feeling. Other students read words such as their names, labels and television ads. However, the foundation of knowledge varies among students, and it is necessary to identify the communication skills that are relevant to reading, such as experiencing, studying, and relating different communications between the self and others.

If Language Experience is to be successful, teachers must be open to sharing and discussing experiences, and students must be comfortable with relating personal experiences and listening to those of other students. Sharing might include dictating an experience to the teacher, who reads it aloud to other students.

Students study communication by learning frequently used words in poetry, drama, and prose. Students listen to, read, and interpret the language of others. They share their own experiences, evaluate the ideas of others, and formulate personal responses.

Some advocates of the Language Experience method support the use of a key vocabulary or key words. These key words can be generated and utilized by:

1. Asking students for the best words they can think of. This encourages them to consider "power words," or words that they use repeatedly in their speech.
2. Having students print the words on tagboard and asking them to name the letters they recognize.
3. Asking students to trace the letters of the words starting on the left and moving from top to bottom.
4. Asking students to do something with the words, for example, they can copy or illustrate the words.
5. Periodically asking students to read their key words to the teacher.
6. Having teachers store words for students in a word box.

Proponents of the Language Experience method believe that the classroom should be a dynamic environment where experiences are generated. In addition to being conducive to communication and sharing, the classroom environment should have materials and supplies available to students, such as books of all kinds and levels, pictures, records, and objects of nature. The teacher needs to be flexible, while establishing limits that everyone can understand and adapt to. Furthermore, students should have space to sit as groups, for individual conferences, and for individual and group activities, as well as blackboard and wall space. The teacher's role is to broaden and enrich the experience base of students at every opportunity.

Very early in their school experience, students are introduced to dictation. Dictation is used not only to help students see that speech can be represented in written form, but also to develop their oral language competency. The teacher plays a key role in eliciting responses from students by structuring key ideas and determining how much should be written in the dictation process. As the teacher writes, students and teacher read the words aloud together. Words, sounds, and letters in words, capital letters, and the functions of words are discussed. Once students have learned to write independently, they can write their own stories. Dictation should be continued for its value in promoting oral language and personal exchanges.

Reading aloud and storytelling are part of every Language Experience classroom. The teacher's and students' enthusiasm and personal involvement in these activities are critical. Comprehension checks are limited to individual student-teacher conferences. Assessment and evaluation are an integral part of this method.

Notes: For students who have experienced failure in traditional programs, the Language Experience method may provide the necessary motivation to stimulate interest in reading. However, it may not provide the teaching sequence and the controlled phonetics instruction that some students with disabilities need; it does not provide enough language and vocabulary enrichment for students with limited English proficiency or receptive and/or expressive language learning disabilities; and it may not be enough for students accelerated in written language.

Teachers who employ this method will need good management and planning skills to develop material and a classroom learning center. In addition, they will need to individualize instruction for the slower readers in the class. They will also need a thorough understanding of the reading process. Ongoing assessment of individual students provides specific data for planning lessons; however, the teacher must know how to use these data in programming for each learner.

LAUBACH METHOD

Method: Laubach Method

Author: Frank Laubach

Sources: Laubach, F., Mooney, K., & Laubach, R. (1981). *Laubach way to reading, Teachers Manual.* Syracuse, NY: New Readers Press, Laubach Literacy International; Curtis, M. B., & Chmelka, M. B. (1994). Modifying the "Laubach Way to Reading" program for use with adolescents with learning disabilities. *Learning Disabilities Research and Practice, 9*(1), 38–43.

Description: Frank Laubach is credited with teaching reading to more than 100 million non-English-speaking people throughout the world and developing word and picture charts in 312 different languages. After 20 years of work worldwide, Laubach developed a literacy program in English, a task made difficult because of the inherent irregularities of the English language.

The principles underlying the Laubach Method include teaching sound-symbol relationships; teaching by association; teaching from the known to the unknown; using familiar vocabulary and meaningful content; repetition; introducing something new each lesson; fostering independent learning; and integrating listening, reading, and writing.

The Laubach Method initially presents learning material using a phonemic approach. Sounds and spellings of basic consonants are introduced first, followed by short vowels, long vowels, irregular spellings, and more difficult reading, writing, and grammar exercises. Each lesson follows a similar format of vocabulary development, phonics and structural analysis, short story reading, comprehension checks, and writing practice.

Students begin by learning the names and sounds of the alphabet letters and the digraphs "ch," "sh," and "th." The Laubach Method uses picture association charts for learning letters, sounds, and key words. After lower case letters are mastered, capital letters are taught; the alphabet is learned in sequence; and the color and number words are learned. By the completion of the first book, students have learned 132 words; they can write letters and numbers

and transcribe letters that their teachers dictate to them.

By the time students complete the third book in the reading series, they have been introduced to 399 words and can begin to practice with functional reading materials such as menus, letters, bills, and ads. When they complete the Laubach reading program, students will have completed fifth-grade reading materials. Readers for supplementary practice have been designed for adult learners. In addition, the *Laubach Way to Reading Software* is available, which provides supplementary exercises designed to improve reading comprehension. Students can use this software once they have completed corresponding lessons in the skill book and have mastered decoding. The software, which consists of four disks, is a set of modified cloze exercises. It encourages students to use syntactic and semantic clues to predict the missing words of a cloze passage. It also gives students practice integrating meaning across sentences and increases students' sight word vocabulary.

Although most of Frank Laubach's work was done in other countries, he was able to develop a literacy program in English, and his work is continued by his son, Dr. Robert S. Laubach. Today many Laubach centers are located in the United States where volunteer tutors teach this method.

Notes: The Laubach method may be used with illiterate adults, high school dropouts, and intermediate grade students in group or tutorial settings. The vocabulary is controlled and the skills are sequenced in small steps. This method recognizes that the adult is a different type of learner, and materials are designed to accommodate this difference.

This method will be effective for some adults with learning disabilities, although it has many advocates as a beginning reading program for adults. Indeed, it is one of the few methods designed specifically for adults who do not read. The software is useful only if students are able to benefit from using a cloze procedure, which is closely tied to an individual's background knowledge.

LET'S READ

Method: Let's Read: A Linguistic Approach

Authors: Leonard Bloomfield and Clarence Barnhart.

Sources: Bloomfield, L., & Barnhart, C. (1961). *Let's read: A linguistic approach*. Boston: Wayne State University Press; Aukerman, R. C. (1984). *Approaches to beginning reading*. New York: John Wiley & Sons.

Description: The authors of Let's Read assert that, to teach reading, teachers must understand certain linguistic facts and principles. They stress that writing is recorded speech. The linguistic approach avoids the pitfalls of many existing methods of teaching reading. This method, in contrast to many others, is based on oral language. It recognizes the phonemic structure but stresses meaning only after students have acquired basic reading skills.

1. *Pre-Reading.* Before students are introduced to books in the Let's Read method, they must recognize all letters, first capitals and then lowercase letters. Letter writing is not taught until reading is fairly well advanced. Letters that might present problems (e.g., "d," "p," "b," "q") are carefully taught and practiced. Students are taught directionality in reading letters, moving from left to right and top to bottom, before they are introduced to books.

2. *Beginning Reading.* Initial reading materials must contain phonetically regular words. For example, "gem" and "got," "cot" and "cent" must not appear together; and silent letters ("knit"), doubled letters ("cell," and "see"), or combination letters ("th," "ea") should not be used. The letter "x" is also not used at this stage because it repre-

sents more than one phoneme. A sequence of introducing letters is recommended.

Reading material includes two- or three-letter words that are grouped according to the five vowel sounds. Two subgroupings are possible within each of the five vowel groups. Words can be grouped by final consonants or by initial consonants. Words are first taught using final consonant groupings because students can watch the initial letters easier than the ending letters. Lessons may proceeds as follows:

a. The teacher points to a word that has been printed in small letters, for example, "can." Students name its letters. Then, with the teacher's prompting, students read the word.

b. Another word with a different initial sound is introduced, and the same procedure is repeated.

c. Students must learn both words and demonstrate that they know them by naming them when the teacher shows them by pointing to the word that the teacher pronounces. Students do not yet write at this stage.

d. Once students learn word patterns, they are introduced to nonsense syllables. These can serve as drill exercises or as mastery tests. Nonsense syllables are described as parts of bigger words, and learning them will help students acquire reading more rapidly.

e. After one final consonant group is learned (e.g., "at"), word pairs are introduced (e.g., "can" and "cat," and "man" and "mat").

Initially, meaning is not stressed in this approach. Words are introduced slowly, and lessons are very brief. No more than two or three new words from the same group are presented in any lesson. Review of past words always precedes introduction of new material.

Subsequent reading lessons are divided into major sections. **First Reading** is significant because it introduces basic reading skills. Each of the lessons has three sections: (a) the words in students' spoken vocabularies and those that are more difficult; (b) practice phrases or sentences; and (c) review exercises. Overlearning and mastery testing are required.

Easy Reading and **More Easy Reading** introduce students to more reading vocabulary and additional letter sounds. These sounds include consonant combinations or consonant sounds that are doubled but keep their regular sounds (such as "qu," signifying /kw/ in "quit". In addition, vowels with regular phonetic manifestations are introduced, as well as two-syllable and compound words. The only irregular words introduced at this time are those that end in a silent "e."

In **The Commonest Irregular Words**, the most common irregular words are introduced. Practice and overlearning of each new word is essential. In subsequent sections, the most common irregular spellings of vowel and consonant sounds are taught. Comprehension is increasingly stressed in activities as reading skills develop.

Notes: Let's Read is built on the student's spoken language. Words are introduced in a systematic fashion. This method takes advantage of the regularity of written language. Students can see and hear the consistency of word patterns, which may be an advantage for disabled readers. Decoding regularly spelled words is emphasized, and oral reading is stressed initially.

Let's Read has been used with a variety of students with reading problems. The method provides practice and frequent repetitions of words. Because picture cues are avoided, students must rely on their decoding skills to unlock words. Many materials are available that are compatible with this method. The vocabulary used in Let's Read is limited and somewhat stilted. Sound-symbol relationships are to be discovered by the students, and blending is not taught, which may be a problem for many disabled students.

Let's Read presupposes auditory memory for speech sounds. Meaning is not stressed initially, and writing is not integrated into the initial stages.

MODALITY BLOCKING

Method: Modality Blocking

Authors: Harold Blau and Harriet Blau

Sources: Blau, H., Blau, H., & Schwalb, E. (1971). Developmental and symptomatic dyslexia: Differential diagnosis and remediation. In B. Bateman (Ed.), *Learning disorders: Vol. 4. Reading* (pp. 343–385). Seattle: Special Child Publications; Blau, H., & Blau, H. (1968). A theory of learning to read. *The Reading Teacher, 22*, 126–129.

Description: Visual Modality Blocking was designed to teach reading to students with dyslexia. It is described as an adaptation of the multisensory Fernald Method (Fernald, 1988). Furthermore, this nonvisual auditory, kinesthetic, and tactile (nonvisual AKT) approach is based on the premise that the auditory modality is in intact, but deficits in the visual modality interfere with learning to read. The authors believe that, if "looking" has not helped a student learn to read, then "not looking" may do so.

Theorizing that some disabled readers suffer from "modality conflict," or "overloading," this method introduces the nonvisual AKT approach as a remedial technique. Some disabled readers, however, may need the Modality Blocking approach prior to or simultaneously with other approaches or methods. This technique may help disabled readers to overcome word recognition problems. Moreover, because Modality Blocking is not a complete method, it must be used in conjunction with another reading method of the teacher's choice. Its procedures are as follows:

I. Students are blindfolded or asked to close their eyes.

2. A word is traced on the students' backs by the teacher, who spells it aloud letter by letter, repeating the task as often as necessary until students can identify the letters and spell the word themselves.

3. Three-dimensional letters may be provided to the blindfolded students so that they can be arranged into the word that has been traced on their backs. Once the letters have been arranged to spell the word, blindfolds are removed and students write the word on paper, the blackboard, or a file card.

Notes: This method is reportedly useful with adolescents and adults who are unable to visualize symbols in their minds. Although little is known about the effectiveness of this technique, a minimum investment in time and resources is needed to ascertain its usefulness with severely disabled readers who seem to make little progress in traditional modes of task presentation.

This technique is designed to increase word recognition skills in disabled readers. Although it is described as useful for students who may have problems with overloading, little empirical research exists to support its use. This technique has appeared in the literature for many years and is probably used most often in clinical settings with severely disabled readers.

MONTESSORI READING

Method: Montessori Reading

Author: Maria Montessori

Sources: Montessori, M. (1965). *The Montessori elementary material.* Cambridge, MA: Robert Bentley, Inc.; Aukerman, R. C. (1984). *Approaches to beginning reading.* New York: John Wiley & Sons.

Description: In Montessori Reading, reading is preceded by writing, and writing is preceded by visual and motor activities that prepare students for writing. Students learn the skills to write before they actually write. By the time they master writing, they are already able to read.

Students are first introduced to motor movements connected with writing by tracing sandpaper letters mounted on smooth cards. They trace first with their index fingers and then with two or more fingers. Students look at the letter while tracing over it and then trace over it with their eyes closed. Later, students trace with sticks to prepare for using writing utensils.

To reinforce their visual memory of letter forms, students place cut-out lower-case letters over letter forms that have been printed on cards. They also construct words from alphabet cards that are referred to as "phonograms" in the Montessori method. And they place vowels on large boards. Vowels that are formed with circles are laid across the top, and those formed with straight lines are laid out across the bottom.

In other activities, students trace over the sandpaper letters while saying the letters' sounds. Multisensory input is used to reinforce this learning. For example, the teacher gives the sound of a letter, and students locate it in the letter box. Next, the teacher holds up the letter card and asks students to give its sound. Consonant sounds must be accompanied by a vowel sound, and once students have learned the muscular formation of a letter, can pronounce the letter sound, and handle a writing instrument properly, they begin to write.

Materials needed to begin reading are strips of paper with the names of objects written on them. These are used in a variety of game formats. Phrases and sentences are taught using simple directions such as, "Walk to the door and open it." Montessori found that children as young as 4 years of age were able to participate in this activity.

One effective technique used by teachers is to write questions on the chalkboard and elicit answers to them as a means of checking reading skills. This technique is used because Montessori does not allow oral reading. Because children work alone at their own pace, there is no structured curriculum in the early grades nor an established time frame. Consequently, students are responsible for their own learning.

The American adaptation of Montessori provides additional suggestions for practicing phonemics. Vocabulary development is promoted by the addition of pictures of common objects. Students are also encouraged to pursue activities that teach word functions.

Notes: Montessori Reading begins by teaching writing and the prerequisite writing skills. It is a one-to-one approach in which students initiate activities. Montessori Reading was designed to teach Italian, which is more phonetically regular than English. This reading method does not encourage much social or verbal interaction, which may affect language development.

NEUROLOGICAL IMPRESS

Method: Neurological Impress

Author: Richard Heckelman

Source: Heckelman, R. G. (1986). Neurological impress method revisited. *Academic Therapy, 21,* 411–420.

Description: Neurological Impress is a method of unison reading between students and teacher. It is intended for intermediate, junior, and senior high school students who have not benefited from remedial instruction. The Neurological Impress method uses assigned reading materials and is not a total program. The unison reading method is best used one-to-one, but it can also be used with groups of students with the aid of earphones and a microphone.

Teachers need to practice before beginning Neurological Impress so that their voices are synchronized with their finger movements. Little additional training is needed to implement this method; however, appropriate materials must be available. For larger groups, film strips and the opaque projector can be used if there is a shortage of ample reading material.

Neurological Impress replaces inaccurate, erratic readings with accurate, fluent readings. Heckelman asserts that word recognition lags behind reading speed and functional reading by 12 to 18 months. Therefore, reading material should be at a level slightly below the student's instructional level. Nevertheless, teachers are cautioned against spending too much time unnecessarily on lower level materials. Students can accelerate rapidly through levels of reading material. Reportedly, some students have progressed several grade levels after only 12 hours of instruction.

When students plateau using this method, teachers sometimes become discouraged. Students can move very rapidly using this method and may quickly reach the limit of their capabilities. When a student does plateau, it is recommended that teachers continue this method for a few hours to ensure optimal performance.

In preparing students for impress reading, the teacher should explain that reading errors and comprehension are not the central concern. Students should practice moving their eyes across the pages, articulating the words as the teacher points to them and reads them aloud. The steps of this method follow:

1. In daily 15-minute sessions, students and the instructor read aloud together. Students are seated slightly in front of the instructor, and the instructor reads slightly louder and faster than the students. Later the instructor will intentionally lag behind the students.

2. The instructor points to each word at precisely the same time it is being pronounced. A time lag between pointing to the word and pronouncing it must be avoided. Later, students will take the lead, pointing to each word as they read it.

3. Emphasis is placed on style, smoothness, the flow of reading, and the sweep from the end of one line to the beginning of the next. Students begin with slightly easier material than they can handle and move rapidly to more difficult material. Initially, the reading rate should be comfortable for the students; this rate will later increase.

4. Errors are not corrected, because word attack and comprehension problems are not a consideration at this point. More importantly, students are being exposed to correct reading processes.

5. Pacing should be used periodically in the practice period. Pacing means speeding up the reading process to push students to faster reading rates. This should be done for a few minutes at a time throughout each reading session.

6. A total of 8 to 12 hours of instructional time divided into daily 15-minute sessions is required.

If students complain initially about not being able to keep up, the instructor should encourage them to continue to try while ignoring all of their errors. The instructor may have to slow down somewhat and read initial paragraphs several times until students are comfortable. However, if students do not show rapid improvement after 4 hours of instruction, another approach may be needed.

A kinesthetic method or an echoing technique are recommended for students with suspected auditory discrimination problems. When teachers use the echoing technique, students are asked to repeat phrases or sentences dictated by the teacher. They begin with short phrases and increase the difficulty of this task until sentences are mastered. They then can return to the impress method.

Notes: The Neurological Impress method may be motivating for students who like one-to-one attention. If rapid progress is noted, students quickly experience success. When oral reading is required, this method may be preferable to the round robin approach where students take turns listening to other students stumble read.

This method is probably most useful for students from third grade to adulthood. It positively impacts reading fluency by providing only correct practices and by teaching students to approach words as whole structures rather than as component parts. In addition, a wide variety of materials can be used, including science text books and magazines. This method is easy to learn; aides and parents can use this method with minimal instruction.

To use this method on a one-to-one basis with numerous students, a teacher will need additional aides, parents, or tutors. Some students may need additional prerequisite training using a kinesthetic or echoing approach. The teacher's auditory input may confuse rather than teach some students.

ORGANIC READING

Method: Organic Reading

Author: Sylvia Ashton-Warner

Sources: Ashton-Warner, S. (1958). *Spinster.* New York: Simon & Shuster; Ashton-Warner, S. (1963). *Teacher.* New York: Simon & Shuster; Aukerman, R. C. (1984). *Approaches to beginning reading.* New York: John Wiley & Sons; McDonald, J. P. (1992). *Teaching: Making sense of an uncertain craft.* New York: Teachers College Press.

Description: Organic Reading is a language experience approach to reading developed by Ashton-Warner in her 24 years of work with Maori children in New Zealand. This method is an outgrowth of insights into the personal needs and feelings of these students. The term "organic" conveys the idea that reading depends on the inner thoughts of students; and, therefore, if it is to be meaningful, reading should be highly personal and relate to each individual's sense of self.

The key word technique that the Organic Reading method employs attempts to reach students at a personal level. It seeks, through the intense personal meaning of selected words, to open students' minds and allow them to express themselves verbally. In describing Organic Reading, Ashton-Warner listed several maxims as being important to prepare students for reading. A key vocabulary centers on two basic instincts, fear and sex. This vocabulary will differ across geographic locations and between races. A key vocabulary will also differ among students. Considerable time and effort are needed on the part of the teacher to discover these vocabularies. Illustrations are not to be used with key words, and the "power of the content" of a word should not be related to the word's length. Each subculture has its own content standard, as well as the standard of the dominant or hegemonic culture.

Key words are those that grow out of everyday experiences and the personal feelings of students. Key words are learned using "One-Look" cards, a type of flash card that has a key word on it that students have dictated and the teacher has written down. Students watch the teacher print the word and then they pronounce it together. Students then trace the word. They work in pairs and teach one another their own words. Eventually, all key words are mixed together, and students search through the stack to find their own words. Once these words have been learned, students take them home. In addition, each student has a word box in which to keep key words.

Spelling and writing become an integral part of this process. Students learn to write their own words and progress to writing sentences based on personal experience and using key words. The teacher assists with sentence writing initially, but eventually the students work independently.

In addition, students write their own books. These books are written from key vocabulary using the organic writing exercises. And, because these books are written by students, careful attention is given to the handwriting, spelling, and punctuation. Much of the writing is done on the chalkboard so that the teacher can monitor the work closely. Furthermore, students read their own books and then one another's. All students' key words are written and read, and all students benefit from this economy of words with expanding vocabularies. Gradually, students are introduced to transitional readers and standard reading books.

Notes: Organic Reading is a child-centered method. The key vocabulary approach may unlock reading for a reluctant reader or for a student who is experientially deprived and cannot relate to traditional classroom reading materials. It can stimulate creativity, and it builds on the spoken vocabularies of students.

There are no materials for this method; therefore, teachers must develop their own or adapt existing materials. This process can be time consuming and unrealistic for teachers with heavy teaching loads. The key word method, although individualized and directed toward personal experiences, does not provide the structure some students need to decode words. The components of this method parallel the components of the Whole Language method. Although these two methods appear to be philosophically aligned, this method is typically not included in the Whole Language literature.

READING RECOVERY

Method: Reading Recovery

Author: Marie M. Clay

Sources: Clay, M. (1985). *The early detection of reading difficulties* (3rd ed.). Portsmouth,

NH: Heinemann Educational Books; Boehnleim, M. (1987). Reading intervention for high-risk first graders. *Educational Leadership, 44,* 32–37; DeFord, D. (1991). On noble thoughts, or toward a clarification of theory and practice within a whole language framework. In W. Ellis (Ed.), *All language and creation of literacy* (pp. 27–39). Baltimore: Orton Dyslexia Society.

Description: Reading Recovery is designed for at-risk first-grade students in need of intensive reading remediation. All first graders should be assessed within the first several weeks of first grade to determine students who are reading at the lowest levels. This program attempts to bring these students to reading levels at their class average in the shortest time possible through accelerated learning and strong holistic teaching.

The Reading Recovery method provides each student with intensive one-to-one learning sessions for 30 minutes every day. These students do extensive reading and writing. This method proceeds along the following framework:

1. *Familiar Reading.* To develop fluency, students read familiar material.
2. *Running Records.* Teachers observe students reading and devise goals and strategies based on these observations.
3. *Writing.* Students are given numerous opportunities to write. Furthermore, they learn to recognize sounds in words, generate new words, increase fluency with familiar words, and gain a phonological awareness of sounds.
4. *New Book Introduction and First Reading.* Students choose a new book to read. Together, the teacher and students read aloud from these books.

This method, which has been used successfully in schools in several states, focuses on the importance of early intervention (i.e., the first grade). Teachers need to receive intensive training in the techniques of this program.

Notes: This method provides remediation to students who need intensive instruction and practice to learn to read. It is intended to be used as an intervention before students experience failure. Students who do not respond to this method will need to be re-evaluated to determine an appropriate method for them.

REBUS READING

Method: Rebus Reading

Author: Richard Woodcock

Sources: Clark, C. R., Davies, C. O., & Woodcock, R. W. (1974). *Standard rebus glossary.* Circle Pines, MN: American Guidance Service; Woodcock, R. W., Clark, C. R., & Davies, C. O. (1979). *Peabody rebus reading program.* Circle Pines, MN: American Guidance Service; Van Oosterom, J., & Devereux, K. (1982). REBUS at Rees Thomas School. *Special Education: Forward Trends, 9*(1), 31–33.

Description: The visual symbolic systems of reading can be divided into two graphic systems. These systems are the standard alphabetic system of a language and the syllabic, or logographic, system. In standard alphabetic systems, the phoneme (sound) or the grapheme (letter) is represented. These systems include traditional orthography (alphabet) and phonemic alphabets such as the International Phonemic Alphabet or i.t.a.

Alphabetic systems rely on the fundamental units of words, that have no meaning, for example, letters or sounds. These units must be combined in various forms (often irregular blends, diphthongs, etc.) in order to communicate whole words or thoughts.

Syllabic, or logographic systems, on the other hand, are complete systems that contain meaning in their constitutive representations. Through the use of pictographs or nonpictographs, these systems convey complete messages as such. In addition, graphic systems may be written or signed. They may have universal or colloquial meanings, and they are frequently thought of as the international language of road signs.

Clark, Davies, and Woodcock produced a pictorial, logographic, and syllabic system for reading which is called Rebus Reading. Rebus Reading is not a new phenomenon strictly speaking, because rebuses have been used in road signs for years. However, the use of rebuses in beginning reading is viewed as a departure from standard procedures for teaching reading, although, historically, rebuses have been used in many beginning reading programs. Many 19th century reading texts used rebuses to help children learn new words. Many early learning books, magazines, and "color and read" books for preschool children continue to use rebuses in game-like formats.

Rebus Reading was originally produced by Clark, Davies, and Woodcock in an experimental instructional material format. The materials included three workbooks that were designed to introduce the rebus pictographs to students. These workbooks were intended to provide the necessary readiness and prereading skills required prior to traditional alphabetic presentations.

The approach used in the rebus learning phases of Rebus Reading is a whole word approach. Words are introduced which are complete morphemes (root words). Pluralization, possession, and tense changes are indicated by the traditional orthographic symbols of "s," "'s," and "ing." As this program progresses, however, morphemes are combined and compounded to produce new words. Morphemes are also combined with individual letters to produce new words (e.g., "b" added to the rebus signifying "and" would be "b" + "and," or the word "band").

Once the basic rebuses are mastered, students are introduced to rebus words in context. First, students read entire rebus stories. As their readings progress, rebuses are placed above the traditional English spellings of words. After a few repeated readings with rebus and word, the rebuses are removed, and students read standard alphabetic forms.

Successful completion of all workbooks and storybooks will provide readers with a vocabulary of 122 words. The content of these words includes concrete nouns ("table," "cat," etc.), concrete verbs ("to hit," "to jump," etc.), adjectives (colors, sizes, etc.), prepositions ("around," "on," "in," etc.), and conjunctions ("and"). Words that cannot be introduced as rebuses, such as "cannot," "I," or "to sing," are introduced in boxes in standard orthographic form. Unlike some other children's books of rebus games, rebuses that might imply the second meaning of a word with multiple meanings (e.g., "I" and "eye") are not used.

Although the basis of the rebus approach to reading is found primarily in instructional material, rebuses can be used as teaching instruments apart from the material. Although it would certainly be easier for a teacher to use the commercially produced materials, rebuses can be drawn from the Standard Rebus Glossary and incorporated into teacher-made materials.

Notes: Rebus Reading provides an alternative reading system based on whole words rather than fragmentary graphemes or phonemes. It is a concrete visual method of teaching reading that can be useful for the early acquisition of reading. For students confused by phonics approaches, students in need of a concrete beginning approach to reading, and those with visual and/or auditory memory deficits, the presentation of pictorial symbols may have advantages. The intangible advantages of Rebus Reading to nonreaders should be considered in evaluating and implementing this method.

The transition to traditional orthography may be difficult for some students. Rebuses tend to be so concrete that more abstract words cannot be introduced. Rebus systems should not be considered a panacea for all reading problems. They are not intended to be used as replacements for traditional orthography, but only as initial teaching strategies.

REMEDIAL READING DRILLS

Method: Remedial Reading Drills

Authors: Thorleif Hegge, Samuel Kirk, Winifred Kirk, and Esther H. Minskoff

Sources: Hegge, T. G., Kirk, S. A., & Kirk, W. D. (1955; 1970). *Remedial reading drills.* Ann Arbor, MI: George Wahr Publisher; Kirk, S. A., Kirk, W., & Minskoff, E. H. (1985). *Phonics remedial reading lessons.* Novato, CA: Academic Therapy Publications.

Description: The Hegge-Kirk-Kirk Remedial Reading Drills were developed for higher functioning individuals with intellectual deficits at the Wayne County Training School. These drills are designed to be used with students who read below the fourth grade level, have evidence of a severe reading disability, can sound blend, have corrected any severe auditory and visual problems, and are motivated and cooperative.

This method is designed so that students can achieve success through mastery-learning in small sequential steps. The short vowel "a" and most consonant sounds are taught before drills begin. Letter sounds are taught by associating the letter form with a common sound (e.g., "t" with the ticking of a clock).

After students have mastered most of the consonants and the short vowels, they learn to sound blend letter by letter by following verbal demonstration. Words are then written on the chalkboard, and students sound out words letter by letter. Several variations of the activity are suggested for students who have difficulty mastering sound-blending. When students can blend three-letter words, they are ready for four-part drill exercises.

Students always begin with Drill I of Part I, reading all the words aloud. Accuracy is stressed over the reading rate. In the first part, only the initial consonant changes, in the second part the final consonant changes, and in the third part both initial and final consonants change. Unlike some methods that combine the vowel with the first or last consonants, each letter in a word is sounded individually.

Students are never rushed, nor are they allowed to skip a drill. Frequent review drills are provided. A grapho-vocal method is also used. Students write a word or letter from memory and, at the same time, repeat the word or sound. When students make errors, the drill is stopped, and students are asked to write the sound and to say it. Students may repeat the exercise several times, finally writing and saying the sound with their eyes closed. Student activities include synthetic phonics (students sound a word and blend it) and analytic phonics (the teacher dictates the words and has students produce the sounds).

Sentences are introduced when students indicate an interest in reading and when sufficient words are learned to read short sentences. The vocabulary is controlled, with sentences constructed from drill words and very few nondrill words.

The authors of this method suggest that older students not be introduced to books until they are ready for second or third grade readers, usually after the first 26 drills, or Part I of the drill book. Any reader with a phonic base is recommended; primers are not recommended and pictures should be eliminated in all readers. Words that are consistently problematic for students are used in word drills. Furthermore, word drills continue after students are reading in books.

Part II of the drills presents certain sound combinations that were previously learned in isolation. Part III includes more advanced sounds and less common sounds that are presented in whole words. By the time students reach Part III of the remedial drills, the emphasis switches to reading and word study, but short drill periods are provided each day. Part IV provides supplementary exercises that teach the exceptions not previously learned, word building practice, and extra practice on sounds that might be confusing (e.g., "b," "d," and "p").

Notes: The Remedial Reading Drills are used for students who have experienced severe reading problems in spite of several years of schooling. It is for students who have not mastered phonics, but who have the auditory ability and sound-blending ability to learn to read. This method has been published in an updated version, *Phonic Remedial Reading Lessons*, authored by Kirk, Kirk, and Minskoff.

This method is used with older students still reading on a first through third grade level. This method is not designed for students who are slow but accurate readers. In addition, special precautions must be taken to teach comprehension and to ensure the transfer from word list reading to story reading.

REPEATED READING

Method: Repeated Reading

Author: Sandra B. Moyer

Sources: Moyer, S. B. (1982). Repeated reading. *Journal of Learning Disabilities*, 15(10), 619–623; O'Shea, L., & O'Shea, D. J. (1988). Using repeated reading. *Teaching Exceptional Children*, 20(2), 26–29.

Description: Repeated Reading is a technique for increasing fluency in connected reading. Several researchers have devised procedures and tested them on individuals or small groups of disabled readers with reported success. These several procedures have slight variations. Moyer outlined the steps she used with one adult:

1. Select a passage of three to four paragraphs or one printed page in length. Individuals should be able to read most of the words in this selection.

2. Ask the person to read the passage once at a rate that ensures a high degree of accuracy.

3. Have the person reread the passage three or four times. Speed should increase each time.

Chomsky used a similar procedure with reading disabled third graders, incorporating these listening activities:

1. Students were asked to listen to a tape-recorded book several times while following along in the text.

2. After the story was completely memorized, a new book was introduced.

3. Word analysis and word recognition were taught using the memorized material. For example, students were asked to pick out words from a page at the request of the teacher. Words could be put on flash cards or used in sentences separate from the story.

A third variation of Repeated Reading was proposed by Samuels (1979) who investigated its effectiveness with delayed readers of average intellectual ability and with individuals with intellectual deficits. This procedure involved the Repeated Reading of a passage until students demonstrated fluency when a new passage was introduced. Listening strategies were incorporated in the early stages of this instruction.

Notes: Repeated Reading is a technique that can be incorporated into other reading methods to increase overall reading speed and accuracy. With the taped listening technique used by Chomsky, students can practice individually with little teacher intervention. This reading technique is useful for delayed readers of normal intelligence, individuals with intellectual deficits, and other individuals with reading disabilities.

SEMANTOGRAPHY (BLISSYMBOLICS)

Method: Semantography (Blissymbolics)

Author: Charles Bliss

Sources: Bliss, C. K. (1965). *Semantography* (2nd ed.). Sydney, Australia: Semantography Publications; Helfman, E. S. (1981). *Blissymbolics*. New York: Elsevier/Nelson Publishers.

Description: Semantography, or Blissymbolics, is a communication system that consists of approximately 100 basic symbols. Although these symbols can be used discretely, they most often are combined to form words. In addition, these symbols function both pictographically and linguistically; they can represent both the concrete and the mutable elements of verb tenses and other parts of speech. The symbols can be arranged to form complete sentences, or they can be combined to convey intricate and subtle meanings usually expressed directly through language.

The first step in employing the Blissymbolics method is to learn the basic symbols. There are 100 symbols, including the numbers 1–10, symbols of mathematical operations, arrows used to show direction, symbols with medical and financial functions, a symbol for "thing," and an "s" symbol to signify action. Other symbols include a bent line to signify a time line, or chronological "direction," and a heart to indicate an emotional meaning. In addition, there are sensory symbols for "eye," "ear," "mouth," "nose," and "hand." All of these symbols can be placed on blocks, flash cards, or boards to facilitate study. Or as Helfman, in her book *Blissymbolics* suggests, blocks can be made to conform to the shapes of the symbols themselves for use with very young children. These blocks can be used later in exercises that combine individual symbols to form more complex units of meaning.

Indeed, the next step in utilizing the Blissymbolics method is to combine symbols to construct meaningful units. A teacher assists students in selecting combinations that are relevant to their needs and within the scope of their vocabularies and intellectual capacities. For a child just beginning to communicate, for example, symbols representing "nose" and "action" might reasonably be combined to produce the concept of "smelling." Combining the "hand" and "action" symbols to produce "handing" might occur at a later stage of learning.

As students become more adept at using Blissymbolics and their communication abilities become more sophisticated, they are encouraged to use more complex symbol combinations to express more abstract concepts. Symbol combinations can be used to read and write stories, thematic compositions, and technical communications. For nonverbal students, communication with symbol combinations can become increasingly more abstract. Verbal students can use symbol combinations to explore the subtleties and nuance of language itself.

Notes: Blissymbolics is a pictorial and linguistic system that can express simple, concrete, and complex, abstract communications. It can be used as an alternative to traditional oral and written communication. Its symbols are varied and versatile. They are capable of graphically expressing subtleties of language that may be difficult for many individuals with disabilities to express otherwise. Thus far, the teaching of Blissymbolics has been limited primarily to individuals with cerebral palsy, aphasia, severe intellectual deficits, or language learning disabilities. Blissymbolics could be used with young children who are beginning reading exploration or with students who have severe learning or sensory disorders.

Symbol systems, like Blissymbolics, generally have been used only with nonverbal disabled children, adolescents, and adults. However, in an age when the use of computer languages, universal road signs, and informational and mathematical languages are increasingly more common, a symbol system like Blissymbolics could serve many uses for individuals with other mild handicaps. Many students, who have difficulties using language appropriately in social settings, might be able to utilize a system like Blissymbolics. In addition, the use of Blissymbolics can assist students with intellectual deficits who also possess poor social skills, students with behavior disorders and inadequate perceptual abilities, and students with sensory impairments, particularly with auditory or visual deficits.

Blissymbolics has not been accepted as a standard communication system except with some students with multiple disabilities. To use Blissymbolics more widely in populations with mild disabilities, specific teaching strategies would need to be developed, as well as instructional materials and assessment devices.

SLINGERLAND MULTI-SENSORY APPROACH

Method: Slingerland Multi-Sensory Approach to Language Arts

Author: Beth Slingerland

Source: Slingerland, B. (1993). *A multi-sensory approach to language arts for specific language disability children.* Cambridge, MA: Educators Publishing Service.

Description: The Slingerland Multi-Sensory Approach to Language Arts is an adaptation of the Orton-Gillingham method (Orton, 1966). It was designed to prevent academic failure and the emotional difficulties that students with specific language learning disabilities can experience as a result of failure.

The Slingerland method is a highly structured, multisensory approach designed to integrate the auditory, visual, and kinesthetic learning modalities used in the development of speech, reading, writing, spelling, and concept building. In addition, it is a remedial technique for young students that incorporates repetition and overlearning. Furthermore, the goals of this method are to develop simultaneously the auditory, visual, and kinesthetic integration necessary to (a) achieve language competence; (b) secure automatic recall; (c) provide students with the tools to become independent learners; and (d) achieve grade level skills.

Slingerland asserts that teachers must receive intensive formal training to implement this method. For example, teachers need to learn the correct pronunciation of phonemes and the correct procedure for forming letters in the air. Teachers learn to form letters with their left hand and backwards, so that they present an appropriate model to students facing them in a classroom. Furthermore, teachers are required to learn to screen for students with specific language learning disabilities using *The Slingerland Screening Tests for Identifying Children with Specific Language Disabilities* (Slingerland, 1989).

During their specialized training, teachers must also prepare supplementary materials. Teachers make, or may purchase, wall charts, sets of small manuscript alphabet cards, spelling rules cards, phonogram charts, and card holders. Teachers must be prepared to introduce skills in the structured manner that Slingerland prescribes.

Learning to Write. Students learn the formation of new letters, practice writing letters previously learned, learn letter connections and capital letters, and internalize the writing skills necessary for copying and written expression tasks. Instructions are specific. For example, to learn the letter "z":

1. Teachers introduce the letter "z" from a wall chart, giving the letter's name, a key word, and the phonetic sound /z/. Teachers model the letter's formation by writing it on the board and then forming it in the air.

2. Students are given pieces of paper that have been folded vertically in three columns and horizontally as many times as needed to accommodate the size of the letter. In the first column, teachers write a model of the letter "z." Students trace the letter with their fingers, the blunt end of the pencil, and the sharpened end of a pencil. Students simultaneously name the letter aloud. After several practices, students copy the letter in the second column while saying its name.

3. After teachers check their work, students fold the paper so that only the third column shows. Students then write the letter from memory while saying its name. Again teachers check students' work. After students have begun to use lined paper, they learn to make letter connections and write capital letters in manuscript and cursive.

Auditory Approach. This aspect of the teaching format employs auditory stimulus initially. Instruction occurs in five steps:

1. The teacher names a letter's phonetic sound. Students name the letter, form it in the air, give its key word, and repeat the letter's sound. The alphabet card with the letter is presented, and students repeat the procedure.

2. Alphabet cards and pocket charts are used to teach blending. In the first two steps, students move from chart holder activities to the chalkboard and then to paper. The third step moves them from oral blending to blending performed on paper.

3. Students use the skills learned in blending to learn to spell. Also, they learn to expand words by adding prefixes and suffixes. Students write phrases and sentences using three types of words: phonetic, or **Green Flag**, words; nonphonetic, or **Red Flag**, words; and words that can be spelled more than one way, **Yellow Flag**, words.

4. Prior to writing, students discuss topics with the teacher's assistance. The teacher indicates the mechanical components of a paragraph on the chalkboard, such as margins and indentations. Students observe the teacher write a paragraph and then copy it from the chalkboard. As students copy, the teacher immediately corrects errors. Students are not allowed to erase their mistakes; instead, they bracket their errors and continue to write.

Visual Approach. In this section, the stimulus is visual, while responses are auditory and kinesthetic:

1. Alphabet cards are used to review letters. The teacher displays a card and asks students to describe the letter on it. Students name the letter, form it in the air, give its key word, and say the letter's sound.

2. Students decode phonetic words through the process of **unlocking**. Words, each with a particular vowel sound, are listed on the chalkboard. Students examine each word and draw lines under the letters that represent the appropriate vowel sound. Students then name the letter, pronounce its phonetic sound, and read the words that contain it.

3. Students read phrases that have been written on the board in manuscript rather than cursive writing. The teacher places the pointer under a word or phrase and reads it aloud; students repeat the phrase. The teacher then names the word or phrase. The student places the pointer under the word or phrase and reads it. If the student has read the phrase correctly, the entire class repeats the phrase in unison.

The teacher then describes a concept and asks students to indicate the phrase that best expresses this concept. A student reads the phrase, and the entire class repeats it. Finally, the teacher has students read various phrases that the entire class repeats.

4. Students are now introduced to books. They study phrasing and the use of punctuation through oral readings. After a guided introduction to books, students are expected to read independently.

Notes: The Slingerland method gives teachers specific information about teaching lessons and preparing materials. Teachers are expected to follow this method's structure as it is described in the manual and taught in workshops. The cost of implementing this method is not significant, and teachers can use a variety of basal readers. This method is teacher-directed, but students are actively involved in the learning process. Furthermore, this method can be used with individual students or groups of students with similar needs.

The Slingerland method was designed specifically for students with particular language learning disabilities. It is not recommended for students with intellectual deficits, behavioral disorders, or global learning disabilities. In addition, teachers are expected to be specially trained before implementing this method. Typically, teachers need to remain enthusiastic about this method, because the repetition and overlearning it requires may negatively impact students' interest in it.

STRUCTURAL READING

Method: Structural Reading

Authors: Catherine Stern and Toni Gould

Sources: Stern, C., & Gould, T. (1965). *Children discover reading*. New York: Random House, L. W. Singer Co.; Stern, C., Stern, M, & Gould, T. (1963, 1978). *Structural reading series*. New York: Random House, L. W. Singer Co.; Auckerman, R. C. (1986). *Approaches to beginning reading*. New York: John Wiley & Sons.

Description: Structural Reading begins with the spoken word. Students listen to initial sounds in familiar words and discover that many of them begin with the same sound. Only when students have learned to listen to sounds in spoken words, do they learn written letters.

Word recognition begins with phonetically regular words that are keyed to pictures. Students see a picture of a cat, for example. They say "cat," see the letters below the picture ("ca," "t"), sound the main part and discern the ending ("t"). This approach, Stern believes, has advantages over alphabetic-phonemic approaches that require students to sound out letters in isolation.

Although Stern's method begins by teaching monosyllabic words, it does not use nonsense words, nor does it present word groups by adding initial sounds to a final letter group (e.g., "c," "an" or "f," "an"). Stern believes that such a technique breaks the words unnaturally and focuses students' attention on the ends of words, which serves to confuse left to right directionality. She also believes that it inhibits the ability of students to learn other words.

When students are introduced to phonetically irregular words, they have already learned how to decode initial and end sounds. They only need to learn middle sounds. Students are reading books without a controlled vocabulary by the end of second grade.

At the prereading stage, students engage in a variety of activities that help them learn initial sounds. Students learn to hear and read initial sounds, write the alphabet letters, and expand their speaking vocabularies. As a reminder to students, consonants are colored blue and vowels red in the printed materials that accompany the Structural Reading program.

Writing is integrated into the reading process. Students make their own Sound Books. Writing, a kinesthetic experience, is believed to be the best way of "fixing" letters in students' minds. A sequence for teaching is presented in the materials.

From Spoken to Printed Word. In first grade, students move from an emphasis on oral language to an emphasis on printed words. Because Stern believes that teaching begins with the spoken word, she does not give books to beginning first graders. She does not condone the use of experience charts either, although she believes that "pictorial" experience charts may be useful for vocabulary building. The following procedure is used to teach words in Structural Reading:

1. The teacher displays pictures of objects representing phonetically regular three-letter words and teaches students the names of the objects if necessary. In oral activities, students match the name of the object with the picture, always breaking the words into their natural parts ("ca" and "t").

2. Students have their first exposure to written words in workbook activities where pictures have accompanying names (e.g., the picture of a cat is accompanied by "ca," "t"). On the bottoms of pages, each picture is reproduced with its initial two-letter blend (e.g., "ca"). Students discover, through discussion, the final sound/letter.

3. Using dominoes containing word parts, students build words dictated by the teacher and by self-dictation.

4. Writing begins by asking students to self-dictate words they have learned. Errors are discussed, and students are encouraged to find and correct their own errors by using the picture dictionary provided.

5. Students learn to blend three-letter words smoothly. They begin reading words without pictures, but the blue and red colors for consonants and vowels are retained.

6. Sight words are introduced, but neither phonic drills nor flash cards are permitted. Students learn sight words in short vowel groups. Colored type is used in the Structural Reading materials to accent new words. The silent "e" is in gold; prefixes and suffixes are green; and silent letters are in broken gray lines. Black is used to signify words that need special attention.

From Reading Words to Reading Sentences and Stories. In learning to read sentences, students are exposed only to words they already know. Students must read with the inflections and fluency. Sentence reading begins after the short "a" sound is learned, which limits the reading content but controls the vocabulary.

Sentence reading begins with the spoken word. A key word is introduced in class discussion, and students write it on the board and read it aloud. This word is then placed in a sentence that students read. To demonstrate their comprehension, students are read a sentence stem and select from two endings the one that best communicates a logical thought. Written responses are also required as comprehension assessments.

Simple supplementary booklets with a single sentence on each page are used to encourage students to illustrate meaning in pictorial form. Experience charts, in which the teacher controls the vocabulary, may also be used to further comprehension.

Silent reading is encouraged, first with inaudible decoding, then with inner decoding, and lastly with automatic sight reading. Easy books of all kinds are made available to students by the end of first grade. In second grade, more word structures are taught, and individual reading is stressed in areas such as science, history, folklore, and adventure.

Students learn spelling rules in Structural Reading. Students are taught to understand the structure of language underlying these rules. Syntax, although not specifically taught, is introduced in the early grades. Students learn that words have particular functions in sentences.

Related reading skills are not overlooked in Structural Reading. Three reading skills are rudimentary: (a) reading to understand directions; (b) reading for detail; and (c) reading to grasp the main idea.

Notes: Structural Reading is an approach that stresses accuracy along with comprehension. The teacher must have a clear understanding of the reading process and a tracking system for monitoring individual student's progress. The color coding may confuse some students. In addition, many disabled students have difficulty learning intuitively and generalizing new knowledge.

SUCCESS FOR ALL

Method: Success for All

Authors: Robert Slavin, Nancy Madden, Nancy Karweit, Laurence Dolan, and Barbara A. Wasik

Sources: Slavin, R. E. (1990). On success for all: Defining "success," defining "all." *Remedial and Special Education, (RASE),* *11*(4), 60–61; Madden, N., Slavin, R. E., Karweit, N., Dolan, L., & Wasik, B. A. (1991). Success for all. *Phi Delta Kappan,* *72*(8), 93–99.

Description: The Success for All method is designed to ensure that all students make it through the third grade with reading skills near their grade levels and thus are prepared to succeed in later grades. Its focus is prevention and early intervention. This method proposes that the enthusiasm and positive self-expectations of young learners are the greatest instructional and learning resources available to educators. Therefore, it attempts to ensure children's success to utilize these resources optimally.

This method attempts to employ all that is known about effective instruction for at-risk students to channel the entire school and classroom organization toward preventing academic deficits, recognizing and intervening where deficits exist, and providing all students with a full and diverse curriculum designed to allow them to build on their fundamental skills. The Success for All method employs an approach that integrates several different components:

Reading Tutors. Tutors are used in one-on-one instruction that supports what students are learning in their regular reading curriculum. Sessions last for 20 minutes daily. Tutors can also work as additional reading teachers to reduce class size.

Reading Program. Reading classes are arranged according to reading levels and contain from 15 to 20 students in each class. By having all students in a reading class at the same performance level, regardless of their grade level, class time and quality are enhanced. Beginning reading classes teach basic comprehension, prereading skills, and story retelling. Later classes stress sound-symbol relationships and reading fluency. Reading classes eventually integrate spelling and writing exercises into their curricula as well as vocabulary building, decoding practice, and reading with partners. Students are also encouraged to take library books home to read, which they share with their classmates in twice weekly "book club" sessions in presentations, summaries, and other formats.

Eight-Week Reading Assessments. The results of regular testing are used to determine students' needs. Their individualized programs can be modified to accommodate their changing needs.

Preschool and Kindergarten. Schools attempt to provide half-day preschool and full-day kindergarten to eligible students. These classes are designed to give children learning experiences and academic readiness.

Family Support Team. These support teams seek to involve parents in their children's educational experience, because this method asserts that parents are integral to the success of students. Teams are comprised of social workers, attendance monitors, and the school's regular staff. They inform parents, help to make them feel comfortable in their schools, and hope ultimately to train them to fill numerous volunteer roles in the school.

Program Facilitator. A facilitator works with the principal at each school to oversee the operation of the Success for All model.

Teachers and Teacher Training. Both teachers and tutors are certified teachers. They receive specialized program training, frequent inservice presentations, and meet in informal sessions where they are encouraged to share problems and solutions, suggest changes, and discuss individual children.

Special Education. Special education teachers sometimes serve as tutors or reading teachers for students with learning disabilities.

Advisory Committee. The school principal, a teacher representative, and the family support staff comprise an advisory committee that meets to review the program's progress. They also identify and remedy problems.

Notes: The Success for All method varies in its implementation from site to site, depending on the needs and resources of the various schools. Nevertheless, this method continues to stress the success of all children; it is committed to preventing learning problems and intervenes vigorously where they do exist.

TAPED BOOKS/AUDIOBOOKS

Method: Taped Books/Audiobooks

Authors: Nancy Mather, Craig Michaels and Gloria Lodato-Wilson

Sources: Mather, N. (1991). *An instructional guide to the Woodcock-Johnson psycho-educational battery—revised.* Brandon, VT: Clinical Psychology Publishing; Michaels, C. A., & Lodato-Wilson, G. (1995). *Learning through listening—An informational guide for educators and parents of students with learning disabilities.* Princeton: Recording for the Blind and Dyslexic; Baskin, B. H., & Harris, K. (1995). Heard any good books lately? The case for audiobooks in secondary classrooms. *Journal of Reading, 38*(5), 372–376.

Description: Taped Books can be used as a remedial approach to enhance the reading fluency of children or adults. It enables students to listen to a text and follow along as it is read to them.

Students proceed with Taped Books through repeated listenings. They can listen to a text as many times as needed for them to read it fluently. Listening sessions can last anywhere from 5 minutes to half an hour, depending on the motivation of individual students. In addition, students progress gradually through increasingly more difficult texts.

Teachers need to consider several factors in helping their students select appropriate texts. For example, the taped books should be read neither too rapidly nor too slowly. Indeed, when possible, tapes should approximate the reading rates of students. Furthermore, teachers must consider the content level of tapes. There is some indication that students benefit significantly from tapes at their frustration level rather than at their independent reading level. In addition, teachers may want to base the selection of taped books upon the interests of their students.

An example of one Taped Book instructional approach follows:

1. During daily 10-minute sessions, students eventually listen to a tape three or four times as they read along with it. Once a week, students read aloud to their teacher.
2. Students record in a notebook any words that are difficult for them.
3. When students have completed listening to a book, they reread their list of difficult words, choose a new book to listen to, and repeat the entire procedure again.

Notes: Reading instruction that incorporates Taped Books is effective with students who have difficulty reading fluently. It is also useful for those with sustained attention deficits and memory difficulties. Taped Books has also been used effectively with students with learning disabilities, educable students with intellectual deficits, students with behavioral disorders, and students with speech and language impairment. These students demonstrated gains in comprehension, word recognition, vocabulary, and knowledge of phonics.

Taped Books can also be used effectively with students who have not experienced success with phonics or with older students who have previously been unable to achieve significant levels of reading success.

TRAUB SYSTEMATIC HOLISTIC METHOD

Method: Traub Systematic Holistic Method

Author: Nina Traub

Sources: Traub, N. (1982). Reading, spelling, handwriting: Traub systematic holistic method. *Annals of Dyslexia, 32,* 135–145; Traub, N., & Bloom, F. (1990). *Recipe for reading.* Cambridge, MA: Educators Publishing Service.

Description: The Traub Systematic Holistic Method was developed from the Traub Tutorial Program, which was designed to assist tutors working with learning disabled readers. The Traub method is a multisensory phonetic approach, a variation of the Gillingham and Stillman: Reading method (Gillingham & Stillman, 1973). This method incorporates many of the principles of instruction found in the literature: (a) diagnosis to determine students' entry level skills; (b) carefully sequenced skills that allow students to achieve mastery and experience success; (c) overlearning, ordering, and rewarding; (d) ability development; and (e) a supportive environment.

This method introduces letter sounds in a sequence that is dictated by auditory, visual, and kinesthetic factors. Letters that are formed by making a circle to the left are in-

troduced first along with the hard "c" and "g" and "l," "h," "t," and "m."

Letter forms are taught by placing a dot on the paper at the point where students begin to write a letter; arrows give the direction in which letters are to be formed. Directionality aids are provided to help students who reverse letters. Specially lined writing paper with two blue parallel lines and two red parallel line between them are used. The spaces between the lines have names: the upper blue line is the "attic," the red parallel lines are the "little red house," and the lower blue line is the "basement." These labels are used to identify the placement of letters in relationship to the lines during writing.

All letters are presented in a prescribed sequence. Students have sets of sound cards. Sounds are introduced with some rather elaborate associative cues to establish sound-symbol relationships. Students respond in unison. Progress is carefully documented.

Materials include sound cards, word cards, phrase cards, sentence cards, storybooks, word games, sequence charts, and writing paper. Teachers make these materials, with the exception of the storybooks, sequence charts, and writing paper.

The sequence of instruction begins with the daily drill of a sound using the phonetic sound cards. Kinesthetic activities can be incorporated for students who have difficulty mastering a sound. The teacher gives the sounds, and students name the letter and write it.

After the drills, new material is presented. Students learn to write and spell new words before they are taught to read them. Students repeat a word the teacher dictates and spell it aloud as they write it. Students also practice reading and blending sounds using the phonetic word cards. Very specific instructions are provided for teaching the sounding and blending of words. The teacher dictates a sentence; students repeat it and spell each word aloud as it is written. Single words are not dictated, only sentences. If there are nonphonetic words in a sentence, they are shown to the students to copy.

After students have learned enough words, they are introduced to phonic storybooks from a list provided by Traub. The reading is teacher-directed and is reinforced by phonetic word games. Students are also given the opportunity to dictate stories to the teacher and make their own books. To encourage reading for meaning, adults read to beginning readers and answer questions or discuss the reading with them.

Notes: The instructions with this method are detailed and sequenced. Activities are suggested throughout for students who have difficulty learning skills such as sound blending. A daily lesson structure is provided. Also, there is a good selection of readers, along with the location in the reading sequence at which they may be introduced. A section of the manual is devoted to older students in which the content is more age-appropriate. Spelling and vocabulary are taught using root words, prefixes, and affixes.

Traub recommends this approach for older students who have problems in spelling and/or reading. Regardless of age or skill level, all students start from the beginning of the program.

UNIFON

Method: Unifon

Author: John Malone

Source: Aukerman, R. C. (1984). *Approaches to beginning reading.* New York: John Wiley & Sons.

Description: The Unifon system is an alphabetic system designed to regularize the English language alphabet. It consists of 40

phonemic representations of the sounds in English. The goal of this approach is to create a system in which each word in the language can be spelled phonetically, and each sound is represented by only one symbol.

All symbols employ capital letters. Long vowels differ insofar as they have an additional horizontal line over them. All doubled letters become single letters in Unifon, if one of the two original letters is silent. All silent letters are eliminated. New Unifon symbols have been created for diphthongs and consonant pairs. No digraphs appear in the Unifon system, and all symbols, having both consonant and vowel sounds, are eliminated. Furthermore, all homonyms are spelled the same way, so that the reader must rely on contextual clues for understanding. Separate symbols have been developed for all remaining combination sounds.

Materials needed to teach the method include charts, a teacher's manual, a Unifon-traditional spelling dictionary, and a beginning text.

Notes: This method has been used for adults with limited English proficiency. Some effort has been made to combine this method with the Basic Language Skills Program (Aukerman, 1984) to create an adult reading program.

The Unifon system has not been widely accepted nor well researched. It places an additional burden on students with disabilities, who will eventually be required to make the transition to traditional English. Students who change schools while learning this system and are entered into a different program will be at a great disadvantage, especially if they are disabled. This system receives little attention in the current literature.

WHOLE LANGUAGE METHOD

Method: Whole Language Method

Authors: Kenneth Goodman, I. Liberman, and A. Liberman

Sources: Goodman, K. S. (1990). The past, present, and future of literacy education: Comments form the pen of distinguished educators, Part I. *The Reading Teacher, 43,* 302–311; Liberman, I., & Liberman. A. (1990). Whole language vs. code emphasis: Underlying assumptions and their implications for reading instruction. *Annals of Dyslexia, 40,* 51–78.

Description: The Whole Language method stresses the wholeness of the integrated language forms (i.e., reading, writing, and oral language) and values meaning in authentic speech and literacy events over language itself.

The philosophy of Whole Language is that active engagement in oral and written language will improve students' reading skills. The assumption is that *emergent literacy,* or the developing awareness of the interrelatedness of speech to writing, occurs naturally in young learners. Therefore, students, learning through the Whole Language method, begin to write as early as kindergarten, often before they learn to read.

The philosophy underlying the Whole Language Method is that, because children learn to talk without special drills or exercises, they will also learn to read simply through immersion in language and books from early childhood. Therefore, acquiring reading skills is part of a child's natural development, in much the same way as learning to walk.

Similarly, only meaningful materials are used to teach reading. The Whole Language method proposes that students will learn whole language more effectively than language broken into words, syllables, and isolated sounds. Students will learn phonics, or sound-symbol relationships naturally as they master the reading of meaningful whole passages.

Teachers who utilize the Whole Language approach can incorporate all of the recommended procedures and techniques, or they can choose to implement only those that are most appropriate for any given situation.

Notes: The Whole Language method is widely used in one form or another, often being incorporated into other instructional methods. Indeed, it has greatly influenced the reading curriculum in many schools.

This approach attempts to provide whole learners with a whole language learning methodology. However, it fails to address some of the concerns of students with reading disabilities and their teachers. It fails to address the language or motor difficulties of some students attempting to learn to write. It naturalizes the process of learning to read, although reading is not innate to humans in the same way, for example, as learning to talk. Therefore, it does not account for the many students who need direct intervention in order to understand the process of reading or for students who have underlying oral language disorders that prohibit them from learning to read "naturally." And finally, by valorizing whole language learning as natural learning, this method, in effect, stigmatizes the many students who need to learn decoding skills before they will learn to read.

For teaching students with reading disabilities, this method will be most useful if it is supplemented with a variety of other instructional approaches and the intensiveness and duration of instruction are calibrated to meet the needs of individual learners.

WORDS IN COLOR

Method: Words in Color

Author: Caleb Gattegno

Sources: Gattegno, C. (1969). *Reading with words in colour*. Berkshire, England: Cuisenaire Co.; Gattegno, C., & Hinman, D. (1966). Words in color: I. The morphologico-algebraic approach to teaching reading. II. The current status of words in color in the United States. In J. Money (Ed.), *The disabled reader: Education of the dyslexic child* (pp. 175–192). Baltimore: John Hopkins Press; Aukerman, R. C. (1985). *Approaches to beginning reading*. New York: John Wiley & Sons.

Description: Words in Color is a synthetic alphabet-phonics program that uses color to reinforce the sounds that comprise words. It is a multisensory, developmental approach for beginning readers that has also been used as a remedial method for students who have experienced reading failure in traditional programs.

This method identifies 48 English language phonemes, each depicted in a different color. Each sound is consistently represented by the same color, regardless of its spelling. For example, the long vowel sound "a," as in "hate," is colored sea green regardless of what other letter or letters are used to represent this sound. In the case of diphthongs, which merge two distinct sounds, such as in the word "quick," the upper half of "qu" is colored gold to represent the first sound /k/, and the lower half is colored light aqua to represent the second sound /w/.

This method's initial instruction uses activities that provide two visual clues, conventional letter configurations and color. There are 29 color-coded word charts that are essential to teaching this method. On the first 21 of these charts, there are 600 words that provide the phonic clues to reading. The remaining eight wall charts contain the phonic codes. The various spellings for each of the 48 sounds are arranged in 48 color-coded columns. The stated purpose of the colored wall charts is to prompt students and aid them in the transfer of this learning approach to traditional printed material. In addition to wall charts, books, cards, worksheets, and a detailed teacher's manual are provided.

This method integrates speech and writing. Phonics instruction is stressed; students learn the sounds of letters rather than letter names. Vowels are introduced one at a time using sound and color. Visual Dictation is used to teach the sound.

After vowels have been mastered, consonants are introduced but are not sounded in isolation. For example, the first consonant introduced is "p," which is written on the chalkboard in dark brown below the vowel sounds already mastered. The "p" is sounded only in combination with vowels. Visual Dictation continues, using combinations and reversals. The teacher points at three sounds in a sweeping movement to indicate the formation of closed, simple syllables.

The Word Building Book introduces words that students build from word tables. Oral dictation is also used with this book. Two sounds of the letter "s" are introduced: "s" as in "is" is colored lilac, and "s" as in "us" is lime green. The double "tt" was introduced previously in the same color as the single "t" to indicate the identity of its sound.

Visual Dictation 2 uses a wall chart with words that the teacher points to to form sentences. "The Game of Transformation" teaches students to change one word to another using one of four operations: **substitution**, such as "test" for "pest"; **reversal**, such as "pets" for "step"; **addition**, such as "step" to "steps"; and **insertion**, such as "pest" from "pet."

After word building exercises, students read short, isolated sentences. They are also introduced to oral dictation and writing. As students progress, they learn new letters and words, read primers and *The Book of Stories* and complete worksheets.

Notes: This multisensory approach may have certain advantages for some disabled students. However, it is not a total reading method. Phonics is taught in a systematic fashion, with much repetition and over-learning. It may be taught in groups or individually to students of any age. Its colors may be motivating for reluctant readers.

This method would not be appropriate for disabled students with auditory, perceptual, and associative problems or for students who have intellectual deficits. The need for students to establish the association between numerous colors and sounds may overwhelm many disabled learners. Students are required to make a transfer from color-coded material to standard print, a generalization that is difficult for many disabled learners to master. This method teaches decoding, with comprehension receiving less attention.

WRITING ROAD TO READING

Method: Writing Road to Reading

Authors: Romalda Spalding and Walter Spalding

Source: Spalding, R., & Spalding, W. (1986). *The writing road to reading: A modern method of phonics for teaching children to read.* New York: William Morrow.

Description: The Writing Road to Reading uses an integrated phonics method that stresses saying sounds and writing them, combining sounds into words, and pronouncing words. The Writing Road to Reading, originally called the Unified Phonics Method, was designed for regular classroom teachers to use at the nursery, kindergarten, or first grade levels. This method is also adaptable for remedial purposes.

Students learn the 70 phonograms and the 29 spelling rules. Writing (kinesthetic), listening (auditory), seeing (visual), and saying (vocal) activities are combined to teach phonograms and words. The Spal-

dings believe that, by teaching spelling prior to reading from books, learning remains in the spelling domain, and meaning, ostensibly the purpose of reading, remains in the province of reading.

The following principles underlie the Spalding method:

1. Spelling is the major deterrent to successful reading and writing in English. Students begin by learning 54 of the 70 common phonograms by saying sounds and writing them.

2. Students write sounds from dictation, saying the sounds of the 150 most frequently used words taken from the Extended Ayres List. Students demonstrate an understanding of words by writing and reading original sentences. Actual reading normally begins after approximately 2 months of instruction.

At the completion of first grade, average students will have learned the 70 phonograms, be able to write 700 of the most frequently used words, and be able to read many additional words. The 1,700 most frequently used words are the basis of word learning. By the time student have mastered the complete list (typically by fifth or sixth grade), they will have been introduced to most spelling problems.

The 70 common phonograms that students learn are letters or letter combinations that represent the 45 basic sounds in spoken English. Of the 70, two thirds have only one sound, 11 have two sounds, and 10 have three sounds. These phonograms are available on 6 × 4-inch cards with key words printed on the back for the teacher's use only. Students learn all of the pronunciations of a single phonogram in the order of their frequency of occurrence in the English language. Handwriting and spelling are integrated and taught with the phonograms.

Handwriting. Because handwriting is stressed from the beginning, the Spaldings include very specific instructions for body positioning and techniques for both left- and righthanded students. For beginning writers, 5/8-inch ruled paper is recommended; beyond second grade 3/8-inch ruled paper is used. For chalkboard writing, 3-inch ruled lines are drawn no higher than the top of a student's head.

To teach lower case manuscript letters, students are taught that all letters sit on a line and are comprised of straight lines and parts of the clock face. After lower case letters have been mastered, some capital letters are introduced. However, if a capital letter is used, students must be able to give the rule for using it.

When all 70 phonograms have been mastered in speech, writing, spelling, and reading, cursive writing is introduced (usually about mid-second grade). "Connected writing" is taught by having students write over the manuscript alphabet using these connecting lines. Once connected writing has been mastered, manuscript writing is no longer used.

Reading. The procedure for integrating handwriting with reading is as follows:

1. The teacher introduces the 26 single letter phonograms in a prescribed sequence, showing the phonogram card, saying each sound, and asking students to repeat each sound in unison. Students write each phonogram immediately after pronouncing it.
2. Students do not learn letter names. Likewise, phonograms containing two or more letters are learned according to their sounds.
3. Students are sent to the blackboard to review their lessons each day. Students who need extra drill are seated near the teacher and are taught the next lesson prior to presenting it to the entire class.
4. Students should be able to write the alphabet sounds from dictation and to recognize sounds when shown their letters.

Spelling. After students master the phonograms and the manuscript writing of the alphabet, spelling is introduced using the Extended Ayres List. The teacher pronounces words normally and uses them in sentences. Students say the phonograms or syllables aloud in unison as they write them. After each word is written, students read it aloud and visually check what they have written.

The most frequently used words are taught first, and most spelling patterns are introduced through word lists. Spelling rules are taught as the need arises; however, memorization is required when no spelling rule governs the choice of a phonogram. Students are introduced to easy books and original sentences after they have learned enough common words to comprehend reading passages fully.

Notebook. Students beyond the second grade keep notebooks which they use as references for phonograms, spelling rules, and pronunciation. Below the third grade, students are introduced to parts of the notebook through blackboard and chalkboard exercises. The purpose of these notebooks is carefully explained, and students of all ages are expected to know and use manuscript writing in their notebooks. The first seven pages are written in the notebook each year by the students. The Spaldings stress the need to teach the pages of the notebook carefully. Students are expected to refer to it continually whenever they are involved in learning activities.

Notes: The Writing Road to Reading is a teacher-directed, multisensory, total language arts approach that requires adherence to the teaching instructions provided. This method may be used with older students, but they are also required to start at the beginning and move as rapidly as possible through the program. Instructions are provided for use of this method with classrooms of students or with individuals. A self-teaching edition for home use is also available for parents.

The rapid pace of this method may discourage teachers from individualizing it. Without sufficient practice, students may not acquire the skills at the level of automaticity needed to become efficient readers.

The lack of controlled vocabulary may not give slow readers the repetitions they need to acquire a reading vocabulary. This method presupposes auditory competency; therefore, students with auditory-related problems, such as discrimination, may have difficulty learning with this method.

REFERENCES

Aukerman, R. C. (1984). *Approaches to beginning reading.* New York: John Wiley & Sons.

Chall, J. S., & Stahl, S. A. (1982). Reading. In H. E. Mitzel (Ed.), *Encyclopedia of educational research* (5th ed., pp. 1535–1559). New York: Free Press.

Fernald, G. (1988). *Remedial techniques in basic school subjects.* Austin, TX: Pro-Ed.

Gillingham, A., & Stillman, B. (1973). *Remedial training for children with specific disability in reading, spelling and penmanship.* Cambridge, MA: Educators Publishing, Inc.

Levine, M. (1994). *Educational care.* Cambridge, MA: Educators Publishing Service.

Orton, J. L. (1966). The Orton-Gillingham Approach. In J. Money (Ed.), *The disabled reader: Education of the dyslexic child* (pp. 119–145). Baltimore: John Hopkins Press.

Samuels, S. J. (1979). The method of repeated readings. *The Reading Teacher, 32,* 403–408.

Slingerland, B. (1989). *Slingerland Screening Test.* Cambridge, MA: Educators Publishing Service.

Traub, N., & Bloom, F. (1990). *Recipe for reading.* Cambridge, MA: Educators Publishing Service.

Van Allen, R., Venezky, R., & Hahn, H. (1975). *Language experiences in reading, level III: Teachers resource guide.* Chicago: Encyclopedia Britannica Educational Corp.

CHAPTER 9

Written Expression Methods

AvaJane Pickering, Ph.D.

CONTENTS

Handwriting Methods   174
▶ Left-Handed Writers'
   Accommodations   174
▶ The Johnson Handwriting Program   174
▶ Learning to Use Manuscript
   Handwriting and Learning to Use
   Cursive Handwriting   175
▶ Keyboarding Skills   175
▶ Progressive Approximation
   Procedure   176
▶ Manu-cursive   176
Spelling Methods   177
▶ Adaptation of Simultaneous Oral
   Spelling   177
▶ Horn Method   178
▶ The Cover-Write Methods   178
▶ Syllable Approach   179

▶ Corrective Spelling Through
   Morphographs   186
▶ Inventive Spelling   180
▶ Making Words   181
Written Composition Methods   181
▶ Clinical Teaching: Written Expression   181
▶ Step-by-Step Revising   183
▶ Strategies for Reluctant Writers   183
▶ Integrated Writing Strategy   185
▶ Computer Writing   185
▶ Integrated Method of Teaching
   Composition   187
▶ Phelps Sentence Guide   188
▶ Sentence Combining   189
▶ Writing Process   191
▶ Writing Fluency   192
▶ The Writer's Workshop   192

Written expression is the encoding of thoughts into words and discourse and is considered the most complex language task (Lerner, 1993). Levine (1994) believes that writing proficiency involves the automatic and precise synchronization of cognitive functions, including organizational skills, memory (declarative and active working), language ability (semantics, syntax, morphology, and pragmatics), graphic motor skills, attention (detailed and sustained), sophisticated ideation, and reasoning and problem-solving skills. In other words, an individual must simultaneously hold an idea in her or his head while formulating words and sentences. In addition, the student must manipulate a writing instrument to execute with exactness the graphic form of each letter. Therefore, in the traditional sequence of developmental language skills, writing is the last topic introduced (except in the whole language model). The subskills of written expression—such as handwriting, spelling, grammar, usage, proofreading, prewriting, mapping, vocabulary, and text structure—are taught using these methods. Sometimes skills are taught in isolation; other times an integrated approach is used.

HANDWRITING METHODS

LEFT-HANDED WRITERS' ACCOMMODATIONS

Method: Left-Handed Writers' Accommodations

Author: H. Howell

Source: Howell, H. (1978). Write on, you sinistrals! *Language Arts, 55*, 852–856.

Description: This method allows left-handed students to adjust their writing techniques designed to fit their unique writing style. Left-handed students should be encouraged to hold the pencil slightly differently from right-handed students, approximately 1 inch higher up on the pencil. Moreover, they should not be taught to hook their wrists when writing; if they already hook their wrists, however, teachers should not attempt to reteach them.

Left-handed students should also be encouraged to slant their papers slightly to the right when they write in cursive. Furthermore, teachers should allow students to slant their letters in a way that makes individual students comfortable in their technique. Many left-handed writers, unlike right-handed students, commonly write their cursive letters either vertically or slanting slightly backwards.

Notes: This program works well for individuals who are left-handed and who are required to write in cursive.

THE JOHNSON HANDWRITING PROGRAM

Method: The Johnson Handwriting Program

Authors: Warren T. Johnson and Mary R. Johnson

Source: Johnson, W. T., & Johnson, M. R. (1986). *The Johnson handwriting program manual.* Cambridge, MA: Educators Publishing Service.

Description: This method is a cursive writing program that emphasizes neuromuscular control strokes that assist students in developing an efficient handwriting technique and a mature style. In addition to simply learning cursive handwriting, students can progress through other manuals provided by this program: *Beginning Connected, Cursive Handwriting* (Levels 1–3), *Let's Print and Spell*, and *Let's Write and Spell*.

Students begin to learn a letter by tracing it in the air or in their books. They write the letter alone, in double-letter combinations, and then in words. These steps are sequential and consist of letters that students have learned already.

Supplementary handwriting and phonetic spelling approaches are designed to assist students with learning disabilities. These supplemental approaches combine perceptual skills with neuromuscular skills to reinforce the learning of handwriting—first as printing and then as cursive—and spelling.

Notes: These programs work together to take students from beginning printing through to the mastery of cursive writing. It is an effective approach for students who can learn both manuscript and cursive, but who also need more intensive practice and a more tightly structured program.

LEARNING TO USE MANUSCRIPT AND CURSIVE HANDWRITING

Method: Learning to Use Manuscript Handwriting and Learning to Use Cursive Handwriting

Authors: Beth H. Slingerland and Marty Alto

Sources: Slingerland, B. H., & Alto, M. (1985). *Learning to use manuscript handwriting.* Cambridge, MA: Educators Publishing, Inc.; Slingerland, B. H., & Alto, M. (1985). *Learning to use cursive handwriting.* Cambridge, MA: Educators Publishing, Inc.

Description: This is a two-part multisensory approach to teaching manuscript or cursive handwriting whose parts can be taught either separately or concurrently. Each of the two parts of this program con-

tains three kinds of materials. A **manual** gives instructions for introducing, teaching, drill and exercise, and reviews all the upper and lower case letters. **Duplicate masters** contain the letter forms and lined and patterned writing paper to practice writing. **All cards** show all the upper and lower case letters individually.

Notes: This program is designed for students who learn with multisensory materials. Consistency is a significant component of this program.

KEYBOARDING SKILLS

Method: Keyboarding Skills

Author: Diana Hanbury King

Source: King, D. H. (1986). *Manual keyboarding skills.* Cambridge, MA: Educators Publishing Service.

Description: This is a multisensory touch typing program that teaches students of all ages how to type quickly and easily. They learn the alphabetic sequence with simultaneous oral spelling. By naming the letter out loud while pressing a key, students establish a conditioned reflex according to King. Students who utilize this method will make rapid progress, whether they are currently enrolled in computer or conventional typing classes. After they have learned the alphabet (typically this can be done in under an hour), students practice typing words, phrases, sentences, numbers, symbols, and punctuation.

Notes: Keyboarding is a life-skills task. This keyboarding program has proven to be successful. It allows students who employ multisensory learning techniques to achieve success, even when individuals have slow processing speeds.

PROGRESSIVE APPROXIMATION PROCEDURE

Method: Progressive Approximation Procedure

Author: Alan M. Hofmeister

Source: Hofmeister, A. M. (1973). Let's get it write. Five common instructional errors in teaching writing. *Teaching Exceptional Children, 6*, 30–33.

Description: The Progressive Approximation Procedure method is a four-step instructional approach to handwriting designed to eliminate mistakes. This method uses a worksheet with a writing model that includes several blank lines for practice. Students are directed to perform the following four-step procedure:

1. Students copy the model on the first blank practice line in pencil and notify the teacher when they are done.
2. The teacher corrects the worksheet and highlights only letters or words that need improvement.
3. Students erase only the incorrect portions of letters or words designated by the teacher and then trace over the entire word or letter.
4. Students proceed to the next blank line and repeat the portions in need of improvement.

These steps can be repeated as often as necessary for students to attain handwriting mastery. In addition, models can be used to accommodate manuscript or cursive letters or short sentences. Moreover, this method provides students with both immediate feedback and practice specific to their individual needs.

Notes: This method provides students with correct practices and can be used across curricula. It can be applied to reading and writing and to life skills. However, it can also be time-consuming.

MANU-CURSIVE

Method: Manu-cursive

Authors: Donald N. Thurber and Rosa Hagin

Sources: Thurber, D.N. (1984). *D'Nealian manuscript: A continuous stroke approach to handwriting.* Novato, CA: Academic Therapy; Hagin, R. (1983). Write right—or left. *Journal of Learning Disabilities, 16*, 266-271.

Description: These approaches teach writing styles that stress the shared motor patterns required to write in manuscript or cursive. The D'Nealian writing style is an example of Manu-cursive writing. It is a continuous-stroke method whose letters are designed to be written with minimal movement. It also employs visual, auditory, and tactile-kinesthetic clues that aid the memory process and ease learning.

The D'Nealian method provides several steps that can be followed in teaching letter formation:

1. The teacher tells students a letter name.
2. The teacher writes the letter in the air and describes aloud the directions for writing it.
3. The teacher and students repeat the directions together while simultaneously writing it in the air.
4. Students practice this letter in short words. Students are expected to make mistakes; therefore, they are discouraged from erasing their work.

Additional steps can be added to this approach to assist students who have difficulty recalling letter formation patterns. For example, the teacher can trace the letter on a student's hand or back while describing its formation. Students, too, can repeat this process by describing the directions while tracing the letter on the teacher's hand.

This approach can be particularly effective in teaching students with learning disabilities. It (a) provides audio descriptions of letter formations; (b) reduces the strokes and eliminates some of the parts required to form letters; (c) increases discrimination among letters; (d) allows for an easy transition from manuscript to cursive; and (d) promotes the acceptance of individuality. The D'Nealian approach provides numbers and both upper and lower case letters, and a recommended phraseology. However, teachers are encouraged to modify the descriptions of letter formations as needed.

Hagin devised a simplified Manu-cursive approach designed for students who have difficulty learning cursive. It focuses on vertical rather than slanted downstrokes and employs instructional motifs designed, for example, to teach joining strokes and pivoting movements.

This approach uses the following five-step technique to practice letter formation:

1. Students trace a letter on a transparency positioned over a printed model.
2. Students write the letter on a transparency positioned over printed lines designed to help students form letters.
3. Students place the transparency with the letter they have written over the original printed model to evaluate their work.
4. Students record the letter they wrote and the motifs they used to practice them.
5. Students continue to copy and participate in spontaneous writing.

This approach may be useful for students who have difficulty manipulating slanted letters and prefer to write their cursive letters with a vertical orientation.

Notes: This method can be beneficial for students with weak motor, memory, visual and auditory skills. However, there may be some students for whom this method may be too complex (e.g., its motifs that teach joining strokes); these students will probably need to use manuscript.

SPELLING METHODS

ADAPTATION OF SIMULTANEOUS ORAL SPELLING

Method: Adaptation of Simultaneous Oral Spelling

Author: L. Bradley

Source: Bradley, L. (1983). The organization of visual, phonological, and motor strategies in learning to read and to spell. In U. Kirk (Ed.), *Neuropsychology of language, reading, and spelling* (pp. 235–254). New York: Academic Press.

Description: The Adaptation of Simultaneous Oral Spelling method is a multisensory approach designed to provide remediation in spelling. This method establishes one-to-one correspondences between the sounds of spoken language and the written symbols that represent them. In the following six-step process students:

1. Select a word.
2. Write the word out or form it using plastic letters.
3. Pronounce the word.
4. Name each letter of the word as they spell it.
5. Pronounce the word again and verify its spelling; repeat steps 2 through 5 twice.
6. Follow this procedure to practice the word for 6 consecutive days.

By establishing one-to-one correspondences, the Adaptation of Simultaneous Oral Spelling method teaches students to (a) label the sounds of speech and their letters, (b) discriminate between different sounds and letters, (3) recall the discrete relationships of specific sounds and letters, and (4) organize them into the sequences that make up words.

Notes: This method accommodates the effective use of auditory memory skills. It allows for words to be spelled without having to be written, and it promotes immediate feedback, since students spell words aloud. Although this method works best for students with weak visual memory skills, it may also function to strengthen and build visual memory through the repetitive use of auditory memory skills. Furthermore, this method can be used with any word list. However, this method may be difficult to master for students who rely primarily on their visual memory skills.

HORN METHOD

Method: Horn Method

Author: E. Horn

Source: Horn, E. (1954). *Teaching spelling.* Washington, DC: American Educational Research Association.

Description: The Horn Method is designed to provide remediation in spelling, particularly for students who overdetermine visual cues in their learning approach. This method focuses on word pronunciation and on teaching the sound sequences that make up the phonic structures of words.

In the Horn Method, students go through the following eight-step process. Students:

1. carefully pronounce each word.
2. examine each word as they pronounce it.
3. say each letter of the word in sequence.

4. recall the word from memory and spell it orally.
5. check their spelling of the word.
6. write the word.
7. check their spelling again.
8. if necessary, all steps can be repeated.

The Horn Method attempts to teach sound sequencing and careful pronunciation as spelling techniques to students who already employ visual techniques but who nevertheless lack spelling proficiency.

Notes: This method provides a systematized spelling system that can be effective for some students with learning disabilities. However, for other students, it may not be detailed enough to benefit them.

THE COVER-WRITE METHODS

Method: The Cover-Write Methods

Authors: Samuel A. Kirk and James C. Chalfant

Source: Kirk, S. A., & Chalfant, J. C. (1984). *Academic and developmental learning disabilities.* Denver: Love.

Description: The Cover-Write Methods are approaches designed to provide remediation in spelling, particularly for students who have difficulty visualizing words. The approach that Kirk and Chalfant describe combines visual, oral, and kinesthetic modalities.

The Cover-Write Method described by Kirk and Chalfant uses the following 11-step approach:

1. The teacher selects a word, writes it on a card, and pronounces it.
2. Students look at the word and pronounce it.

3. Students look at the word, vocalize the name or sound of each letter, and trace each letter of the word in the air.
4. The word is removed; students pronounce the word and trace it in the air.
5. If necessary, repeat step 3.
6. Students continue to trace the word in the air and to pronounce it until they are prepared to write it.
7. Students write the word from memory and pronounce it. If students write the word incorrectly, they can continue to trace it.
8. Students are taught a new word following the same procedure.
9. Students trace the first word and write it repeatedly from memory.
10. Students record the word in a notebook for later review.
11. Students use these words in any number of various writing assignments.

By tracing the words in the air, students employ large muscle movements that may reinforce word retention. However, this kinesthetic technique does not provide students with distinct visual imagery of words. Teachers can better use visual imagery by modifying the kinesthetic function and having students trace over the words themselves.

Notes: This method employs the multisensory memory skills involved in the task of spelling. Because it can be broken down into smaller steps, this program can be modified easily to fit the needs of individual learners; writing can be done, for example, on a computer or on paper instead of in the air. However, this method can also be time-consuming, and some teachers may find some parts of this method difficult to implement.

SYLLABLE APPROACH

Method: Syllable Approach

Author: Regina Cicci

Source: Cicci, R. (1980). Written language disorders. *Bulletin of the Orton Society, 30,* 240–251.

Description: The Syllable Approach method is designed for remediation in spelling, particularly for students with auditory processing difficulties. The method isolates word parts by teaching students to disassemble and assemble words by syllables. This method assumes that students will progress from syllable recognition to recognition of the words these syllables comprise.

The Syllable Approach requires the teacher to present students with syllables printed on flash cards. Students examine each flash card and say the corresponding syllable after the teacher pronounces it. Students practice and learn many syllables separately. Syllables are then placed in sequence together to form words. Students see the words, hear them, and pronounce them themselves. The words are gradually introduced on paper, divided into their constitutive syllables, and typed.

The process of spelling words is similar to the flash card approach. Students hear a word, pronounce it themselves by its syllables, and then write the word in syllables. If students are unable to divide words into syllables, the teacher can pronounce words by their separate syllables as students write them down. The Syllable Approach method is most effective when teaching words that have consistent, regular grapheme-phoneme correspondences.

Notes: This method provides students with a system that allows them to spell multisyllablic words. It can also be used across many curricula with students of all ages. However, some students who have difficulty sequencing will be unable to follow the appropriate order of syllables needed to reconstruct words.

CORRECTIVE SPELLING THROUGH MORPHOGRAPHS

Method: Corrective Spelling Through Morphographs

Authors: Robert Dixon and Siegfried Engelmann

Source: Dixon, R., & Engelmann, S. (1980). *Corrective spelling through morphographs.* Chicago: Science Research Associates.

Description: Corrective Spelling Through Morphographs is an intensive 1-year program for learners from the fourth grade through adulthood. It is designed for students and adults who have not experienced success with other spelling approaches. This method includes 140 twenty-minute lessons that cover more than 12,000 words, including numerous problem words.

Corrective Spelling Through Morphographs teaches students basic units of meaning in written language, called "morphographs," which are always spelled the same. By employing morphographs—word bases, prefixes, and suffixes—students learn strategies that build and improve their spelling skills. Students master a variety of these morphographs and a manageable set of rules for combining them. At the same time, they learn analytical techniques and rules of generalization that can be applied to words in this program and outside of it.

Notes: This program adds a language morphology component as a strategy designed to strengthen the traditional components of phonemic awareness and visual memory. It is especially beneficial for individuals who use language effectively and can reason well enough to know when to apply its rules.

INVENTIVE SPELLING

Method: Inventive Spelling

Authors: Michael Tanner and Faye Bolton

Sources: Tanner, M. (1992). *Classroom research by classroom teachers.* Flagstaff: Northern Arizona University Reprographics; Bolton, F., & Snowball, D. (1993). *Ideas for spelling.* Portsmouth, NH: Heinemann; Goodman, K. S. (1990). The past, present and future of literacy education: Comments from the pen of distinguished educators, Part I. *The Reading Teacher, 43,* 302–311.

Description: Kenneth Goodman's whole language movement in writing instruction emphasizes the communicative role of writing over its mechanically correct application. A significant component of this whole writing methodology is Inventive Spelling. Inventive Spelling promotes the acquisition of spelling skills through the natural development of language learning. It attempts to increase children's exposure to language by immersing them in different communicative positions, as listeners, talkers, readers, and writers. The rigors of spelling can negatively impact the process of writing and the development of writing skills. Therefore, individuals are asked to write words without regard for conventional spelling correctness. In this way, the task of spelling correctly will not discourage learners from attempting to write. Furthermore, the immersive approach this method employs will allow many students to improve their spelling skills simply as an effect of developing their overall language skills.

Notes: This method can be effective in encouraging reluctant students to write. In addition, older students and adults can use it effectively with computers, particularly when the spell check is used. This allows learners to observe corrections visually. These visual cues can also strengthen and improve memory.

This method may not be effective for some students with learning disabilities. It does not promote visual memory for students with memory deficits. It does not stress the phoneme-grapheme relationship necessary to understand phonics approaches; and it encourages wrong spelling practices. In addition, students with language disabilities who do not have whole language capabilities and need intensive direct instruction may not be able to participate effectively in this method's immersion approach.

MAKING WORDS

Method: Making Words

Authors: James W. Cunningham and Patricia M. Cunningham

Source: Cunningham, P. M., & Cunningham, J. W. (1992). Making words: Enhanced the invented spelling-decoding connection. *Reading Teacher, 46,* 106–115.

Description: Making Words is a spelling method designed to assist students in developing phonemic awareness and a working knowledge of how the alphabet operates. This method is designed to be used as a supplement to regular writing activities.

For this task the teacher selects several eight-letter words that should be of some interest to students. The teacher makes lists of 12 to 15 smaller words that can be made from the eight letters of each primary eight-letter word. The teacher gives students the eight letters of a primary word in a scrambled order. The students are instructed to assemble two- and three-letter words from their letter groups. Longer and longer words can be made, and eventually students will be asked to discover and assemble the original word from which their letters are derived.

The other smaller words that can be formed from the primary eight-letter word should possess the following characteristics: They should conform to patterns the teacher wishes to stress. For example, there should be instances when words can be formed by rearranging the same letters in different places, showing students the importance of ordering letters when spelling words. The primary words should also be divisible into smaller and larger words. In addition, their letters should be usable to form proper names so that students can practice capital letters. The derived words should also be words that are already part of students' listening vocabularies. Besides these word characteristics, teachers need to focus on the operation of letter patterns, modeling, and explaining to students how rearranging just two letters in a word or substituting only one letter for another, changes the word.

Notes: This Making Words spelling task can be performed by individual students, or it can be an activity that involves the entire class as participants with the teacher prompting students and directing the activity at the head of the class. For example, the letters can be displayed on the chalkboard and smaller letters distributed to students. In this way, different students can present various words to the class or groups of students can collaborate to form different words.

WRITTEN COMPOSITION METHODS

CLINICAL TEACHING: WRITTEN EXPRESSION

Method: Clinical Teaching: Written Expression

Authors: Doris Johnson and Helmer Myklebust

Source: Johnson, D., & Myklebust, H. (1967). *Learning disabilities: Education principles and practices.* New York: Grune & Stratton.

Description: The Clinical Teaching: Written Expression method is a remediation approach that focuses on disorders of formulation and syntax. This method was developed for students who can communicate orally, copy, revisualize, spell, and comprehend what they read, but who are otherwise unable to put their thoughts on paper meaningfully.

Clinical Teaching: Written Expression has five procedural steps designed to help students improve their compositional skills: (a) awareness of errors, (b) ideation and productivity, (c) concrete to abstract ideas, (d) punctuation, and (e) grammar.

To improve **error awareness**, students write sentences and listen to a teacher read them aloud. When students identify errors, corrections are made. Students then read the sentences aloud and silently. To encourage **ideation** and **productivity** in written expression, the teacher must provide a classroom environment that is conducive to spontaneous verbal interaction. Verbal language is converted into writing in the Clinical Teaching: Written Expression approach. For example, students talk about their experiences, feelings, and emotions and then incorporate them into written compositions.

In addition, this method employs four hierarchical stages to help students advance in their writing from considering **concrete to abstract ideas**. In the **concrete-descriptive** stage, students write simple sentences describing the attributes of size, space, and color or the general appearance of various objects. Pictures can be used to stimulate ideas and encourage more complex thinking.

In the **concrete-imaginative** stage, students attempt to extract meaning from pictures or experiences. In the **abstract-descriptive** stage, students first develop stories in more detail and then develop concepts of chronology and sequence. Film strips or picture sequences can be used to teach these concepts and to encourage students to think about them. Students can produce simple plays using a tape recorder; students assume character roles, record a conversation, and transcribe it.

In the final stage, the **abstract-imaginative** stage, students develop stories that incorporate plot, setting, continuity, occasional figures of speech, and some reference to moral values. Teachers need to be involved to motivate students and assist them in developing imaginative and interesting narratives.

In addition, activities are described for teaching students **punctuation** and **grammar**. Some students will need to be taught the significance, names, and positions of various punctuation marks. Furthermore, students with written expression disorders may also need special help with grammar. Exercises use concrete imagery to teach nouns, verbs, adjectives, and adverbs. Students also construct their own books or outlines that use pictures and words to denote parts of speech.

Notes: The Clinical Teaching: Written Expression method may be used with students of normal intelligence who have written language disorders. Because it is a teacher-directed method that builds on students' experiences, it is appropriate for "turned-off" students who have previously experienced failure in written expression tasks. This method promotes teaching to the readiness levels of students and considers the rate and amount of writing relevant to each student's needs. In addition, the procedures for teaching the symbol systems of punctuation and grammar may be helpful for students with visual-spatial problems. For example, exercises are designed to teach the names and locations of the various punctuation marks.

Although the psychoneurological basis of this method has been challenged, its procedures can enhance the ideation and productivity of written expression. Furthermore, creative teachers can adapt this method to accommodate it to their own teaching philosophies.

This method relies heavily on the "translation" of experience into auditory language and then to written expression. Therefore, to benefit fully from this method, students must have adequate auditory and visual processing skills, motor skills, and language skills. Where language deficits are noted, remediation must occur before this method can be applied. This method promotes structural grammar over alternate systems. Because it is not a total method, teachers will need to develop the materials and teaching strategies. Further information on Clinical Teaching can be found in the chapter on Seminal Methods.

STEP-BY-STEP REVISING

Method: Step-by-Step Revising

Author: B. L. Cohen

Source: Cohen, B. L. (1985). Writing: A new approach to the revision process. *Academic Therapy, 20,* 587–589.

Description: The Step-by-Step Revising method is a revision process used with high school age students with learning disabilities. This structured approach provides students with many opportunities for instructor feedback and opportunities to revise their work. Students use the following seven-step process:

1. Students complete a writing assignment.
2. The teacher comments on the first draft without making corrections.
3. Students read their papers aloud to other students.
4. Students receive feedback from the other students and then reorganize and revise their papers.
5. Students complete a second draft, which the teacher corrects by marking with a check on the lines containing an error. Teachers can designate lines containing more than one error with numbers that correspond to the number of errors in a line.
6. Students make the corrections the teacher has indicated and complete a third draft of their papers. Teachers make additional corrections and final comments.
7. Students complete their final drafts, taking the teacher's comments into consideration and making corrections.

The Step-by-Step Revising method is intended to be employed with many writing assignments. By incorporating it throughout an academic year, its process can be learned. In addition, students may choose from their final drafts one paper to revise further and complete as a final writing assignment that incorporates accumulated and refined revisions. This method, with its prescriptive structure and its focus on repeated revisions, may be useful in teaching revising skills to students with language learning disabilities.

Notes: This approach provides students with immediate feedback from several sources (teacher and students). It also generates a more diverse writing experience by requiring students to distribute their writing to other students for peer review, and to the teacher. Furthermore, because feedback comes from various sources, students may derive a broader perspective from the feedback they receive. However, some students may not have an appropriate critical background to evaluate the content or skill levels of their peers' writing. In addition, some sensitive students may react negatively to exposing their work to the critical scrutiny of their peers.

STRATEGIES FOR RELUCTANT WRITERS

Method: Strategies for Reluctant Writers

Author: Gerard Giordano

Sources: Giordano, G. (1982). CATS exercises: Teaching disabled writers to communicate. *Academic Therapy, 18,* 233-237; Giordano, G. (1983). Readiness skills for disabled writers. *Academic Therapy, 18,* 315-319.

Description: Strategies for Reluctant Writers was designed to help students develop beginning writing skills. By building on these fundamental skills, it also attempts to develop fluency, or the ability to write simple declarative sentences with ease. Furthermore, this method asserts that getting students to write is the first goal when working primarily with reluctant writers. Skills are carefully sequenced from simple to complex, emphasizing the gradual progression through levels of communicative competency. In addition, this method privileges personal content in writing activities.

Giordano provides prewriting and remedial exercises intended for use with reluctant writers or students with limited writing skills. The following are sample activities:

1. *Scribbling.* This prepares students for the motor movements required for handwriting. Practice may begin as simply as fingerpainting and move to the use of pencils or crayons. The teacher can model either manuscript or cursive writing.

2. *Imitation.* Students copy words or parts of words. The teacher may write down what students say to them and then have students copy part of their dialogue.

3. *Tracing.* Students dictate sentences, and the teacher transcribes them. Students select one or two words from these sentences and trace them with a yellow marker.

4. *Completion.* The teacher writes a sentence and says the words as they are written. The teacher then pauses before the final word of the sentence and has students choose an appropriate response from one or two word cards.

5. *Automatic Writing.* The teacher chooses a word that students can easily write, for example, their first names. Students write their names next to their favorite items in a list or catalog. Students can also choose from among written sentences and write their names beside their favorite one.

6. *Ordered Writing.* The teacher might have students describe in writing the beginning, middle, and end of an experience. This activity is designed to develop passage comprehension.

7. *Incomplete Sentence Exercises.* The teacher presents students with various incomplete sentences. Initially, possible responses can be provided for them to choose from; later they can create their own.

8. *Paraphrasing.* Students can write synopses of lower grade books for other students who have difficulty reading. Or students can rewrite various sentences for different reading audiences.

9. *Dialogue.* Students write dialogue for cartoon or fictional characters. Cartoons can be provided for them by deleting the dialogue from newspaper cartoons and enlarging them. Students could then fill in the deleted dialogue with their own.

10. *Correspondence.* Students write in personal notebooks. The teacher reads these notebooks and responds to their content. The teacher can direct individual students appropriately or model writing strategies for them.

Once students have developed some interest in writing and have acquired some basic skills, they can engage in other activities that will increase their participation. Activities are designed to improve students' automaticity, ability to manipulate written syntax, and construction of both simple and more complex sentence patterns. Giordano asserts that writing develops naturally if students are provided with opportunities to explore and record their personal experiences for others to share. Gradually, as writing fluency increases, students will give much of their attention to expressing more complicated ideas.

Notes: This method divides the writing skills into small increments, which simultaneously allows students to experience immediate success and teachers to ascertain where any trouble spots in the writing process occur. This program can also be modified for students who do not progress adequately by substituting keyboarding for handwriting.

INTEGRATED WRITING STRATEGY

Method: Integrated Writing Strategy

Author: Edwin S. Ellis

Sources: Ellis, E. S. (1994). Integrated writing strategy instruction with content-area instruction: Part I—Orienting student to organizational devices. *Intervention in School and Clinic, 29,* 169–179; Ellis, E. S. (1994). Integrated writing strategy instruction with content-area instruction: Part II—Writing processes. *Intervention in School and Clinic, 29,* 219–228.

Description: This method attempts to assist students with writing difficulties to develop and organize their thoughts prior to writing. It relies on cognitive mapping, or webbing, and graphic organizers to indicate important ideas and their relationships to other ideas. These modalities also function as excellent planning sheets for organizing writing ideas.

Students are encouraged to list their ideas quickly and then to expand, organize, and structure them. Teachers construct graphic organizers to help students begin to recognize relationships among ideas. Students also begin to recognize common organizational patterns, text structures, and rhetorical strategies (e.g., compare and contrast or cause and effect).

Initially, teachers must model and cue students with the use of organizers. Gradually, however, they will learn to use these strategies independently. Mapping, for example, begins with brainstorming. Its purpose is to increase background knowl-edge, which also assists students in retrieving prior knowledge. During the brainstorming or free association stage, the focus is on divergent thinking and the rapid generation of ideas. Value judgments are not made at this stage, as all ideas are viewed as pertinent and worthwhile. The following steps may be used to introduce graphic organizers:

1. During brainstorming, students write one- or two-word cues to represent concepts or ideas as they are generated.
2. When no more ideas are being generated, students return to their cues and elaborate the ideas they represent.
3. Students can group or categorize ideas and then color code them.
4. Or students can write their ideas on a graphic organizer developed for their particular textual and rhetorical strategy (e.g., compare and contrast).
5. Students develop paragraphs for each category and expand on their ideas.

As students become more familiar with the use of cognitive mapping and graphic organizers, teachers can help them to categorize their ideas as they generate them. Once students have mastered the construction of their own organizers, they benefit from explaining their topic ideas to others and organizing their ideas.

Notes: This method benefits individuals who gain from visual organization presentations. Once individuals have learned to use cognitive mapping and graphic organizers for their own writing, they can then use this technique for classes, such as history and science.

COMPUTER WRITING

Method: Computer Writing

Authors: Catherine Cobb Morocco and Susan B. Neuman

Source: Morocco, C. C., & Neuman, S. B. (1986). Word processors and the acquisition of writing strategies. *Journal of Learning Disabilities, 19*(4), 243–247.

Description: Computer Writing uses word processing as a tool for teaching writing to students who have difficulty with written composition. It provides an easy way to edit writing; it stimulates social communication, which in turn generates ideas for writing; and it enhances self-esteem. For these reasons, Computer Writing has evolved as a method that uses computers to teach the writing process.

Typically, teachers focus attention on strictly mechanical errors in writing. However, they might better serve their students by giving greater attention to the process of writing, because it is the process that students with learning disabilities are unable to master. Morocco and Neuman contend that these students are unable to master the writing process because they lack the cognitive strategies to implement it. In fact, it is the ability to apply cognitive strategies to the writing process that distinguishes successful from unsuccessful learners. The Computer Writing method uses computers to adapt the teaching of the writing process to students with writing disabilities.

Many students with learning difficulties have trouble planning a writing project. Frequently, they are unable to generate ideas, formulate topics, anticipate audiences, and organize information. To begin to correct these inabilities, students initiate their writing by brainstorming on a word processor. The authors assert that students are more willing to take risks on computers; therefore, students make more frequent attempts at generating ideas. Collaborative brainstorming is also encouraged.

In addition, the "public" nature of the word processor allows the teacher to participate in the process in a positive but unobtrusive manner. The teacher can encourage students to ignore editing and to focus, instead, on generating words and phrases that develop an idea or concept. The teacher might raise pertinent questions or type insightful responses on the word processor to direct and model the writing process. To help students explore their own ideas and better express them, a teacher might read aloud to students what they have already written. Teachers can ask questions that seek to clarify the students' ideas or help students to elaborate their ideas. The teacher's role in this process is to be interactive without being intrusive.

With Computer Writing, students compose their writing projects on the computer. The computer facilitates the process of composition because its features allow students to reorganize and physically rearrange their texts with little effort. For students who are learning to explore ideas and organize thoughts, using a word processor to edit sentences and organize paragraphs diffuses the frustration and alleviates the sense of drudgery they sometimes feel. The teacher can discuss ways to organize a composition and direct students on how to use sentences to develop and pursue ideas. The students can use the word processor to organize and reorganize their compositions as they work toward sequencing their thoughts logically and completing them. On the word processor corrections and revisions are quickly and easily made.

Notes: The advantages of using the computer are twofold. First, the writing process is simplified because editing is easier. Second, the public nature of the computer allows the teacher to monitor students in the writing process and to act as an audience, providing vital feedback to students about their work.

Conversely, teachers may be tempted to use the computer only as an editing tool and overlook its importance in developing the writing process. In addition, equipment is expensive, and each student must have access to one to use this method effectively.

Morocco and Neuman conclude that computers do not automatically engage the student in the learning process. If students use computers to compose interesting first drafts, they appear to remain engaged in the writing process. However, if computers are used only to practice writing drills or to focus on editing during the draft stage, students tend to disengage from the writing process. Intervention too early to correct problems with writing mechanics during the process of composition may inhibit the students' creative thinking.

INTEGRATED METHOD OF TEACHING COMPOSITION

Method: Integrated Method of Teaching Composition

Author: William Kerrigan

Source: Kerrigan, W. J. (1979). *Writing to the point: Six basic steps* (2nd ed). New York: Harcourt Brace Jovanovich.

Description: The Integrated Method of Teaching Composition is a six-step process designed to help students produce written compositions. This method provides students with specific information about how to develop word connections, phrases, clauses, sentences, and how to use contrast to develop ideas.

The Integrated Method is designed to teach students to integrate the constitutive elements of composition while generating a composition. This method is procedural and focuses on both the structural and thematic elements of composition. Students are taught, for example, to construct a thematic sentence before beginning the composition. Likewise, for each paragraph, they write a topic sentence that is thematic and relates to or elaborates on the initial thematic sentence. Students then write detailed sentences within each paragraph that develop that paragraph's topic sentence.

The Integrated Method uses the following six-step process as a clear, methodical approach to teaching students the elements of composition. Students:

1. Write a simple, declarative sentence. This sentence should be thematic (i.e., it should express an idea or contain a theme); it should allow for elaboration. The sentence should begin with a subject, make only one statement, and contain no detail.

2. Write three sentences about the first sentence. Each of these three sentences must relate directly and clearly to the idea or theme expressed in the target sentence. They are intended to elaborate the target sentence. It is useful, therefore, to point out and explain words vital to the relationship between these expository sentences and the sentence they are elaborating. In addition, students should be encouraged at this point to ask questions about the sentence they are elaborating.

3. Write four or five additional sentences about each of the three elaborative sentences generated in step 2. Step 3 is an elaboration of step 2. Sentences in this step should follow the same elaborative procedure as sentences in step 2. In addition, they should continue to maintain an expository relationship to the initial target sentence.

4. Make specific, concrete statements about each four or five sentences generated in step 3. Students should add details to sentences that provide them with color, interest, and rhetorical vitality. At this point, students should be encouraged to use examples and anecdotes without straying from the central theme. This step is particularly helpful in building vocabulary while developing writing skills.

5. Write a clear, transitional statement about the preceding paragraph in the first sentence of the paragraph that follows. Effectively teaching this procedure will help students to link their thoughts in a chain-like progression, not only between sentences in a paragraph, but between the paragraphs in a composition.

6. Write sentences that refer clearly to the sentences that immediately precede them. This can be done by repeating words, using synonyms and antonyms, or by using pronouns that refer to antecedents in the preceding sentence.

Notes: The Integrated Method of Teaching Composition is appropriate for teaching regular and remedial students from junior high school through college. This method is useful for adolescents with writing disabilities because it is structured and provides opportunities for students to use their creative ideas and experiences in writing. The method also provides opportunities for students to build their vocabularies.

This method presupposes enough cognitive ability to generate and elaborate on ideas. Students with good abstract verbal abilities should benefit from it. The steps may need to be written out in simplified form and distributed to students who can refer to them until they internalize the process.

PHELPS SENTENCE GUIDE

Method: Phelps Sentence Guide

Authors: Trisha Phelps-Gunn and Diana Phelps-Terasaki

Sources: Phelps-Gunn, T., & Phelps-Terasaki D. (1982). *Written language instruction: Theory and remediation.* Rockville, MD: Aspen Systems Corporation; Phelps-Teraski, D. & Phelps, T. (1980). *Teaching written expression: The Phelps sentence guide program.* Novato, CA: Academic Therapy.

Description: The Phelps Sentence Guide is an adaptation of the Straight Language/-Fitzgerald Key and uses an interactive approach to teach language skills. The Phelps method teaches students to generate sentences in a communicative context. This approach stresses the purpose of communi-

cating clearly in writing as it teaches the important relationship of proper structure to coherent and meaningful content.

Like the Fitzgerald Key (Fitzgerald, 1949), the Phelps Sentence Guide consists of columns, each of which corresponds to a word class (e.g., nouns, verbs, etc.). However, unlike the Fitzgerald Key, which employs a geometric symbol system, the Phelps method uses separate columns for different language elements, such as nouns and verbs. These are labeled according to their functions.

The Phelps Sentence Guide attempts to internalize the process of structuring sentences through practice in an interactive forum. This method seeks to inculcate in students a process of writing that is coherent and that functions for the student almost automatically. Building upon Laura Lee's (1975) interactive approach to teaching oral language, this method incorporates teacher-directed interactions into its writing program. For example, a teacher might ask, "Who is going to the store?" while pointing to appropriate word class columns. Students are not allowed to respond with sentence fragments, such as "He is" or "She is," but are required to form complete sentences of their own with their responses.

The Phelps Sentence Guide is divided into nine segments that progress through developmental increments. In Stage I, students generate simple sentences in a controlled interactive environment. Students are encouraged to use words from all the word classes that appear in the language element columns. A teacher asks questions designed to promote sentence expansion and elaboration. Imagery, or the use of descriptive language to create a "picture" in a reader's mind, is also taught. Spelling is taught with a method like Fernald's (1943).

In Stages II and III, students are taught to elaborate their use of subjects and predicates. The goal of these stages is to teach students to be specific rather than general, to use precise subjects and predicates to enhance their communicative skills and eliminate guesswork by readers. To encourage the use of precise subjects, the sentence guide provides students with descriptive predicates. These predicates require students to select subjects that appropriately match the predicate's actions and details and optimize a sentence's meaning. Likewise, to encourage the use of descriptive predicates, the sentence guide provides students with subjects that evoke, for example, specific actions, circumstances, or settings. This arrangement compels students to choose predicates that appropriately complement or modify a specific subject.

In Stage IV, students are taught editing skills by learning specific error types and then seeking to locate them in written examples. Initially, this editing focuses on identifying sentence fragments and nondescriptive or vague subjects and predicates, examples of poor writing that students have already been taught to recognize.

The last five stages of the Phelps Sentence Guide provide students with instruction and practice in editing skills and composition that are progressively more advanced and more demanding. In Stage IX, for example, the last stage, students focus on abstract composition. They learn to write about their feelings and emotions. In addition, students are taught complex sentence structures that enable, for example, the communication of difficult abstract causalities, the "whys" of particularly complicated actions, conditions, and ideas.

Notes: The various stages of the Phelps Sentence Guide method allow students to advance through a developmental sequence that is progressively more challenging and complex. Students learn each phase thoroughly, however, before moving to the next. In addition, the interactive approach and its communicative paradigm impress on students the structuring of complete sentences. This method seeks to internalize the process of composition through its constitutive elements, making writing itself more accessible to students.

Teachers who use this method must individualize the program for students; therefore, the teacher must be thoroughly familiar with all of its aspects. For example, the rate at which students progress through the various stages will vary considerably depending on the extent of students' disabilities, and teachers need to prepare for this. In addition, this method of instruction should be coordinated and integrated with other programs students are already being taught.

The Phelps Sentence Guide provides visual representations, focuses on the structural elements of language, and other cues. This is helpful for students with language disorders, students with auditory processing deficits and other learning disorders, and students with hearing impairment. In addition, the program has reportedly been successful with aphasic adults in therapy.

SENTENCE COMBINING

Method: Sentence Combining

Author: C. Cooper

Sources: Daiker, D. A., Kerek, A., & Morenberg, M. (Eds.). (1985). *Sentence combining: A rhetorical perspective.* Carbondale. IL: Southern Illinois University Press; Nutter, N., & Safran, J. (1984). Improving writing with sentences combining. *Academic Therapy, 19,* 449–455; Cooper, C. (1973). An outline for writing sentence-combining problems. *English Journal, 62,* 96–102.

Description: Sentence Combining is a method of teaching writing skills that can be used as a supplement to other writing curricula. This method builds on students' existing linguistic knowledge to teach them to create and develop more sophisticated sentence patterns. The instructional benefits of Sentence Combining include a greater awareness of how writing works. It also provides a model for revising and editing during the writing process and for the development of better sentence composition. Sentence Combining is a method that provides controlled practice in integrating hand, eye, and cerebral activities while composing. Cooper suggests that controlled practice functions to reduce the overload caused by taxing the short-term memory.

Sentence Combining has evolved out of generative-transformational grammar. Traditional grammar treats the main clause as the fundamental unit. Supplements are added to it to structure more complex linguistic forms. For analysis, generative-transformational grammar uses the kernel sentence as its basic semantic unit. The kernel sentence contains a noun phrase and a verb phrase and consists of surface and deep structures. Typically, the syntactical arrangement of any sentence constitutes its surface structure. Its deep structure is its underlying meaning, or the semantic content of a sentence. Transformational grammar focuses on the relationship between deep and surface structures at their location in the sentence. It proposes rules that can be applied systematically to govern the generation of complex and meaningful sentences.

In the Sentence Combining method, students combine two or more kernel sentences to build complex sentences. There are three procedures that students can use to structure these more complex sentences: **coordination**, **embedding**, and **complementation**. For example, students match two kernel sentences like "Mary washed her hair" and "Mary combed her hair." In the **coordination** procedure, students link these two kernel sentences, as in: "Mary washed and combed her hair." Using the **embedding** procedure, one kernel sentence is subsumed by a second. For example, "Sara works at Ensign School" and "Sara is a teacher" combine to form, "Sara who works at Ensign School is a teacher." **Complementation** is a procedure that functions to fill empty or inadequate parts of a sen-

tence with the purpose and significance that result in better sentences. This procedure operates to give sentences generally greater semantic value. Words such as "that," "for," and "what" initiate the complementation procedure. For example, "That the boy yearns is sad," "For the boy to yearn is sad," "The boy's yearning is sad," and "What the boy is yearning for is sad," are all examples of the expository aim of complementation.

The different procedures of the Sentence Combining method teach students to embed kernel sentences into main statements. The purpose of this practice is to develop the writing skills characteristic of a cognitively mature writer. However, one caution is that Sentence Combining is not representative of how the mind itself operates to develop discourse.

Notes: Sentence Combining was developed as a controlled practice approach to written language to help students develop fluency with linguistic patterns. It provides a systematic methodology for students to use to explore topics and revise work. An adapted version of this method should be considered for students with learning disabilities. The procedures of Sentence Combining are highly systematic, and the overloads that can result from implementing this system are problematic for some students.

Sentence Combining may be an effective way to teach writing to normal populations; however, there is some question regarding the extent to which procedural transfer to students' writing occurs. Also, the causal relationship between syntactical restructuring and semantic improvement in composition is questioned. Furthermore, questions continue to arise regarding the effectiveness of Sentence Combining as a remediation approach. Students with higher cognitive abilities appear to benefit more from this method than students with lower cognitive abilities. Although Sentence Combining may increase students' ability to combine syntactical units, it does not guarantee that the semantic quality of these units will also be improved. In addition, it is not known if these gains will be sustained over time. Sentence Combining remediation also requires more time than most special educators usually have with students.

WRITING PROCESS

Method: Writing Process

Authors: Jacqueline Moulton and Mary Stering Bader

Source: Moulton, J. R., & Bader, M. S. (1985). The writing process: A powerful approach for the language-disabled student. *Annals of Dyslexia, 35,* 161–173.

Description: The Writing Process method was developed to teach writing to students with language-learning disabilities who do not spontaneously develop the strategies needed to write proficiently. This method details the stages through which students must progress in generating writing projects. These stages include prewriting, planning, drafting, revising, and proofreading.

In the **prewriting** stage, students generate ideas and specific details that provide the contextual foundation of written compositions. Vocabulary building, word retrieval, and brainstorming can help to generate writing topics. In addition, the examination of photographs, stories, and dramas can be used as a mechanism to stimulate and motivate students to write. A teacher can assist students by helping them to develop outlines that sequence events and generate lists of descriptive words for chosen topics. Students are encouraged to produce prewriting notes that flush out topical and contextual possibilities. They are not concerned with spelling, organization, handwriting, and so forth.

The **planning** stage helps students develop a clear, consistent point of view and organize the development of their ideas around a central topic. This process develops out of simple or elaborate outlines. Or a teacher, for example, can discuss the communication triangle that explains the dynamic relationship between the writer's purpose, the writer's point of view, and the writer's audience. In addition, students can use the notes produced in the prewriting stage to develop their focal topic in an orderly fashion.

At the **drafting** stage of the writing process, students develop working drafts of their projects based on their prewriting notes and planning efforts. Organization and ideas are emphasized in the drafting stage; spelling, punctuation, and handwriting, however, are not stressed. For students with language-learning disabilities, this can be a difficult stage, because working with the flow of ideas and the mechanics of writing can sometimes cause problems. However, by privileging the flow of ideas over the mechanics of writing, this stage can relieve some of the anxieties that students typically associate with the writing process.

For the **revising** stage to be effective, teachers need to actively encourage students to revise their work. Teachers can read drafts and prepare lists of questions and comments. While examining drafts, for example, teachers might ask questions such as, "How well does this draft address its topic?" "Does this draft follow a plan?" "Is this draft well-written and does it use specific skills?" In addition, teachers can meet with students to discuss the strengths and weaknesses of their drafts. Students can make notations on their drafts in colored pencil, indicating suggested changes or modifications. Teachers, however, do not need to bring all of the problems in a draft to the attention of students, particularly those that are superficial or only secondary to a project's thesis.

Teachers can provide students with specific **proofreading** guidelines to help them locate spelling, punctuation, and capitalization errors. Furthermore, these guidelines can be developed according to the individual needs of students. Some students, for example, may need line-by-line guidance and feedback. The goal of proofreading and revision is to improve writing skills, not to produce a mechanically perfect paper.

Using this method, students who are motivated to write will learn strategies to enhance the writing process. It is important, however, that teachers encourage and support students in the writing process.

Notes: The Writing Process method teaches a system that students can apply to their compositions in a variety of situations. This method is for students with language-learning disorders who have the abstract thinking skills, vocabulary, and cognitive abilities to organize and develop ideas. Many of these students have good verbal skills, but may also have writing-related expressive disorders that inhibit their ability to communicate well without significant intensive instruction.

WRITING FLUENCY

Method: Writing Fluency

Authors: R. V. Houten, E. Morrison, and M. MacDonald

Source: Houten, R.V., Morrison, E., & MacDonald, M. (1974). The effects of explicit timing and feedback on compositional response rate in elementary school children. *Journal of Applied Behavior Analysis, 7,* 547–555.

Description: This method is intended to help students develop writing styles that are rapid and fluid. It is recognized that, as the writing demands on students increase, the importance of writing fluency also increases greatly. This method attempts to es-

tablish the motor patterns that rapid, legible writing requires. This kind of automaticity is an effect of consistently repeated practice.

The method attempts to increase the rate and fluency of writing through daily timed writing. The following steps are used:

1. The teacher writes a topic on the board.
2. Students write about the selected topic for 10 minutes. They attempt to write more words each day than they did the previous day.
3. At the conclusion of each timed period, students count the number of words they wrote and record this total on the top of their papers. Words from repetitious or incomplete sentences are not counted.
4. The teacher verifies the score totals and records them on a chart.
5. As options, the teacher can elect to evaluate papers on their mechanical aspects, vocabulary, number of ideas, development of ideas, or rhetorical unity.
6. The teacher returns the compositions to students with feedback on their writing.

Notes: This method may be helpful when used with reluctant writers. However, students who have only limited experience with selected topics may be unable to achieve significant levels of fluency.

THE WRITER'S WORKSHOP

Method: The Writer's Workshop

Authors: Charles MacArthur, Shirley Schwartz, and Steve Graham

Sources: MacArthur, C., Schwartz, S., & Graham. S. (1991). A model for writing instruction: Integrating word processing and strategy instruction into a process approach to writing. *Disabilities: Research and Practice, 6,* 230–236; Graham, S., Harris, K., MacArthur, C., & Schwartz, S. (1991).

Writing instruction. In B. Wong (Ed.), *Learning about learning disabilities* (pp. 309–343). San Diego: Academic Press.

Description: The Writer's Workshop is an approach designed to help students with learning disabilities to improve their writing. It focuses on establishing a social context in which student writing is shared among peers. This stresses the communicative function of writing and makes the writing experience more meaningful. The method also provides cognitive strategies for writing and encourages students to use word processing to ease the physical tasks of writing and editing.

Advocates of the Writer's Workshop cite instructional research which shows that students with learning disabilities can learn to write successfully if they are provided with a supportive classroom environment, meaningful writing tasks, and instruction in the writing process. Specifically, this method stresses the social context of the classroom. A community of writers is established in the classroom, which motivates students to write purposefully for an actual audience. In addition, the instructional approach of the Writer's Workshop is incorporated in a process approach to writing.

The instructional routine of this method follows the same general format every day:

1. *Status of the Class.* The teacher asks students what they plan to accomplish in their writing for that day and records their responses.

2. *Mini-Lessons.* The teacher briefly instructs students in various writing skills or process strategies.

3. *Sustained Writing.* Students should spend the bulk of the workshop on their writing.

4. *Conferencing.* The teacher meets briefly with students during their writing time. These are one-to-one conferences in which the teacher interacts with students, providing them with instruction specific to their individual needs. Students use these conferences to discuss their writing projects with the teacher, their plans and progress. The aim of conferencing is to teach the skills necessary to write independently.

5. *Sharing.* At the end of the writing period, students read their work-in-progress aloud to their peers. In this way they learn the effects their writing has on an audience. In addition, the teacher can use these opportunities to model questions that gradually promote among the students the ability to evaluate writing. The sharing session can be expanded to include a broader audience from outside the workshop as students become more confident in their abilities to write.

6. *Publishing.* This is designed to motivate students. It can be done by displaying students' work on bulletin boards, or students can plan and publish their own literary journal for distribution between friends and family.

In addition, students are taught a strategy for organizing the content of their writing. This strategy attempts to provide students with an awareness of what constitutes clear writing: setting, character, purpose, action, tone, and descriptive language are all emphasized. Furthermore, teachers model a strategy designed to situate students in the writing community. Students learn to function cooperatively, to be positive when reviewing the work of peers, to evaluate the work of peers, and to help them to revise it. Teachers must work actively to model this strategy; however, as students master the strategy for themselves, teachers gradually decrease their own participation in this process.

Word processing is another key element of the Writer's Workshop method. It facilities the process of writing by easing the physical task of writing itself. Composition, revising, editing, publishing, and collaborative work are all made easier with computers. This process recognizes, however, that word processing itself brings with it secondary concerns. This method suggests that three students for every computer will provide sufficient access for each student in the workshop. Therefore, access to computers may be limited, and scheduling can then become a burden to teachers and students alike.

Also, to work with moderate fluency, students must be proficient at typing and at the basic operations of word processing. This may require additional work with typing tutorials and instruction in the basic commands of word processing—edit, save, print, and so forth— for students to be able to function at a rudimentary level. If students have difficulty accomplishing the tasks of typing and word processing, they may become frustrated as well with the more arduous task of writing.

Notes: This method provides students with a stable instructional routine that allows them to focus on their writing tasks, rather than on what various writing assignments might require of them. In addition, the method's concrete approach emphasizes writing's communicative function by promoting purposeful writing for actual audiences. The strategies this method employs encourage students to write independently and teach them the skills and strategies necessary to do so.

REFERENCES

Fernald, G. (1943). *Remedial techniques in basic school subjects*. New York: McGraw-Hill.

Fitzgerald, E. (1949). *Straight language for the deaf.* Washington, DC: Volta Bureau.

Lee, L., Koenigsknecht, R., & Mulhern, S. (1975). *Interactive language development teaching.* Evanston, IL: Northwestern University Press.

Lerner, J. (1993). *Learning disabilities: Theories, diagnosis, and teaching strategies* (6th ed.). Boston: Houghton Mifflin.

Levine, M. (1994). *Educational care*. Cambridge, MA: Educators Publishing Service.

C H A P T E R

10

Study Skills Strategy Instruction

Pamela Pruitt, Ph.D.

C O N T E N T S

▶ Semantic Mapping **196**
▶ Reciprocal Teaching **197**
▶ The Keyword Method **198**
▶ Advance Organizers **199**
▶ Listening Skills **200**
▶ Modified Self-Questioning Training **202**
▶ Modified Graphic Organizer **203**

▶ Multipass **204**
▶ Five Step Method for Taking Lecture Notes **206**
▶ Study Guides **207**
▶ Learning Strategies **207**
▶ SQ3R **209**

Study skills are a critical component of the curriculum for students at all grade levels. The ability to use study skills is particularly important for students struggling to keep up with the demands of the secondary education curriculum; however, the acquisition of study skills should be a process that is developed, refined, and maintained throughout a student's educational career. (Polloway & Patton, 1993).

Unfortunately, students with mild disabilities often lack effective study techniques to enable them to experience success in general education classrooms. Specifically, these students may experience academic problems because of poor organizational and information-processing skills (Polloway & Patton, 1993) and deficiencies in the areas of note-taking, test- taking, and time management (Smith & Dowdy, 1989). In addition, Pany and Jenkins (1978) reported that students with disabilities exhibit deficits in reading comprehension and vocabulary acquisition. Further, problems have been noted in the area of memory skills (Torgeson, 1984).

Clearly, students with mild disabilities need direct and systematic instruction study skills to develop a repertoire of learning strategies that will enable them to respond appropriately to the demands of the classroom. Through the use of effective study skills, students with disabilities will be able to demonstrate more active learning patterns and display proactive approaches to academic tasks (Olson & Platt, 1996).

Study skills include "those competencies associated with acquiring, recording, organizing, synthesizing, remembering, and using information ideas found in school" (Devine, 1987, p. 5). Study skills include strategies such as note-taking, organizers, study guides, maps, and techniques to help students recall and retrieve information. Learning strategies are often considered to be a subset of study skills (Ellis, Sabornie, & Marshall, 1989). Learning strategies emphasize learning how to learn, providing instruction in meaningful contexts, and giving students opportunities to accept responsibility for their own learning (Olson & Platt, 1996). Learning strategies include metacognitive skills, such as self-questioning techniques; metacomprehension strategies; and reciprocal teaching.

This chapter will discuss a variety of study skills and learning strategies, models, and methods. They are representative of practices that have proven to be effective in school settings for not only students with mild disabilities, but also their nondisabled peers.

SEMANTIC MAPPING

Method: Semantic Mapping

Authors: Dale D. Johnson, Susan D. Pittelman, and Joan E. Heimlich

Source: Johnson, D. D., Pittelman, S. D., & Heimlich, J. E. (1986). Semantic mapping. *Reading Teacher, 39,* 778–783.

Description: Vocabulary instruction is a fundamental component of the elementary curriculum and is particularly important for students who are having difficulty learning to read. Students with deficits in reading frequently encounter difficult or unfamiliar words, which adversely affects their ability to bring meaning to text. Students need to be given effective strategies to facilitate their vocabulary development and reading comprehension.

Semantic Mapping may be used as a pre-reading strategy to give students a general overview of a reading selection and help them master key vocabulary and build on their prior knowledge about the topic under study. In the implementation of this strategy, the educator and students interact to develop a visual representation of the key concepts of a reading selection. The educator introduces the students to a key concept, assists them in expanding and building on the concept through the identification of related words, and connects the new words to the experiences and prior knowledge of the students. This enables them to more fully understand and integrate the information in the reading selection.

Johnson, Pittelman, and Heimlich suggested the following guidelines for developing a semantic map:

1. The educator selects an essential vocabulary word or key concept from the reading selection.
2. The key word is written on the chalkboard, a chart, or a transparency.
3. The class is directed to brainstorm and identify words that are associated with the key word. These words are recorded and arranged in categories by the educator.
4. The students then work individually for several minutes, generating additional words that are related to the key word.
5. The students orally present their individual lists, adding their words to the map developed by the class. As work on the map proceeds, the educator has an opportunity to clarify concepts, provide the definition of new words, discuss multiple meanings of words, and determine what students do and do not understand.
6. The students recommend labels for the categories on the semantic map.
7. The semantic map is discussed by the educator and the students. The educator assists the students in forming relationships between new and old words, building on their prior knowledge and experiences.

Notes: Semantic Mapping also can be used as an effective alternative to conventional postreading activities. After reading a selection, constructing a semantic map provides students with an opportunity to expand on the vocabulary, identify and summarize the main concepts, draw conclusions, and link the new information with their prior knowledge and experiences. The semantic map also can be used by the educator to check for comprehension.

In addition, Semantic Mapping can be used as a prewriting activity to help students organize thoughts and information. The map can serve as a structure for story development, with category headings functioning as main ideas and the related concepts as the content of the written assignment.

Further, Semantic Mapping is beneficial for students with mild disabilities, students receiving remedial reading instruction, adults with reading deficits, and with typical students. Semantic Mapping strategies have been found to be effective for both elementary and secondary students.

RECIPROCAL TEACHING

Method: Reciprocal Teaching

Authors: Annemarie Sullivan Palincsar and Ann L. Brown

Source: Palincsar, A. S., & Brown, A. L. (1986). Interactive teaching to promote independent learning from text. *Reading Teacher, 39*, 771–777.

Description: Reciprocal Teaching is a metacognitive instructional strategy that focuses on teaching students how to learn. This teaching method is designed to promote both comprehension of text and comprehension monitoring. In Reciprocal Teaching, the educator and students take turns assuming the role of teacher, engaging in a dialogue to jointly construct the meaning of text.

Four strategies that enhance text comprehension and comprehension monitoring are shared by the participants in Reciprocal Teaching. These strategies include **predicting, question generating, summarizing**, and **clarifying. Predicting** enables students to speculate what the author will discuss in the text, gives students a purpose for reading, and creates the opportunity for them to link new and prior knowledge. **Question generating** enables students to recognize information that provides the material for a good question and to formulate and answer the questions generated. In **summarization**, students identify the important information in a passage and are guided by the educator to integrate the content across sections of the text. **Clarification** involves perceiving when comprehension is not occurring and taking action to bring meaning to the text. Achieving competency in the utilization of these strategies is not the goal of Reciprocal Teaching. Rather, the strategies provide a way to encourage students to read for meaning and to monitor their understanding of the passage being read.

Students receive guidance in the utilization of these four strategies through interactive instruction. Palincsar and Brown recommended the following steps for effective implementation of Reciprocal Teaching:

1. *Explanation.* In initiating instruction in Reciprocal Teaching, the educator describes the strategies to the students and explains why they are learning the strategies, in what situations the strategies may prove useful, and how they will learn the strategies.

2. *Instruction.* Instruction is provided to the students on each of the four strategies: predicting, question generating, summarizing, and clarifying. Each strategy is defined for the students, and the educator makes sure the students are at least minimally competent in the utilization of each strategy before dialogue begins. Approximately one day of instruction is given on each strategy.

3. *Modeling.* During the first few days of Reciprocal Teaching, the educator models the technique for the students, demonstrating how each of the four strategies may be used during reading through use of interactive dialogue.

4. *Guided Practice.* As instruction proceeds, the educator gives increasingly more responsibility to the students to engage in and sustain the dialogue.

5. *Praise.* The educator evaluates and monitors the performance of the students as they implement the Reciprocal Teaching strategies and commends the students for their efforts.

6. *Teacher Judgment.* The educator provides further instruction and modeling as indicated by his or her judgment.

Notes: The most important aspect of Reciprocal Teaching is its interactive quality, with continuous interactions among the educator and students as together they attempt to bring meaning to the text. The educator's role is to promote the students' mastery of the strategies and then to gradually decrease his or her support, encouraging the students to employ the strategies independently.

Reciprocal Teaching is an effective strategy for either individual or small group instruction. Further, as students become proficient in the use of the strategies, they can apply the strategies to different contexts without teacher assistance. Reciprocal Teaching also can be utilized in peer tutoring situations and can be used to enhance content area instruction.

THE KEYWORD METHOD

Method: The Keyword Method

Author: Margo A. Mastropieri

Source: Mastropieri, M. A. (1988). The keyword method. *Teaching Exceptional Children, 20,* 4–8.

Description: Memory plays a significant role in the academic achievement of students and is often an area of difficulty for students with mild disabilities. Deficits in memory skills affect the organization, storage, and retrieval of information. Research indicates that systematic mnemonic instruction is a powerful technique to strengthen the retention of information.

The Keyword method is a mnemonic strategy specifically designed to enhance the initial learning and retention of facts and fact systems. The major features of this method include utilizing both auditory and visual prompts, as well as visual imagery, to promote recall and understanding of information.

Mastropieri suggested that the following three steps should be followed in the implementation of the Keyword method:

1. *Recoding.* In the recoding component, an unfamiliar vocabulary word is changed to an acoustically similar keyword. The keyword selected must be familiar to the student, and it should be easy for the student to create a mental picture of the word. For example, Mastropieri suggested that an appropriate keyword for the word, *apex,* would be "ape." This is a well-known word that sounds like apex and is simple for students to visualize.

2. *Relating.* In the relating component, the new keyword is meaningfully connected to its definition through an interactive visual image. The keyword and its meaning are pictured doing something together. For example, the definition for apex is the highest point; therefore, Mastropieri suggested that visualizing an ape sitting on the highest point of a rock would be a relevant image.

3. *Retrieving.* In the retrieving component, the student is able to recall the meaning of the original vocabulary word by following a series of simple steps. First, the student is directed to remember the keyword for the original word (i.e., ape for apex). Second, the student is asked to recall the visual image of the interaction between the keyword and its definition (i.e., an ape sitting on the highest point of a rock). Third, the student is asked to state the definition of the original word (i.e., the definition of apex is the highest point).

Notes: Students need to be encouraged to incorporate their newly acquired vocabulary into their working language. Therefore, educators should create multiple opportunities for the students to use this vocabulary across a variety of contexts. This may be done through the use of practice exercises that require students to complete written sentences using the new vocabulary words or through prompting the verbal usage of the words.

The Keyword method is appropriate for use with both elementary and secondary students. Further, the Keyword method may be used in any context in which the memorization of facts or fact systems is required, including language, science, and social studies.

ADVANCE ORGANIZERS

Method: Advance Organizers

Author: R. Keith Lenz

Source: Lenz, R. K. (1983). Using advance organizers. *The Pointer, 27,* 11–13.

Description: Many secondary students with mild disabilities are receiving the major portion of their academic instruction in general education classrooms. The demands of the secondary curriculum require that these students acquire information from textbooks and from classroom lectures and discussions. Students with mild disabilities, however, often lack the information-processing skills to enable them to organize and comprehend content area materials. Therefore, educators need to employ a variety of instructional methods to assist students in the acquisition of these skills.

The Advance Organizer is an instructional technique that may be used by the educator to introduce students to a lesson or learning task (i.e., a classroom activity or project, lecture, reading assignment, or video). The Advance Organizer presents a structured overview of the information to be presented prior to the students' actual participation in the learning activity.

Lenz recommended that the following 10 steps be followed in the development of an advance organizer:

1. The students are informed by the educator that they will be receiving an overview of the learning activity in the form of an advance organizer. The ways that the students will benefit by using the advance organizer are then described.
2. The major topic and subtopics that will be covered in the learning activity are identified.
3. The students are given an organizational framework of the learning activity through a visual or oral format, such as an outline, list, or narrative.
4. The actions that will be required of the students and the educator to successfully complete the learning activity are described.
5. The concepts to be learned are related to information previously mastered and to new information.
6. The specific and broad concepts that will be learned through the activity are described.
7. The concepts are clarified through the use of examples, nonexamples, and analogies.
8. The active participation of the students should be encouraged by demonstrating the relevance of the new information to their lives.
9. New and difficult vocabulary should be introduced and defined.
10. The expected outcome should be described by stating the objectives of instruction and relating outcomes to evaluation procedures.

After completion of the above steps, the educator may commence instruction.

Notes: The Advance Organizer is a powerful tool that specifically addresses the organizational difficulties experienced by students with mild disabilities. The retention of information related to content area materials can be substantially improved through the use of this technique. However, the benefits to students will be realized only if students are activated to attend to the advance organizer. It is critical, therefore, that educators both utilize the methodology and motivate the students to actively respond.

The Advance Organizer method is easily implemented by general educators providing instruction to students with mild disabilities in general education classrooms. However, preservice and inservice training in the development and use of advance organizers is recommended to maximize the benefits of the technique.

LISTENING SKILLS

Method: Listening Skills

Authors: Suzanne Robinson and Deborah Deutsch Smith

Source: Robinson, S., & Smith, D. D. (1981). Listening skills: Teaching learning disabled students to be better listeners. *Focus on Exceptional Children, 13*, 2–15.

Description: The ability to obtain information through the process of listening is a fundamental communication skill. Educators typically presume that listening skills will develop automatically along with other types of communication skills. Research has indicated, however, that students with disabilities exhibit atypical listening skills, often remembering less of what they heard than their normal peers and failing to monitor whether or not they understood what they heard. Listening Skills methodology, therefore, should be incorporated into the curriculum, particularly for students who have deficits in this critical area of communication.

Robinson and Smith proposed a model to define and sequence listening abilities and to provide guidelines for initiating instruction. The authors classified listening skills into the following three major components: (a) input—the words, sounds, and nonverbal messages conveyed by the speaker to the listener; (b) listening—prerequisite skills (attention, ability to hear, and competence in the usage of language), comprehension of the input, and the ability to remember what was heard; and (c) output—the motoric, written, or verbal response of the listener.

Robinson and Smith suggested that modifying the input of the speaker is an effective strategy for facilitating the development of listening skills. The educator can modify the message given to the student to solicit his or her attention, accommodate the level of language proficiency, or advance the student's memory or comprehension abilities. The following intervention strategies were developed by the authors to modify speaker input:

1. *Attention*. The educator may solicit the student's attention by cuing him or her to listen or by alerting the student to the importance of the information about to be given. Further, reducing the amount of extraneous stimuli in the classroom will facilitate listening skills.

2. *Language Proficiency*. The educator must be aware of the student's syntax and vocabulary levels and modify the input to the appropriate levels by (a) decreasing the complexity of the language used, (b) restating or clarifying the message given, or (c) simplifying the syntax.

3. *Memory*. The educator may increase the student's retention of information by (a) using high- frequency words; (b) controlling the length of the message, linguistic structure, and serial position of the message; (c) grouping information in associated categories or by semantic membership; or (d) being aware of the relevance of the message to the life of the student.

4. *Comprehension*. The educator should use all of the components that promote listening and adjust to the competence level of the student.

Robinson and Smith also recommended several strategies educators can utilize to modify the listening behaviors of students. Instruction in the following cognitive and task approach strategies is recommended for students who are experiencing difficulty with listening:

1. *Attention*. A combination of instructional strategies including peer and teacher modeling, verbal rehearsal, and reinforcement appear to enhance listening skills of students.

2. *Language Competence.* Instructional strategies designed to increase language competence include: (a) expanding the student's vocabulary, (b) extending the student's awareness of multiple word meanings, and (c) increasing syntactic skills.

3. *Memory.* Basic memory and organizational skills include (a) rehearsing information gathered during the listening situation, (b) clustering or chunking information, (c) coding, (d) visualizing the information, (e) asking questions, (f) recognizing organizational cues, (g) rehearsing and summarizing information after listening, and (h) organizing information to develop categories.

4. *Comprehension.* Students should be given the opportunity to practice three levels of comprehension: literal, critical, and appreciative. In addition, students need instruction in recognizing nonverbal messages.

By requesting verbal, motoric, or written responses before and after listening, the educator can evaluate the student's proficiency with the listening comprehension strategies. The educator can use the information obtained through evaluation to continue, modify, or discontinue instruction.

Notes: The Robinson and Smith model builds a sound structure for the development of memory and attention skills, which are difficult for students with cognitive deficits. It also builds receptive skills and expressive skills through its attention to developing verbal, motoric, and written responses. This process is a practical approach to move students into higher order responding skills, which encourages their ability to receive and also to apply new skills. However, educators should use caution when demanding higher order listening skills because of the prerequisite developmental sophistication.

MODIFIED SELF-QUESTIONING TRAINING

Method: Modified Self-Questioning Training

Authors: Bernice Y. L. Wong and Wayne Jones

Source: Wong, B. Y. L., & Jones, W. (1982). Increasing metacomprehension in learning disabled and normally achieving students through self-questioning training. *Learning Disability Quarterly, 5,* 228–239.

Description: Metacomprehension refers to an individual's awareness of and ability to monitor his or her reading comprehension and is an important skill in facilitating students' ability to gain meaning from text. Typical students regularly monitor their comprehension of material and apply appropriate corrective strategies, such as rereading or paraphrasing, if they fail to understand what they have read. Students with mild disabilities, however, often do not employ such strategies when they are unable to comprehend the meaning of the text.

Wong and Jones developed a Modified Self-Questioning Training program based on a model by Andre and Anderson (1979). The Modified Self-Questioning Training was designed specifically to enhance the reading comprehension of students with learning disabilities. The self-questioning technique requires that students identify the main concepts in a reading selection and develop questions about these concepts. Because identifying the main concept is a prerequisite skill for using this strategy, Wong and Jones advised that students be given pretraining sessions that focus specifically on this skill prior to initiating the Modified Self-Questioning Training program. When the criterion of 80% accuracy is reached on identifying the main concept, the students proceed to the self-questioning training.

Wong and Jones recommended that 2 days of instruction on the self-questioning technique be provided for the students. Procedures for instruction are identical for both days. The training sessions incorporate the following procedures:

1. The students are given an explanation of the purpose of metacomprehension training and provided with the following steps to implement the technique:
   a. Why are you studying this passage?
   b. Locate the main idea/ideas in the passage and draw a line under it/them.
   c. Generate a question about the main idea, following the guidelines for a good question.
   d. Develop an answer for your question.
   e. Look over the questions and answers you generated and note how each question and answer provides you with additional information.
2. The students then are presented a booklet that contains eight short paragraphs. The educator uses the first paragraph in the booklet to model the self-questioning technique by underlining the main concept and developing a question by paraphrasing the main idea.
3. The students are directed to finish the remaining paragraphs in the booklet using the same procedure.
4. The educator provides the students with immediate feedback after completion of their booklets.
5. After a 5-minute break, the students are given a reading passage containing five short paragraphs. The educator uses a di-

rect instruction approach to teach the students to implement the self-questioning technique with this longer format. A 9 centimeter margin on the right side of the passage provides space for the students to write questions developed by the educator during the modeling of the technique.

6. After a 3-minute break, students receive a new reading passage, again containing five short paragraphs. The students also are given a prompt card that describes the five steps in the self-questioning technique and defines the criteria for a good question. Students are instructed to use the self-questioning technique with the reading passage. The educator gives corrective feedback on the students' work.

7. The students are given another passage with five short paragraphs. This time, however, the prompt cards are removed while the students progress through the self-questioning process. Again, to conclude the activity, the educator provides corrective feedback. These same procedures are followed on the second day of self-questioning training, using new materials. Both training sessions are concluded with a discussion of the usefulness of the technique.

Notes: Modified Self-Questioning Training substantially improves the ability of students with mild disabilities to identify key concepts in a reading passage and generate questions about these key concepts. This technique would be appropriate for both reading or content area instruction and appears to be most useful for upper elementary students and above.

Educators should be aware of the importance of providing students with a rationale for using techniques such as self-questioning. When students receive information about the purpose of a skill, when and where the skill can be used, and how to monitor its use, the skill is learned more easily and can be generalized to other contexts.

MODIFIED GRAPHIC ORGANIZER

Method: Modified Graphic Organizer

Author: Donna E. Alvermann

Source: Alvermann, D. E. (1983). Putting the textbook in its place—Your students' hands. *Academic Therapy, 18,* 345–351.

Description: Students with mild disabilities frequently have reading deficits and do not have strategies to enable them to acquire knowledge from text. This problem is heightened in the content areas because of the difficulty level and format of content area textbooks. The Graphic Organizer is a strategy to alleviate some of the difficulties students have when interacting with a text. The Graphic Organizer, first developed by Barron (1969) and Earle (1969) and modified by Alvermann, is a tree diagram that contains terminology related to a particular concept. Empty slots are provided in the diagram to make it necessary for students to search for and write in information. The Modified Graphic Organizer has the following benefits: (a) it motivates students because there are few words to manage, and words that are included serve as cues to information the students are expected to locate; (b) it facilitates retention of information; and (c) it informs students what the educator considers to be important information in the text.

Alvermann recommended the following eight-step procedure for developing a Modified Graphic Organizer:

1. The educator selects a four-to-five-page section of the text that addresses a key concept to be taught. The use of an entire chapter of a textbook should be avoided.

2. The educator then chooses words from the selected reading material that are significant to the key concept being taught. The selected words are written on index cards or small pieces of paper.

3. The educator organizes the selected words into a diagrammatic arrangement to depict a relationship between the words and the key concept.

4. The educator transfers the diagram to paper, deleting some words and substituting empty slots. Guidelines for determining which words to delete are: (a) retain the key concepts, (b) exchange empty slots for words that are parallel in their relationship to the problem, and (c) omit unfamiliar words to encourage students to explore the text in search of the missing words.

5. The educator makes a copy of the graphic organizer for each student. In addition, the graphic organizer is drawn on the chalkboard or on an overhead transparency.

6. The educator discusses the modified graphic organizer with the students prior to presenting a reading selection, focusing on the usefulness of the organizer to the students and discussing the key concepts and unfamiliar vocabulary.

7. Students are asked to read the textbook selection and fill in the empty slots in the graphic organizer.

8. The educator and the students discuss the completed graphic organizer.

Notes: The major function of a graphic organizer is to facilitate the students' ability to acquire knowledge from a textbook. As students become more proficient at using graphic organizers, the educator may consider involving them more in the actual development of the organizer. When students are involved in this process, they will likely feel more ownership of the organizer and be more motivated to use it. Students also may create their graphic organizers and pair up with other students to validate each other's organizer.

MULTIPASS

Method: Multipass

Authors: Jean B. Schumaker, Donald D. Deshler, Gordon R. Alley, Michael M. Warner, and Pegi H. Denton

Source: Schumaker, J. B., Deshler, D. D., Alley, G. R., Warner, M. M., & Denton, P. H. (1982). Multipass: A learning strategy for improving reading comprehension. *Learning Disability Quarterly, 5,* 295–304.

Description: Students with mild disabilities often have difficulty meeting the curricular expectations of the secondary general education classroom. Students experiencing academic problems should be provided with an instructional model that teaches them specific learning skills to augment their ability to manage the demands of the secondary curriculum. Students with mild disabilities often have deficits in reading comprehension, which impede their ability to be successful in general education classes. Multipass is a learning strategy specifically designed to improve students' reading comprehension by giving them an effective method to interact with and comprehend content area textbooks.

The Multipass Strategy is divided into three substrategies: (a) survey, (b) size-up, and (c) sort-out. Each of these substrategies gives students a specific purpose for making a "pass" through the reading assignment.

The goal of the **survey pass** is to acquaint students with the text. Students are asked to (a) read the title of the chapter, (b) read the introductory paragraph, (c) scan the table of contents to determine the relationship of the chapter to adjacent chapters, (d) read the subtitles in the chapter and observe the organization of the chapter, (e) examine the illustrations and their captions, (f) read the summary paragraph, and (g) paraphrase the information obtained during the survey pass.

The objective of the **size-up pass** is to assist students in obtaining information without reading the chapter in its entirety. Students are directed to examine the chapter questions to determine which facts appear to be most significant. In addition, they are asked to place a check mark next to any question they are able to answer. After completion of this process, students are asked to (a) examine the chapter for contextual cues (i.e., bold print, italics), (b) develop questions from the contextual cues, (c) answer the questions by skimming the surrounding text, and (d) paraphrase the answer to the questions without looking at the book. Students then are asked to paraphrase the information they found in the chapter.

The purpose of the **sort-out pass** is for students to test themselves over the information presented in the chapter by answering the end-of-chapter questions. Students should carry out the following steps for questions they cannot answer: (a) decide which section of the chapter is likely to contain the needed information, (b) skim the section for the correct response, (c) consider another section of the chapter if the answer was not located, and (d) skim that section of the chapter. The process continues until the response is located. During the training procedure, educators should use two sets of materials, one at the student's current reading-ability level and the other at his or her grade level. The steps involved in the instructional procedure include the following:

1. *Determine the Student's Current Learning Habit.* The educator assesses the student's current performance level of the Multipass Strategy using both levels of material. The results of the assessment are discussed with the student.

2. *Describe the Learning Strategy.* The educator provides an overview of the steps involved in the Multipass Strategy, providing a rationale for the use of each step.

3. *Model the Learning Strategy.* The educator acts out each step of the Multipass Strategy, verbally describing the thought process involved in each step.

4. *Verbal Rehearsal of the Learning Strategy.* The educator requires the student to verbally rehearse the steps of the strategy with a criterion of 100% accuracy with no prompts.

5. *Controlled Materials Practice.* The educator directs the student to follow the steps using materials at his or her reading-ability level.

6. *Positive and Corrective Feedback.* The student is given feedback by the educator regarding his or her proficiency in using the Multipass Strategy. If criterion is not reached, steps 5 and 6 should be repeated.

7. *Evaluation.* The evaluation procedure used in step 1 is repeated using different chapters in both reading-ability level and grade-level materials. If criterion is reached on both sets of material, the educator may choose to terminate instruction. However, if criterion is not reached, the educator may continue instruction by following the next three steps.

8. *Grade-Level Materials Practice.* The student employs the steps of the Multipass Strategy with the grade-level materials.

9. *Positive and Corrective Feedback.* The student is given feedback by the educator on his or her competence at using the Multipass Strategy. If criterion was not reached, steps 8 and 9 should be repeated.

10. *Test.* When the student meets the criterion on the grade-level materials, the evaluation procedure used in steps 1 and 7 is repeated using different chapters in both reading-ability level and grade-level materials. This serves as the final evaluation of the student's skills.

Notes: The Multipass Strategy is a promising method to increase the ability of students with disabilities to derive meaning from content area texts. Students with mild disabilities were able to master this complex learning strategy and their examination grades covering textbook information showed substantial improvement. However, the authors cautioned that the effectiveness of this method is yet to be determined for students whose reading level is below fourth grade. The authors speculated that the Multipass Strategy may increase younger students' success with ability-level materials, but may be less effective with grade-level materials. Further, the practicality of the Multipass Strategy is questionable because instruction is provided to students on an individual basis.

FIVE-STEP METHOD FOR TAKING LECTURE NOTES

Method: Five-Step Method for Taking Lecture Notes

Authors: Bernice Jensen Bragstad and Sharyn Mueller Stumpf

Source: Bragstad, B. J., & Stumpf, S. M. (1987). *A guidebook for teaching study skills and motivation*. Newton, MA: Allyn and Bacon.

Description: The ability to take succinct, intelligible notes during classroom lectures or presentations is a skill that enhances the academic success of students. Further, note-taking often is a required task in secondary general education classrooms. However, note-taking may be a difficult and laborious task for students with disabilities because of their lack of organizational skills, inability to identify key concepts, and deficits in written language. Systematic instruction in note-taking could significantly enhance the students' abilities to master this critical skill.

Bragstad and Stumpf recommended the following five-step method for instructing students to take notes on lectures or presentations:

1. *Surveying*. The students may be given an advance organizer or an overview of the material that will be covered in the educator's lecture or in the presentation. This will give them a preview of the key concepts. Students may take notes on the main ideas and thus be more aware of what information to expect.

2. *Questioning*. The educator should encourage the students to adopt a questioning attitude to help them focus on the lecture or presentation. Strategies that might be employed by the educator include (a) modeling a questioning procedure for the students and (b) setting up opportunities for students to role-play and practice questioning procedures. Questions that students might be encouraged to ask themselves during a lecture include (a) what is the key

concept in this presentation, (b) what information am I supposed to know when the lecture is finished, and (c) what is being conveyed about the topic?

3. *Listening*. The educator should recommend that students use appropriate listening strategies to help them listen for content, organization, and main and supporting statements. The students may need additional instruction in appropriate listening skills to enhance their ability to gain information from the presentation.

4. *Organizing*. The educator may assist the students to organize the material presented by using the chalkboard, an overhead transparency, or handouts to order the content in an outline or graph format. The educator may provide the skeleton for the students' notes by writing the key concepts on the board or develop a diagram or map of the information on an overhead transparency. In addition, the educator may choose to help students organize the material by giving them verbal cues, such as "It is important that you remember this point . . ." or "The main idea is . . ." The educator also may reiterate an important point or say it with increased emphasis.

5. *Reviewing and Revising*. Students should be given an opportunity to review their notes as soon after the lecture as possible. This gives them an chance to make additions or deletions while the material can be easily recalled.

Notes: Note-taking typically is a required activity in secondary general education classrooms. However, systematic instruction in note-taking is rarely provided. Many students with mild disabilities take incomplete notes or no notes at all; therefore, it is essential that educators provide instruction in note-taking skills and reinforce the use of those skills. However, before skill instruction can begin, the educator may have to convince the students of the importance of taking notes (Olson & Platt, 1996). Olson and Platt suggested that students might be asked to take notes on a presentation and use this activity as a pretest to demonstrate to the students that improvements are needed in their note-taking abilities.

In addition, educators need to be cautioned that note-taking may be nearly impossible for students whose written language competence is at a very basic level. The educator may need to make modifications to the note-taking task for use with these students.

STUDY GUIDES

Method: Study Guides

Author: Thomas G. Devine

Source: Devine, T. G. (1987). *Teaching study skills*. Newton, MA: Allyn and Bacon.

Description: Students with mild disabilities often exhibit deficits in their ability to organize information. The use of Study Guides that present information in a structured format may be beneficial for students experiencing organization difficulties. Study Guides can perform several functions. They can serve as a map to guide students through an auditory or visual exercise, help with comprehension of content area textbooks, provide an opportunity for students to take notes, and increase the effectiveness of homework assignments.

Devine recommended that the following guidelines be used in developing Study Guides:

1. *Keep the Study Guide Simple.* A study guide should be explicit and to the point. The study guide may lead the students through a reading assignment and identify the information to focus on, what to skim, and what to remember. The educator may use the study guide to ask questions, provide suggestions for thought or creative activities, or give directions for taking notes.

2. *Use a Variety of Question Formats.* Study Guides should include questions at the factu-

al level (i.e., who? what? when? where?), the interpretive level (i.e., why?), and the applied level (i.e., what may you infer from this?).

3. *Provide an Opportunity to Take Notes.* Study Guides may be used to develop students' note-taking skills if the educator includes opportunities for them to locate and record key concepts, summarize paragraphs, and outline material.

4. *Develop the Study Guide Based on the Unique Attributes of the Class.* Study Guides should be constructed based on the educator's knowledge about the strengths, needs, and personal characteristics of the individuals in the class.

5. *Encourage Divergent Thinking.* An effective study guide should include questions, comments, and suggestions that value and foster divergent thinking, promote critical reading-thinking skills, and provide opportunities for inference-making, inference-testing, predicting, and anticipating outcomes.

6. *Structure Homework.* The educator can use the study guide to focus and direct the students' homework, rather than simply giving them a reading assignment.

Notes: Study Guides are effective tools in helping students organize both visual information (i.e., reading assignments) and auditory information (i.e., audiotapes, videotapes, and lecture). Study Guides also are beneficial in guiding students through homework assignments and in reviewing material for examinations.

Study Guides may be developed using a variety of formats, depending on the age and ability level of the students, the subject matter, and the individual needs of the students.

LEARNING STRATEGIES

Method: Learning Strategies

Authors: Gordon Alley, Donald Deshler, Edwin S. Ellis, B. Kenz, Jean B. Schumaker, and F. Clark

Sources: Alley, G., & Deshler, D. (1979). *Teaching the learning disabled adolescent: strategies and methods.* Denver: Love Publishing; Ellis, E., Deshler, D., Kenz, B., Schumaker, J., & Clark, F. (1991). An instructional model for teaching learning strategies. *Focus on Exceptional Children, 23*(6), 1–23.

Description: Learning Strategies is based on the premise that the knowledge requirements to function adequately in society are flexible and changeable. Therefore, students must learn strategies to adapt to these rapidly expanding demands. Often students learn an isolated body of facts and skills but are unable to apply them.

By using Learning Strategies, students learn how they perform tasks, memorize new strategies, and apply them to the novel tasks. Teachers teach students to apply new strategies using materials that are less demanding than those in the regular classroom. Later, learning strategies are applied to regular classroom materials.

A seven-area model includes the skills of reading, listening, writing, thinking, social interaction, mathematics, and speaking. Each of these areas is broken down into numerous subareas such as vocabulary development, study skills, problem-solving, self-awareness, organizing, time management, word finding, oral speaking, critical listening, appreciative listening, and so on. Specific strategies are presented for different subareas. The following examples illustrate some of these strategies:

1. *Strategies for Questioning.* Students are taught to ask questions regarding procedures (how something should be done), tasks (what will be done), information acquisition (what are the facts about something), and understanding (why something is or should be done). Students are presented with answers to their questions which they analyze in depth.

2. *Strategies for Self-monitoring.* Students check their own papers. They read the work backward for errors in spelling and editing irrelevant words.

3. *Strategies for Managing Time.* Because the efficient use of time is important for learning, all assignments are timed by clocks, stopwatches, or other timing devices. Students list tasks to be done, set priorities, and define long- and short-term goals; they make and analyze logs and design schedules.

4. *Strategies for Accomplishing Tasks.* To accomplish tasks that are classroom-oriented, students are taught to follow a sequence of strategies. They read tasks or problems, decide what information is relevant, and make an hypothesis as to the outcome of a problem. After they work through the problem, they compare their solution with their hypothesis and check their answers.

5. *Strategies for Problem Solving.* Once students' problem-solving styles have been identified, teachers help students improve their techniques. Students identify the information involved in a task, analyze the problem and the emotional reaction evoked by the problem, and set goals to resolve the problem. By brainstorming, students select a feasible solution. A course of action is determined, and the specific steps and resources necessary to complete the solution are determined. After the plan has been accomplished, students evaluate the strengths, weaknesses, and gaps of their problem-solving strategies.

Notes: Learning Strategies is applicable to many students with mild handicaps and slow learning students who have logic and reasoning deficits.

A system of generalization must be provided to ensure the carryover of Learning Strategies to social situations and various setting. Teachers must monitor students' performance and provide feedback; otherwise, the impact of this method may be lost. In addition, administrative support and support from regular classroom teachers is necessary. Student cooperation is crucial. Learning Strategies helps students to learn to advocate for themselves. This method is a total way of teaching rather than a supplement to an existing curriculum; remedial activities are not taught.

SQ3R

Method: SQ3R

Author: Francis Robinson

Sources: Robinson, F. (1961). *Effective study* (rev. ed.). New York: Harper & Row; Graves, M. F., Cooke, C. L., & LaBerge, M. (1983). Effects of previewing difficult short stories on low ability junior high students' comprehension, recall, and attitudes. *Reading Research Quarterly, 18,* 262–276; Irvin, J. L., & Rose, E. O. (1995). *Starting early with study skills: A week-by-week guide for elementary students.* Needham Heights, MA: Allyn & Bacon.

Description: SQ3R is a study skill technique designed to assist students in systematically approaching the reading of content areas. This technique can be introduced as early as third grade, depending on the reading skills of students. However, reading meaningfully in content materials does require specific study skills.

SQ3R stands for survey, question, read, recite, and review. In implementing this approach, students are taught first to **study** the assigned reading, to check its length, headings, titles, and so forth to get a broad introduction to its content. Second, students jot down or frame **questions** that emerge from the preceding survey. For example, subheadings may be rephrased as questions. Third, students **read** to answer their own questions. They have now examined the assignment twice, once to survey it and formulate questions about it, and again to seek to answer those questions. Fourth, after students have read the material, they return to their questions and attempt to **recite** them mentally, in writing, or in peer

discussion groups. Fifth, students should **review** the materials again later to facilitate better retention. This technique can be modified somewhat for students with learning disabilities.

Notes: The SQ3R method provides a systematic approach for students to acquire information from reading content area materials. This is a particularly useful strategy for individuals with learning disabilities, inactive learners, and students who approach studying in a random, unorganized fashion. Furthermore, this technique can be used by students who have adequate reading skills beginning in the fifth grade and continuing through secondary school and college.

SQ3R is most appropriate for students with learning disabilities who have average or above average reasoning skills, because it requires both the analysis and synthesis of information. In addition, this technique presupposes minimal reading ability—at about the fourth grade level—because content area texts are generally written at specific grade levels. However, the SQ3R method can be adapted for individual students. For example, textbook cues such as italics and underlined words, classroom cues such as previewing, and other instructional cues can and should be incorporated into the SQ3R method for individuals with learning disabilities. Students must receive instruction on when and how to use this technique. Moreover, it is important to keep the technique simple and not cognitively consuming.

REFERENCES

Andre, M. E. D. A., & Anderson, T. H. (1979). The development and evaluation of a self-questioning study technique. *Reading Research Quarterly, 14,* 605–623.
Barron, R. F. (1969). The use of vocabulary as an advance organizer. In H. L. Herber & P. L. Sanders (Eds.), *Research on reading in the content area: First year report* (pp. 29–39). Syracuse, NY: Syracuse University Press.

Devine, T. G. (1987). *Teaching study skills*. Newton, MA: Allyn & Bacon.

Earle, R. A. (1969). Use of the structured overview in mathematics classes. In H. L. Herber & P. L. Sanders (Eds.), *Research on reading in the content area: First year report* (pp. 49–58). Syracuse, NY: Syracuse University Press.

Ellis, E. S., Sabornie, E. J., & Marshall, K. (1989). Teaching learning strategies to learning disabled students in postsecondary settings. *Academic Therapy, 24*, 491–501.

Olson, J. L., & Platt, J. M. (1996). *Teaching children and adolescents with special needs*. Englewood Cliffs: Prentice-Hall.

Pany, D., & Jenkins, J. R. (1978). Learning word meanings: A comparison of instructional procedures. *Learning Disability Quarterly, 1*, 21–32.

Polloway, E. A., & Patton, J. R. (1993). *Strategies for teaching learners with special needs*. New York: Merrill.

Smith, T. E. C., & Dowdy, C. A. (1989). The role of study skills in the secondary curriculum. *Academic Therapy, 24*, 479–490.

Torgeson, J. K. (1984). Memory processes in reading disabled children. *Journal of Learning Disabilities, 12*, 396–401.

CHAPTER

11

Transition Methods

Donna Wandry, Ph.D.

CONTENTS

▶ Life Skills Instruction (Falvey)   212
▶ Life Centered Career Education   213
▶ Life Skills Instruction (Cronin)   214
▶ Bridges ... from
   School to Work Model   216
▶ Community Vocational
   Training Program   217
▶ Job Training and Tryout Model   219
▶ Job Development   220
▶ Community Transition Team Model   220
▶ Interagency Agreement Development:
   Vocational Education Model   222
▶ Parent Case Management   224
▶ ChoiceMaker   225
▶ Self-determination   226
▶ Career Portfolios   226
▶ McGill Action Planning
   System (MAPS)   227

Since the passage of the Education for All Handicapped Children Act (EHA), Public Law 94-142, in 1975, Individualized Education Programs (IEPs) have been a requirement of law for all children and youth with disabilities found eligible for special education. Subsequent amendments to the EHA—now entitled the Individuals with Disabilities Act, (IDEA) (Public Law 101-476)—added a new component to the IEP requiring a statement of needed transition services (Wandry & Repetto, 1993). Specifically, each student must have, beginning no later than age 16, a delineation of services needed to prepare for postschool outcomes such as employment, postsecondary education, adult services, independent living, and community participation [The Individuals with Disabilities Act, 20 U.S.C. Chapter 33, Section 1401 (a)(19)].

In reaction to this legislative language, emerging programs aimed at building best practice in transition planning and implementation have covered an extremely wide gamut. It has been difficult to reach consensus on a definition for transition services and what comprises the most effective approach to developing the services. Although IDEA defined transition services as noted above, professionals have suggested a definition of transition as a "change in status from behaving primarily as a student to assuming emergent adult roles in the community" (Halpern, 1994, p. 17) as a framework to guide future work. Halpern further notes that this change in status requires the participation and coordination of school programs, adult service agencies, and natural supports within the community, and that these partnerships should start during the elementary and secondary years.

Although varying definitions and frameworks surround the area of transition, several core indicators of quality transition programs have emerged in the literature (Halpern, 1992; Rusch & DeStefano, 1989; Wehman, 1990). These quality indicators are (a) effective and timely transition planning, (b) interagency collaboration, (c) family and student involvement, (d) appropriate curriculum and instruction, (e) inclusion in school, (f) adult services and community involvement, and (g) systematic personnel training.

This chapter offers a cross-section of curriculum and instruction models that reflect the current thinking in the field of transition. These models are not exhaustive, but rather represent emerging practices in this relatively new and still evolving area of educational responsibility to youth with disabilities.

LIFE SKILLS INSTRUCTION

Method: Life Skills Instruction

Author: Mary A. Falvey

Source: Falvey, M. A. (1989). *Community-based curriculum: Instructional strategies for students with severe handicaps* (2nd ed.). Baltimore: Paul H. Brookes.

Description: For many students with special needs, particularly those with severe disabilities, a community-based curriculum approach is highly appropriate. The underlying premise for such an approach is that some individuals find it difficult to transfer and generalize knowledge to settings where a skill is typically used. The result may be that, although a student can perform a skill in class, he or she may not be able to do so in the real world in which the skill is actually needed. According to Falvey, "community environments frequented by the student and by his or her family now and in the future should be the environments used to directly teach" (p. 92).

In the community-based curriculum approach, students initially learn and practice a skill in the classroom. Eventually, they practice the skill in the community or home setting. Falvey and her fellow researchers and authors developed a rationale and concrete model for creating a community-based approach to instruction.

Within this curriculum, several key issues and strategies for community-based instruction for persons with severe disabilities are outlined. The main components are:

1. *Partnerships with Parents and Significant Others.* Principles of effective partnerships with families are delineated. In addition, specific strategies for joint decision-making are noted.

2. *Assessment Strategies.* General parameters and strategies for assessing the skill repertoire and needs of students with severe disabilities are suggested, with the intent of guiding chronological age-appropriate and functional education planning. Guidelines for gathering formal and informal information (including ecological data), along with sample tables and charts, are included.

3. *Community Skills.* This section provides a rationale for developing and implementing community-based educational programs. Potential legal, administrative, programmatic, logistical, and financial barriers are outlined, accompanied by strategies for overcoming such barriers if they occur.

4. *Specific Content Instruction.* Specific strategies for developing and implementing community-based instruction for persons with severe disabilities are included for the following content areas: (a) domestic skills, including social and sexual skills training; (b) recreation skills across ages and environments; (c) employment skills, with an emphasis on integrated and supported employment; (d) motor skills development; (e) communication and interaction skills; and (f) inclusion issues related to developing educational programs within chronological age-appropriate regular education schools.

Notes: The rationale for providing instruction in individually relevant environments is clear in light of poor generalization and transference skills among students with disabilities. However, meeting the ecologically individual needs of every student may prove to be a daunting task. This approach is admirable in that it moves instruction from the classroom into the community. However,

teaching in generic community environments still cannot totally assure transference into the specific environments of students. The tendency to regard instruction as a school-driven practice disregards the parent as instructor in the home environment.

LIFE CENTERED CAREER EDUCATION

Method: Life Centered Career Education

Author: Donn Brolin

Source: Brolin, D. (Ed.). (1991). *Life-centered career education: A competency-based approach* (3rd ed.). Reston, VA: Council for Exceptional Children.

Description: The Life-Centered Career Education (LCCE) curriculum is the core of a comprehensive model designed to guide professionals in planning for and implementing individualized transition programming. The original curriculum model, developed in 1978, has undergone systematic revision and improvement since its inception. Recently developed products related to the basic curriculum structure include new instruments for (a) assessing student competency levels in adult domains (knowledge and performance batteries) and (b) individualizing curriculum planning.

The curriculum model reflects the more global interpretation of the term "career education" as not being synonymous with vocational education but rather with the concept of the person as a whole. Although Brolin recognizes that planning for work success is a primary need for the vast majority of students, he recognizes that a career is more than just an occupation. Therefore, the model incorporates other affective and life skills that are vital to productive work activity in the community and home. Brolin's interpretation of career education conceptualizes career development in distinct stages (awareness, exploration, preparation, and assimilation) that are to be addressed at specific points throughout the school years and beyond. Life skills, affective skills, and general employability skills are integral parts of that development.

Therefore, the LCCE is built around three major adult domains that should be infused into the educational program of students with special needs: daily living, personal-social, and occupational skills. Within those three domains, a set of 22 major competencies and 97 subcompetencies are identified. The intent of the curriculum model is not to plan daily lessons, but rather to provide a framework for a comprehensive set of career development skills.

The first of the three primary domains, daily living skills, has nine major competencies: (a) managing personal finances; (b) selecting and managing a household; (c) caring for personal needs; (d) raising children and meeting marriage responsibilities; (e) buying, preparing, and consuming food; (f) buying and caring for clothing; (g) exhibiting responsible citizenship; (h) using recreational facilities and leisure time; and (i) community mobility. Competency areas in the second domain, personal-social skills, are (a) achieving self-awareness, (b) acquiring self-confidence, (c) achieving socially responsible behavior, (d) maintaining good interpersonal skills, (e) achieving independence, (f) achieving problem-solving skills, and (g) communicating with others. The third curricular domain, occupational guidance and preparation, focuses on the following major competencies: (a) knowing and exploring occupational possibilities; (b) selecting and planning occupational choices; (c) exhibiting appropriate work habits; (d) seeking, securing, and maintaining employment; (e) exhibiting sufficient physical-manual skills; and (f) obtaining a specific occupational skill. The 97 subcompetencies, grouped under their respective major competency areas, are hierarchically arranged according to their performance difficulty. This arrangement does not imply rigidity. The competencies are relevant either for separate course content or infusion into regular curricular structures.

Each competency unit contains three sections: objectives, activities/strategies, and adult/peer roles. No specific grade level is suggested for the use of the competencies and subcompetencies in instructional planning. To assist the professional in determining the students' levels of mastery in relation to the competency structure, master forms for a Competency Rating Scales and a LCCE Inventory are available. To assist in individualized planning, an LCCE Individualized Education Program master form also is included.

In addition to the basic curriculum, the model includes a trainer's manual to guide school districts in implementing the LCCE. The training packet includes the content and materials for over 30 hours of inservice training.

Notes: The Life-Centered Career Education model and its related curriculum are extremely relevant to the skill and information needs of students with special needs as they prepare for the demands of adult life. Because of the emphasis on infusion of LCCE content into current curricular structures, it would be difficult to use this model in its fullest sense without the support of school district administrators. However, the model is invaluable in IEP planning for adult outcomes and provides a well-organized, thorough format for general competency assessment and related instruction. The suggested activities and strategies are easy to implement and interesting for students.

LIFE SKILLS INSTRUCTION

Method: Life Skills Instruction

Authors: Mary E. Cronin and James R. Patton

Source: Cronin, M. E., & Patton, J. R. (1993). *Life skills instruction for all students with spe-*

cial needs: A practical guide for integrating real-life content into the curriculum. Austin, TX: Pro-Ed.

Description: The need for providing instruction in daily living skills is supported by both legislative language and providers who are aware of the difficulties individuals with special needs have in dealing with the challenges of day-to-day experiences. Special education personnel are faced with the task of incorporating Life Skills Instruction into already crowded curricular demands. The concept of curriculum content integration, with its underlying philosophy of teaching functional skills within traditional content, is espoused in this model. The conceptual framework is derived from an appraisal of likely outcome environments. It applies a top-down curriculum development process based on an accurate analysis of these likely environments. The model provides a framework for balancing functional and traditional curriculum content. It also incorporates suggestions for making the task more successful and lists resources to assist in the practice. The major content areas are summarized below.

1. *Overview of Existing Curricular Options.* In this section, the authors address curricular themes, including academic content coverage, remediation, regular class support, and adult outcomes. These themes are discussed in terms of their major features and functional relevance. Attention is given to balancing the need for students to be integrated academically with the need to provide instruction in more functional content.

2. *Domains of Adult Life.* This section organizes the daily demands of living into clusters of adult function domains. The domains include (a) employment/education, (b) home and family, (c) leisure pursuits, (d) community involvement, (e) physical emotional health, and (f) personal relationships and responsibilities. These domains are further explored through 23 subdomains and 147 major life demands, with the intent that these components be used to create instructional goals and objectives, courses, and activities.

3. *Integration of Adult Function Content into Traditional Curriculum.* Supporting the philosophical basis for this model, a continuum of five basic curriculum constructs (with accompanying rationale, procedure, and examples) is presented. The authors' message is that teaching of life skills can be done, to some extent, regardless of the educational environment in which students are placed. A sample matrix representing how the six major domains and their subcomponents can be introduced into traditional curriculum subject areas is included.

4. *Instructional Considerations/Materials Selection and Development.* The importance of a combination of classroom- and community-based instruction is clear, given the presence of those terms in the definition of transition in IDEA. In addition, the selection of appropriate materials for use in these settings is crucial. This section stresses factors to consider in selecting materials based on real-life task correlation, commercial availability, and linkages to community-derived resources. Specific guidelines for materials analysis are presented to guide the practitioner.

5. *Guidelines for Planning, Implementing, and Maintaining a Life Skills Program.* This section offers a practical guide for educators considering modification or alteration of traditional curricular programs. Suggestions for getting started include seeking administrative support and additional funding, facilitating personnel development, and developing a pilot curriculum. Implementation guidelines include development of appropriate content, community involvement, and dissemination.

6. *Supporting Resources.* Extensive appendixes include the following information: (a) materials lists (including publisher, age level, and reading level) across the 23 subdomains developed by the authors, (b) publisher's addresses, (c) potential field experience sites for community-based instruction with accompanying competency checklists, (d) sample transition plan formats, (e) sample permission letters, and (f) an annotated resource list of pertinent books and journal articles.

Notes: This method is relevant to any practitioner who is striving to blend Life Skills Instruction with prescribed curriculum content. Although educators are becoming more concerned with outcomes-oriented instruction, the dependence on traditional academic courses and curricular content is a continuing foundation. Concurrently, trends in state competency testing enforce the growing inclusion of students with disabilities in academically based performance measures. With these constraints, it will continue to be a challenge for special educators to find a balance between the two seemingly dichotomous curriculum foci. The options presented in this text are practical alternatives for professionals to consider in finding that balance.

Although suggestions for implementing a type of curricular systems change at the school, district, and state level are included, they are extremely sparse in light of sophisticated systems change models. Professionals who are considering such systemic change will find insufficient guidance in this document.

BRIDGES . . . FROM SCHOOL TO WORK MODEL

Method: Bridges . . . from School to Work Model

Authors: George P. Tilson, Richard G. Luecking, and Mark R. Donovan

Source: Tilson, G. P., Luecking, R. G, & Donovan, M. R. Involving employers in transition: The Bridges model. *Career Development for Exceptional Individuals, 17*(1), 77–89.

Description: The Bridges . . . from School to Work model was originally conceived under the auspices of the Marriott Foundation for People with Disabilities, a charitable ac-

tivity of the Marriott Corporation. The Marriott Foundation was established to foster the employment of young persons with disabilities. It is an outgrowth of the corporation's awareness of poor employment prospects of these youth and the uncertainty of business regarding how to work with this applicant group. The Bridges program was designed to address these concerns through its pilot site in Montgomery County, Maryland, the home of Marriott Corporation. Since its inception, the model has been replicated in San Francisco, Chicago, Washington, D.C., and Los Angeles. The model promotes cooperation with (a) local schools in the referral of youth with disabilities and (b) employers in competitively paid internships. Primary characteristics of the program are as follows:

1. *Participant Eligibility.* Students participating in the program represent all disabilities and levels of severity. They are referred to the program by special educators during the last 2 years of high school; the only criteria for acceptance into the program are a demonstrated interest in participating fully and a school schedule that can accommodate working. Participant characteristics and necessary accommodations throughout the entire process (referral, orientation, job search, and job placement/support) are based on individual needs, not disability. In addition, the participant pool closely reflects the racial profile of the respective communities in which Bridges operates.

2. *Orientation and Training of Employers, Youth, and Families.* The Bridges program requires that participating youth and their families attend orientation sessions regarding the program, employer expectations, and family expectations in support of the participant. In addition, the model stresses training for managers and co-workers in disability awareness, accommodations, and strategies for integrating youth into the workplace.

3. *Job Development.* Commitment from the employers is sought and fostered at all levels from top administration to co-workers. To that end, the model utilizes introductory sessions for community leaders, elected officials, and representatives of business at the executive and senior management levels. At a more specific level, a cadre of Employer Representatives conducts job development activities across a range of employers and occupational areas. This is coupled with any awareness training that may be needed to address concerns related to the hiring of persons with disabilities.

4. *Internship-Intern Matching Process.* Employer Representatives are charged with analyzing potential work sites according to factors such as required skills, workplace culture, and pace of operation. In addition, they work individually with the interns to determine their skills, characteristics, and work experiences, as well as any potentially necessary accommodations. Once viable matches are made between available work sites and intern profiles, internships of 2 to 6 months in duration are established. Interns are "hired" during the internship phase at competitive wages.

5. *Internships.* During the internship, ongoing support and evaluation are offered in the work site by the Employer Representative. Regularly scheduled conferences with the employer and intern give information on attendance, work performance, and general work behaviors. Interventions are given as needed and documented. The Employer Representatives serve as liaisons to monitor intern success and provide guidance in building natural supports with co-workers. They also advocate for permanent employment beyond the internship period.

6. *Follow-up Activities.* To document intern success and project effectiveness, data are collected prior to, during, and after the internships. Yearly follow-along data trace the status of the interns regarding employment, education, independent functioning, and related variables. Data indicate that the program has enjoyed an internship completion rate of 82%, and a subsequent employment rate of 86% either within the host companies or in other settings.

Notes: The Bridges . . . from School to Work program has presented a successful model for preparing youth with disabilities for employment. The strengths of the model are centered on the intensive efforts to match job requirements with student profiles, the emphasis on student strengths rather than deficits, and the collaborative relationships built with all worker and administrative levels of the employment setting. Because of the need for employers to commit to paid internships, this model presents a challenge in that regard. In addition, the model is fully implemented only in cities where a local community organization with a strong record of fostering the employment of persons with disabilities is identified by the Foundation and charged with the implementation of the model.

COMMUNITY VOCATIONAL TRAINING PROGRAM

Method: Community Vocational Training Program

Authors: Shepard Siegel, Karen Greener, J. Prieur, M. Robert, and R. Gaylord-Ross

Source: Siegel, S., Greener, K., Prieur, J., Robert, M., & Gaylord-Ross, R. (1989). The community vocational training program: A transition program for youths with mild handicaps. *Career Development for Exceptional Individuals, 12*(1), 49–64.

Description: The Community Vocational Training Program (CVTP) was developed in the San Francisco Unified School District with the intent of training and placing high school seniors with mild disabilities in permanent employment and postsecondary schools. It incorporates, as its foundation, best practices in improving school- based performance, training work behaviors, and developing social skills. By creating an experiential whole for students, the CVTP is able to build on its key components: (a) a willingness to make demands on the students, (b) a school-based Employment Skills Workshop, (c) an intensive community classroom supervision at work sites, and (d) commitment of staff during and beyond the last year of high school. The key components of the program are outlined below.

1. *Recruitment.* Working in collaboration with the program manager, an employee of the school district, classroom teachers refer seniors to a semester-long training program. Referral criteria for students include a motivation to work, parent support, good attendance records, some prevocational or vocational training, and some ability to alphabetize (for clerical positions); students must meet at least three of these criteria to qualify for admission to the program. On tentative admission, students must interview with the CVTP manager. They may be screened out at this point for aggressiveness, lack of punctuality, immaturity, or other discriminating behaviors. Once the successfully admitted intern candidate and the instructor decide which of the previously developed employment sites is suitable, the candidate is interviewed by the potential employer. Employers interview two candidates for each position. Students who are not successfully admitted are encouraged to reapply if they are at least one semester away from graduation. The overriding result of the recruitment process is a program that makes demands on the students, school personnel who make informed referrals of the students, and employers who have a vested interest in the success of the students.

2. *Job Site Activities.* The interns (5–12 at each work site) work 3 hours a day, 4 days a week. Initial supervision is by the site instructor, who assigns them job tasks. On-site instruction in generic job-keeping skills (attendance, punctuality, appropriate grooming, handling authority, giving and following instructions, asking for help, honesty, and responsibility) is delivered; this is in addition to the interns' worksite task responsibilities. Formative evaluation that assesses

attendance, social skills, and work quality and quantity is guided by at least two vocational objectives and one social objective for each intern. After a 3-week period, interns who have made substantial progress toward those objectives qualify for a minimum wage stipend underwritten by the State Department of Education and the Employment Development Department. Interns who have not made progress are terminated from the program. Successful interns who demonstrate the highest levels of independence may leave the original worksite and have experiences at satellite sites. Permanent job placement at training sites is not assumed, because the sites are used primarily for instruction purposes. However, a training site is encouraged to hire productive interns. Other program practices to help individuals secure ongoing employment include release time from the CVTP site for job interviews and a CVTP-provided "supported job search."

3. *Employment Skills Workshop.* One day a week, interns attend this workshop intended to address transitional needs. The core of the workshop is built on the CVTP "Pyramid of Transition," a hierarchy of skills that lead to permanent employment. The value of each skill builds on the mastery of the previous one, starting with attendance and followed by social skills, job-keeping skills, job skills, and job search skills. Discussion topics relevant to these skills are integrated with an affective curriculum that encourages team-building through group process, role plays, and similar techniques.

4. *Staff Roles.* The personal commitment of the on-site instructor is crucial to the success of the model. In addition to supporting intern efforts in the workplace, the instructor also plays a key role in fading his or her supports, thus encouraging natural co-worker supports to the intern. The instructor also coordinates ongoing evaluation, is the program's liaison to employers, and maintains the credibility of the program. In addition, the instructor advocates for job placement at the training site and delivers any education necessary to co-workers on the nature of disability and the philosophy of natural co-worker supports once program support has been withdrawn.

Notes: The Community Vocational Training Program presents a well-rounded approach to facilitate the movement from high school to employment for students with mild disabilities. Although the concern regarding "creaming", or serving students who have potential for being successful without intervention, is a possible criticism of this program, the authors see the success of the program as being contingent on students' having certain qualifying behaviors. It might be interpreted that the greater responsibility, then, rests with the school and home environments to stress the acquisition of these qualifying behaviors long before the need to exhibit them in the workplace.

JOB TRAINING AND TRYOUT MODEL

Method: Job Training and Tryout Model

Authors: Debra A. Neubert, George P. Tilson, and Robert N. Ianacone

Source: Neubert, D. A., Tilson, G. P., & Ianacone, R. N. (1989). Postsecondary transition needs and employment patterns of individuals with mild disabilities. *Exceptional Children, 55*(6), 494–500.

Description: The authors presented an overview of the Job Training and Tryout (JT&T) model, which was initially developed as a federally funded model demonstration project to provide services to individuals aged 18–30 who have learning disabilities and mild mental impairments. The program is delivered in several phases: (a) initial client intake; (b) an 8-week employability skills course consisting of vocational assessment, community-based exploration, and training

in social and job-seeking skills; (c) two job tryouts, or internships, at community employment sites; (d) structured job search support; (e) competitive job placement with formalized follow-up support; (f) job club; and (g) job change and advancement.

1. *Client Eligibility.* Individuals accepted in the program are referred by special education teachers, vocational rehabilitation counselors, or family members. Eligibility criteria include (a) special education placement with a classification of mild mental retardation or severe learning disability, (b) ability to use or desire to learn how to use public transportation, and (c) desire to obtain permanent employment.

2. *Research Foundation.* The authors conducted research within the scope of the model demonstration project. The participants in the original research included 39 females and 27 females, with a mean age of 22 years. The diverse sample included individuals of Anglo, Black, Hispanic, and Asian ethnicity. The participants completed an employability skills class and then conferenced with staff and family members to discuss the person's employability skill level and develop an action plan for job placement. Project staff then assisted participants in job search and interviewing. Subsequent to employment, assistance was offered in the form of work station organization, modifications of work task guides, clarification of workplace policies, and monitoring of social/interpersonal behaviors. Support time and follow-up throughout the course of employment were gradually faded. Data were then analyzed to determine staff support needs, job-related difficulties, and job retention/job change patterns.

Notes: The JT&T model is innovative in its efforts to provide not only job-seeking and on-site supports, but also to provide supports as necessary to negotiate movement within a job or between jobs. The recognition that persons with disabilities are equally as desirous of job mobility as their nondisabled peers is crucial in programming for vocational needs. It would have been interesting to note any natural co-worker supports that were developed in the course of workplace situations and whether they had any effect on the desire to change jobs or the ease with which such changes occurred.

JOB DEVELOPMENT

Method: Job Development

Authors: Dale DiLeo and Dawn Langton

Source: DiLeo, D., & Langton, D. (1993). *Get the marketing edge: A job developer's toolkit.* St. Augustine, FL: Training Resource Network.

Description: The authors developed this resource in response to requests from professionals assisting persons with disabilities in employment venues; the primary need was a framework to provide practical job development and marketing strategies. The desire was to move away from the "beg-place-pray" philosophy to presenting job seekers with disabilities as persons with skills that will contribute to the bottom line of productivity for employers. The resulting resource is comprised of two parts: (a) strategies for meeting employer needs and (b) methods for understanding the needs, preferences, and skills of each potential worker so effective work matches can be made.

Part One: Marketing Principles for the Employment of People with Disabilities. This part of the framework draws a close corollary between non-profit and for-profit organizations in their shared need to present themselves as entities that will successfully meet the needs of their consumers. Several strategies for job developers are described to (a) engage in a planning process for worksite development, (b) build networks and relationships with the business community, (c) incorporate business needs into the planning structure, and (d) create dissemination and media tools to most effectively advertise their services.

Part Two: Personalized Job Development. This section draws a parallel with the first, in that relationships with the consumer are stressed. However, the concept of the consumer is enlarged to include not only the business community, but also the prospective employee being served by the job site developer. To that end, attention is given to creating a full vocational profile of the prospective employee, based on casual interactions, formal and informal assessment, and engagement in a form of "futures planning" with other individuals involved in the prospective employee's life.

Using this information, job connections are sought through business relationships developed during the first phase. Strategies for facilitating effective job matches, involving job seekers in the search, and negotiating with employers for commitment to hiring are delineated.

Notes: The long-used philosophy of "Please hire the handicapped" is replaced effectively in this model. The basis of this "new" philosophy is built on a viable labor pool with a historically low rate of employment and a high desire to work—persons with disabilities who have the capabilities to fill employers' needs. This model redefines the task of marketing from trying to "sell" a prospective employee to a hesitant employer to "selling" the idea that worksite developers who seek employment opportunities for persons with disabilities provide a valuable service to the business community. By establishing an organization with a clear mission and a plan for action, human service providers can establish a strong, equitable presence in the consumer community they serve—their clients and their business partnerships.

COMMUNITY TRANSITION TEAM MODEL

Method: Community Transition Team Model

Authors: Andrew S. Halpern, Michael R. Benz, and Lauren E. Lindstrom

Source: Halpern, A. S., Benz, M. R., & Lindstrom, L. E. (1992). A systems change approach to improving secondary education and transition programs at the secondary level. *Career Development for Exceptional Individuals, 15*(1), 109–120.

Description: The authors of this systems change model focused on two key aspects of transition planning as put forth in the Individuals with Disabilities Education Act: (1) planning for individual students through the IEP process and (2) planning for program capacity to support service needs for those individual students. They also perceived that a substantive systems change model would be needed to facilitate the growth in service capacity. Guided by conditions that predecessors (Becklund & Haring, 1982; Hord, Rutherford, Huling-Austin, & Hall, 1987) had indicated must exist for such a model to work, the Community Transition Team Model (CTTM) was developed in Oregon.

Development of Program Standards. Program standards that provide the foundation of the model were gleaned primarily from a statewide survey of secondary special education and transition programs, and supported by an intensive literature review. The five principal areas of need were identified as (1) appropriateness of curriculum and instruction in terms of a balance between functional and academic content, (2) barriers to regular education/special education coordination and mainstreaming, (3) lack of assigned responsibility and parent participation in charting transition services, (4) documentation of student planning process and outcomes, and (5) need for adult services that provide assistance across the broad spectrum of living domains. A sixth category of administrative support was added to complete the final foundation.

These areas of need were used to create a set of standards by which existing programs could be assessed. The standards also pro-

vide the context for building from baseline in initiating changes in the local program or community. The original 71 standards were trimmed to 38 streamlined standards. They provide the frame of reference for program evaluation as well as the cornerstone for establishing procedures to facilitate any indicated systems changes needed. The entire set of standards and procedures comprise the Community Transition Team Model.

Description of the Model. The fullness of the CTTM is realized through local community transition teams or councils. These entities are usually comprised of persons with disabilities and their families, adult agency personnel, members of the general public (including employers), and school personnel. This local control is central to the successful implementation of the model, in that the set of 38 standards is used to set the framework for change. The local community team members use that framework to chart specific objectives and actions for change within their setting. The objectives emerge from a needs analysis once a working team is selected through a team-building process.

As objectives for change are being considered, the teams decide whether (a) they are going to take a person-centered, "wraparound" approach to build services collaboratively for a specific individual (and therein create the avenues of communication that can facilitate subsequent collaborations), or (b) they are going to focus on building the systemic collaborations that will then become available to meet individual needs. Once the approach is decided, tasks, timelines, resources, and responsibilities are delineated. Oversight of the phases of the CTTM model is conducted by an outside "change facilitator" until local control for action can be achieved. This resource remains available for continuing technical assistance and evaluation of outcomes. A crucial component of this local control is the willingness of teams to network with other community teams in information-sharing and support.

Material available to assist in the use of the model include a team leader's manual, a facilitator's manual, and a computerized data management information system that assists in the needs analysis, planning, and evaluation phases of the model. The latter also is supported by a user's manual.

Notes: Formation of a multidisciplinary team to address any area of services to persons with disabilities is often fraught with barriers due to different "languages", funding constraints, and case management assignment, among others (Sarkees & Scott, 1987). While all concerned have the best interest of their respective clientele as a priority, this shared interest does not automatically overcome interagency collaboration barriers. The CTTM model is efficient in its approach to "cut through" personal agendas and barriers and set concrete goals that reflect the collective perspectives of the individual team members. An outside facilitator and a clear process add to the effectiveness of this model. Although some of the indicators may need to be updated to reflect societal and cultural changes, the format itself is strong.

A challenge to teams implementing this model is to avoid selecting too many identified needs to address. A possible failure for any team using the CTTM approach is not in the processes leading to action plan development, but in the inability to effectively handle too many responsibilities at once as it tries to build collaborative partnerships through implementation of that action plan.

INTERAGENCY AGREEMENT DEVELOPMENT: VOCATIONAL EDUCATION MODEL

Method: Interagency Agreement Development: Vocational Education Model

Authors: Lloyd W. Tindall, John Gugerty, Elizabeth E. Getzel, JoAnn Salin, Gabrielle B. Wacker, and Carol B. Crowley

Source: Tindall, L. W., Gugerty, J., Getzel, E. E., Salin, J., Wacker, G. B., & Crowley, C. B. (1981). *Handbook on developing effective linking strategies: Vocational Education models for linking agencies serving the handicapped*. Madison: University of Wisconsin-Madison, Vocational Studies Center.

Description: In the words of the authors, "the purpose of this handbook is to assist State and local level personnel to develop effective linking strategies which will help meet the vocational education needs of handicapped students" (p. 3). The intent of this framework is not to focus exclusively on vocational education in our public school structures, but also on those professionals and agencies that may be involved in any phase of vocational education in its broader sense. Because of the inclusion of providers in and outside the school structure, the process requires effective interagency linkages. Tindall and his colleagues went to extensive lengths to address one aspect of interagency collaboration that they felt was key to that collaboration, namely, the formation and implementation of written interagency agreements. This handbook covers strategies for establishing and developing interagency agreements, the role of the Individual Education Plan (IEP) and the Individual Written Rehabilitation Plan (IWRP), guidelines for cross-agency inservice training, cost considerations, and strategies for program implementation and evaluation.

As with other professionals addressing interagency collaboration, Tindall and his colleagues placed great importance on bringing the right people "to the table" to form a team that will effectively address service collaboration needs. Tindall et al. have limited their focus to those who will be involved in providing and receiving vocational education and related services. However, a caution is extended that agency participants must have either the authority to commit resources from their respective agencies or the means to move up through the chain of command to procure that commitment. Professionals who do not have this channel, but who have interest, should be encouraged to join informal work teams that stem from the formal team structure.

The authors stress that the focus of the initial meetings of the team should be to establish a formal linkage committee and to select a sponsoring agency to serve as a catalyst for building the sought partnerships and giving a collective credibility to this possibly fragmented group. This group addresses the actions needed to overcome barriers related to attitudes, conflicting interagency policies and regulations, unclear intraagency operations, and environmental barriers such as participant logistics.

Writing a Local Agreement. Strategies for writing a local agreement reflect the need to clearly address such contingencies as referral procedures, financial responsibilities, functions of operating personnel, administrative relationships, and methods for information exchange. The model includes guidelines for negotiating a formal written agreement, as well as necessary components such as facilitative language. Suggestions for incorporating agreed upon service patterns into IEPs and IWRPs also play a key role in the model.

The need for inservice training is stressed in both early stages of cooperation and after the local agreement is written and being used to implement programs. Gugerty suggested that the lack of comprehensive inservice training for involved personnel may have contributed historically to the difficulty of maintaining linkages. Clear and thorough strategies for setting up and conducting an interagency workshop are included in this model.

Implementing a Local Agreement. Tindall stresses in this model that state level intera-gency teams must provide leadership and serve as role models in the development of interagency agreements. Even when local agreements are in place, the movement must still be cautious and supportive for the newfound collaboration to sustain itself.

Ongoing efforts to overcome personal agendas, conflicts, and fear of new practices must occur. Clarity concerning role definitions and projected tasks and timelines must exist. Accountability to the group process can be facilitated by holding public meetings and disseminating open statements concerning progress and barriers that occur.

Notes: Although this framework was constructed 15 years ago, its tenets and components are extremely timely. The challenges to building interagency linkages have yielded slow, yet steady, progress. As more pieces of federal legislation include language mandating interagency collaboration (most commonly through council structures), the practice of interagency agreements will continue to grow as a tool for cementing cross-agency cooperation. One might argue that the emphasis placed by the authors on the responsibility of agencies at the state level to serve as models for collaboration through written agreements is not enough; it would seem that state level personnel are sometimes restricted by the boundaries set at the national level.

In a similar vein, the authors charged local linkage teams with the responsibility of facilitating good communication among members, especially in the arena of interpersonal interaction. It was also suggested that each agency know what the others do. However, it might have been beneficial to address the need for intra-agency communication-building to assure a smooth flow of information from lower to upper ranks within particular agencies.

Finally, it must be noted that the use of interagency agreements, as delineated by the authors, places an emphasis on systemic change from the global to the specific (individual client) perspective. This might not find favor with those who support the wraparound perspective, which uses individual client planning as a catalyst for global systemic change.

PARENT CASE MANAGEMENT

Method: Parent Case Management (PCM)

Author: Staff

Source: Staff. (1991). *Parent case management: Self-determination and empowerment for persons with disabilities.* Minneapolis: University of Minnesota Institute on Community Integration.

Description: Since the 1960s, parent participation has been commonly included in model programs for children with disabilities. The intention has been to empower parents with certain rights and responsibilities that provide some influence over the services received by their children (Mallory, 1986). Since parental participation in the special education process was mandated by Public Law 94-142 (Education for Handicapped Children Act) in 1975, and reconfirmed in Public Law 101-476 (Individuals with Disabilities Education Act) in 1990, parents have been expected to be involved in assessment, planning, and evaluation (Brantlinger, 1987; Leyser, 1988) in the school settings. The underlying assumption of P.L. 94-142 was that the best way to ensure that each individual with disabilities would receive an appropriate education was to involve those most closely associated with that person; these individuals are perceived as having the person's best interests at heart in formulating individualized education planning (Winton, 1986).

These philosophies guided the formation of the Parent Case Management model. The purpose of the model is to give parents and other family members information that would enable them to have a positive influence over the type and quality of services their children with disabilities receive.

Description of the Model. Parents participating in the program commit to a series of training seminars designed to give them key information and fulfill particular objectives concerning their roles in their children's program. Primary objectives of the training include being able to (a) describe what case management means; (b) identify human and civil rights and responsibilities of persons with disabilities; (c) demonstrate effective use of resources and how to match resources to needs; (d) describe how to keep appropriate records; (e) demonstrate proper procedures for letter writing and effective meetings; (f) identify appropriate functional goals, health care issues, and technology issues; and (g) describe appropriate means to communicate with special education and related services professionals.

Training content includes materials in the areas of legislation, financial information, record-keeping, functional goals, services and resources, service acronyms, and technology. Evaluation is based on a pre-and posttraining survey that includes open-ended questions regarding any family role changes in case management issues as a result of involvement in the PCM model.

Notes: Although the Parents as Case Managers model is geared toward school age-students with developmental disabilities, it has relevance for transition from school to adult life as well. The literature supports parental involvement in educational processes during the school years (Boone, 1992; Gallagher & Vietze, 1985). Brofenbrenner (1974) suggests that, without ongoing family involvement, any effects of intervention appear to erode fairly rapidly once the program ends. In this light, the family is seen as the primary entity that contributes to meeting an adult son's or daughter's needs for continued and ongoing services (Johnson, Bruininks, & Thurlow, 1987). Thus, parents can be perceived as the ultimate advocates and case managers for their children as the one constant in a lifetime of service providers (Goodall & Bruder, 1986). Researchers (Wandry, 1992) are investigating this family case management role as youth exit school and enter adult service programs.

CHOICEMAKER

Method: ChoiceMaker

Authors: James E. Martin and Laura H. Marshall

Source: Martin, J. E., & Marshall, L. H. (1995). ChoiceMaker: A comprehensive self-determination transition program. *Intervention in School and Clinic, 30*(3), 147–156.

Description: Martin and Marshall built the ChoiceMaker model on the language put forth in P.L. 94-142 (Education for All Handicapped Children Act of 1975) and in the Education of Handicapped Children special education regulations of 1977 that mandated student participation in IEP meetings "whenever appropriate." Despite this call for student participation, its occurrence has been rare. In response to the need for well-grounded student participation, ChoiceMaker, a socially validated self-determination curriculum, assessment, and instructional program was developed.

Description of the Model. The ChoiceMaker curriculum addresses self-determination areas such as self-awareness, self-advocacy, self-efficacy, decisionmaking, independent performance, self-evaluation, and adjustment. The curriculum is divided into three phases: (1) selecting goals, (2) expressing goals, and (3) taking action on the goals.

The first section, selecting goals, teaches students to articulate their own interests, needs, and abilities in the context of classroom- and community-based experiences. During the second phase, expressing goals,

students learn how to relate their profile, as determined during the first phase, to the management of their own IEP meetings. Finally, during the third phase, taking action, students learn how to break their goals into manageable objectives and determine strategies for achieving them. In each section, teaching goals and objectives addressing various transition domains are presented.

The assessment component is a criterion-referenced tool matched with the curriculum. It contains teacher ratings of student skills in the three curriculum areas prior to instruction. Corresponding lesson packages, as described above, are used to implement the instructional needs as determined through assessment. The model follows a curriculum infusion philosophy that is appropriate for general or special education populations (with the exception of the self-directed IEP lesson plan).

Notes: Students' participation in their educational planning has, as is also true of family participation, been granted largely only "lip service." Despite the fact that the planning decides the daily ebb and flow of a student's life, as well as has implications for adult success, transition planning is in danger of becoming an "administrative paper shuffle" (Martin & Marshall, p. 148). The importance of student ownership of planning sessions is undisputed. However, the authors appear to dismiss other attempts to include the student within a vision-based context as inappropriately dependent on input from significant others rather than the student. A clear delineation must be made between students with learning disabilities for whom the ChoiceMaker was intended and students with more severe cognitive disabilities with whom vision-based techniques may be most commonly used. Regardless of the delineation, it is clear that transition planning, or any educational planning, must include proactive participation and leadership from the student consumer as well as from well-meaning professionals.

SELF-DETERMINATION

Method: Self-determination

Authors: Sharon Field and Alan Hoffman

Source: Field, S., & Hoffman, A. (1994). Development of a model for self-determination. *Career Development for Exceptional Individuals*, 17(2), 159–169.

Description: Field and Hoffman have responded to the need, as noted in legislation and federal protocols, for models that promote self-determination among individuals with disabilities. The ensuing model was constructed using validation exercises such as (a) literature reviews; (b) interviews defining self-determination, its components, and supporting or hindering factors; (c) student observations; and (d) focus groups across three states reviewing and critiquing model content.

Description of the Model. The overall theme of the model is one of defining and achieving goals based on a foundation of knowing and valuing oneself. In addition, it requires the individual to recognize both alterable and unalterable variables in his or her life and to exhibit self-determination in altering those variables that can be influenced.

In the central theme of the model, five major components are defined: (1) Know Yourself, (2) Value Yourself, (3) Plan, (4) Act, and (5) Experience Outcomes and Learn. All of these components are seen as interactive and mutually sustaining, suggesting that value-centered beliefs and concrete skills will not be effective if not exercised in concert.

The first component, **Know Yourself**, is structured to encourage individuals to develop an understanding of their own strengths, needs, and preferences, as well as a knowledge of the range of options available to them. The second component, **Value Yourself**, is designed to build the self-knowledge that students have the right to pursue their desires and to enhance this knowledge in terms of self-acceptance and self-esteem regardless of personal limitations.

The third and fourth components, **Planning** and **Action**, are designed to teach concrete skills that will assist students in seeking what they desire. This is accomplished through the generation of long- and short-term goals, as well as a series of enabling steps. Then it is necessary to build the confidence of individuals so they will take risks in achieving these goals, objectives, and steps. Skills in negotiation, conflict resolution, and persistence are an integral part of this component. The fifth component, **Experience Outcomes and Learn**, is based on an evaluation of what self-determination has accomplished and is used in turn to encourage further instances of risk-taking.

Although the intent of this model is to serve as a guide for further development of strategies and materials, the authors also have developed and field-tested a curriculum based on the model. They further suggest that it be used as a tool for further research and a guide for local development efforts in operationalizing the components of self-determination described in the model.

Notes: The model appears to achieve a good balance between development of the more nebulous qualities of self-esteem and concrete risk-taking behaviors. Because of the conceptual nature of the model, it is difficult to determine the populations for whom it would be most beneficial. It may be undesirable for individuals who are seeking a discrete set of goals and instructional activities. However, the undefined nature of the model allows variations in specific content as the components are operationalized by various consumers.

CAREER PORTFOLIOS

Method: Career Portfolios

Authors: Michelle Sarkees-Wircenski and Jerry L. Wircenski

Source: Sarkees-Wircenski, M., & Wircenski, J. L. (1994). Transition planning: Developing a portfolio for students with disabilities. *Career Development for Exceptional Individuals, 17*(2), 203–214.

Description: Current educational reform relies on sets of indicators or skills that every student who leaves our educational system should possess to pursue employment or further education (The Secretary's Commission on Achieving Necessary Skills, 1991). To address this need, student portfolios are used to document the levels of proficiency achieved by students in these skill areas. Sarkees-Wircenski and Wircenski have taken this basic premise of student portfolios and enlarged it to include a validated set of competencies necessary for successful transition from school to adult life for students with disabilities.

The Career Portfolio concept was the result of this effort. Although the Career Portfolio was designed to chart student performance specifically in vocational education, it contains statements of mastery in other adult domains as well. Following development and field validation, the portfolio was divided into five primary domains: (1) 31 employability skills necessary to obtain and maintain a job, (2) 18 work-related social skills that enable a person to establish positive relationships in the workplace, (3) 17 independent living skills necessary to function independently in the community, (4) 34 generalizable basic academic skills that can transfer across job settings, and (5) 8 job-specific skills that allow a person to be an effective worker in specified jobs or occupational fields.

Structure and Uses of the Portfolio. Following a cover page that provides student information and a list of the five competency areas and their subskills, a rating scale is included to measure student proficiency across a continuum ranging from "no exposure/knowledge" to "ability to perform independently and in a job-ready fashion." The scale is completed by instructors, and presumably (al-though the authors did not mention it) passed on with the student to subsequent settings. This provides a longitudinal assessment of progress in specific skills.

Suggested uses for the portfolio are as (a) an informal assessment tool before placement into a vocational program, (b) a baseline for generation of IEP goals and objectives, (c) an indicator for effective matches between skills and job demands, (d) a vocational counseling tool, and (e) an effective documentation in a job interview.

Notes: The authors have presented a clear model for a concept that appears to be taking root rapidly among schools. Although the use of such a portfolio is limited among the general education population, it is growing among special educators. More sophisticated examples can be found in local school districts, where the portfolio document is used as a transition planning sheet complete with timelines, tasks, and staff responsibilies. Major challenges to using a transition portfolio include the need for acceptance of the document and the process by all involved school and agency staff, as well as the commitment to use the information to plan consecutively related IEPs throughout the years.

McGILL ACTION PLANNING SYSTEM (MAPS)

Method: McGill Action Planning System (MAPS)

Authors: Susan Stainback, William Stainback, and M. Forest

Source: Stainback, S., Stainback, W., & Forest, M. (1989). *Educating all students in the mainstream of regular education* (pp.51–55). Baltimore: Paul H. Brookes.

Description: The McGill Action Planning System (MAPS) was developed as a systems approach to assist school teams in planning for integration of new students into regular education classrooms. However, it has significant implications for the integration of students with disabilities into the community and adult life. The model revolves around the inclusion of students, parents/family members, professionals familiar with the student, and friends or other informal supports. The inclusion of family members is seen as particularly important, because they know most about the person and may be perceived as the one constant in that person's life (Goodall & Bruder, 1986). The family members also can use this opportunity to strengthen their support needs through friends and significant others in attendance. The MAPS process can also be seen as an opportunity for the planning team, often for the first time, to become aware of the family's desires for the future successes of their child.

The focus of MAPS is to create a plan for the student to be integrated into the school (again, integration into adult life domains can be seen as a broader interpretation of the entire integration philosophy). The MAPS meeting is seen as crucial to this process. At the meeting, key questions are asked and input is sought from all in attendance. These questions and their intent are briefly described:

1. *What is the student's history?* This is an opportunity to summarize key milestones in the student's life that may impact future outcomes. By gathering different perspectives from the student and others in his or her life, a more complete profile of significant occurrences can be generated.

2. *What are your dreams for the student?* By asking this question, individuals with disabilities and their family members have the opportunity to articulate a vision for future activities. These can reflect not only immediate outcomes in the school setting, but desires concerning adult domains such as living arrangements, employment interests, and social interactions.

3. *Who is this person?* Team members are encouraged to describe attributes, strengths, and needs of the individual. Besides the opportunity to share insights from varying perspectives, this interaction can provide a way for the person to reveal self-esteem issues that can affect future attempts at self-determination.

4. *What would an ideal day for this person look like?* Although this model was created with school inclusion in mind, the implications for future adult activities are clear. This is an opportunity for team members to envision a successful lifestyle for the individual, and to consider what needs to happen to enhance the possibilities of such success occurring.

Notes: The McGill Action Planning System provides an ideal opportunity for students and families to take leadership in planning for their needs and desires as part of the educational process. The inclusion of students, family members, friends, and other informal supports is a refreshing addition to this process, which has seen continuing growth in subsequent related models.

By using such a model, educators can take a back seat in the team structure and serve as facilitators rather that primary controllers of the educational planning process. The depth of information gleaned from such a "visioning" activity will be invaluable in creating instructional goals and objectives that are the most relevant to the student being served.

REFERENCES

Becklund, J. D., & Haring, N. G. (1982). *Strategies for change in special education: Maintaining and transferring effective innovations.* Seattle: University of Washington Press.

Boone, R.(1992). Involving culturally diverse parents in transition planning. *Career Development for Exceptional Individuals, 15*(2), 205–221.

Brantlinger, E. (1987). Making decisions about special education placement: Do low income parents have the information they need? *Journal of Learning Disabilities, 20*(2), 94–101.

Bronfenbrenner, U. (1974). Is early intervention effective? *Teachers' College Record, 76,* 279–303.

Gallagher, J. J., & Vietze, P. M. (1985). *Families of handicapped persons.* Baltimore: Paul H. Brookes.

Goodall, P., & Bruder, M. B. (1986). Parents and the transition process. *Exceptional Parent, 16*(2), 22–28.

Halpern, A. (1992). A systems change approach to improving secondary special education and transition programs at the community level. *Career Development for Exceptional Individuals, 15*(1), 109–120.

Halpern, A. (1994). Transition of youth with disabilities to adult life: A position statement of the Division on Career Development and Transition, The Council for Exceptional Children. *Career Development for Exceptional Individuals, 17*(2), 115–124.

Hord, S. M., Rutherford, W. L., Huling-Austin, L., & Hall, G. E. (1987). *Taking charge of change.* Alexandria, VA: Association for Supervision and Curriculum Development.

Individuals with Disabilities Act, Public Law 101-476, 20 U.S.C. Chapter 33, (1990). (Available from the Superintendent of Documents, U.S. Government Printing Office, Washington, DC 20402.)

Johnson, D. R., Bruininks, R. H., & Thurlow, M. L. (1987). Meeting the challenge of transition services planning through improved interagency cooperation. *Exceptional Children, 53,* 522–530.

Leyser, Y. (1988). Let's listen to the consumer: The voice of parents of exceptional children. *The School Counselor, 35,* 363–369.

Mallory, B. L. (1986). Interactions between community agencies and families over the life cycle. In R. R. Fewell & P. F. Vadasy (Eds.), *Families of handicapped children* (pp. 317–356). Austin, TX: Pro-Ed.

Rusch, F., & DeStefano, L. (1989). *Secondary transition intervention effectiveness: Fourth annual report.* Champaign, IL: Transition Research Institute.

Sarkees, M. D., & Scott, J. L. (1987). *Vocational special needs* (2nd ed.). Homewood, IL: American Technical Publishers.

The Secretary's Commission on Achieving Necessary Skills. (1991). *What work requires of schools: A SCANS report for America 2000.* Washington, DC: Department of Labor.

Wandry, D. (1992). *The effect of a training module on parental knowledge and self-perception in transition case management collaboration skills.* Unpublished doctoral dissertation, University of Florida, Gainesville.

Wandry, D., & Repetto, J. B. (1993). *Transition planning in the IEP.* Washington, DC: National Information Center for Children and Youth with Disabilities.

Wehman, P. (1990). School-to-work: Elements of successful programs. *Teaching Exceptional Children, 23*(1), 40–43.

Winton, P. (1986). Effective strategies for involving families in intervention efforts. *Focus on Exceptional Children, 19,* 1–11.

CHAPTER

12

Computer Methods

Renet Lovorn Bender, Ph.D.

CONTENTS

▶ **Computer Proficiency** 232
▶ Teaching Keyboard Skill 232
▶ Hunt and Peck Typing 233
▶ Touch Typing 233
▶ Positions of Fingers 233
▶ Pseudo-Keyboards 234
▶ Using Computer Software to
Teach Touch Typing 234
▶ **Teaching Students the Basics
of Computer Use** 236
▶ Computer Operator's License 236
▶ Computer Instructions Chart 236
▶ **Software Organization** 238
▶ Color Coding of Software 238
▶ Individual Student Folders 239
▶ Computer Control of Student
Access to Programs 239
▶ Notebook of Computer Use 240
▶ **Computer Methods
for Teachers** 240
▶ Placement of Computers in
the Classroom 240
▶ Scheduling of Computer Time 241
▶ **Integration of CAI** 242

▶ Guidelines for Implementation
of CAI 242
▶ Integration of CAI 244
▶ Matching Learning Characteristics
of Students with Attributes of
Computer Software 244
▶ **Software Evaluation** 249
▶ Software Selection by List 249
▶ Applications Evaluation
of Software 249
▶ Evaluation of Multimedia
Software 258
▶ **Assistive Technology** 259
▶ Speech Synthesizers 259
▶ Speech Recognition Systems 264
▶ Switching Systems 265
▶ Joysticks 265
▶ Touch Screen 265
▶ Touch Tablets 266
▶ Screen Magnification Systems 266
▶ Braille Access Systems 266
▶ Muppet Learning Keys 267
▶ Intellikeys 267

In classrooms, teachers are almost always expected to teach students with varying levels of knowledge and ability. This is particularly true in today's inclusive classrooms. The proper use of computers and Computer Aided Instruction (CAI) can be of considerable help to teachers in schools and other institutional settings. The use of computers can assist teachers in totally restructuring the methods of instruction. For example, if a student needs more work on spelling than other students, the teacher should utilize CAI to assist the student. The student gets the individual attention he or she needs to keep up with the rest of the class, while the teacher has more time for other individualized lessons. The benefits of using computers include, both significantly enhanced learning for students (Dailey & Rosenberg, 1994; Higgins & Boone, 1990; Keyes, 1994), and more job satisfaction for teachers.

This chapter is written as a reference guide for the use of computers and CAI in the classroom. It is intended for teachers at all grade levels. The main goal is to be of service to teachers by (a) being mindful of the needs of teachers and students in the classroom; (b) being careful not to overload the reader with unnecessary technical information while presenting practical classroom methods; and (c) writing methods that, not only give good results, but can be implemented in small increments of time.

There are three sections in this chapter. The first section, Computer Proficiency, contains methods to teach students how to use computers and to become self-reliant in their use of computers. For example, this section contains methods to teach students keyboard skills and methods to set up the computers and software so that students can use it with minimal teacher supervision.

The second section, Computer Methods, contains methods for the use of computers in the classroom. For example, this section contains methods to match computer software attributes to students' learning characteristics, help choose the right software for students, and use computers in classroom lessons.

The third section, Assistive Technology, describes hardware and software that are available to help disabled students. For example, this section contains methods for alternative interaction with computers other than regular keyboards. When looking at this section, educators should keep in mind that, although assistive technology was designed for disabled students, other students will enjoy this technology too.

COMPUTER PROFICIENCY

Teaching students to use computers can be a rewarding task when students realize a goal of self sufficiency with respect to using computers. The methods enumerated in this section are specifically designed to help students attain this goal.

TEACHING KEYBOARD SKILLS

Keyboard skills are some of the most important skills students need when using instructional software (Bitter, Camuse, & Durbin, 1993; Lewis, 1993). Lack of these skills can cause students to become frustrated at the time it takes to perform a task. However, keyboard skills should not be a prerequisite for computer use. As students use computers more frequently and become frustrated by having to hunt for keys, the need for keyboard skills will become apparent to them and they will become more motivated to learn these skills.

When young students begin using CAI, one of the first things they learn is that, in order to communicate with the computer, one uses a keyboard. Most programs for very young students use only a few keys: the **enter** or **return** key, the **spacebar**, and the **arrow** keys. It is only when students begin to use the computer for writing, that they must learn the location of the letter keys. When students are first learning to use the keyboard, it may be beneficial for them to use an alternative keyboard, such as *IntelliKeys* or *Muppet Learning Keys*. These keyboards arrange the keys in alphabetical order (see Assistive Technology). But, at some point, students must use standard keyboards which have the QWERTY, or standard, configuration.

Students with skills on the level of the early grades usually begin to interact with the computer using the hunt and peck method on the keyboard. Some of these students will become very adept in this method. However, if the long-term goal is for students to use word-processing software, they should be taught a quick and efficient method with which to interact with the keyboard.

HUNT AND PECK TYPING

Method: Hunt and Peck Typing

Description: In the hunt and peck method of typing, both index fingers are used to type. This method requires constant looking between the page or computer screen and the keyboard.

Notes: Although some people become fast typers using this method, they will not be able to match the speed that can be obtained using the touch typing method below.

TOUCH TYPING

Method: Touch Typing

Description: In touch typing, students learn the location of keys on the computer keyboard by touch. It is the most efficient keyboard method for most students.

Notes: The problem that many teachers face is that teaching touch typing to stu-

dents requires time, usually at the expense of other subjects. One possible solution is to teach touch typing as a part of the writing curriculum (Lewis, 1993). Have the students perform their writing assignments on the computer using a word-processing package and mark 3–5 minutes of the lesson time for instruction in touch typing. It is exciting for students to learn locations of keys and then immediately use the keys in the writing lesson. Furthermore, Bitter, et al. (1993) suggest that older students should take personal or business typing classes offered by schools. The standard method of teaching typing in these classes is touch typing. See methods below on finger position and pseudo-keyboards.

POSITIONS OF FINGERS

Method: Positions of Fingers

Author: J. A. Van Dorn

Source: Personal communication

Description: The teaching of keyboard skills can begin as soon as students' hands are large enough. Students should be taught that the fingers of the left hand are placed on the ASDF keys and those of the right hand on the JKL; keys. This particular row of keys is called the home row. The students' thumbs should be resting lightly on the spacebar. From this position, students will learn the remainder of the keys. With washable ink, the teacher writes letters on the students' fingers so that they can remember which keys are pressed by which fingers. Students start with only the letters contained in the home row of the keyboard. New rows are added as the students' proficiency increases. The only letters on the students' fingers are the keys that they have learned. As new keys are learned, they are added to the fingers. Figure 12–1 shows which fingers are used to press which keys

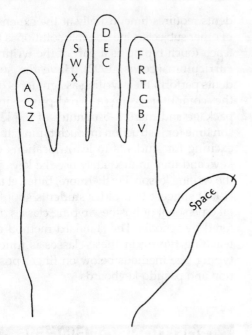

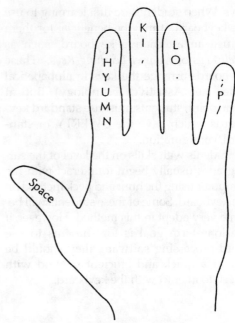

Figure 12–1. Finger positions for keyboarding.

when students have learned the letter keys. On the students' right index finger are the letters JHYMNB on their left middle finger at the letters EDC.

PSEUDO-KEYBOARDS

Method: Pseudo-Keyboards

Description: Pseudo-Keyboards are a piece of paper or cloth on which a keyboard is drawn. These are easy and inexpensive to make. Moreover, Pseudo-Keyboards are ideal for teaching the entire class or groups of students touch typing when the number of computers in the classroom is limited.

Notes: An advantage of Pseudo-Keyboards is that the students can take them home for practice. Adding music with a slow enough beat to type to is also fun for the entire class.

USING COMPUTER SOFTWARE TO TEACH TOUCH TYPING

Method: Using Computer Software to Teach Touch Typing

Authors: Renet L. Bender and W. N. Bender

Source: Bender, R. L., & Bender, W. N. (1996). *Computer-assisted instruction for students at-risk for ADHD, mild disabilities, or academic problems.* Boston: Allyn and Bacon.

Description: Software packages are available to help teach students keyboard skills. Most of this software starts by demonstrating and/or describing how each key should be pressed. Some of these programs show a keyboard on the screen and demonstrate keystrokes by highlighting specific keys. As the students practice with these new keys, they receive immediate feedback on their accuracy. A few of the programs do not accept an incorrect keystroke. Generally, programs that teach keyboard skills contain practice drills that emphasize accuracy and speed. Most keep a record of the students' performance so the student and the teacher can see how they are improving.

One example of a software package to teach young students keyboard skills is *Type to Learn* by Sunburst Communications. This software is available for Apple, Macintosh, IBM, and IBM-compatible computers. *Type to Learn* uses pictures of two hands on the computer screen to demonstrate the key strokes to students. The fingers on the computer screen wait for the student to follow them before moving to the next key stroke. Most directions are given as words and symbols so the program can be used with prereaders.

This program is easy to use and has appealing menus and graphics. The main menu displays five options. The first option is **Learn New Keys** which teaches students new keys. The second is **Games** which contains games to reinforce the new keys the student has learned. The next is **Scratch Pad** which is a simplified word-processing program that allows the student to use only the keys that have been mastered so far in the lessons. The fourth is **Speed Up** which provides text at the top of the screen for the student to copy. The final option is **Good-bye** which exits from the program. *Type to Learn* uses colorful graphics and an errorless learning feature to keep students motivated. It also has a teacher management option that allows teachers to individualize and maintain records using a Change Option menu. This program comes with a detailed manual explaining all parts of the program. The manual also includes a section for teachers with suggestions for using *Type to Learn* in their classroom, and a section for use with exceptional students, including gifted students. The manual contains numerous forms and charts for teacher use and detailed descriptions of the lessons.

Another program that teaches keyboard skills is *Junior Typer* by Aquarius Instructional. This software is available for Apple, Macintosh, IBM, and IBM-compatible computers. It can also be purchased through Edmark. *Junior Typer* uses the techniques of showing a keyboard on the screen and demonstrating the keystrokes to facilitate exercises for letter combinations, numbers, word phrase combinations, and sentences. This program uses menus that allow teachers to choose the skills on which the students need practice. Furthermore, each student's progress is tested and recorded. This program is appropriate for the skill level of elementary grades.

A software program for students from kindergarten through 8th grade skill level is *Talking Fingers* by California Neuropsychology Services (marketed by Cambridge Development Laboratory). This program uses speech sounds with finger strokes on the keyboard to teach students, not only keyboard skills, but also word-processing and phonics. The software consists of several parts. One part, **Typing Challenges**, uses graphics that display two imaginary keyboard houses with rooms on different floors (representing the rows of keys) inhabited by characters. The characters come alive to guide students through the mystery of the keyboard. Another part of this software package, **Discovery Textwriter**, is a talking word processor that can be used with students who are just learning to read. *Talking Fingers* is currently available for use with Apple, Macintosh, IBM, and IBM-compatible computers.

Mavis Beacon Teaches Typing! (available for Apple, Macintosh, IBM, and IBM-compatible computers) by Software Toolworks (marketed by Cambridge Development Laboratory) is another program that is widely used in classrooms.

Notes: The software packages described above are just a sample of the many packages on the market designed to help students at all skill levels learn keyboard skills. Teachers should keep in mind that the use of computer software to teach keyboard skills is just one teaching method of many. Most teachers find that a combination of teaching methods achieves the best results. Addresses for the companies mentioned above are included in the appendix.

TEACHING STUDENTS THE BASICS OF COMPUTER USE

Teaching students keyboard skills is not sufficient for them to feel confident in using a computer. Students need to learn how to use a computer properly. This learning experience can be both frightening and exciting to students. Everyone at one time or another has forgotten how to use a computer or has forgotten a particular command needed to do something. Here methods are presented for teaching students how to operate a computer and helping them remember the steps in its operation. In short, if a student forgets a step in the operation of a computer, methods are suggested that allow that student to "look up" what to do. This is an aspect of computer use that is often overlooked in computer applications instruction for students at all levels. Nevertheless, it is one of the most important aspects of computer use, in that, if the student can solve his or her own problems, the teacher will have more time to concentrate on individualized instruction. Obviously, this also fosters student independence, and the students gain a feeling of self-confidence about using computers.

Several basic steps must be taught to students, regardless of the system used. These basic steps include:

1. *Turning on the Computer and the Monitor.* Some computers and monitors have their power switches in obscure places. Others are plugged into a power bar (a portable outlet that has 6–10 plug-ins) that also has an on-off switch. Students must learn to do this as a first step.

2. *Adjusting the Contrast and Brightness of the Monitor.* These dials are easily changed by curious students and by anyone cleaning the classroom. Students should be taught to adjust these controls for their comfort.

3. *Putting a Diskette/CD in the Computer.* Depending on the size of diskettes the system uses, students need to know which side of the floppy disk is the top and how to lock the disk drive (if they are using an older computer). Instruction should also include teaching students how to handle disks and CDs. For example, students should be taught not to touch the actual disk, and that they should handle the CDs from the edges. They are going to be curious about what a floppy disk looks like inside. Therefore, cut one open and have it available for them to inspect. Students should be taught not to leave floppy diskettes in the sun—they may melt. Leave a floppy disk outside during a hot day and show students the result. Furthermore, students need to know if a diskette is required in the disk drive before they turn the power on (this is true for older computers).

COMPUTER OPERATOR'S LICENSE

Method: Computer Operator's License

Author: R. B. Lewis

Source: Lewis, R. B., (1993). *Special education technology: Classroom applications.* Pacific Grove, CA: Brooks/Cole.

Description: When teaching students the operation of a computer, some teachers issue what is called an operator's license, which is similar to a driver's license. With this method, students are shown individually how to operate the computer. They practice for awhile, and when they feel they are ready, they demonstrate their ability to operate the computer. For some at-risk students, teachers may wish to have them demonstrate their new skills for the entire class to help them build confidence. On successful completion of the "licensing" test, students are awarded their operators' licenses. Figure 12–2 is an example of such a license.

COMPUTER INSTRUCTIONS CHART

Method: Computer Instructions Chart

Author: R. L. Bender

Source: Bender, R. L., & Bender, W. N. (1996). *Computer-assisted instruction for students at-risk for ADHD, mild disabilities or academic problems*. Boston: Allyn & Bacon.

Description: Because many at-risk students demonstrate memory problems, teachers should put a Computer Instructions Chart nearby, to remind students of the basic steps in using the computer. These charts can take several forms. For example, if the students have reading skills, the teacher can make a poster that enumerates the steps and place it on the wall behind the computer. Figure 12–3 is an example of such a chart.

Computer Operator's License

Name: _____

Date: _____

Computer: _____

Sign off on each of the steps of operation as the student demonstrates proficiency.

1. _____

2. _____

3. _____

4. _____

I hereby certify that _____ has demonstrated the

  ability to operate a computer. I hereby authorize _____ to

  use the computer.

Date _____

Signature _____

Figure 12–2. Computer operator's license.

AT THE BEGINNING:

1. Put the disk in the disk drive (the slot in the front of the computer).

   Top up (the top is the side with the label).

   Metal part goes in first.

2. Turn on the computer.

   The switch is on the back right; you switch it up.

3. Turn on the monitor.

   The switch is on the front right; you push it.

4. Adjust the contrast and brightness.

   These knobs are blue and are on the front of the monitor.

AT THE END:

1. When finished, take the disk out of the disk drive.
   (Press the blue button under the disk drive.)

2. Turn the computer off.

3. Turn the monitor off.

4. Replace the software in its proper place.

Figure 12–3. Computer instructions chart.

If writing the basic steps is not appropriate for students, the teacher may wish to make a poster using pictures (these are also available from some educational materials companies). One option is to draw pictures of the steps, for example, drawing the power switch and using an arrow to indicate which way the students are supposed to push it. The teacher can draw a picture of a diskette being placed in the disk drive. The teacher also can cut pictures out of magazines or use snapshots of students performing these tasks. No matter which option is chosen, the basic steps in some form should be posted by the computer so that, if the students forget the steps, they will not be upset or embarrassed.

SOFTWARE ORGANIZATION

The final aspect of teaching students to use a computer is setting up the software so that the student does not need the teacher's help to begin a computer assignment. The strategy that is chosen should be based on the skill level of the students. Several methods for organizing software are discussed. Teachers should combine these methods as necessary.

COLOR CODING OF SOFTWARE

Method: Color Coding of Software

Author: R. B. Lewis

Source: Lewis, R. B. (1993). *Special education technology: Classroom applications.* Pacific Grove, CA: Brooks/Cole.

Description: This is a method designed for prereaders. The teacher puts colored dots on each software package. All of the items that belong to a particular package will have the same color dots. For example, a teacher could put blue dots on one program, (i.e., put blue dots on the disks, manual, and anything else that goes with that software). He or she could then place a chart on the wall with the students' names or pictures and the same color dots as those on the students' software. When the teacher wants a student to work on the computer with a particular software program, he or she tells the student to use the correctly colored software.

Notes: The problem with color coding is the restriction in the number of software programs that can be used because of the limited availability of colors. One solution to this problem is to use a combination of color coding and students' names or pictures. In this case, each box of software would not only have a color associated with it, but also a list of names or pictures. If a teacher uses this method, the software could be arranged on the shelves by color. For instance, all of the red color-coded software could be on one shelf and all the green-coded software on another. Pictures of the students can be placed nearby or on the appropriate software.

INDIVIDUAL STUDENT FOLDERS

Method: Individual Student Folders

Authors: R. L. Bender and W. N. Bender

Source: Bender, R. L., & Bender, W. N. (1996). *Computer-assisted instruction for stu-dents at-risk for ADHD, mild disabilities, or academic problems.* Boston: Allyn and Bacon.

Description: In this method a folder is created for each student. In the folder, the teacher places copies of either the cover of the manual or the box for the software the student will use. The student then has to match the copied page with the manual cover or box of software. When using this option, the teacher will need to show at-risk students how to match these pages to the software.

COMPUTER CONTROL OF STUDENT ACCESS TO PROGRAMS

Method: Computer Control of Student Access to Programs

Author: R. L. Bender

Source: Bender, R. L., & Bender, W. N. (1996). *Computer-assisted instruction for stu-dents at-risk for ADHD, mild disabilities, or academic problems.* Boston: Allyn and Bacon.

Description: A computer option for teachers is *KidDesk* (Macintosh, IBM, and IBM-compatible computers) by Edmark. This is a program which functions as an interface between the student and the computer to make using the computer easier. Using *KidDesk*, teachers can control which programs on the hard drive students can use. The teacher creates an icon (picture) on the main screen for each student who is to use the computer and decides which program he or she will be able to access. Students gain access to programs by clicking the mouse on their icon. They then see another screen containing icons for the software they are allowed to use. All student choices in *KidDesk* are graphical and require no reading skills. Using *KidDesk*, students can run software programs or explore the interactive desk accessories which include a talking clock, interactive calendar, a working calculator, and a message machine.

Notes: The time for setting up *KidDesk* can be minimized by adding one student each day. In this manner, the teacher does not feel overwhelmed, and the setup is completed fairly quickly.

NOTEBOOK OF COMPUTER USE

Method: Notebook of Computer Use

Authors: R. L. Bender and W. N. Bender

Source: Bender, R. L., & Bender, W. N. (1996). *Computer-assisted instruction for students at-risk for ADHD, mild disabilities, or academic problems.* Boston: Allyn and Bacon.

Description: If students have minimal reading skills, in addition to the above options, the teacher can create a notebook for them. To create a notebook, the teacher should include one page for each computer program that the student is using. The students should use the notebook to keep a record of their performance with each software program. The teacher should encourage students to make notes about the software programs in their notebook. It is extremely important that students realize that all software is different and computers are different. If students have difficulty in the use of a particular software program, have them make a note in their notebook concerning this difficulty. They should include their thoughts on how to avoid the difficulty in the future.

Notes: This method teaches students valuable problem-solving skills. If they encounter a problem, students should check their notebooks to see if they have had this problem before; if so, they can read in their notebook what to do. If they have not had this problem before, they should call the teacher, solve the problem, and then write notes on how to solve the problem in the future. This will dramatically decrease the number of students asking the teacher the same questions over and over. Teachers may want to have the students break into groups once a month and share with the group the problems they have encountered and their solutions.

Keeping a notebook that contains notes on how to use different computer systems and software is a common practice in industry and business where employees interact with several different systems. Although it is not realistic to expect all students to enjoy their "notebook" activity, a few students will become quite adept at identifying and solving these types of problems. Some may begin to help others solve computer or software problems. In one special education classroom, a student with learning disabilities became the class "problem-solver" based on this notebook idea. He gained both self-respect and confidence as he helped other students (and, on occasion, the teacher) with their computer use problems.

COMPUTER METHODS FOR TEACHERS

Effective use of computers in the classroom starts with the teacher. This section contains methods to help teachers integrate computers into their classrooms. Methods for placement and scheduling of computer time and for evaluating software are discussed.

PLACEMENT OF COMPUTERS IN THE CLASSROOM

Method: Placement of Computers in the Classroom

Authors: G. G. Bitter, R. A. Camuse, V. L. Durbin, and R. B. Lewis.

Sources: Bitter, G. G., Camuse, R. A., & Durbin, V. L. (1993). *Using a microcomputer in the classroom* (3rd ed.). Boston: Allyn and Bacon; Lewis, R. B., (1993). *Special education technology: Classroom applications*. Pacific Grove, CA: Brooks/Cole.

Description: The computer should be placed at the side or back of the classroom. (It should be in the back of the classroom only if the classroom is not too deep.) This placement is preferable for several reasons.

1. The teacher needs to be able to monitor the students when they are using the computer, while still leading instruction elsewhere in the class. If the computer is placed in a cubbyhole, the teacher may be unable to do so.
2. Graphics and sound from the computer and software can be distracting to the other students. A pair of headphones is recommended so that the rest of the class will not hear the sounds. Most teachers place the computer on the side of the classroom and either turn the sound off or instruct the students to use headphones. Headphones are only available for computers that have sound boards with speakers or speech synthesizers.
3. If a student makes an error, the computer should not be placed so that the entire class can see that the student made an error. This can be embarrassing to students.
4. Side placement, along the walls, also serves to protect the computer more than central placement. If overtly aggressive behavior does erupt in the classroom, resulting in overturned centrally located desks, the computer may fall on someone.
5. Most classrooms have electrical outlets located on the walls.

SCHEDULING OF COMPUTER TIME

Method: Scheduling of Computer Time

Author: W. N. Bender

Source: Bender, R. L., & Bender, W. N. (1996). *Computer-assisted instruction for students at-risk for ADHD, mild disabilities, or academic problems*. Boston: Allyn and Bacon.

Description: Scheduling of computer time varies considerably depending on the students' abilities and size of the class. For example, if a student has a difficult time staying on task, a teacher would not want to schedule that student for 30 minutes of computer time. Instead, the student could be scheduled for three blocks of 10–15 minutes of computer time, separating the computer time by other noncomputer activities. Another option would be to schedule that student, along with a peer tutor, for 30 minutes of CAI time.

Many at-risk students have difficulty remembering what they are supposed to do with the computer unless these skills are practiced frequently. If students feel confident in their ability to use the computer, it will be easier to have them work with a computer. Therefore, at-risk students will probably do better if they have contact with the computer every day, or perhaps twice a day. If there is only one computer in the classroom, schedule the students as frequently as possible, perhaps for 10–15 minutes every other day, depending on their disabilities and the number of students, rather than 30–45 minutes once a week. This will help the students feel more comfortable with working on their own on the computer. The time spent monitoring CAI use will decrease as the students' confidence grows.

Notes: When students are comfortable using CAI software, the teacher can post a written CAI schedule on the wall and let the students be responsible for using the computer and CAI when they are scheduled. The teacher also can make students responsible for monitoring their CAI time and quitting on time. Figure 12–4 depicts a form you can use in your scheduling of computer time.

INTEGRATION OF CAI

As teachers begin to enhance their skills in Computer Aided Instruction (CAI), they must consider the needs of individual students as the primary basis for software selection. A teacher's second concern must be implementation of CAI with the content of effective instructional principles (Malouf, Jamison, Kercher, & Carlucci, 1991a, 1991b, 1991c; Vockell & Mihail, 1993). Instructional options for students are virtually endless if the use of CAI is well grounded in effective learning principles.

GUIDELINES FOR IMPLEMENTATION OF CAI

Method: Guidelines for Implementation of CAI

Authors: D. B. Malouf, P. J. Jamison, M. H. Kercher, C. M. Carlucci, E. L. Vockell, and T. Mihail.

Sources: Malouf, D. B., Jamison, P. J., Kercher, M. H., & Carlucci, C. M. (1991a). Computer software aids effective instruction. *Teaching Exceptional Children, 23*(2), 56–57; Malouf, D. B., Jamison, P. J., Kercher, M. H., & Carlucci, C. M. (1991b). Integrating computer software into effective instruction. *Teaching Exceptional Children, 23*(3),

Day _____

Student Name	CAI to Use	Start Time	End Time

Figure 12–4. Classroom CAI schedule.

54–56; Malouf, D. B., Jamison, P. J., Kercher, M. H., & Carlucci, C. M. (1991c). Integrating computer software into effective instruction (part 2). *Teaching Exceptional Children, 23*(4), 57–60; Vockell, E. L., & Mihail, T. (1993). Principles behind computerized instruction for students with exceptionalities. *Teaching Exceptional Children, 25*(3), 39–43.

Description: Figure 12–5 summarizes the guidelines for implementation of CAI in the classroom from the above sources.

Notes: In the context of these effective instructional principles, CAI can be applied to numerous learning problems demonstrated by at-risk students. Further, research has demonstrated that appropriate use of CAI is at least as effective as the whole group instruction which is typically provided in most mainstream classes (Perry & Garber, 1993; Raskind, 1993; van Daal & van der Leij, 1992). Effective teachers will implement CAI instruction with these guidelines in mind by concentrating on the particular learning characteristics of individual students.

Mastery Practice	Pacing	Immediate Feedback
1. Use programs that specify exact steps and teach them clearly and specifically.	1. Use computer programs to provide self-paced, individualized practice.	1. Use programs that provide immediate feedback.
2. Show the relationship of computer programs to steps in the direct instruction process.	2. Use computer programs that provide game-like practice for skills that require much repeated practice.	2. Use programs that provide clear, corrective feedback.
3. Use programs that provide extra help and practice toward reaching objectives.	3. Use computer programs that provide varied approaches to practicing the same activity.	3. Select programs that ask higher level questions.
4. Use programs to stimulate and enrich students who reach objectives early.	4. Use programs that individualize the pace of instruction, because wait time is likely to be better than with traditional instruction.	4. Use programs that have management systems to monitor student progress.
5. Use record-keeping programs to keep track of student performance.		5. Use record-keeping programs.
6. Use computer programs to provide repeated practice and facilitate memorization.		6. Use computers to communicate feedback.
7. Use programs designed to develop memory skills.		7. Teach students to use the computer as a tool to manage and assist learning.
		8. Use programs that teach thinking skills.
		9. Teach generalization of thinking and study skills across subject areas.

Figure 12–5. Guidelines for implementation of CAI.

INTEGRATION OF CAI

Method: Integration of CAI

Author: R. L. Bender

Source: Bender, R. L., & Bender, W. N. (1996). *Computer-assisted instruction for students at-risk for ADHD, mild disabilities, or academic problems.* Boston: Allyn and Bacon.

Description: Computers are most useful when integrated into the classroom. Also, research has shown that CAI is very effective if it is properly evaluated, modified, and integrated into the class (Gardner, Taber-Brown, & Wissick, 1992; Malouf et al., 1991a, 1991b, 1991c). Appropriate modification of software should facilitate its integration into the curriculum.

The following suggestions should help teachers modify and integrate CAI into their classrooms in a reasonable amount of time and without stress on either teachers or students.

1. To begin, select one program or software package that is appropriate for several students. Modify the software as needed for the chosen students. This may be as simple as increasing the time allowed for responses or typing in the students' names. Decide on an appropriate amount of time for the students to use this software in one sitting. Then select the days of the week that the students should work on this subject. Remember that some students may forget how to use computers if not used at least on a biweekly basis. Plan CAI use for several students who are likely to enjoy the experience. Others in the class will then request their "turn" on the computer.

2. Before moving on to other software, get the bugs out (i.e., eliminate any problems with the software). Evaluate the software. Is it helping the students? Have the students progressed to the next level? Does the software require teacher intervention for a student to have access to the next instructional level? Is the amount of time allotted adequate? Is the student bored or frustrated with the software?

3. Move on to other software. After the above evaluation questions have been addressed and any problems resolved, choose a second piece of software. Some teachers make the mistake of jumping in with 20 pieces of software and overwork themselves trying to get set up initially. They may become frustrated and cease CAI use altogether. Remember that the computer is a tool, not a substitute teacher, and you, as the teacher, know best how to teach your students. Do not over extend yourself initially. Know the software well.

4. Learn more about the software already in the room as a first step. If software is already in the classroom and is not being used to its full capabilities, start with a piece of this software. Then, after identifying areas in which to use CAI, search for additional software to meet those needs.

5. Spend 10 or 15 minutes every other day before or after class becoming familiar with the CAI programs. Modify or evaluate the CAI software. Most software is written so that modifications do not have to be made at one time. Set aside regular times each week to work on integrating software into the classroom. This time can be spent individualizing or evaluating software, obtaining software, or evaluating students' performances with the various software they use. A regularly scheduled time will help you, the teacher, become quite familiar with the CAI programs.

6. For older students, require one or two written assignments each week to be completed on a word processing package. This will help to change the students' attitudes towards writing, and in the process, they will become very comfortable with the computer.

MATCHING LEARNING CHARACTERISTICS OF STUDENTS

Method: Matching Learning Characteristics of Students with Attributes of Computer Software

Authors: R. L. Bender and W. N. Bender

Source: Bender, R. L., & Bender, W. N. (1996). *Computer-assisted instruction for students at-risk for ADHD, mild disabilities, or academic problems.* Boston: Allyn and Bacon

Description: Almost all students can benefit from the use of computers in their educational programs. However, to efficiently use Computer-Assisted Instruction (CAI) with students, teachers first need to identify the learning characteristics of their students.

Figures 12–6 and 12–7 are forms designed to help teachers identify common learning characteristics among students and to identify which students have these learning characteristics. Based on the learning characteristics of students, teachers may find that some students will learn better if they have step-by-step elaboration of tasks, models of task completion, concrete examples, shorter assignments, and other modifications.

CAI can assist teachers in making each of these instructional modifications. For example, if a particular student is having dif-

Attention Characteristics:

1. How long does this student work on a task at his or her reading level? _____

2. How often does this student complete assigned work in class? _____

3. How often does this student fail to turn in homework? _____

4. Does this student have other particular attention behaviors? _____

_____

_____

Behavior Characteristics:

1. Does this student disrupt the class? _____

_____

2. How frequently is this student disciplined in class? _____

_____

3. The last time you disciplined this student, what was he or she doing? _____

_____

4. Describe this student's disruptive behavior. _____

_____

_____

Memory Characteristics:

1. Is this student able to remember things from a few minutes ago? _____

_____

Figure 12–6. Learning characteristics of my students. *(continued)*

(continued)

2. Is this student able to remember concepts from one day to the next?

_____

3. If no to questions 1 and/or 2, what types of things does the student have problems remembering? _____

_____

4. How often do you have to repeat lessons for this student? _____

_____

Subject Variations:

1. What subjects are this student's strengths? _____

_____

2. What subjects are this student's weakness? _____

_____

3. Are there any tasks that this student cannot do? (Such as seatwork, discussions, etc.) _____

_____

Academic Modifications:

1. Is this student on grade level in reading, math, and language arts? _____

2. What modifications do you make for this student in your teaching methods? _____

_____

_____

_____

3. Are there any other modifications that you think may work? _____

_____

_____

_____

Figure 12–6. *(continued)*

ficulty solving word-problems in mathematics, a computer program that helps the student solve word-problems by dividing the task into four steps may benefit this student. Figure 12–8 is a form designed to help teachers identify the attributes of a computer program for instructional purposes.

Figure 12–9 helps teachers match the learning characteristics of students listed in Figure 12–7 with the attributes of computer software listed in Figure 12–8. Two characteristics of students are not shown in Figure

Notes

1. Low level of frustration

2. Lack of interest

3. Short attention span

4. Easily distracted

5. Short- and long-term
   memory recall problems

6. Different rates for
   learning the same content

7. Variations in subject
   strengths and weaknesses

8. Poor fine motor
   coordination

9. Overlapping disabilities

Figure 12–7. Characteristics displayed by students.

1. Does this software allow you to change the response time for the student? _____

2. Does this software have a high level of repetition? _____

3. Does the student receive immediate reinforcement for correct answers? _____

4. Does the software use graphics and sound adequately to help keep the student on task? ____

5. Can this software be used in time lengths appropriate for this student? _____

6. How many questions are presented in sequence? _____

7. Does the software instruct the student to get teacher help? _____

8. How does the software deal with an incorrect response? _____
   _____

9. If the student gives an incorrect response, does the software review the student on the material or keep recycling the questions the student has missed? _____

   Which do you prefer? _____
   _____

10. What other software characteristics are important to you? _____
   _____

Figure 12–8. Attributes of computer software.

Students' Characteristics	Computer Attributes
Low frustration level	Variable response times High repetition Immediate reinforcement
Lack of interest Short attention span Easily distracted	Use of graphics and sound Frequent reinforcement
Different rates for learning the same content	Variable response times
Short- and Long-term memory recall problems	Variable response times Frequent repetition Use of graphics and sound

Figure 12–9. Matching student's learning characteristics and computer attributes.

12–9. One, variation in academic subjects, is addressed by the software chosen, and the other characteristic, poor fine motor coordination, is discussed in a later method using assistive technology.

SOFTWARE EVALUATION

Before looking at a piece of software, teachers should consider several questions. What is the content area in which you are interested in using CAI? What are the academic levels of the students included in this lesson? What is the intended use of the software? What are the learning objectives of the lesson(s) for which the software may be used? Armed with the above information, teachers are now ready to locate software and perform evaluations on the software.

Software selection and evaluation are acquired skills, and, when teachers master these skills, effective utilization of CAI software is greatly enhanced. This section provides several methods to aid teachers in the evaluation of software.

SOFTWARE SELECTION BY LIST

Method: Software Selection by List

Description: When buying software for the classroom, teachers typically are given a software catalog with the titles of the software, a brief description, and price. Using this information, teachers are expected to choose software appropriate for their students.

Notes: This system for software selection is clearly not optimal. However, even with this limited information, teachers can narrow down the choices of software and then request demonstration copies for more extensive evaluation.

APPLICATIONS EVALUATION OF SOFTWARE

Method: Applications Evaluation of Software

Authors: R. L. Bender and W. N. Bender

Sources: Bitter, G. G., Camuse, R. A., & Durbin, V. L. (1993). *Using a microcomputer in the classroom* (3rd. ed.). Boston: Allyn & Bacon; Lewis, R. B. (1993). *Special education tech*nology: Classroom applications. Pacific Grove, CA. Brooks/Cole. Maddux, C. D., Johnson, D. L., & Willis, J. W. (1992). *Educational computing: Learning with tomorrow's technologies*. Boston: Allyn and Bacon.

Description: There are five types of CAI software, namely, initial instruction, mastery practice, simulations, problem solving, and word-processing software. When evaluating CAI software for use in the classroom, several software attributes should be considered, regardless of the type. There are also software attributes that should be considered when evaluating a particular type of CAI software.

Many forms are available to help teachers in evaluation of software. Some of these forms can be used for all types of CAI software (Lewis, 1993; Maddux, Johnson, & Willis, 1992); others are designed to be used for particular types of CAI software (Bitter et al., 1993). The authors chose a modification of one form with different sections for particular types of CAI software. Teachers may wish to modify the form in Figure 12–10 for their individual needs.

Content and Type of CAI. The content of a CAI software package may seem a bit obvious, but consider two packages named *Call the Parrot* and *Glowy*. Looking solely at the names of the software, teachers have no idea what the content of these two packages is. In fact *Call the Parrot* teaches students the directions of north, south, east, and west; and *Glowy* teaches students critical thinking

SUBJECT:

Area: _____

Topic(s): _____

Program Name: _____

Publisher: _____

Address: _____

Telephone: _____

Price: _____

Brief Description of Software:

Rate the remaining topics between 0 and 5, with 0 indicating poor (or no) and 5 indicating excellent (or yes).

CONTENT	**RATING**
1. accurate content	_____
2. accomplishes stated objectives	_____
3. age appropriate	_____
4. skill level appropriate	_____
TOTAL FOR CONTENT	_____
(total possible)	20

PRESENTATION	**RATING**
1. program bug free	_____
2. clear instructions	_____
3. appropriate reinforcement	_____
4. appropriate use of color and graphics	_____
5. appropriate use of sound	_____
6. variable pacing	_____
7. appropriate sequencing	_____
8. readability of text appropriate for user	_____
TOTAL FOR PRESENTATION	_____
(total possible)	40

Figure 12–10. CAI software applications evaluations.

TEACHER USE   RATING

1. keeps useful performance records   _____
2. curriculum objectives stated clearly   _____
3. suggestions for integration into curriculum _____
4. no need for instructor assistance   _____
5. interesting follow up activities or projects suggested _____
6. teacher manual is useful   _____
7. prerequisite student skills clearly stated _____
8. adequate documentation   _____

TOTAL FOR TEACHER USE   _____
   (total possible)   40

USER FRIENDLINESS   RATING

1. instructions are reviewable at any time   _____
2. students can exit the program at any time _____
3. students can restart program where they stopped _____
4. allows correction of typing errors   _____
5. incorrect selection of keys does not cause the program to crash _____
6. clear summary of program operations provided _____
7. requires no computer knowledge   _____
8. high student involvement   _____

TOTAL FOR USER FRIENDLINESS   _____
   (total possible)   40

Initial Instruction and Master Practice:

ATTRIBUTES   RATING

1. provides students with performance record _____
2. student controls rate of presentation   _____
3. student controls sequence of lesson   _____
4. student controls selection of lesson   _____
5. student can choose style of presentation   _____
6. can review previous screens of information _____
7. errorless learning feature   _____
8. does not require student to manipulate disk drive _____

(continued)

9. random generation of problems   _____

TOTAL FOR INITIAL INSTRUCTION AND
MASTERY PRACTICE ATTRIBUTES   _____
   (total possible)   45

Simulation:

ATTRIBUTES	**RATING**
1. realistic simulation of events	_____
2. students do not need to refer to reference manuals	_____
3. high student involvement	_____
4. encourages cooperation	_____
5. time of simulation is appropriate	_____

  TOTAL FOR SIMULATION ATTRIBUTES   _____
  (total possible)   25

Problem Solving:

ATTRIBUTE	**RATING**
1. skills required of student are clearly stated	_____
2. skills the program enhances are stated	_____
3. beginning skill level explains the basic steps for problem solving	_____
4. skills helped by the program can transfer to other content areas	_____
5. problems are randomly generated	_____
6. reviews the problem or the basic steps to problem solving when a student misses a problem	_____

TOTAL FOR PROBLEM SOLVING ATTRIBUTES   _____
  (total possible)   30

Word-Processing:

ATTRIBUTES	**RATING**
1. documentation provides index and table of contents	_____
2. Clear, nicely formatted screen displays	_____
3. incorrect selection of commands does not make the program crash	_____
4. menus and help features make the program user friendly	_____
5. clear and useful summary of commands provided	_____
6. accepts abbreviations for common responses	_____

Figure 12–10. *continued*

7. operation of program does not require student to turn the computer on and off   _____

8. commands easy to learn   _____

9. allows easy deleting, moving, and underlining of text   _____

10. has word wrap feature   _____

11. protective features to avoid loss of files   _____

12. entire width of text can be seen on the monitor   _____

13. loading, saving, and printing files is easy   _____

14. use of word-processing program does not require intermittent access to master disk   _____

TOTAL FOR WORD-PROCESSING ATTRIBUTES   _____
(total possible)   70

TOTAL POINTS   _____
(total possible)   310

RECOMMENDATION FOR THIS SOFTWARE:

skills for addition, subtraction, and whole-number concepts. It takes more knowledge than merely the name and "reading the wrapper" to understand software content.

When considering the content area of a CAI package, teachers should consider the objectives of the software. Do the stated objectives match the objectives of the curriculum plan for students? If not, can the CAI objectives be modified to meet teacher's objectives? Is the content material accurate? Questions like these help teachers plan more effective use of the CAI program.

CAI software is screened initially by content area and type. The type of software also helps with the initial screening. Note that a CAI program can be classified as more than one type.

Age Appropriateness and Skill Level of CAI Software. Other important aspects of CAI software include age appropriateness (Gardner, Taber-Brown, & Wissick, 1992) and the skill level. Suppose a teacher wants to drill a 13-year-old on vocabulary. If this student

has the skill level of a student in second grade, the teacher would not drill him or her on software with a skill level at fifth grade. Furthermore, the teacher should be cognizant of how appropriate the material is. Software that drills a student, using nursery rhymes, will not appeal to a 13-year-old student.

Presentation of Material. To use CAI effectively, the software should help keep the student on task. Keeping a student on task involves several factors some of which relate to the presentation methods chosen. Among these factors, are graphics and auditory systems. Most effective CAI software uses a combination of the above.

Other aspects of presentation include how the program handles correct and incorrect answers, pacing, and sequencing. Teachers should ask several questions regarding the presentation.

1. *Is the program free of bugs?* A program is said to have a "bug" if it has an error in the program. Some bugs are harmless and

go unnoticed. An example of this is if the documentation tells the student to press RETURN to enter an answer, and by trial and error, the student discovers he or she must press RETURN twice to enter the answer. At the other extreme, a bug in a program can cause it to crash (i.e., the computer will stop performance in the middle of the program). For example, if the program crashes when the ESC key is pressed, the program has a major bug.

2. *Do the directions make clear what type of response is expected?* There is nothing more frustrating to a teacher or students than responding to the questions in the program in the appropriate manner and having the program say that an error was made. Another problem is when a teacher or student is responding appropriately to a question and the program does something unexpected (not mentioned in the documentation).

3. *What happens when a wrong answer is given?* When a wrong answer is given, it is more helpful to students if the program helps them to discover what is wrong with their answers rather than asks students to repeat the missed question. A program that just tells the student to "try again" is not very helpful in instructing the student. It may also result in a teacher spending more time monitoring that particular CAI program.

4. *What happens when a wrong answer is given?* When a student consistently gives wrong answers, the program should either review the content material or tell the student to summon the teacher. Also, the program's response is related to the type of CAI package. For example, teachers should expect an initial instruction program to review the content material, while a mastery practice program would instruct the student to summon the teacher.

5. *Does the software do anything that is distracting to students?* With at-risk students, care should be taken to choose software that does not distract the student. These students are often easily distracted and find it difficult to stay on task. Loud noises or extremely flashy graphics can break a student's concentration. Therefore, both of these features should be avoided with students who are easily distracted. A teacher may wish to try these programs once or twice with a particular student to determine if the program overly excites him or her.

6. *Is the CAI software self-paced or can the teacher vary the pacing?* Pacing is the rate at which new material is introduced (i.e., the amount of time the student is given to answer questions). Programs can have automatic pacing or pacing can be determined by the teacher. The most flexible CAI programs will have both.

7. *Does the student have control over* the sequencing? Sequencing represents the sequence of presentation of the material. That is, when a student is working on a lesson, some CAI programs allow the student to choose particular exercises in the lesson according to the student's individual curiosity. If a teacher uses CAI software that has student-controlled sequencing together with performance summaries, she will find that students will usually make wise decisions concerning the exercises they need to work on and he or she will spend less time monitoring students.

8. *Can the student review the directions?* The student should have the option of reviewing the directions at the beginning of the lesson or at any point during the lesson. This is particularly important for students who have difficulty with short- or long-term memory and for students with attention problems.

Method of Instruction. The method of instruction includes feedback, reinforcement, and the range of ability the program accommodates (Vockell & Mihail 1993). All of these are important features because their proper use will prevent students from becoming frustrated and anxious.

CAI programs should always give students immediate feedback. If a student answers correctly, the software should tell the student that he or she answered the question correctly and provide other reinforcement as necessary. If a student answers a question incorrectly, the software should tell him or her to try again, to review the material, or to summon the teacher. Immediate feedback is one of the main reasons for using CAI software, instead of pencil and paper worksheets. Immediate feedback can motivate students when they are answering questions correctly, and it can prevent students from getting wrong ideas if they are answering questions incorrectly.

Reinforcement is a type of feedback, but it should be more than that. For example, consider the following two CAI software packages. The first package says "Good job!" every time a correct answer is given, and "Try again" every time a question is answered incorrectly. The second package gives one of six congratulatory messages when a question is answered correctly. After answering four consecutive questions correctly, it displays colorful fireworks going off on the screen. After a question is answered incorrectly, this software package gives one of three messages that, in effect, tell the student that his or her answer was wrong and to try again. Furthermore, after a question is missed three times, the CAI instructs the student to summon the teacher.

Most teachers would prefer the second CAI package. It behaves more like we expect a teacher to act. Furthermore, if the responses of the software become predictable, the reinforcement will lose potency, and the students will not like to use that particular software.

Further, the amount of reinforcement offered is a crucial concept. If a program offers reinforcement too frequently for a particular student, the reinforcement loses its value. If a program offers too little reinforcement, the student's interest in the lesson will decrease. A CAI program should offer just enough reinforcement to motivate each student to continue. For this reason, effective CAI packages let a teacher vary the reinforcement level from one student to the next.

Some software will show the most interesting graphics and sound effects when a student makes a mistake or a series of mistakes. Students quickly learns that it is more fun to respond with incorrect answers rather than correct answers. Thus, CAI programs may reinforce the wrong ideas. This problem rarely occurs but should be considered.

Management of Student Performance. Computer management and assessment of students can be made easier by CAI software. When evaluating a CAI package, a few items should be noted. Does the software automatically keep student performance records? Is every student answer stored, so that a teacher can recheck the student's work and do an error analysis on a problem-by-problem basis? Are the records stored on disk? Is the information useful and complete? Are the records secure? These questions are important when monitoring student performance and should be included in any applications evaluation.

Documentation. Good documentation is necessary for effective use of any CAI package. Documentation includes instructions on installation and running of the CAI software. The hardware requirements, discussed above, are delineated as are the goals and objectives, prerequisite skills, and skill levels of the software. Furthermore, most documentation for CAI software includes suggestions for its use in the classroom, student worksheets, and lesson plans. The documentation also should specify how to set up student records and modify pacing and reinforcement. Clearly, documentation is an important aspect of CAI software. Good documentation will aid a teacher in setting up the software in a minimal amount of time, whereas inadequate documentation can lead to frustration and wasted time.

User Friendliness. User friendliness is a term that all teachers have heard. Think about the "ideal" CAI software. Students should be able to use it with minimal teacher interaction. The software should have clear, on-screen directions. Students should be able to exit the program at any time and restart the program later at exactly the same point in the program. An interesting example of this is the simulation software, *Oregon Trail*. In the Macintosh version, students are able to stop the simulation and exit at any time. Furthermore, they can restart the program without starting over. This is not true for the Apple IIe version of the same software. The result is that students always have to start over, and they never reach Oregon using the Apple version. This feature is particularly important with simulation software because this type of software is usually used over several class periods or lessons.

A few other things that can cause difficulties with students also should be checked:

1. Does the program allow correction of typing errors?
2. Are loading and running instructions clear?
3. Does incorrect selection of keys cause the program to stop running?

All of the above problems are common to many types of CAI software. If a program is poorly designed in any of these areas, more of the teacher's time will be spent monitoring students. This leaves teachers and students feeling frustrated, anxious, and reluctant to use the computer.

Characteristics of Specific Types of CAI Software. Characteristics common to all types of CAI software were discussed in the last section. In this section, attributes that are more specific to different types of software are presented. Although some of the attributes discussed below are relevant to all types of CAI, these attributes are a major concern with certain software types.

INITIAL INSTRUCTION AND MASTERY PRACTICE. Both initial instruction and mastery practice use traditional techniques for teaching students during the initial instruction and mastery practice phases of learning. When evaluating these two types of CAI software, a teacher should also give consideration to the following attributes.

After a practice session, students should be provided with information about their performances. This information can motivate students and lets them know which areas they need to work on. Perhaps the teacher could chart the students' correct answers daily and provide extra reinforcement when the number of correct answers increases. This is a very effective instructional technique, because students love to see charts of their own performance increases.

Students should be allowed to read new information and directions for the program at their own rates. Most CAI programs accomplish this by asking students to press a key after they have read the screen of information. This prevents the student from getting frustrated and anxious about how to use the program. If the pacing is controllable, the teacher may allow the students to go at their own speeds until their competence increases. The pace is then increased.

In some cases, it is appropriate to allow students to choose particular exercises in a lesson, a particular lesson, or the style of presentation. For example, some students may prefer lessons with a game-like format similar to a maze, while others may prefer puzzle-like formats. Effective CAI offers both.

Students should be able to review previous screens of information. For example, *Rocky's Boots*, by the Learning Company, is a program that teaches students general problem-solving skills. The goal of the program is for the student to use given components to build machines that solve certain problems. For the student to attain the ability to build machines, they must learn certain skills and rules. *Rocky's Boots* is structured so that, at any time, the student can review previous information concerning the skills and rules of building machines.

A potential problem with any older CAI software is intermittent operation of a single disk drive. When using older software, students may be asked to turn the disk over. Software should be selected which does not require this of students. Most modern software does not have this requirement.

Errorless learning features, which help students to avoid making errors and improve performance, are excellent for initial instruction and mastery practice CAI software. It can be extremely difficult for at-risk students to learn new material or to attain competence in certain material. The errorless learning procedures can help a student learn new material or practice on material without becoming frustrated.

SIMULATIONS. Realistic simulation of events is an important characteristic. Most simulations are similar to real life but vary in the details. For example, on the real *Oregon Trail*, the settlers had to contend with Indians and Outlaws, but these are not mentioned in the simulation. Teachers should take notes on how the simulation program differs from real life and discuss these differences with students after the simulation is over. The students may be able to point out a few other places where the simulation and real life differ. This is a very effective, postsimulation learning activity for at-risk students.

Simulation activities can be very complex for at-risk students to learn. Teachers should check the available references in the school library. They should also provide reference material while the students are working with the simulation. Many teachers find that students who are usually reluctant to use an encyclopedia for ordinary school reports will utilize it much more frequently to support a CAI simulation activity.

Another characteristic of simulations is that they call for high student involvement. Simulations are flexible in that one student, a group of students, or the entire class can participate. Teachers should also consider how well the program encourages cooperation between at-risk students and others.

Finally, the time requirement of the simulation should be noted. Most simulations require longer than a class period to use. It is important to find out if the CAI simulation can be broken down easily into class lessons.

PROBLEM-SOLVING. Problem-solving software can be subject-specific or non-subject-specific. When using this type of software, a teacher should be careful to note the skills required of the student. It can be frustrating for students to have problems forced on them before they have adequate skills.

One attribute of problem-solving software that should be considered is whether or not the beginning skill level in the CAI program takes the student through the basic problem-solving steps.

A teacher should note the problem-solving skills for which the software is designed. Are these general skills or subject-specific skills? Can the skills be used in other areas? If a teacher wants the skills to generalize to other areas, he or she should discuss generalization with the students. Start by asking, "In what other situations could you use these skills?"

In subject-specific problem-solving software, there is usually a given set of problems for the student to solve. A teacher should ask several questions about the presentation of these problems. Are the problems generated randomly? In other words, does the information in the problems change and are the problems presented in a different order every time the program is used? After using the program a few times, have the students memorized the problems and their order? A teacher will wish to avoid any problem-solving software that allows students to memorize the problems and their solutions.

What happens when the student misses a problem? Does the software review the information in the problem? Does the software help the student through the basic steps of problem-solving? Or does the software just repeat the problem until the student gets it right? If problem-solving software repeats a problem that the student just missed, and if the student misses the problem a second time, the software should instruct the student to summon the teacher.

WORD PROCESSING. The attributes to be evaluated in a word-processing package concern the operation of the program and the documentation. When evaluating these attributes, a teacher should always bear in mind the abilities of his or her students.

First, the documentation should be complete. It should include an index, a table of contents, and full instructions on utilization. The information concerning the installation and running of the program should be written in clear steps that are easy to follow. The information concerning the use of the program should be clear with step-by-step commands for performing the operations. There should be numerous examples. A "quick reference card" which describes most commands is helpful. These are extremely useful after students have mastered the basics of the word-processing program. These quick references tend to get misplaced, so several copies should be made. A copy of the quick reference can be taped by the computer students are using.

When editing text, clear and helpful headings should appear at the top of the screen. For example, when using WordPerfect, by WordPerfect, Inc., the headings at the top of the screen include File, Edit, Search, and a few others with pull-down menus. The menus and help features help make the program user friendly.

Another consideration is that incorrect selection of commands should not cause the program to crash. Furthermore, the program should accept abbreviations for common responses. For example, it should accept N for no.

Operation of the program should not require students to turn the computer on and off. The commands should be easy to learn. Use of the program should not require intermittent access to the master word-processing disk.

Deleting, moving, underlining, and justification of words, sentences, and paragraphs should be quick and easy. The entire width of the document should appear on the screen. It should contain protective features that prevent loss of files and simple methods to load, save, and print files.

Notes: All of the attributes of CAI software discussed above are combined into a comprehensive software evaluation form that teachers may use. We encourage teachers to use and modify the form seen in Figure 12–10 to meet the needs of students. Teachers might keep a file of the evaluations so that they may be shared with others.

Instruction using multimedia is promising, but unless the motivational properties of the program are effective, the full benefits will not be obtained. Keller and Keller (1994) combined four components of interactivity with the primary features of a motivational design model into a checklist that can be used to design and evaluate multimedia programs.

EVALUATION OF MULTIMEDIA SOFTWARE

Method: Evaluation of Multimedia Software

Authors: B. H. Keller and J. M. Keller

Source: Keller, B. H., & Keller, J. M. (1994, March). *Meaningful and motivating interactivity in multimedia instruction: Design and evaluation guidelines.* Presented at 11th International Conference on Technologies in Education, London.

Description: Interactivity is defined as the kind, amount, and timing of interaction in an instructional program. Furthermore, interactivity can be divided into four areas:

1. *Learner Control.* Learner control involves the pacing, sequencing, and selection of the instructional material by the student. For example, this includes what selections students can make and when material is reviewed.
2. *Stimulus Characteristics.* Stimulus characteristics include the material and how it is presented.

3. *Learner Responses.* Learner responses include emotional responses as well as mechanical responses such as solving problems and note-taking.
4. *Consequences.* Consequences include the actions the program takes as a result of student responses.

The motivational design model used is the ARCS model (Keller, 1987a, 1987b). This model has four criteria that must be met for a lesson to stimulate and sustain the motivation to learn in a student. First, the student's attention must be obtained. Second, the lesson must build relevance by connecting the lesson to the student's experiences. Third, the lesson should allow the students to build confidence that they will succeed in the lesson. Fourth, the students must receive some degree of satisfaction from their learning experience.

The checklist in Figure 12–11 combines the components of interactivity with the ARCS model of motivational design. The checklist consists of two parts. The Management Interactivity section applies to learner control. The second part, Instructional Interactivity, applies to the motivational responses in the student and the feedback the student receives.

Notes: This checklist contains 49 questions to aid teachers in the selection of multimedia software that will motivate their students. Even the most exciting software can become boring when the novelty expires.

ASSISTIVE TECHNOLOGY

Students with poor fine motor skills or physical disabilities may not be able to use, or start directly with, a standard keyboard. For these students, teachers may need to obtain a touch-screen, so they can use the computer like the other students while working on their motor skills. It may be helpful to use a modified keyboard that has keys considerably larger than those on a standard keyboard. An example is the IntelliKeys Expanded Keyboard by IntelliTools which is discussed below. At no time should a student's disability or lack of fine motor skills prevent him or her from working on computers like the other students.

Although a detailed description of assistive technology is beyond the scope to this chapter, it is important to note several methods. This technology is important because, it not only enables students with disabilities to participate in class, but students without disabilities also enjoy using it.

The types of assistive technology described in this section include speech recognition systems, switches, joysticks, touch tablets, screen magnification systems, braille access systems, and alternative keyboards. Information on the hardware (equipment) discussed can be found in the sources listed.

SPEECH SYNTHESIZER

Method: Speech Synthesizer

Author: R. Lewis

Source: Lewis, R. (1993). *Special education technology: Classroom applications*. Pacific Grove, CA., Brooks/Cole.

Description: A substantial portion of newer software for at-risk students uses the Echo speech synthesizer produced by Echo Speech Corporation. This device allows the computer to "talk" to students. The Echo speech synthesizer has several versions depending on the type of computer. For example, the Echo II is designed for Apple IIe and Apple IIGS computers, and the Echo LC for Apple IIc/IIc+ computers and the Macintosh LC when running in Apple IIe emulation mode. The Echo PC II is designed for IBM and IBM-compatible computers, and the Echo PC is for all computers.

MOTIVATING INTERACTIVITY IN MULTIMEDIA

(The MIM Checklist)

Bonnie H. Keller & John M. Keller

INTRODUCTION

This checklist contains motivational tactics that have been demonstrated to have a positive motivational effect when used appropriately in interactive multimedia instruction. The purpose of the checklist is to assist in planning and evaluating multimedia instruction with respect to interactivity. There are two major parts to the checklist. The first pertains to those tactics that apply primarily to learner control over managing the multimedia instructional program, and the second pertains more to features that affect the degree of motivation in the instructional interactivity.

Each item in this checklist has been categorized as to whether its primary effect is on stimulating or maintaining attention (A), establishing relevance (R), developing confidence (C), or building satisfaction (S) in the learner. Some items may appeal to more than one of these categories. For additional information on this approach to identifying and categorizing motivational tactics, see the reference at the end of this checklist.

INSTRUCTIONS

Three columns are provided for your use. You may modify them to suit your requirements.

Applies? Put a check in this column if a given tactic applies to the given program of multimedia instruction. There are numerous criteria that may be used to make this decision.

Present? This column can be used when reviewing progress during development or when evaluating finished products. It simply indicates whether a given tactic has been incorporated as planned. It the tactic is included in the materials, but was not checked as applying to the audience, then consider removing it.

Rating? Use any rating scale that you wish. For example, a simple S for satisfactory or U for unsatisfactory works in some situations. In others, reviewers prefer to use a five point scale ranging from excellent (exceeds requirements) to unacceptable.

Figure 12–11. The MIM Checklist.

MANAGEMENT INTERACTIVITY

1. Pacing: Program characteristics that allow learner control over pacing.

___ ___ ___ 1.1 Learners have control over when and how fast to move through the program or have the option to exercise such control if desired. (A,S)

2. Override: Program characteristics that allow learners to override, or interrupt, the program sequence.

___ ___ ___ 2.1 Learners have access to system help at all times. (C)

___ ___ ___ 2.2 Learners may exit instructional presentations or practice exercises when they wish. (S)

3. Selection: Program characteristics that allow learner control over sequencing and structure.

___ ___ ___ 3.1 System navigational skills are prerequisite or an easy tutorial is provided. (C)

___ ___ ___ 3.2 Instructional framework and levels are as easy as possible to move through (include only the levels required for course complexity). (C)

___ ___ ___ 3.3 Learners may review presentations and practice as often as they wish. (C)

___ ___ ___ 3.4 Diagnostic checkpoints are provided before major portions of instruction and practice, and learners who perform satisfactorily may move ahead. (A,S)

___ ___ ___ 3.5 Learners have access to the main menu as often as possible. (A,S)

___ ___ ___ 3.6 A predetermined selection and sequence is recommended but not required. (A,R,S)

INSTRUCTIONAL INTERACTIVITY

4. Internal Motivation: Program characteristics to stimulate motivated internal learner responses:

___ ___ ___ 4.1 Mystery, paradox, or inquiry is used to introduce segments which may be inherently less interesting to learners. (A)

___ ___ ___ 4.2 Instructional segments are varied in length and speed. (A)

___ ___ ___ 4.3 Appealing and clear graphics are provided to break up text blocks and/or to communicate information. (A)

___ ___ ___ 4.4 Adequate time is allowed for covert responding. (A, C)

(continued)

____ ____ ____   4.5   Role-plays, games, and simulations have characters and settings appropriate for characteristics of learners, and their interests and contain content and applications related to the objectives. (A, R)

____ ____ ____   4.6   Scenarios and case studies contain human interest (good characterizations), realistic situations, problems appropriate for the objectives and content, and are appropriate for current skill levels of learners. (A, R, C)

____ ____ ____   4.7   Examples are provided for all relevant learner contexts. (R)

____ ____ ____   4.8   The relationship between program content and dealing with common fears and misconceptions is made explicit. (C)

____ ____ ____   4.9   Introductions or overviews are provided at unit or module levels. (C)

____ ____ ____   4.10   Examples are sequenced from easy to difficult. (C)

____ ____ ____   4.11   Summaries of content are provided at key break points. (C)

____ ____ ____   4.12   Humor is used if content may induce fear, tension, or boredom for learners. (C, S)

5.   Overt Responses: Program characteristics to stimulate motivated overt learner responses.

____ ____ ____   5.1   Requests for meaningful overt learner responses are interspersed within tutorials. (A)

____ ____ ____   5.2   Program prompts are provided after a designated interval. (A)

____ ____ ____   5.3   Learner roles are varied through use of role-plays, games, and simulations in addition to tutorial presentations. (A)

____ ____ ____   5.4   Physical response types (touch screen, keyboard, type-in, capture, reorganize) are varied without causing confusion. (A, C)

____ ____ ____   5.5   Cognitive response types (select, identify, match, recall, answer, create, etc.) are varied without causing confusion. (A, C)

____ ____ ____   5.6   Response selections are appropriate for objectives, content, and skills. (R)

____ ____ ____   5.7   Responses require application of content. (R)

____ ____ ____   5.8   An opportunity is provided to allow learners to personalize objectives or to add some of their own. (R)

____ ____ ____   5.9   A variety of instructional resources available (glossary, encyclopedia, expert files, etc.) is available. (C)

Figure 12–11. *(continued)*

Applies?   Present?   Rating?

____ ____ ____   5.10 Directions are simple and clear. (C)

____ ____ ____   5.11 Adequate time is allowed for learner response. (C)

____ ____ ____   5.12 Practice examples are sequenced from easy to difficult. (C)

____ ____ ____   5.13 Learners are given at least two chances to respond to practice items. (C)

____ ____ ____   5.14 Appropriate tangible "takeaways" are provided such as job aids, handouts, certificates, etc. (S)

____ ____ ____   5.15 The number of examples and practice exercises are appropriate for the learners. (C, S)

Applies?   Present?   Rating?

6.   **Feedback. Program characteristics to sustain motivation through feedback.**

____ ____ ____   6.1   Feedback is appropriate for learner characteristics. (A)

____ ____ ____   6.2   Feedback style varies without causing confusion. (A)

____ ____ ____   6.3   Feedback relates practice exercises to job or real-life applications when appropriate. (R)

____ ____ ____   6.4   Corrective feedback focuses on tasks and content, not on personal traits of learners. (C)

____ ____ ____   6.5   Confirming feedback is used to reinforce correct answers. (C)

____ ____ ____   6.6   Knowledge of results (KOR) is provided for drill and practice. (C)

____ ____ ____   6.7   KOR plus correct answers are provided where problem types or difficulty levels vary. (C)

____ ____ ____   6.8   KOR, correct answers, and rationale are provided for evaluative, analytical or synthesis practices. (C)

____ ____ ____   6.9   Feedback is provided as soon as possible after practice. (C, S)

____ ____ ____   6.10 Feedback for simulations show the results of learner decisions as realistically as possible. (R)

____ ____ ____   6.11 Clues are provided after wrong responses for content that is complex, or for learners for whom the content is difficult. (C)

____ ____ ____   6.12 Appropriate review and/or new study is recommended or required for remediation. (C)

(continued)

Applies?   Present?   Rating?

____   ____   ___   6.13 Level of feedback (KOR, correct answers, rationale, remediation) is
appropriate for objectives and content. (C)

REFERENCE

For information on the ARCS model and its application to software design, see Keller, J. M. & Suzuki, K. (1988). Use of the ARCS motivation model in courseware design. In Jonassen, D.H. (Ed), *Instructional designs for microcomputer courseware*. Hillsdale N.J: Lawrence Erlbaum Associates.

Figure 12–11. *(continued)*

Both the Echo LC and the Echo PC are stand-alone devices. This means that teachers simply plug them into a particular port on the computer. The Echo II and the Echo PC II consist of boards that are installed inside the computer. Obviously the stand-alone versions are easier to install, but with good instructions, teachers have installed both types. In either case, there will also be an external speaker and a jack for headphones.

SPEECH RECOGNITION SYSTEMS

Method: Speech Recognition Systems

Author: R. Lewis

Source: Lewis, R. (1993). *Special education technology: Classroom applications*. Pacific Grove, CA., Brooks/Cole.

Description: Speech recognition systems are the opposite of speech synthesizers. The goal of speech recognition systems is for the computer to recognize continuous human speech and to act on spoken commands. Unfortunately, human speech has numerous variabilities and complexities of semantics, all of which can cause problems for speech recognition systems.

The current technology allows these systems to recognize discretely spoken words if they are separated by a pause. Therefore, the user must carefully enunciate each word or command. When commands are spoken in this manner, speech recognition systems give a 60 to 90% accuracy rate (Church & Glennen, 1992). Examples of speech recognition systems include Voice Connection's *Introvoice V, VI*, and *Micro Introvoicer* for IBM and IBM-compatible computers; Covox, Inc.'s *Voice Master* for Apple II series computers; and Dragon System's *DragonDictate* available for IBM and IBM- compatible computers. These systems may be integrated into a computer system using an interface card, special software, and a headset.

Notes: With most of the systems mentioned above, the users must train the computer to recognize their voices. This is done by repeating a particular word several times and allowing the computer to analyze it. Developing just a 100-word vocabulary may take hours. Furthermore, the computer is trained only for that particular person. An exception to this is the speech recognition system, *DragonDictate*. This system incorporates phonetic models that are used in speech recognition. By doing this, *DragonDictate* relieves the user from having to train the speech recognition system with new words. One advantage, therefore, is that the *DragonDictate* system can be used by several people.

SWITCHING SYSTEMS

Method: Switching Systems

Author: G. Church and S. Glennen

Source: Church, G., & Glennen, S. (1992). *The handbook of assistive technology*. San Diego: Singular Publishing Group.

Description: A switch is a device similar to a light switch; it is either open or closed, controlling the flow of electricity. Students with severe motor control problems can use switches to operate computers, toys, and communication devices. For example, switches may be used for game access or as a substitute keyboard. Using a switch with a computer for game access usually requires a "game I/O switch interface." This interface is a box-like device that is physically interposed between the computer and the switch. Many companies offer switch interfaces for game I/O access.

Single-, dual-, and multiple-switch access methods have been designed to be used in place of a standard keyboard. When switches are used in place of a keyboard, a keyboard emulator is required. The emulator is a software program that translates information from the switches to the computer so that the computer thinks the information is coming from a keyboard.

JOYSTICKS

Method: Joysticks

Authors: G. Church and S. Glennen

Source: Church, G., & Glennen, S. (1992). *The handbook of assistive technology*. San Diego: Singular Publishing Group.

Description: Joysticks are often used with computer games, graphing programs, and educational programs. A joystick is a stationary box with a stick that moves in two directions. Any movement of the stick results in the x,y coordinates of the position being sent to the computer. Modified joysticks are available for physically disabled students. For example, KY Enterprise has a mouth-operated joystick. Lovejoy Electronics produces a light-activated joystick emulator (to use with a penlight mounted on the student's head) for the Apple II series and IBM and IBM-compatible computers. This is a light-activated device that, as far as the computer is concerned, acts like a joystick.

TOUCH SCREEN

Method: Touch Screen

Authors: R. Lewis

Source: Lewis, R. (1993). *Special education technology: Classroom applications*. Pacific Grove, CA., Brooks/Cole.

Description: This special screen fits over the monitor screen. It allows the student to select his or her answer by touching the screen. It is an important device for students with extremely poor fine motor skills who may have difficulty typing their answers on the keyboard. The touch screen allows these students to use the computer like other students, which can improve their self-confidence. Moreover, the touch screen can be used as a beginning step in teaching students keyboard skills. The touch screen easily attaches to the monitor with velcro strips and typically is installed by the teacher.

TOUCH TABLETS

Method: Touch Tablets

Authors: G. Church and S. Glennen

Source: Church, G., & Glennen, S. (1992). *The handbook of assistive technology.* San Diego: Singular Publishing Group.

Description: Touch tablets are similar to the touch screens discussed above except that they are a flat surface that can be placed on a table, desk or in a student's lap. Touch tablets are plastic membranes that sense the position of a pointer or a finger on the surface. Touch tablets can replace a mouse or a keyboard and are produced by several companies. For example, Koala Technology has a Koala Pad for Apple II series and IBM and IBM-compatible computers. MicroTouch produces UnMouse for Macintosh series, IBM, and IBM-compatible computers. Depending on the make of the computer, special software may be required to use a touch tablet.

SCREEN MAGNIFICATION SYSTEMS

Method: Screen Magnification Systems

Author: G. Church and S. Glennen

Source: Church, G., & Glennen, S. (1992). *The handbook of assistive technology.* San Diego: Singular Publishing Group.

Description: Screen magnification systems are designed to alter output of information from the computer to a person. These systems are usually used for students with visual impairments. Depending on the system, they can magnify characters from 2 to 15 times their normal size. Screen magnification systems can be hardware (equipment that is attached to the monitor or computer), software, or a combination of the two.

The simplest and cheapest way to magnify the computer screen is by the use of a fresnel lens, which is basically an adjustable lens that can be attached to any standard computer monitor. One example of a fresnel lens is *Compu-Lenz* which is produced by AbleTech Connection for use with any computer monitor.

For some students, the fresnel lens may not give enough magnification. The next step to consider is specialized software. This type of software not only allows users to choose the amount of magnification, but also allows them to zoom and magnify part or all of the computer screen. Most of these software packages cannot be used with all computers and graphics programs. So this should be checked before purchasing a software-based magnification system. Examples of this type of software include *inLarger* by Berkeley System for Macintosh series computers and *MAGic* and *MAGic Deluxe* produced by Microsystems Software for IBM and IBM-compatible computers.

BRAILLE ACCESS SYSTEMS

Method: Braille Access Systems

Author: G. Church and S. Glennen

Source: Church, G., & Glennen, S. (1992). *The handbook of assistive technology.* San Diego: Singular Publishing Group.

Description: Braille is a system of writing for the blind that consists of characters represented by patterns of raised dots. Braille-access systems enable students with visual impairments to use computer systems. These systems include devices such as braille-style keyboards, terminals, speech synthesizers, and braille printers.

For a computer to accept braille input and produce braille output, a combination of software and hardware is needed to act as a translator between the student using braille and the computer. Because both the input and output must go through this translator, computers with braille access systems are slower than computers without these systems.

MUPPET LEARNING KEYS

Method: Muppet Learning Keys

Author: R. L. Bender

Source: Bender, R. L. & Bender W. N. (1996). *Computer-assisted instruction for students at-risk for ADHD, mild disabilities, or academic problems.* Boston: Allyn & Bacon.

Description: Muppet Learning Keys (by WINGS for Learning/Sunburst Communications) is an alternative keyboard on which keys are arranged in alphabetical order. It requires no additional hardware to install, but can be used only with software written specifically for it. Muppet Learning Keys is available for Macintosh, Apple, and IBM PS/2 computers.

INTELLIKEYS

Method: Intellikeys

Author: R. L. Bender

Description: Intellikeys, by IntelliTools, is another alternative keyboard that allows modifications for students. It was designed for young students and students with disabilities. The keyboard is basically a plastic membrane. The teacher has a choice of six overlays. Overlays are plastic covers that are placed over the membrane and dictate which locations on the membrane do specific functions. Custom overlays can be designed for specialized applications.

By sliding an overlay into the IntelliKeys keyboard, the teacher tells the device which setup to use. The keys on each overlay are specially designed to be large enough for students with physical disabilities and easily comprehended by students with learning disabilities. Furthermore, IntelliKeys has features which allow the teacher to adjust the responsiveness of the keyboard. For example, one adjustment allows the teacher to determine if multiple repeated letters will appear when a key is held down. IntelliKeys, with its large keys and colorful overlays, appeals to all students, not just students with disabilities.

Intellikeys is plugged into the keyboard port of the computer. It is available for Apple IIe computers with an IntelliKeys IIe card, Apple IIGS computers, and most Macintosh, IBM, and IBM-compatible computers. Teachers can use IntelliKeys with any software, which is a distinct advantage over Muppet Keys.

REFERENCES

Church, G., & Glennen, S. (1992). *The handbook of assistive technology.* San Diego: Singular Publishing Group.

Dailey, E. M., & Rosenberg, M. S. (1994). ADD, computers and learning: Using computers to help children with ADD become efficient learners. *Attention!, 1*(2), 8–16.

Gardner, J. E., Taber-Brown, F. M., & Wissick, C. A. (1992). Selecting age-appropriate software for adolescents and adults with developmental disabilities. *Teaching Exceptional Children, 24*(3), 60–63.

Higgins, K., & Boone, R. (1990). Hypertext computer study guides and the social studies achievement of students with learning disabilities, remedial students, and regular education students. *Journal of Learning Disabilities, 23*(9), 529–540.

Keller, J. M. (1987a). Strategies for stimulating the motivation to learn. *Performance and Instruction, 26*(8), 1–7.

Keller, J. M. (1987b). The systematic process of motivational design. *Performance and Instruction, 26*(9), 1–8.

Keller, B. H., & Keller, J. M. (1994). *Meaningful and motivating interactivity in multimedia instruction: Design and evaluation guidelines.* Presented at 11th International Conference on Technologies in Education, London, March 27, 1994.

Keyes, G. K. (1994). Motivating reluctant students: The time on computer program. *Teaching Exceptional Children, 27*(1), 20–23.

Lewis, R. B. (1993). *Special education technology: Classroom applications.* Pacific Grove, CA. Brooks/Cole.

Maddux, C. D., Johnson, D. L., & Willis, J. W. (1992). *Educational computing: Learning with tomorrow's technologies.* Boston: Allyn and Bacon.

Malouf, D. B., Jamison, P. J., Kercher, M. H., & Carlucci, C. M. (1991a). Computer software aids effective instruction. *Teaching Exceptional Children, 23*(2), 56–57.

Malouf, D. B., Jamison, P. J., Kercher, M. H., & Carlucci, C. M. (1991b). Integrating computer software into effective instruction. *Teaching Exceptional Children, 23*(3), 54–56.

Malouf, D. B., Jamison, P. J., Kercher, M. H., & Carlucci, C. M. (1991c). Integrating computer software into effective instruction (part 2). *Teaching Exceptional Children, 23*(4), 57–60.

Perry, M., & Garber, M. (1993). Technology helps parents teach their children with developmental delays. *Teaching Exceptional Children, 25*(2), 8–11.

Raskind, M. (1993). Assistive technology and adults with learning disabilities: A blueprint for exploration and advancement. *Learning Disabilities Quarterly, 16,* 185–196.

van Daal, V. H. P., & van der Leij, A. (1992). Computer based reading and spelling practice for children with learning disabilities. *Journal of Learning Disabilities, 25,* 186–195.

Vockell, E. L., & Mihail, T. (1993). Principles behind computerized instruction for students with exceptionalities. *Teaching Exceptional Children, 25*(3), 30–43.

APPENDIX

12-A

SOFTWARE SOURCES

Aquarius Instructional
P.O. Box 128
Indian Rocks Beach, FL 34635
813-595–7890

Edmark Educational Print and Software Catalog
P.O. Box 3218
Redmond, WA 98073-3218
800-362–2890

IntelliTools
5221 Central Ave.
Suite 205
Richmond, CA 94804
800-899–6687

MECC Educational Software
6160 Summit Drive North
Minneapolis, Minnesota 55430-4003
800-685–MECC

Special Times
Cambridge Development Laboratory, Inc.
86 West Street
Waltham, MA. 02154
800-637–0047

Sunburst Communications
101 Castleton Street
P.O. Box 100
Pleasantville, NY 10570-0100
800-321–7511

The Learning Company
6493 Kaiser Drive
Fremont, CA 94555
800-852–2255

CHAPTER

13

Seminal Methods

Carol Weller, Ed.D.

CONTENTS

▶ Psychopathology and Education
of the Brain-Injured Child   **272**
▶ TALK   **276**
▶ ITPA Remediation   **277**
▶ Clinical Teaching   **280**
▶ Perceptual-Motor Match   **286**
▶ Developmental Visual Perception   **288**

▶ Method for Brain-Injured and
Hyperactive Children   **289**
▶ Neurological Organization   **292**
▶ Precision Teaching   **294**
▶ Instrumental Enrichment   **295**
▶ Orton and Gillingham: Reading   **298**

Seminal methods are methods that serve as foundations for developing other methods, have stood the test of time, or exist today with few changes throughout their history. Two analogies aptly describe seminal methods. The first is Latin. Although Latin is a dead language in that it is no longer written nor spoken by a culture, its grammar forms the basis of many Romance languages including English. Like Latin, seminal methods form the roots from which new methods can be generated. The second analogy is reminiscent of the phoenix. To paraphrase a quotation from Lester Mann (1979), "Methods have always made the phoenix look like a bedraggled sparrow. You cannot kill them. They simply bide their time in exile after being dislodged by one of history's periodic attacks upon them and then return, wearing disguises or carrying new noms de plume, as it were, but consisting of the same old ideas, doing business much in the same old way" (p. 539).

Bender (1992) postulated that most training approaches associated with seminal methods were futile efforts that lacked conclusive research support. He listed Frostig's Visual Perception Training program, Doman and Delacato's Neurological Organization approach, Getman's method for Readiness, Kirk and Kirk's psycholinguistic methods, Barsch's Movigenic Curriculum, Kephart's perceptual-motor approaches, and Cratty's Motor Skills approach as examples of these methods. Being somewhat gentler, Lovitt (1989) termed seminal methods as historical. His list included methods such as Strauss and Lehtinen's training programs for brain-injured, Fernald's approach to synthetic phonetic reading, Kephart's techniques for perceptual-motor match, Cruickshank's use of stimulus reduction, and Orton and Gillingham's procedures for teaching lateral dominance and reading. Lovitt also listed Kirk and Kirk's psycholinguistic methods; Minskoff, Wiseman, and Minskoff's ITPA materials to alter psycholinguistic components; Haring's behavioral techniques; Lindsley's precision teaching; Becker, Engelmann, and Carnine's methods for direct instruction; Meichenbaum's cognitive behavior modification; and Myklebust and Johnson's strategies for teaching auditory language, reading, written language, arithmetic, and nonverbal language methods as historical.

For purposes of this chapter, both unsubstantiated and historical methods are considered classic seminal methods. Methods will be drawn from the domains of instruction, language, visual, motor, behavior, and neurological. In addition, one seminal method for teaching cognitive processing will be included. Some methods, considered seminal or historical by many, are included in other chapters of this book because aspects of these early methods are still in use today (e.g., Direct Instruction and Slingerland methods).

PSYCHOPATHOLOGY AND EDUCATION OF THE BRAIN-INJURED CHILD

Method: Psychopathology and Education of the Brain-Injured Child

Authors: Alfred Strauss and Laura Lehtinen

Source: Strauss, A. A., & Lehtinen, L. E. (1947). *Psychopathology and education of the brain-injured child*. New York: Grune and Stratton. Reprinted and revised as Strauss, A. A., Lehtinen, L. E., and Kephart, N. (1989). *Psychopathology and education of the brain-injured child*. Austin, TX: Pro-Ed.

Description: The method is based on the premise that students who have sustained injury to or infection of the brain before, during, or after birth will exhibit behaviors that inhibit a normal learning process. These behaviors—hyperactivity, distractbility, short attention span, cognitive (learning) disorders, and perceptual disorders—seriously limit a student's ability to acquire knowledge in a typical manner. From the premise that reduction of environmental stimuli can alter learning and attention, methods for teaching reading, mathematics, and handwriting emerged.

According to the authors, all students who meet biological, medical, or behavioral criteria for brain damage require reduced stimuli learning environments. Classrooms, instructional materials, and instructional methods are modified to restrict extraneous stimuli and heighten relevant ones. Teachers reduce the stimuli produced by dress, such as avoiding bracelets, earrings, and dangling necklaces. The classroom houses a minimum of pictures, bulletin boards, murals, and other visually stimulating materials. Classrooms are located away from the distractions of playgrounds and windows are covered across the lower quarter with paint or paper. Students are provided with individual work cubicles that face a blank wall. They work in this space, which can be enclosed if necessary, until gradual reentry into group work is possible. Extraneous stimuli are reduced in instructional materials. Borders and pictures are cut away to expose only essential information. A "window" (a piece of cardboard with a slit) is moved down a page one line at a time to reduce distractions during reading.

While some stimuli are reduced, others are heightened. Letters or words being learned are highlighted by color, and teachers' instructions are given in clear audible tones. Large motor activities are provided to release tension and small motor activities are used to channel appropriate responding.

Reading. Reading readiness is promoted through various activities. Classrooms and instructional materials are carefully organized and free from unnecessary distractions. Language development is emphasized if a deficiency is evident. Perceptual activities are part of the readiness instruction. Such things as visual discrimination of forms, spatial relations, figure ground, and integration of parts into a whole configuration are incorporated into the activities.

Cues or prompts are used as needed to aid in the learning process.

Auditory skills are promoted through oral activities that focus on sounds and sound discrimination of letters in isolation and in words. Students then move to selecting pictures that represent various beginning sounds. Blending is taught and reinforced in a similar manner. After auditory discrimination is established, the visual symbols of the sounds are introduced. Short vowels are assigned a color to aid in building associations of letter name, sound, and color.

After learning letter forms, students receive a set of alphabet cards that are used in various activities such as building words from a model. Handwriting is incorporated into these activities as soon as possible.

Reading is taught as an analytical process emphasizing word accuracy. Word study stresses analysis of the visual and auditory components of words. Words are copied, built from letter cards, written on the chalkboard, and practiced in many other ways to draw attention to the attributes of words. After about a dozen words are learned, appropriate book reading is introduced and comprehension checks begin. Students are encouraged to subvocalize as they read, but silent reading is not emphasized until oral reading is fluent and the rate equals that of their speech. Students write words and sentences that are being learned and also dictate short stories to the teacher which are typed and read back to them. Teaching aids such as book markers or fingers are used to help students track their reading.

Writing. Writing readiness is aimed at developing visual-motor abilities. Activities begin with tracing lines and geometric forms placed in various positions and drawn in assorted colors. The purpose of this variety is to increase attending behavior. The next step is copying the lines and forms onto paper. Body movements that copy the pattern and writing in clay are encouraged. The authors believe that clay furnishes the resistance that develops motor-kinesthetic ability.

Teaching cursive writing was thought to be too difficult for this population. With cursive writing, students are more apt to see words as a unified whole rather than a string of letters. Although cursive writing results in better spacing between words, manuscript writing improves discrimination between letters. Formal writing begins with learning letters in isolation. The first letter taught is *m* because it requires abductor movements. Letters that require adductor movements, inward and across the body are taught next. These letters *i, u, w, t,* and *s* are followed by *e* and *l*. Letters that require both abductor and adductor movements are taught next (*a, o, d, c,* and *g*). The remaining letters are taught according to individual needs. Wide spaced writing paper, large beginner pencils, and sometimes pencil grasps are used.

If necessary, motor re-education is provided for students with coordination and spatial relation problems. Cues such as outlining the writing space with colored or heavy black lines are suggested. These cues are faded until the student is able to write without them.

As students write a letter, they repeat its phonetic equivalent. They first learn the short vowel sounds for *a* and *o* and then long vowel sounds for *i, o,* and *u* to avoid confusion of the five short vowel sounds. When students can copy a group of letters, they are taught to combine two letters. They are not allowed to prolong the copying process to the exclusion of learning to write letters from memory. A set of cards with the letters correctly formed on wide lines is provided. Students look at a letter, turns the card over, and write it from memory, check for errors, and proceed to the next card. Eventually cards with two and three letter combinations are introduced.

Mathematics. The method also focuses on acquisition of number concepts. The goal is to develop a scheme of visual-spatial organization emphasizing the whole-part relationship. Number concepts evolve as a result of the inherent organizational ability of a student. Differentiation and organization occur continuously. Visual-spatial relationships develop as students move from the concrete to the abstract level.

According to the authors, arithmetic is based on two assumptions. First, some students do not spontaneously develop an understanding of number concepts. Second, visual-spatial organization is one skill underlying the ability to calculate. If this scheme is dysfunctioning, problems in mathematics will result. Although visual perception dysfunction is not the only factor that affects mathematics performance, it is the most difficult to overcome.

Before number concepts are introduced, students must have appropriate readiness skills. Readiness is promoted in a systematic fashion, closely directed by a teacher using an uncluttered, simplified approach. This is particularly important for highly distractible or hyperactive students. Environments that are minimally distracting, tasks that are at a level designed for success, materials that are devoid of clutter, and appealing devices such as pictures and color without purpose are avoided.

Before students count objects, they develop number awareness. Groups of 2, 3, or 4 objects are viewed as gestalts. A configuration is seen as "lots" or "many." Thus a quantitative concept is emerging prior to counting. Once students learn to count, number awareness becomes more precise. Numbers, names, and their sequence are learned so students begin to conceptualize units within the group as well as the group as a whole. Later students are taught to see subgroups within groups. As organizational capacity improves, students discern that a group has a defined number of units without counting.

1. *Counting.* Number names are learned in relationship to the quantity they represent. Part of the discrimination process is

seeing the parts that comprise the whole. Counting dots through a slotted card, counting objects that must be manipulated, and touching objects as they are counted are used to prevent students from racing through the task, skipping "counters," and showing no understanding of correspondence.

2. *Grouping.* Counting is introduced in which students are required to make groups or sets (i.e., 3,4,5). To inhibit preservative behavior in which a student is unable to stop at the required number, a card with the required number of dots is provided. The task of drawing sets of objects is controlled similarly by using templates with the appropriate number of cutouts.

3. *Combining Numbers.* At this point, a student is exposed to tasks that show that groups of dots can become part of a larger group. The student is still not writing number symbols. Exercises include a task such as

$$+ \because$$

The student counts the dots and records the answer in dots. If perseveration is evident, a circle is drawn around the dots to help the student see the whole. When students can count to six and group units of six, the number symbol is taught, always working with concrete and semiconcrete forms. Tracing is used if necessary.

Recalling symbols for writing or verbally can be a difficult task for some students. One suggestion offered is that the student be provided with a cue card containing all the numbers. For children who confuse parts of numbers (e.g., the upper half of 2 and 3), the authors suggest differentiating the top half of each number by color. Other techniques are also provided for minimizing confusion and aiding in recalling numbers.

4. *Number Relationships.* Students must learn the relationship of one number to another: Is more than? Less than? Is 7 closer to 9 than to 4? The difficulty lies in the ability of the students to see objects or dots as total configurations without counting first. Many activities are suggested to teach students to identify configurations at a glance and draw or construct configurations on demand.

5. *Addition and Subtraction.* The abacus becomes the basis for preparing students for simple addition. After learning to identify the rows from 1 to 10 and their relationships to one another, students practice addition with sums below 10. To help students switch from addition to subtraction, special strategies may be needed. Devices such as a simplified slide rule in which dots on the insert can be "taken away" in a subtraction task are helpful aides. Written problems of mixed facts are presented in random order rather than in alternating rows of addition and subtraction.

6. *Further Skill Development.* Numbers up to 20 are learned, using the same procedures as learning numbers from 1 to 10. The concept of "tens" is introduced and, after mastery is achieved, addition with sums above 10 and subtraction are taught, again using the abacus. Although concrete materials continue to be used, students begin to see relationships and short cut the process. In all cases, rote memorization without understanding is unacceptable. Manipulatives and other devices are not removed until students show a firm grasp of the number concepts and relationships.

Notes: Early criticisms of the method often did not lie with the method itself, but with the lengths to which it was sometimes carried. To understand Strauss' conception of teaching in a stimulus-reduced classroom, it is necessary to place this environment in its proper time frame. At this time, Strauss and Lehtinen were working with severely brain damaged students who were highly distractible and hyperactive. Through stimulus reduction, they found some of these behaviors to be decreased. Today situations may exist in which overloaded and explosive students can profit from the method's original techniques. When the method was first written, is was designed for severely brain injured children. Later it was also recommended for minimally brain injured students (those meeting behavioral, but not neurological criteria). In the newly reprinted and revised method, these problems were solved and the method became appropriate for most students with learning and behavioral difficulties.

TALK

Method: TALK

Author: Richard Dever

Source: Dever, R. (1978). *Teaching the American language to kids: TALK*. Columbus, OH: Charles Merrill.

Description: TALK is a systematic framework of the English language that can be used with any student who requires special assistance in learning English as a first language. TALK makes the assumption that students with language disorders are no different from normal children in their developmental language sequence. This method provides teachers with a way to use current language behavior to predict the future course of linguistic development.

TALK is divided into two components. First, the method presents a plan to systematically assess linguistic development. Second, the method offers a program for teaching the English language. Assessment is conducted using one of two types of analysis: a long-procedure that transcribes every construction and function of language or a short-procedure that relies on identification of developmental sequences. The latter procedure focuses on linguistic milestones. When the approximate level of development becomes apparent, intensive observation of specific functions and constructions begins. Both long and short procedures focus on one construction or function at a time until a judgment can be made about a student's control of the element.

When the linguistic level of students is determined, the second component of TALK

is used. The method concentrates on teaching the form of the language that is spoken by most people and adapts to local usage whenever necessary. It teaches sentence patterns by developing habits through drill. After students develop the patterns, emphasis is placed on using them in life situations. A conscious attempt is made to have students use English in a grammatically correct manner, but seldom, if ever, are rules verbalized.

A description of a checklist for the short method of analysis illustrates some of the linguistic constructions presented in TALK.

1. Ability to use intransitive and transitive clauses in imperative (predicate or predicate-object), declarative (predicate-object or subject-predicate-object), and adverbial functions;

2. Ability to use equative constructions with the subject-be-complement function, transitive constructions with indirect objects, and coordinated clauses with and, so, or, but; deletion of forms in the second clause that would repeat those in the first clause;

3. Ability to move tense in questions, particularly when the question contains clauses that require the passive voice, the perfective tense, or modals and when the question calls for tense changes dictated by changes in wh-words;

4. Ability to insert clauses appropriately when the clause is used as a direct object, with gerunds, or as an adverbial modifier; when the clause beginning with a wh-word is used as a direct object, adverbial modifier, object restrictive modifier, or subject restrictive modifier; and when the clause must be in the passive voice with either get or be forms;

5. Ability to use semantic functions appropriately in one- or two-word sentences. Functions include: those found in comments, actions, greetings, or other substantive functions; relational functions such as nonexistence, rejection, cessation, or disappearance; and combination functions such as denial, location, or recurrence;

6. Ability to use functors and fillers in verb phrases that are negative contractions, accompanied by other auxiliaries, or with contracted forms of do, and in inflections for the regular past, irregular past, or regular and irregular third person singular;

7. Ability to use functors and fillers of noun phrases including those with pronoun substitutions and determiners, articles, adverbial modifiers, limiters, or inflections for the regular plural, the irregular plural, the possessive, and the comparative/superlative.

Notes: TALK is a method that is no longer in print. Teachers who choose to use it must order it through Inter-Library loan. TALK is one of the most comprehensive of all linguistic methods. No linguistic functions or constructions are omitted from the method, and lessons are presented for each. The long and short linguistic analyses are thorough and provide assessment strategies to isolate constructions that need training. The presentation of the linguistic constructions and functions taught in TALK follows a normal language development sequence. The author contends that all students learning language must utilize this sequence and that deficits in basic constructions dictate the beginning point of instruction.

ITPA REMEDIATION

Method: ITPA Remediation

Authors: Samuel Kirk and Winifred Kirk

Source: Kirk, S. A., & Kirk, W. (1974). *Psycholinguistic learning disabilities: Diagnosis and remediation.* Urbana: University of Illinois Press.

Description: The ITPA remediation methods are based on the *Illinois Test of Psycholinguistic Abilities* which was experimentally produced in 1951 by Sam Kirk, and

revised in 1968 by Kirk, McCarthy, and Kirk (1951, 1968). The method supports the contention that, when ideas and intentions are verbally or nonverbally transmitted, they must be received and interpreted to be understood. Primary to this transmission are underlying language processes critical to social and academic functioning. If these processes are not intact, a program of remediation is to be instituted as early as possible. Using these methods Kirk and Kirk purport that teachers can interrelate the reading, spelling, writing, and arithmetic disabilities of students with major process disabilities that underlie them. Once this relationship is ascertained, teachers train deficit areas through remediation.

Nine general and specific guidelines are used for remediation. Overlearning, periodic review of progress, appropriate reenforcement, and avoidance of overloading are employed.

1. Use testing to determine what students can and cannot do; use teaching to impart important skills. Recognize the difference in these procedures and keep them separate.
2. Concentrate on training deficit areas. Work on the assumption that deficits can be remediated and turned into strengths.
3. Do not ignore the areas of strength. Do not use compensatory strategies, but employ strengths to develop weak areas. Do not allow strengths to become weaknesses.
4. Use appropriate multisensory presentations. Visual, auditory, verbal, and motor modalities should be used concurrently or simultaneously. Students should read, spell, trace, and recite words to learn them. Some stimuli should be removed if overloading occurs.
5. Organize the remediation program so that prerequisite deficits are trained first. Reception abilities should be trained before expression abilities. Deficits that underlie reception, such as discrimination, should be taught before the method is begun.

6. Make use of feedback and encourage students to use feedback. Both external and internal feedback information should be monitored and remediation proceed accordingly.

7. Deficit areas should be developed in the most natural environment possible to ensure generalization to usable life situations.

8. Begin remediation as early in a student's educational career as possible. Preschool and kindergarten years are preferable.

9. Individualize instruction to the specific strengths and deficits of students. Group for instruction only if student needs are alike. Otherwise one-to-one tutoring is necessary.

The ITPA is composed of two psycholinguistic components called levels: representational and automatic. The representation level is composed of language processes that involve complex symbolic concepts such as understanding (reception), interpreting (association), and manipulation of meaningful symbols (expression). The representational level includes semantics, abstraction, problem solving, categorization, ideation, and reasoning. The automatic level involves less voluntary, habituated language processes. These processes include the ability to use closure, rote or short-term memory, phonemes, and perceptual speed. These abilities are identified as nonsemantic or nonmeaningful processes which require little conceptual ability or mediation analysis.

In both the representational level and the automatic level, there are several subsets of processes. The representational level involves reception, association, and expression in both the visual-motor channel (pictures, words, objects or signs) and auditory-verbal channel (symbols and morphemes). Organization and association of information are addressed, and students are required to express themselves through either vocalization (auditory output mode) or movement (visual output mode). The automatic level includes closure and sequential short-term memory. Auditory-verbal and visual-motor channels are remediated. Activities include: (a) grammatic closure (ability to use spoken grammar proficiently); (b) auditory closure (ability to recognize and say a word when only parts are heard); (c) sound blending (ability to verbally combine two or more discrete phonemes into a morpheme); and (d) visual closure (ability to motorically identify common objects from incomplete presentations). Two sequential memory skills, visual sequential memory and auditory sequential memory, address the ability to recall a sequence of stimuli and to reproduce them in the same order they were presented.

Illustrative Activities. Ranging in application from preschool to high-school students, the following activities illustrate the method:

1. *Auditory Reception.* Auditory discrimination activities are used for teaching and understanding spoken messages. Students listen to voices and identify emotions such as anger or surprise from the tone of voice. Teachers ask students questions about a story that has been read to them. Speech sounds and understanding of single words are taught by providing motivation for listening. Guessing games, deliberate misstatements (e.g., dogs fly), finishing a story, listening for pitch and tones in music, and reading many stories geared to the student's interests are suggested. Students attach meaning to words by learning all parts of speech. Demonstrations, categorizing words, overlearning, and meaningful speech are taught in lessons. Teachers model and reinforce conversational speech that is commensurate with the level of strength or deficit. They use a moderate pace of speech, emphasize important words, use an appropriate sentence length, and present simple sentence structures.

2. *Visual Perception.* Pictures, objects, and games develop visual perception. Activities included facial-feature matching games, animal picture matching, lotto games, card sorting games, picture and shape puzzles, object sorting, button sorting, copying

beaded designs, duplication of patterns, table setting, object-to-picture matching, and sightseeing trips. The concepts of shape, color, number, position, size, and name are taught through games. Matching geometric shapes to like shapes (cracker shape to napkin shape), "open and shut" pictures (doors open and doors shut), singular and plural form sorts (one of something vs. two of something), and large and small sorts (putting all small things and all large things together to form groups) are suggested. Awareness of action is promoted by keeping folders of simple action pictures and facial expressions, detecting absurdities in pictures, identifying body parts, following directions from visual cues, and playing pantomime games. Action songs, finger plays, acting out simple rhymes and stories, and playing simple imitative movement games are also suggested. For older students teachers use film strips, science experiments, graphs, maps, building plans, and objects and events in nature. Students match states to capitals, play word-matching games, use arithmetic flash cards, find smaller words in large words, and work jigsaw puzzles of maps and pictures.

3. *Auditory Association.* Students listen to two words such as *apple* and *orange* or *hot* and *cold*, and tell how they are the different, alike, or opposite. They group words such as *cow*, *horse*, *barn*, and *tractor*. They identify absurdity in sentences such as "It was sunny yesterday, so I played in the rain." Guessing games and graphic representations lead to association of verbal concepts. Teachers emphasize differences and similarities liberally in lesson presentations and talk through logical situations asking questions related to outcomes of events, stories, and behaviors.

4. *Visual Association.* Students categorize pictures of clothing, items of furniture, pictures of objects in a store and various types of stores, pictures of animals and their habitats, and uses of objects. They classify groups of pictures related to a given subject (hunting, fishing, racing, etc.) and word

cards or number cards into related piles (all the numbers which when added total under ten). They sort hand tools needed to build a table, use measurement tasks and jigsaw puzzles, arrange coins by size or value, arrange books on a shelf from tallest to shortest, place historical events in chronological order, use crossword puzzles, and play commercial card games.

5. *Verbal Expression.* For verbal expression students imitate single words and sentences, define words that are geared to their level of vocabulary, and vocally express ideas at length without prompting. Teachers train articulation skills by using a mirror for students to watch the movements of the body when speaking. They teach sounds by making liberal use of auditory and tactile cues, use cuing for word retrieval ("This is a dr ." [dress]), and use pictures to represent words and stimulate recall. Students engage in imaginary telephone conversations, tape recordings, impersonation of other students, dramatizations, puppetry, and songs. Adequate opportunities for practice and listening are provided.

6. *Manual Expression.* Pantomimes, (e.g., what can be done in school? at home? on a trip?); finger plays; manipulation of blocks, dowels, cans, cylinders, and lock boards; dramatic play; and familiar stories and nursery rhymes are taught. Music time includes movement and action songs, guessing songs, and movement to music. Students perform charades of action (driving a car, riding a bicycle, playing a sport, putting on makeup), illustrate parts of stories, complete squiggles to make puzzles, draw faces from ovals, and model with clay. They tell stories with gestures and devise skits related to objects (a pencil for a skit about secretaries; a piece of chalk for a skit about teachers). Students also portray famous persons by pantomiming their inventions and sing action songs.

7. *Auditory Sequential Memory.* For auditory sequential memory students memorize finger plays, poems, and songs. They recite nursery rhymes, repeat dramatic gestures, and imitate finger tapping. They play following direction games that gradually increase in number of directions and complexity, group elements of sequences into clusters, and use motor responses (pushing a buzzer) to identify the clusters. Teachers make sequences as meaningful as possible (phone numbers and meaningful phrases), teach syllable counting in words, and meaningful elements in sequences (meet and meat).

8. *Visual Sequential Memory.* To enhance visual sequencing and memory, students reproduce patterns (necklaces that duplicate a model; paper chains), arrange calendars, recreate simple scenes, make toothpick pictures, design art projects from pipe cleaner sequences, fit shapes to a pattern, and use flannel board patterns to tell a story. They play memory games that have visual cues such as packing a suitcase with all the items necessary for a trip, repeat action sequences after hearing several directions, and find missing parts of a sequential pattern. Students write words to be recalled, organize visual information into clusters, and review assignments on a daily basis. Story pictures, sequence designs, tracing, completing shapes, and arranging object and pattern in logical order are also used. Teachers ask students to observe a number of letters, words, or sentences in a certain order or pattern, then reproduce the order. Students arrange pictures in a series, follow mazes, play anagrams games, arrange colors to make a rainbow, and fill in omitted words to make a story complete. Students make daily class schedules, maps of the school, and floor plans.

9. *Grammatic Closure.* Teachers employ imitation of grammatically correct sentences to teach closure. Lessons include plurals, negatives, pronouns, tenses, possessives, commands, questions, comparisons, advanced sentence structures, and embedded sentences. Using rehearsal, teachers have students think, say, and think a word again before answering questions. Choral responses from the group are added for ad-

ditional reinforcement. Intensive verbal practice for words needed in environmental situations is provided.

10. *Visual Closure.* Puzzles are used to identify the whole of a visual stimulus by looking at component parts. Teachers provide shape puzzles, domino halves, split animal puzzles (where the top of an animal is matched to the bottom), and dot to dot puzzles. They teach identification of necessary parts through hidden pictures, incomplete pictures, and rapid recognition of functional words (stop or danger). Tachistoscope presentations, quick presentations of words on flash cards, charts and graphs from social studies and math texts, maps (especially those of space and astronomy), and worksheets of incomplete words are used. Words from areas of interest or from spelling and reading lists are included.

Notes: Despite the fact that some researchers have considered the ITPA method controversial, because the Illinois Test of Psycholinguistic Abilities lacks validity, the method itself offers many important activities for teaching written and spoken language. The method was one of the earliest attempts in special education to address and teach the processes of language. It was developed for students between the ages of 2 and 10 having language difficulties related to linguistics, reading, spelling, or writing. The processes of discrimination, association, sequencing, categorization, closure, figure-ground, reauditorization, revisualization, and memory addressed by the method are critical abilities that all students must possess during their early schooling. Emphases on multisensory presentations of material, use of feedback in teaching, development of abilities in natural environments, and individualization of instruction are strengths of this method.

CLINICAL TEACHING

Method: Clinical Teaching

Authors: Doris Johnson and Helmer Myklebust

Source: Johnson, D. J., & Myklebust, H. R. (1967). *Learning disabilities: Educational principles and practices.* New York: Grune and Stratton.

Description: Clinical Teaching is a concept of remediation that considers multidimensional interventions to ameliorate learning difficulties. The method is guided by fundamental assumptions involving integration (strengths), deficits (weaknesses), tolerance levels, readiness, and sensory modalities. By identifying and teaching the behaviors associated with these assumptions, teachers develop integration of student learning. Clinical Teaching does not assume that the same teaching methods can be applied to every student, but suggests specific strategies for students with disorders of auditory language, reading, written expression, spelling, handwriting, arithmetic, and nonverbal skills.

The intervention strategies for each of these disorders rest on the assumption that there are strata of central nervous system function which must be recognized and trained. Perception, a gross primitive form of discrimination, is the first of these strata. At this level, students show difficulties in distinguishing one form from another. If this level is impaired, difficulties in higher levels will occur. The second stratum, imagery, is the relationship of information that has already been received to information that is currently being received. Imagery is the focal point of memory and must be present for new learning to become meaningful in light of past experiences. Imagery leads to the third stratum of experience, symbolization. Symbolization consists of verbal and nonverbal abilities that represent experience. Words, numbers, and letters are symbols that stand for thoughts and ideas. The understanding and use of symbols is necessary for oral and written communication. Symbolization leads to the highest stratum—conceptualization. Conceptualization is the ability to abstract and recognize relationships among experiences. Cause and effect, behavioral consequences, logic, and reasoning skills are manifestations of conceptual abilities.

Basic to these strata is a medical or psychoneurological consideration. If there are neurological dysfunctions, sensory disorders (hearing or sight), or problems of physical causation, remediation of problems must be guided by these factors. The following twelve principles of teaching, articulate the interaction of these factors with levels of central nervous system function.

1. Individualize to the experiential and learning deficits.
2. Teach to the level of experience (perception, imagery, symbolization, conceptualization).
3. Teach to the disorder (nonsocial-nonverbal, social-nonverbal, verbal).
4. Teach to readiness of strength and deficit patterns.
5. Teach input before output.
6. Teach to the tolerance level while avoiding overloading.
7. Use multisensory input to stimulate the central nervous system.
8. Teach to the deficits to remediate them.
9. Teach to the strengths to keep them strong.
10. Avoid teaching perception unless a deficit is clearly evident.
11. Control attention, distractibility, hyperactivity, rate of learning, and size of task.
12. Teach to the interaction of verbal and nonverbal tasks (e.g., visual and linguistic components of reading).

Auditory Language. The method describes remediation strategies for two types of auditory language disorders: receptive and expressive. Receptive language is the input ability a student possesses which underlies expressive ability. Expressive language is the output of information in response to stimuli that have been received and integrated. Before remediating expression, teachers must ascertain if reception is intact. If the problem is only expressive, teaching is begun. If the problem is receptive language affecting expression, reception and expression activities are meshed.

Receptive Language. Educational procedures for training receptive abilities include the following:

1. Input precedes output and students who lack early training will be farther behind than those who receive training in the early years.

2. Teach meaning units and key concepts first. Instead of teaching complex sentence patterns, use single words and phrases as teaching stimuli. Reduce the length of commands and cues to aid association of words to meanings.

3. Use simultaneity when teaching language. Time the presentation of spoken words and experiences to gain recognition and association.

4. Repeat concepts of language until learning and retention of key concepts is achieved.

5. Select vocabulary in keeping with student experience. Colloquial and geographically specific words, nonsense syllables, and words that sound similar should be avoided. Be sure students understand the concept of vocabulary words, explain multiple meanings, and semantic concepts.

6. Teach parts of speech sequentially. Teach nouns in the following order: (a) concrete nouns that name an object; (b) concrete nouns that name body parts; (c) concrete nouns that can only be named in miniature; (d) concrete nouns that can only be shown in pictures; (e) abstract nouns of group names; and (f) abstract nouns that denote value. Teach verbs in the following sequence: (a) verbs that describe simple activities that can be acted out; (b) verbs that describe actions that occur over long periods of time; (c) past tense; and (d) future tense. Teach adjectives by connecting them with nouns, using opposites, making concrete comparisons by size and shape, and denoting sensory characteristics (smell, taste, distance, space). Teach prepositions by placement position when possible. For prepositions with nonconcrete referent (of, for, etc.) model them in multiple situations.

7. Teach the significance of listening; listen to stories for the main idea, ask true-false questions, complete questions, discuss verbal absurdities, and give numerous directions orally.

8. Train memory by gradually increasing the length of material to be remembered. Use exercises with tape recorders, memory games, and songs.

Expressive Language. Educational procedures for teaching expression include the following:

1. Teach reauditorization (recall of words). Use sentences with the word to be recalled omitted; paste pictures of words to be recalled on cards for students to keep in a file; practice word associations and antonyms; present words in series; show visual cues (pictures or initial letters); rapidly name lists of familiar objects; incorporate words in a variety of sentences and meaning units; and teach auditory self-monitoring techniques.

2. Teach auditory motor integration to students who can understand and recall words, but have difficulty associating the words they wish to use with the patterns of speaking. Inventory sounds and words currently used and teach new words that are similar. Use visual and tactile/kinesthetic cues for words and concentrate on modeling and imitation of proper tongue, teeth, and lip placement when speaking.

3. Teach syntax and sentence formation to students who have difficulty with word order and grammar. Teach sentence patterns, questions, and statements with visual cues and facial expressions; emphasize important words in a sentence through vocal inflection and pitch changes; play scrambled sentence games; and tell sentence stories with words missing.

Reading and Written Expression. Two components of clinical teaching, reading and written expression, are described in detail in this text in the chapters on reading and written expression methods.

Spelling. The authors purport that spelling deficits are the result of an inability to revisualize words. Thus materials are suggested that are clear and readable. Heavy large block print, color cues, and tactile materials that maximize visual memory abilities are used. Students with attention and visual memory problems are provided verbal cues ("ready" and "next") or visual prompts (a pen light).

Several activities are suggested that allow students to work through the sequence of recognition, partial recall, and total recall. For example, recognition of correctly spelled words can be practiced using a multiple choice exercise. Partial recall can be taught using incomplete words such as *laugh*, l_ugh, l__gh, lau__, and so on. Total recall can be taught using activities that require writing a word from memory. Students with severe spelling disorders may need alphabet charts and key-word lists of their own to complete classroom assignments.

Handwriting. Handwriting begins with teaching prewriting skills. Students are taught correct pencil grasp using large size pencils, crayons, or felt tip pens with grips if needed. If good auditory ability is present, learners verbalize the teacher's instructions for holding a pencil properly. If auditory skills are weak, but kinesthetic ability is good, students close their eyes and the teacher guides their hand movements.

Paper position is also taught with special attention given to the slant of the paper for left-handed writers. For hyperactive students, papers are anchored to the desk top. Posture is taught and appropriate desks and chairs are provided for each student. Chalkboards are positioned so that students can maintain good writing posture while using them.

Before teaching handwriting, an assessment of each student is necessary to determine discrimination abilities between letters, a prerequisite skill for copying that must be taught if it is lacking. Students are asked to imitate motor patterns without a verbal command and then with a verbal command. Student close their eyes and their hand movements are guided until the pattern can be reproduced unassisted. From this information, five individualized teaching procedures are used.

1. Students form visual impressions of vertical strokes and circles by watching the teacher form these patterns on a chalkboard. A pen light can be used to further illustrate the movement pattern: up, down, left, or right. For verbal learners, teachers vocalize the patterns.

2. After visual impressions have been practiced, kinesthetic movement is developed by having students close their eyes and write in the air or chalkboard with a finger. Initially, motor movements should be large to emphasis kinesthetic action. The same spatial plane is used, either vertical or horizontal. Switching between the two is not acceptable.

3. Each new pattern is introduced visually, then kinesthetically, and finally in combination. To integrate and coordinate visual and kinesthetic learning, students perform activities with their eyes closed and then opened to compare performances. In addition, students work from large motor to fine motor activities and are taught to use sequenced movements. Arrows or other cues are used as needed and repetition reinforces movement patterns. Materials such as sand, stencils, and crayons are used to provide visual feedback. Verbal cuing is used for students for whom it is appropriate. Learning is further reinforced by using templates and stencils in a variety of activities.

4. Students are now introduced to letters and numbers. Each form is introduced by describing its shape and discussing its component parts thoroughly. Directional cues are practiced until forms are written automatically. Manuscript writing is taught first. After students can read and write manuscript successfully, they learn cursive writing using the same techniques.

5. Spacing is taught by having students identify run-on words. Anagrams are used to make sentences without spaces between words and students are taught to separate words. Handwritten sentences can also be used. Once students recognize spacing problems, they are asked to write sentences. Erasure and correction procedures are also taught so that students are always working from clear models.

Nonverbal Skills. Teaching nonverbal skills employs remediatation of social perception, self-perception, and adaptive behavior disorders. The method suggests remediation procedures for understanding the social environment, gestural communication, temporal-spatial concepts, and motoric interaction. Several strategies are employed to teach these skills. Pictures are used to identify concepts of size, color, shape, and separation of foreground from background. Pictures are studied for gestalt and detail, jigsaw puzzles are completed, and dot-to-dot pictures are drawn. Action pictures are described and inferences drawn about what will happen next, what happened before, and why the action is taking place. Gestures are identified in the pictures and imitated to convey their meaning.

In addition to pictures, a student's body becomes a teaching strategy. For self-perception activities, the body is moved to the left and right, various distances through space, used to communicate through gestures, and placed into various positions and orientations. Body parts are named and moved on command. For person-perception activities, students observe their actions in a mirror, identify parts of their bodies on life-size outlines, and construct models of their bodies from clay. With peers as stimuli, they identify body parts, differentiate body sides, estimate the time it takes to perform actions, read gestures, and observe facial expressions. Students observe and imitate the adaptive skills of others practicing humor, social judgment, proxemics, tone of voice, and attending. They minimize distractibility, hyperactivity, perseveration (repetitive behaviors), and disinhibition (random internal shifts in trains of thought) by requesting reduced stimulation when needed, resting frequently, learning to control and delay responding, and removing themselves from overloading situations. Until students become adept at utilizing these behaviors, teachers intercede with instruction and modeling as needed.

Arithmetic. Johnson and Myklebust designed their method for teaching arithmetic to students with nonverbal disorders. Characteristics of the population are described in depth along with educational procedures, beginning with the development of nonverbal concepts of quantity, order, size, space, and distance. To teach these concepts, concrete materials are recommended to develop numerical thinking. Presentations through auditory rehearsal and verbal interaction are used. Seven concepts are introduced in small sequential steps and must be clearly understood to avoid rote learning.

1. *Shape and Form.* To develop quantitative reasoning, students are taught shapes and sizes, learning how they are similar and different. Materials such as puzzles, pegboards, and formboards are used. Students are introduced to two-dimensional figures because blocks, cubes, and other three-dimensional objects confuse many students.

2. *Size and Length.* For students who are unable to perceive differences in size and length, learning activities similar to those described for shape and form are used. Students are asked to arrange objects by order of their size, length, and so forth. Auditory input is used to facilitate learning.

3. *One-to-One Correspondence.* To understand the concept of numbers, students must be able to count meaningfully. Activities to teach this concept include: using a pegboard to match rows of pegs; matching activities using auditory input (e.g., the teacher taps out sounds and students lay out the given number of objects); using tactile input when the number of objects is small enough to make the tasks feasible;

running errands requesting a specific number of objects; and writing numbers above or on pictures of objects.

To complete these activities, students must be taught to count. The authors discuss the underlying factors that may be impeding the development of this skill and suggest some procedures. For example, students may be asked to close their eyes and concentrate on counting to the beat of a drum, open their eyes and repeat the activity, and then write a line on the paper for each beat. Counting objects for which a motor response is required is also suggested. Students need to understand that ordinal numbers represent positions in a sequence. Ordinal counting (first, second, third, etc.) is introduced by lining up objects and teaching the concepts of *how many* and *where*.

4. *Visual Symbols.* Students with math disorders have difficulty integrating auditory symbols with a visual representation and either or both of these with a quantity. Activities are geared to teaching integration. For example, if students do not understand that the spoken word, *"four"* is the same as the written numeral,*"4,"* they may not be able to write numerals from dictation. Materials such as large cardboard blocks numbered 1 to 10 are laid out for a walking activity and a number line is used to teach visual-auditory integration. Dot configurations of numbers and large dominoes on which the numbers are indented can be used to teach the relationship of visual symbol to quantity.

5. *Conservation of Quantity.* Concept Manipulatives are used to teach the concept of conservation. Activities using paper cut into 1- to 10-inch strips for teaching concepts of length are suggested. Grouping and regrouping of shorter length strips to equal the length of a longer strip can be used. Similar activities using Cuisinaire rods may be appropriate.

6. *Visualizing Groups.* Another problem evidenced by students with arithmetic disorders is the inability to visualize groups of objects. A tachistoscope is suggested as one

means of increasing this ability. The tachistoscope can be used to flash a configuration of dots on a screen. Students name the number of dots or circle the corresponding pattern on a worksheet. Color and size cues are used to facilitate learning.

7. *Other Activities.* The authors do not overlook the importance of understanding the language of arithmetic. Students must understand the meaning conveyed in mathematical symbols as well as terminology such as "more than" and "less than." Suggestions for teaching math symbols as well as for the alignment of numbers are included.

Students with memory dysfunction need props for retaining the sequence of mathematical operations. They are encouraged to verbalize operations. If additional help is needed, cues like dots indicating where a procedure begins, arrows to show directionality, and cards with the steps written out are suggested. Gradually the cues are faded and eventually eliminated.

Problem solving is another area that can be difficult for students. The authors recommend beginning with concrete examples and moving toward abstract concepts. Again the process is verbalized. Number sentences which are numerical interpretations of written problems are used. Activities such as these help students systematize their approach to problem solving.

Notes: Several of the assumptions of the Clinical Teaching method have shaped the thinking in the field of learning disabilities. The assumptions of strengths-weakness patterns, sensory modality input-output, and interaction of verbal-nonverbal tasks are commonly held precepts of good teaching. Critics of the method would contend that, although the strategies of clinical teaching may be sound, the premise of central nervous system involvement is unscientific, untenable, and unnecessary.

Teachers should be aware of the history of Clinical Teaching. It was based on a model of learning to describe the auditory/verbal reception and expression problems of aphasic students (i.e., severely language disordered). The model was extended to include visual, auditory, and tactile reception, as well as verbal and motor expression. The model later served as the basis for the psycholinguistic model described by Kirk, McCarthy, and Kirk (1968).

The model was used also in the development of psychoneurological models that describe subtyping for children with learning disabilities. These models led to the development of a theory that identifies both subtypes (Verbal Organizational Disorders, Nonverbal Organizational Disorders, Global Organizational Disorders, Production Deficit Disorders, and Nonspecific Learning Disorders) and severity levels (mild, mild-to-moderate, moderate, moderate-to-severe, and severe) within the population of children, youth, and adults receiving services in classes for the learning disabled (Weller, 1987; Weller, Crelly, Watteyne, and Herbert, 1992).

PERCEPTUAL-MOTOR MATCH

Method: Perceptual-Motor Match

Author: Newell Kephart

Source: Kephart, N. (1971). *The slow learner in the classroom* (2nd ed.). Columbus, OH: Charles E. Merrill.

Description: Perceptual-Motor Match provides a comprehensive program of early childhood motor and visual motor intervention. The program teaches students gross and fine motor skills and visual perceptual skills that must match them. This match was purported to enhance academic skills of reading, handwriting, spelling, and mathematics. Because the motor experiences of an infant are considered the foundations of development, the Perceptual-Motor Match is based on motor and visual responses. According to Kephart, all behavior is basically motor and develops from muscular activity. Thus, higher forms of behavior such as visual learning and academic abilities are based on lower forms of motor behavior. Kephart suggested seven motor activities and three visual activities to enhance visual-motor perception:

1. *Posture.* Posture is the basic movement pattern from which all other movements originate. For students to develop properly, posture must be flexible, controlled, and easily adjusted. Children will not be able to perform if an underlying postural pattern has not been acquired.

2. *Laterality.* Laterality is the perceptual awareness of left and right and is developed and learned from the manipulation and coordination of movement of the two sides of the body. Laterality is the basis of the spatial world and must be mastered before other spatial skills are acquired.

3. *Directionality.* When laterality has been internally mastered, concepts of left and right extend to external space use (directionality). Directionality, ocular (eye) control, and perception of the midline (imaginary line which divides the body into top and bottom, right and left, forward and backward) become coordinated for use in academic skills such as reading from left to right and writing from the top to the bottom of a page.

4. *Body Image.* Establishing one's body as a point of reference to the environment is called body image. Body image is learned from observing the movement of various body parts and understanding the relationship of various parts to others. It is a prerequisite to advanced motor patterns and academic skills.

5. *Motor Generalization.* Unintegrated patterns of posture, laterality, directionality, and body image are of little use if they do not generalize to the environment. Students are taught that: (a) balance and posture master spatial demands of the environment, (b) locomotion masters motor demands of the environment, (c) contact (exploration of objects through handling and manipulation) brings meaning to the physical environment, and (d) receipt and propulsion allow manipulation of the moving environment. With these four motor generalizations students move in an organized manner to explore environmental stimuli.

6. *Perceptual Processing.* In addition to motor generalizations, perceptual processes must be mastered. These include receiving and organizing sensory input, integration of this input with prior learned skills, the ability to scan or translate the input and motor patterns into an output response, effective use of output and feedback from the output once a response has been made, and use of long-term and rote memory to coordinate the process of learning.

Motor behaviors are taught according to verdicality and prosthesis. Verdicality is performance dependent on the laws of nature with outcomes contingent on these laws (e.g., failing to balance and falling down). Prosthesis is an artificially imposed means of problem solution (e.g., counting boards, number lines, writing with typewriters). Verdicality and prosthesis are used in lesson designs for perceptual-motor and perceptual-motor-match activities.

Perceptual motor activities use walking boards, balance boards, trampolines, and exercises to teach balance, laterality, and directionality. A walking board is a section of two-by-four approximately 8 to 12 feet in length, with the ends of the board securely held by brackets. Students walk backward, forward, and sideways on the board. A balance board is a square of wood about 16 inches by 16 inches set on a 3-inch high post. Students balance on the board, jump, and bounce balls. A trampoline is used to teach muscular control, dynamic balance, and coordination of muscular activity.

Other activities can be used in perceptual motor training. Body image is enhanced through activities such as angels-in-the-snow. Students lie on the floor on their backs with arms to the side and feet together. From this position, arms and legs are moved in specific directions.

Perceptual-motor match activities join motor movements with perceptual processes in a series of coordinated and purposeful movements. Activities for perceptual-motor matching begin with gross motor tasks of walking, running, jumping, rolling a ball, or throwing at a target. Later fine motor tasks such as hand-eye coordination, following a line with eye and hand, placing pegs or shapes in boards, scribbling, and screwing nuts on bolts are used. Next, fine motor tasks of tracing around shapes or templates are used.

Integration Activities. Several visual-perceptual training activities are used to integrate sensory information with motor information. The method suggests three visual-perceptual activities.

1. *Visualization.* Visualization tasks in which students selects familiar objects from a bag and describe or name them without looking are used. Ocular control is trained by following a moving light with the eyes, hitting or bouncing a ball, and using diacritically marked rhythm patterns in reading. Chalkboard training, scribbling, and finger painting are used to teach large, unrestricted movements, hold the wrist away from the writing surface, and make smooth and flowing movements. Directionality activities teach students to connect dots from left to right, up to down, and read clocks. In addition, these activities teach students to cross their midlines (imaginary axes of the body) without stopping or changing hands.

2. *Visual Orientation.* Visual orientation is taught by drawing circles with each hand and both hands simultaneously. Students make parallel circles, draw "lazy" (on-their-sides) eights, trace circles on the chalkboard, outline templates, trace on paper, copy, and reproduce circles from memory. Geometric shapes, letters, numbers, and words are similarly taught.

3. *Form Perception.* Form perception (differentiation of the elements of form) is taught by matching objects of like shape, color, and size. Time is devoted to symbolic matching and includes letters, numbers, and words. Matching is followed by manipulation. Form boards for fitting shapes into depressions in the board, simple puzzles, letters modeled from clay, making forms with sticks, and using the body to emulate forms are suggested. Activities use pegboards to teach form constancy, shape or line reproduction, multiple form construction, and interlocking form arrangement. Building blocks and construction sets are also used to construct forms and form designs.

4. *Figure-Ground.* Figure-ground activities such as locating objects in the room; finding pictures camouflaged by other pictures; finding different sizes, colors, textures, and attitudes in designs; and finding forms within other forms are suggested. Cutting, pasting, sorting, coloring, and drawing activities teach integration of patterns with visually processed information.

When these perceptual abilities are joined to motor movements in a meaningful manner, a "perceptual motor match" is attained; however, other perceptions are necessary to complete learning. These include form perception (connection of shapes to referents), space discrimination (estimate and use of space as referents), and time discrimination (orientation to time as referent). These skills facilitate use of letter and word shapes, spaces in handwriting and spelling tasks. time concepts, and numerical constructs.

Notes: Kephart began his work with Strauss studying the motor skills of children with brain-damage and cerebral-palsy. When Kephart became the Director of the Purdue Achievement Center for Children in West Lafayette, Indiana, he was confronted with students who had milder learning problems. Because these students had accompanying motor difficulties, Kephart hypothesized that motor and learning difficulties were related. Historically, the motor perceptual method of Kephart was a standard

from which other perceptual motor methods were derived.

DEVELOPMENTAL VISUAL PERCEPTION

Method: Developmental Visual Perception

Author: Marianne Frostig

Source: Frostig, M., and Maslow, P. (1973). *Learning problems in the classroom: Prevention and remediation.* New York: Grune and Stratton.

Description: Developmental Visual Perception is based on the premise that visual perception is involved in most actions and behaviors of individuals. Deficits in visual perception result in difficulties not only with academics, such as reading and writing, but also in social and behavioral adjustment. According to the author, maximum visual perceptual development occurs between the ages of $3\frac{1}{2}$ and $7\frac{1}{2}$ years. A lag in visual perceptual development during this time results in difficulties recognizing objects and their relationships to one another. These distortions contribute to an unstable, unpredictable environment, clumsiness, ineptness, and faulty interpretation of visual symbols such as shapes, letters, and numbers.

To identify students' degree and type of visual perceptual impairment, Frostig, Maslow, LeFever, and Whittlesey developed the Marianne Frostig *Developmental Test of Visual Perception* (1964). The test assesses five areas of visual perception: visual-motor coordination, figure-ground perception, perceptual constancy, perception of position in space, and spatial relationships.

Structured Activities. Once students have been assessed, remediation in areas of weakness is begun. Structured activities are used to strengthen visual perception abilities in each area:

1. *Visual-Motor Coordination.* Some 90 sequential worksheets, coordinating fine motor skills and visual perception, are used for coloring, tracing, and drawing straight, curved, and broken lines between boundaries. Physical exercises such as catching a bean bag, rolling and catching a hoop, cutting, pasting, and free-style drawing are also used.

2. *Figure-Ground Perception.* Figure-ground is the ability to select a central figure from background stimuli. Sorting objects of different sizes and shapes, identifying objects in the classroom and other "busy" situations, pencil and paper tasks for tracing lines and identifying figures on complex backgrounds, recognition of intersecting and hidden figures, figure completion, and assembling incomplete figures are activities used for students who are inattentive, disorganized, and unable to concentrate on critical aspects of configuration.

3. *Perceptual Constancy.* Perceptual constancy activities emphasis the unchanging properties of shape, size, and form regardless of color, texture, mode of representation, or angle. Initial exercises consist of matching and sorting objects of similar shapes and sizes but different colors and textures. Exercises are provided on worksheets for matching, discrimination, and categorizing various forms. Letter, word, and number recognition using different print types, manuscript, and cursive writing are also suggested.

4. *Perception of Spatial Relations.* Spatial relations is the ability to perceive the position of two or more objects in relationship to self and others. Exercises include placing colored blocks, pegs, and marbles in patterns and duplicating three-dimensional block designs. Worksheets provide practice in figure completion, recall of sequence, assembly of parts, and figure copying.

5. *Position in Space.* Position in space involves the relationship of an object to an observer. Perception of behind, in front, above, below, and to the side are emphasized. Exercises include games of identification and movement of body parts, location of body parts on others and dolls, assembling puzzles of people, completing partially drawn figures, and copying positions from models and pictures. Worksheets are used to develop directional skills of right, left, over, under, behind, and before. Letters such as *b* and *d*, words such as *was* and *saw*, and numbers such as *24* and *42* and *6* and *9* are included on the worksheet.

Frostig provides guidelines for the program. According to the author, activities should be based on individual needs, students should move at their own pace and not be required to complete the entire program, the program should be used individually in an informational rather than judgmental manner, and students should complete activities only after they have been modeled. Mistakes are immediately observed and corrected by teachers.

Notes: When used solely for visual perceptual training, this method has several merits. It is an appropriate choice for students with difficulties in fine motor skills, particularly those involved in tasks such as sewing, cutting, and pasting. In the early days of special education, only Frostig materials were available to many teachers. In these situations, teachers often expected the Frostig worksheets and ditto pages to accomplish total remediation of learning problems. Although the method did not accomplish total remediation, it still has merit for some young students with visual impairments and learning disabilities who experiences visual perception difficulties.

METHOD FOR BRAIN-INJURED AND HYPERACTIVE CHILDREN

Method: Method for Brain-Injured and Hyperactive Children

Author: William Cruickshank

Source: Cruickshank, W. M., Bentzen, F. A., Ratzeburg, F. H., & Tannhauser, M. T. (1961). *A teaching method for brain-injured and hyperactive children.* Syracuse, NY: Syracuse University Press.

Description: The method for Brain-Injured and Hyperactive was designed for students defined as hyperactive who manifest the following symptoms of brain-injury: (a) distractibility (inability to control attention to stimuli), (b) motor disinhibition (inability to refrain response to stimuli), (c) dissociation (inability to see objects as a whole), (d) figure-ground disturbance (inability to separate foreground from background), (e) perseveration (inability to shift from one task to another), and (f) inadequate self-concept and body image. These students are taught in an environment free of extraneous stimuli with maximum structure in schedule, program organization, teaching procedures, and instructional materials.

Stimulus-reduced classrooms consist of a series of study cubicles which are large enough to hold two persons comfortably. The cubicles are built against the walls of the classroom with dividers reaching from floor to ceiling. Dividers are insulated with sound-proof material. Headsets are used with recorders and phonographs. Lighting over the study area is incandescent (not fluorescent) to avoid flicker. The walls are painted the same pastel color as the floor, ceiling, bulletin boards, and storage areas and are unbroken by lines, tile holes, and seams. Furniture is the same color as the walls, floor, and ceiling and excessive chrome and shiny distractions such as hinges or knobs are avoided. An open uncluttered space at the center of the room is used for small group work. All materials that are not in use are kept in the desk. Worksheets, art projects, and so on are displayed in the cubicle, but only if they serve the purpose of the present lesson. Cabinets, free of clutter as well as distracting hinges and other hardware, are used to store all materials not being used for lessons.

In contrast to the bland surroundings, instruction uses one exciting stimulus at a time. Vivid colors are used to highlight material to be learned; auditory instructions are given clearly, authoritatively, and loudly through headsets. Teaching begins with fine motor and perceptual activities that engage students directly in tasks and fix their attention on the learning processes involved. Instructional materials that are free of unnecessary detail are used to enable students to focus on the task. Tasks of visual discrimination, auditory training, motor training (gross and fine), tactile discrimination, and perception of smell are taught. When students have mastered these tasks; writing, mathematics, reading, and art are introduced along with auditory and motor skills.

Handwriting. Once adequate motor and coordination skills have been gained, handwriting activities begin. Formal writing starts with letters that require movements away from the body, those seen as being developmentally easiest for students: *m, i, u, w, t, s, n, o, l;* followed by *h, k, b,* and *a.* To begin, students write large letters, at least three spaces high, with top and bottom lines drawn in contrasting colors. Letters can be shortened and colored lines faded as the student develops handwriting skills. Students write with felt-tipped pens, crayons, and pencils. For those who have great difficulties with coordination, large writing tools are suggested. In the beginning, writing letters is combined with reading activities. Several suggestions using colored dots, arrows, dot-to-dot activities, and color coding are available if a student is having difficulty producing legible handwriting.

Reading. In beginning reading, students learn to associate letter sounds with pictures. Several pictures representing an initial sound are used for practice with the teacher exaggerating the beginning consonant sound. Activities are designed to reinforce learning such as having students cut out and mount their own pictures that begin with a particular sound and write the letter form under it. Students are introduced to various shapes and forms of the letter as seen in books and magazines. The letter name is also taught, using cursive writing or printing, never manuscript.

Next, activities using a pocket chart introduce dissimilar "sound pictures" so that students can begin to discriminate letter forms and sounds. The pocket chart is also used to display letters that have been learned. All consonant sounds are introduced in the same manner. First, initial sounds are taught, then final consonant sounds.

After several consonant sounds are introduced, one vowel sound is taught so that students can begin to read words. Short vowel sounds are taught after consonant sounds because this sequence is easier for students with weak auditory perceptual skills. Vowel sounds are taught by associating them only with their letter forms; picture cues are not used (e.g., a as in apple). Two or three sounds are written on the board, each in a different colored chalk, to teach blending.

Word families are taught using picture word cards and a pocket chart. Students sound a word, phoneme by phoneme, and place the appropriate letter in the slots on the chart. Gradually the picture card is faded and students work with only the words. One vowel, which may be colored, is practiced until it has been mastered and read in many word families. During this time, students also learn to spell words orally and in written form. Sight words are taught as needed and incorporated into short sentences which the teacher helps the student read. Color words, number words, and words needed to follow simple directions are used as beginning sight words.

Language development is integrated into the method because of its importance in learning to read. Prepositions, adverbs, adjectives, and verbs are taught in action-type games to develop vocabulary and comprehension. Story reading, storytelling, and film strips are used to motivate students. Chart stories help students see the relationship between verbal and written language, provide a group activity, and offer an opportunity for students to recognize words that they have learned in context. When students have learned all of the words from a book, they then are given the book to read.

Arithmetic. Students must be introduced to the concept of arithmetic and numbers in a fashion that does not increase hyperactivity and distractibility. Thus it is necessary for teachers to develop their own manipulative materials. The first activities to which students are introduced use sets of cards of various shapes and colors. The sets are: color-pattern cards using domino patterns to represent numerals 1 through 6, each of a different color; two-color matching cards representing the six primary and secondary colors; multicolored domino cards; solid color domino cards; and black and white domino cards. Various activities of matching patterns, colors, and configurations are used to teach form and number concepts.

Additional cards are designed to introduce and teach numbers. Activities include matching exercises, recognizing the relationship between dot configurations and the numeral, and matching the two. Once students have mastered these skills, the teacher prepares a desk chart with three columns. The first column is for the numerals 1 through 6, the second is for the dot configurations, and the third remains blank for later insertion of number names. Each number continues to have appropriate color coding that has been carried throughout all the materials used in previous activities where color is indicated.

The first worksheets are activities that reinforce what the student has learned. For example, students may be asked to draw dots representing a given numeral or vice versa. Worksheets are uncluttered and have a small number of items on them to encourage completion and avoid unnecessary distractions.

Teaching one-to-one correspondence in counting uses the same color coding, dot configurations, and numerals. Several materials are used to teach this concept; pegboards, counting beads, bead boxes, and an abacus are suggested materials. When students have mastered counting with one-to-one correspondence, grouping is introduced using blocks. Blocks are assembled to represent groupings of 1 through 6. Students are taught to analyze configurations. For example, they may be shown a pattern of three blocks and asked how many more are needed to make a pattern of four. Later the plus sign (+) is introduced with the word and allowing students to compute simple problems using color-coded numbers and dots configurations.

When students have mastered addition tasks, subtraction is introduced. The numerals 7 through 10 are used and each is written in a different color. Many worksheets are provided with cues supplied as needed for the students as they move into column addition and simple story problems. After students learn to write the numerals 1 to 50, add to 10, tell time, subtract 10 through 19, add by 10s, count money, count by 5s, carry and borrow, count by 2s, multiply and divide, learn elementary measurements, the dollar sign, and the decimal point, they are able to work from an arithmetic text with teacher assistance.

Art. Art begins with visual discrimination activities that require coordination of eye and hand. Geometric forms of different colors are matched and sorted; teacher-made puzzles are assembled; stenciled geometric forms are colored; pegboard designs are reproduced; 1-inch cube blocks to duplicate designs drawn on 1-inch graph paper are assembled; pictures, letters, and numbers are sorted by similarities and differences; and geometric forms are reproduced from memory.

Auditory Skills. Auditory training activities that involve listening skills and sound discrimination are used. Students distinguish environmental sounds, count the number of times sounds are heard, identify loud and soft sounds, and follow directions presented orally. Teachers read poems and stories to students who identify rhymes and main ideas. Music (listened to, sung, and pantomimed) is employed for training memory, rhythm, and rhyme.

Motor Skills. Motor training begins when students have made sufficient adjustment to the structure of the program and achieved a degree of success. Teachers provide explicit directions for outdoor gross motor games such as kick-ball, tag, Red Rover, London Bridge, and relays. Indoors, directions are provided for calisthenics, balancing, marching, walking, tossing, and skipping activities. Fine motor activities such as folding, cutting, pasting, tapping, lacing, and tying are also taught indoors. Activities such as making holiday pictures, murals, and displays are used. Teachers direct students through each step of activities such as opening paste jars, cutting on lines, and forming designs. The exact amount of materials that are needed for a given activity are provided. Tasks for mixing color to form hues, simple wood working, and weaving are taught. These activities are enhanced by tactile games that require identification of objects by touch and texture and olfactory games that require identification of objects by smell.

Notes: Cruickshank influenced the thinking of the field of special education with this method. Whether accepted or disavowed, the method has provided mental stimulation and discussion for years. Cruickshank tended to view the method as an intervention that was appropriate for many students. A more reasoned view would be to reduce stimuli based only on individual needs. Although the method may have a positive effect on the behavior of some students subject to intense overload, for many it may only be an effective, short-term step for developing environmental coping.

NEUROLOGICAL ORGANIZATION

Method: Neurological Organization

Authors: Robert Doman, Glen Doman, and Carl Delacato.

Source: Delacato, C. H. (1966). *Neurological organization and reading.* Springfield, IL: Charles C. Turner.

Description: Neurological Organization was based on two major premises: patterning and dominance. Patterning was advocated by Temple Fay in 1948 to train movement among children with cerebral palsy. It was used only with young children between the ages of birth and 5 years and employed the theory that ontogeny recapitulates phylogeny (i.e., development of an individual repeats the principal points of the development of the species). Patterning was used by physical therapists based on a physician's prescription and was prescribed only until children began to walk. Doman, Doman, and Delacato (1966) revised Fay's intentions to include dominance and suggested that Neurological Organization be used with students of any age having learning needs. They implied that this method would be appropriate for students with learning disabilities, developmental disabilities, and sensory impairments. They also purported its usefulness for teaching children below the age of 5 to read and for promoting giftedness in the young.

Neurological Organization is sensory-motor-based and presents techniques that are intended to organize the brain and central nervous system (CNS) to remediate learning disorders. According to the authors, some million students under the age of 18 have nonprogressive or minimal brain damage that results in special learning needs. As a result of brain damage and factors such as environmental deprivation, inappropriate treatment procedures, and misdiagnosed psychosis, these students suffer their entire lives from disorders that debilitate them. With these assumptions in mind, the authors proposed a method to alleviate learning disorders through organization of the CNS; thereby increasing the neurological age of students who participated in the method.

The method involves providing information to the CNS in several different ways through multiple inputs. Outputs are patterned (movement by others of a passive body) in mobility, dominance, expression, and language. Of these, motor receives the most emphasis.

Processing information is measured by the *Developmental Profile*. This profile is a hierarchial system developed by the Institute for the Achievement of Human Potential to pretest and posttest changes in the neurological age of individuals involved in the program. At the lowest level of the profile are behaviors that are primitive to the CNS. These behaviors include reflexive movements associated with the medulla and spinal cord. Next is the pons level, which includes crawling and responses to threatening situations; then the midbrain level, which includes creeping, grasp, appreciation, and creation of meaningful sound; and lastly the cortex level, which includes functions of walking, differentiation, use of words, and identification of visual information. When this level is reached, the CNS culminates in an organized manner for academic tasks.

Doman, Doman, and Delacato (1966) purported that damage to the CNS will be indicated symptomatically by gaps in *Developmental Profile* scores. Therefore, the profile is used to dictate the beginning point for remediation. Once this point is established, five principles are used:

1. *Supply Basic Bits of Information to the CNS for Storage.* This principle involves the bombardment of all senses with stimulation. Students are stroked with different textures, presented with different intensities of colors, presented with different tones and sounds, or presented with different smells and tastes. No response is expected, but it is assumed that this principle will reawaken a sluggish or disorganized CNS.

2. *Apply Procedures to Program the Brain.* Assuming the brain has been aroused to readiness in the first step, the second step supplies information in coordinated patterns. Students' bodies are passively moved in the behaviors of higher mobility that are lacking. If students do not spontaneously creep, they are moved through the patterns of creeping. The student is bombarded with speech and auditory information; visual stimuli of written words, letters, and numbers are shown; and hemispheric dominance (sidedness) is established using several techniques. These techniques include: (a) the nondominant hand is used in gross motor skills of throwing, catching, and pointing; (b) the nondominant hand is used in fine motor skills such as picking up and manipulating objects, making circles, and drawing horizontal lines across the midline; (c) sleeping with the nondominant hand in line with the dominant eye; (d) restraining the normally dominant hand during waking hours; (e) occluding the dominant ear that is not in accordance with the dominant eye until the formerly nondominant ear becomes dominant; (f) restricting music in the environment when the dominance of the ear is left and the eye is right to prevent excessive right hemisphere use and encourage left hemisphere development; (g) using gross motor kicking exercises with the nondominant foot until it becomes the dominant one; and (h) using sleep patterns in which the knee is bent upwards toward the dominant eye. In this pattern, the dominant eye is also turned toward the dominant hand. The nondominant hand and leg are extended and the nondominant eye is occluded by the bed or pillow. No response is required, but it is assumed that the brain is being organized to carry out these behaviors at a later time.

3. *Apply Procedures That Demand an Immediate Response.* Students are asked to respond to stimuli from all sense modalities. No longer passive recipients of patterning, students use the skills of head turning and pushing with the dominant hand, moving the dominant foot, or looking with the dominant eye. Responses are simplistic and mobility is not required.

4. *Apply Procedures That Allow Response to Previous Programming.* Students are ex-

pected to respond to certain environmental stimuli with appropriate movements. These movements include mobility, grasp, release, pointing, naming, speaking, and reading words. The movements are required in the presence of stimuli that have been programmed previously and in the same manner they were programmed. Academic abilities and higher order movement skills are expected to spontaneously emerge as a result of prior patterning.

5. *Apply Procedures That Improve the Physiological Environment of the CNS.* Two procedures were purported to improve the physiological environment of the CNS. First, the student breathes into a paper bag for several seconds to rebreathe carbon dioxide. Then the bag is removed. It was assumed that the increased in-rush of oxygen replacing the carbon dioxide in the brain would be beneficial. Second, spinal taps were used to alleviate the excess pressure of cerebrospinal fluid in the brain, relieve compression in the CNS, and increase the plasticity of the brain for learning.

Notes: Of all the methods used for development, none has received more criticism or generated more controversial debate. Censured by the American Medical Association, acclaimed by parents and the popular press, the method has been the focus of heated arguments for many years. Teachers who teach students involved in Neurological Organization should be aware of these controversies. Familiarity with the method may prepare teachers to better advise and counsel parents who encounter publicity about such programs.

PRECISION TEACHING

Method: Precision Teaching

Author: Ogden R. Lindsley

Source: Lindsley, O. R. (1971). From Skinner to precision teaching: The child knows best. In J. B. Jordon & L. S. Robbins (Eds.), *Let's try doing something else kind of thing.* Arlington, VA: Council for Exceptional Children.

Description: Precision Teaching (PT) is a method of gathering and analyzing data to determine progress, regression, and maintenance of behavior. Behaviors are specified, their frequency of occurrence is counted, their upward or downward trends are analyzed to determine movement toward a desired goal, and the environments in which they operate are changed to facilitate reaching that goal. Use of this sequence provides a systematic plan for evaluation of student behavior change and the teaching environment. Through continuous measurement of a student's behavior, teachers gain consistency in scheduling, lesson planning, sequential presentation of the components of instruction methods, and criteria for changing from one method to another.

Precision teaching begins with identifying the behavior to be changed (pinpointing). The behavior must have a discrete beginning and end (movement cycle), must be observable, repeatable, and be able to be changed. Each occurrence of the behavior is counted (tallied or marked in some manner) and converted to a frequency measure. To derive this measure, the amount of time available to do the behavior is divided into the number of behaviors that occur. The frequency for each day is derived, plotted on a Precision Teaching Six-Cycle Logarithmic Chart, and analyzed.

Analysis takes place over time (days, weeks, months) on the parameters of acceleration (increase), deceleration (decrease), and maintenance. If behaviors are not changing in accordance with the desired parameter or are changing too slowly, an environmental change is initiated. Changes include modification of antecedents to behavior (stimuli, methods, teaching strategies, directions) and changes of consequences (reinforcements). The effect of these changes on the desired behavior is then analyzed.

Precision Teaching is a convenient and continuous form of data keeping and analysis designed specifically for use in public schools. Based on the principles of operant conditioning, PT can be used to measure changes in academic, linguistic, social, interpersonal, and adaptive behaviors. Students can be taught to count and chart their own behaviors, and the method can be integrated with any method of behavior management. Because it is a versatile yet precise system of measurement, Precision Teaching can compliment any teaching plan.

Notes: Lindsley used Precision Teaching strategies in creative ways. For example, being first in line or setting in a favorite set could effect behavior positively. Like Lindsley, several authors have discussed the advantages of using Precision Teaching in classroom settings. These authors include; Lovitt (1981, 1982, 1986) and Kunzelmann, Cohen, Hulten, Martin, and Mingo (1970). By applying PT practices, teachers carefully pinpoint important instructional behaviors, monitor student efforts related to those behaviors, and chart student progress on the Six-Cycle Logarithmic Chart. These procedures have been used to deal with self-management, reading, arithmetic, expressive language, and other curricular areas.

INSTRUMENTAL ENRICHMENT

Method: Instrumental Enrichment

Author: Rueven Feuerstein

Source: Feuerstein, R. (1980). *Instrumental enrichment: An intervention program for cognitive modifiability.* Baltimore: University Park Press.

Description: Instrumental Enrichment (IE) is a comprehensive method for redeveloping cognitive processes through mediated learning experiences (MLE). Teachers and students encounter stimuli and interact with them, verbalize the processes needed to monitor these interactions, and practice the logical and cognitive rules of learning what the environment has to offer.

IE is based on the premise that students possess retarded performances rather than retarded abilities. These performances are remediable given proper instruction in cognitive skills. As students understand and can verbalize what processes are, how processes are used, and why certain processes are chosen, they will be able to perform not only the basics of learning, but also the higher level skills of elaboration and application needed in a variety of learning situations.

Feuerstein described three cognitive processes necessary for learning: (a) the input phase, (b) the elaboration phase, and (c) the output phase. If deficient, these phases, singly or in combination, require mediated instruction using MLE.

Input phase problems affect the quality and quantity of information an individual gathers and include perceptions that are blurred, sweeping, impulsive, or unsystematic. Problems stem from impairments in temporal concepts; conservation of consistencies of size, shape, quantity, or distance; verbal discrimination; spatial orientation; systems of spatial reference; accurate and precise means of gathering information; or the capacity to deal with more than one source of information in an organized manner.

Elaboration phase deficits include difficulties using available information to move toward appropriate responding. Problems in this area include inadequacy in perceiving that a problem exists, inability to define the problem clearly, inability to separate relevant from nonrelevant cues, lack of or impairment in hypothetical thinking strategies, deficits of organizing planning behavior, and lack of spontaneous comparison of one stimuli to another. These problems are accentuated by a narrow mental field, episodic grasps of reality, or lack of verbal concepts in the individual's cognitive repertory.

Output problems interfere with the adequate communication of the solution to a problem. They may occur independently or when input and elaboration phases are inadequate. Specific output phase deficits include trial and error responding, impulsive or acting-out behaviors, blocking, or egocentric modes of communication. Difficulties with projection of relationships, lack of precision and accuracy in selection responses, or lack of verbal communication tools also contribute to these difficulties.

To correct cognitive problems in input, elaboration, and output, IE uses a series of "instruments" that students complete through group interaction. These instruments do not concentrate on content, but on the processes and strategies that can be learned from them. Teachers use verbal probes to elicit student thought. For example, given a configuration of dots, students are asked to describe how they may be connected. Descriptions of the type, angle, length, direction, orientation, and outcome of the lines are obtained. Once a connection is described, discussion begins about why certain dots were selected (relevance), why certain dots were ignored (irrelevance), what would have happened if a different connection had been selected (alternative), how beginning and ending points were determined (sequences), and how different persons can approach the connection differently (executive planning).

Mediated instruction of one instrument may take from one class period to several weeks with emphasis continually placed on strategies of solution rather than the solution itself. Several subgoals for modification of deficit processes and strategies are included. For each subgoal the teacher and students verbally interact about the cognitive logic required for completion.

I. *Correction of Deficient Cognitive Functions.* In this subgoal, a variety of basic input, elaborative, and output processes are attacked. Blurred perceptions are organized through activities of dot organization, figure comparison, following numerical progressions on number lines, and logic exercises. Students are asked to sequence events for the relationship of what happened first to what happened next and taught to use two or more sources of information that require the integration of temporal and spatial information. Stories about trials in which students act as jurors, listen to all evidence, and render a verdict and solution are used. Analytic perception exercises using wiring diagrams, numerical progressions, and verbal, pictorial, numerical, and symbolic cues are used.

2. *Correction of Planning Behavior.* Impulsivity in responding without thorough planning is inhibited by activities that recognize the end goal and the strategies necessary to attain that goal. Verbal temporal planning activities ("John left late. It takes 20 minutes to get where he is going. How could he have gotten there on time?") are often used. Transitive relationships ("Father is 3 three years older than mother. Mother is three times the age of Joe who is 12. How old is father?") are also taught. Activities involving numerical planning, such as composing a numerical formula and plotting it correctly on a graph, decrease impulsivity in planning.

3. *Acquisition of Vocabulary and Cognitive Habits.* Vocabulary acquisition is not the names of things found in the environment, but the names of processes and conceptual relationships necessary for cognitive learning. Precise vocabulary enables students to label the thought processes used to organize information and employ elaboration, logic, and reasoning. Through these activities, cognitive habits are produced by repetition of the basic processes needed for learning until they are automatic. Strategies are repeated in a variety of different but related tasks to avoid single-strategy perseveration, boredom, and to reinforce analytical and critical consideration skills.

4. *Production of Insight.* Insight is taught through teacher-student discussion. Dialogues include the analysis of functions necessary for proper completion of task, in-

vestigation of types of errors and the reasons for these errors, and formulation of an efficient, economic strategy for task mastery. The need for cognitive functions, strategies, and insight in life as well as academic learning situations is discussed.

5. *Creation of Task and Intrinsic Motivation.* Teachers work with students to enable the task and completion of the task to become the reinforcing agent. As tasks progress from simple to complex, students are made aware that difficult problems are being worked. Students identify themselves as solvers of problems, users of cognitive skills, and knowledgeable learners rather than passive knowledge receivers. As active participants in learning, students' self-perception, perception of others, planning strategies for self, and evaluation and organization of self-learning are enhanced and organized. Cognitive strategies and motivation become intrinsic and generalizable to other learning situations.

Notes: Instead of approaching students with inefficient learning as having static intellectual, psychological, cultural, or physiological problems, IE views them as having an unfulfilled potential. Through IE and MLE, training is provided in as many input, elaboration, and output processes as possible. Processes that require extra help are trained in the program. Maximum educational opportunity is offered. The dynamic nature of learning is emphasized. All individuals are systematically taught processing and cognitive abilities. As such, the method is appropriate for students Feuerstein calls culturally undernourished, intellectually understimulated, and psychologically blocked from learning (i.e., all individuals with disabilities).

Instrumental Enrichment was developed in Israel and is used in other countries such as Canada and the United States. Although IE and MLE are similar to methods such as the Cognitive Functional Approach by Meichenbaum (1983), they differ in terms of comprehensiveness and focus. In addition, specialized teacher training is needed before IE instruments can be purchased.

Teachers who receive the training must be committed to the philosophy, pace, and goals of the method. Teachers must repeat one lesson numerous times before students can progress to the next lesson of a given instrument. If teachers are unwilling to follow the pace of the method, maximum success cannot be attained.

ORTON AND GILLINGHAM: READING

Method: Orton and Gillingham: Reading

Author: Samuel Orton and Anna Gillingham

Sources: Orton, S. T. (1937). *Reading, writing and speech problems in children.* New York: W. W. Norton; Orton, J. L. (1966). The Orton-Gillingham Approach. In J. Money (Ed.), *The disabled reader: Education of the dyslexic child* (pp. 119–145). Baltimore: John Hopkins Press; Orton, J. L. (1976). *A guide to teaching phonics.* Cambridge, MA: Educators Publishing Services.

Description: Orton recognized developmental reading disorders and formulated principles of diagnosis and remediation as early as 1925. Anna Gillingham developed the teaching procedures based on these principles, which subsequently influenced educational methods and procedures.

Orton saw reading as a stage of language development which was preceded by spoken language and expressed through written language. He associated language with the development of a hierarchy of integrations in the nervous system. This hierarchy resulted in cerebral dominance, or unilateral control, by either one of the two hemispheres of the brain. Orton proposed that developmental reading deficits occurred when this normal process of language development was impeded.

Several characteristics that reading-delayed students typically demonstrate, such as letter transpositions and reversals, are indicators of problems in the associative process. Orton noted problems of mixed laterality in delayed readers, leading him to the conclusion that mixed dominance was disrupting the reading process. He suggested that mirror images interfere with students' abilities to build the associations necessary for learning to read.

Orton proposed two underlying principles as teaching methods for reading-disabled students. First, it should be a multisensory approach in which students use tactile and kinesthetic input simultaneously with their visual and auditory modalities. Second, students are to be taught beginning with smaller units of language that are gradually fused with larger units.

The Orton and Gillingham reading method begins by teaching letter names and sounds through visual, auditory, and kinesthetic associations which are reinforced by speaking and writing activities. Oral spelling is taught simultaneously to establish auditory to visual linkages. Sound-blending letters into words is begun after letter names and phonemes are firmly established. Nonsense words are used if students have learned the short words by sight and need additional practice. Pointing to words is allowed if directionality or sequencing problems are noted. Instruction proceeds systematically to longer sound units, more complex word patterns, and multisyllable words, phrases, and sentences. The Orton-Gillingham approach requires five lessons a week for a minimum of two years.

Notes: Orton's contributions are widely recognized in the area of developmental reading disabilities. Although other methods are more complete and easier to use, Orton contributed substantially to understanding and teaching students with reading disabilities.

Orton's work laid the foundation for many remedial methods. His principles were developed into teaching procedures, but they lacked the specificity of later methods.

REFERENCES

Bender, W. N. (1992). *Learning disabilities: Characteristics, identification, and teaching strategies.* Needham Heights, MA: Allyn & Bacon.

Doman, R., Doman, G., & Delacoto, C. H. (1966). *Neurological organization and reading.* Springfield, IL: Charles E. Thomas.

Fay, T. (1948). Neurophysical aspects of therapy in cerebral palsy. *Archives of Physical Medicine, 29,* 327–334.

Frostig, M., Maslow, P., Lefever, D. W., & Whittlesey, J. R. B. (1964). *The Marianne Frostig Development Test of Visual Perception.* Palo Alto: Consulting Psychologists Press.

Kirk, S. A., McCarthy, J. J., & Kirk, W. D. (1951). *Illinois Test of Psycholinguistic Abilities* (Experimental Ed.). Urbana: University of Illinois Press.

Kirk, S. A., McCarthy, J. J., & Kirk, W. D. (1968). *Illinois Test of Psycholinguistic Abilities* (rev. ed). Urbana: University of Illinois Press.

Kunzelmann, H. P., Cohen, M. A., Hulten, W. J., Martin, G. L., & Mingo, A. R. (1970). *Precision teaching: An initial training sequence.* Seattle: Special Child Publications.

Lovitt, T. C. (1981). Charting academic performances of mildly handicapped youngsters. In J. M. Kaufman & D. P. Hallahan (Eds.), *Handbook of special education* (pp. 270–304). Englewood Cliffs, NJ: Prentice-Hall.

Lovitt, T. C. (1982). *Because of my persistence, I've learned from children.* Columbus, OH: Merrill.

Lovitt, T. C. (1986). Oh! That is too too solid flesh will meet . . . The erosion of achievement tests. *The Pointer, 30*(2), 55–57.

Lovitt, T. C. (1989). *Introduction to learning disabilities.* Needham Heights, MA: Allyn & Bacon.

Mann, L. (1979). *On the trail of process.* New York, NY: Grune & Stratton.

Meichenbaum, D. (1983). Teaching thinking: A cognitive-functional approach. In *Interdisciplinary voices in learning disabilities and remedial education.* Austin, TX: Pro-Ed.

Weller, C. (1987). A multifaceted hierarchical theory of learning disabilities. In S. Vaughn & C. Bos (Eds), *Issues and future directions for research in learning disabilities* (pp. 113–122). San Diego: College-Hill Press.

Weller, C. Crelly, C. Watteyne. L., & Herbert, M. (1992). *Adaptive language disorders of young adults with learning disabilities.* San Diego: Singular Publishing Group.

Index

A

ABDs of reading method, 128–129
Abstract application, teaching, 120
Abstract-descriptive stage of written expression, 182
Abstract-imaginative stage of written expression. 182
Academic acceleration for gifted student, 51–53
Academic competitions for gifted students, 60
Acceleration for gifted students, 50, 51–53
    administrative, 51–52
    classroom, 52
    correspondence courses, 53
    extracurricular programs, 53
    mentorships, 52–53
Achievement-based curriculum (ABC) and project I CAN, 67
Activity-based intervention for early childhood, 25–26
Adaptation of simultaneous oral spelling, 175–176
Administrative acceleration for gifted students
    combined classes, 51–52
    concurrent enrollment, 52
    credit by examination, 52
    early entrance, 51
    skipping grade levels, 51
Adolescents with visual impairments, daily living skills for, 104
Adult topic continuance questions, use of, 10
Advance organizers, 199–200
    development of, 200
Advanced placement for gifted students, 52
Affection training for preschool children, 45–46
Alphabet Relay, 78

Alphabetic systems, 155–156
Alternative modes of reading, 107–108
Animal, Vegetable, Mineral, 77
Antecedent events, managing, 84
Applications evaluation of software
    aspects of presentation, other, 253–255
    CAI software applications evaluations, 250–253
    characteristics, 256–258
    management of student performance, 255
    types of software, 249–250
    user friendliness of, 255–256
Assistive technology
    Braille access systems, 266–267
    intellikeys, 267
    joysticks, 265
    muppet learning keys, 267
    screen magnification systems, 266
    speech recognition systems, 264–265
    speech synthesizers, 259, 264
    switching systems, 265
    touch screen, 265
    touch tablets, 266
Aquatics for individuals with disabilities, 65–66
Arithmetic
    for brain-injured child, 291
    clinical teaching of, 284
    direct instruction, 112–114
Around the World, 75
Art, teaching for brain-injured child, 292
Assertive discipline, 82
Assessment strategies for students, 213
Astronomy, 76
    Planets, 76
Attention, and listening skills, 201
Audio books, 165–166

Auditory approach to reading, 161
Auditory conceptual function, as key to reading and spelling problems, 129–130
Auditory dyslexia, 134
Auditory language method, 281–282
Auditory reception, for understanding spoken messages, 278, 279
Auditory sequential memory, 279–280
Auditory skills, for brain-injured child, 292
Autism, developmentally based instruction for child with, 40–41
Automatic writing, 184
Autonomous learner model (ALM), for gifted student, 53–54

B

Ball-stick-bird method for reading, 130–131
Basic language skills program, 131–132
Beginning reading, 149
Behavior disorders, developmentally based instruction for child with, 40–41
Behavior modification, 83–85
Behavioral interventions
    assertive discipline, 82
    behavior modification, 83–85
    bibliotherapy, 89
    biofeedback, 92–93
    contingency contracting, 85–86
    creative arts therapy, 89–90
    recreation and leisure interventions, 91–92
    self-behavior management, 87–88
    skillstreaming, 82–83
    social competence, 88–89
    token economy, 86–87
Bibliotherapy, as behavior intervention technique, 89
Biofeedback, 92–93
Blissymbolics, or semantography, 159–160
Body Alphabet, 78
Body skills
    curriculum, 73
    motor development curriculum for children, 73
Braille access systems, 266–267
Braille code for individuals who are visually impaired, 105–107
Brain-injured children
    psychopathology and education of, 272–276
    teaching method for, 289–292
Bridges from school to work model, 216–217
    follow-up activities, 217
    internship-intern matching process, 217

internships, 217
job development, 216–217
orientation and training of employers, youth and family, 216
participant eligibility, 216
Bruininks-Oseretsky Test of Motor Proficiency, 73

C

CAI, *see* Computer aided instruction
Carden method for reading, 132–133
Career portfolios, concept of, 226–227
    structure and uses of, 227
Case management, parent, 224–225
Chance and probability, as area of mathematical activity, 117
Child relationship enhancement family therapy (CREFT), 35–37
    process, 36
    training process, 36–37
Child with special needs, *see* Early childhood interventions for child with special needs
Childhood, early, *see* Early childhood
Children with visual impairments
    cognitive and communicative development in, 102–103
    daily living skills for, 104
Chisanbop method, 110–111
ChoiceMaker model, 225
    description of, 225
Classroom acceleration for gifted students
    advanced placement, 52
    continuous progress, 52
    curriculum compacting, 52
    self-paced instruction, 52
    subject-matter acceleration, 52
    telescoping, 52
Classroom
    computer methods in, *see* Computer methods in classroom
    computer proficiency in, 232–242
Client eligibility for job training, 219
Clinical teaching, 280–286
    reading, 133–134
    written expression method, 181–183
Closed circuit TV (CCTV) for people with functional vision, 107
Cloze procedure for reading, 135–136
Cognitive and communicative development in infancy and early childhood, 102–103
Color coding of software, 238–242
ColorSounds, 136
Come and Go, 78

Communicative context, teaching in, 14
Communicative development in infancy and
    early childhood, 102–103
Communicative intentions, 14
    responding to, 15
Communicative interventions with individuals
    with severe disabilities, 17
Community, 76
    Grocery Shopping, 76
Community Match Race, 75–76
Community skills, 213
Community transition team model, 220–222
    description of model, 221
    development of program standards, 221
Community vocational training program
    (CVTP), 217–219
    employment skills workshop, 218
    job site activities, 218
    recruitment, 218
    staff roles, 218–219
Competency Rating Scales, and LCCE
    inventory, 214
Complementation in writing, 190
Composition, integrated method of teaching,
    187–188
Comprehension, and listening skills, 201
Computer aided instruction (CAI), integration
    of, 242–249
    guidelines for implementation, 242–243
    integration, 244
    matching learning characteristics of students,
        244–249
Computer instructions chart, 237–238
Computer methods in classroom
    assistive technology, 259–267
    methods for teachers, 240–259
    proficiency, 232–240
Computer methods for teachers
    applications evaluation of software, 249–258
    evaluation of multimedia software, 258–259
    guidelines got implementation of CAI,
        242–244
    integration of CAI, 244
    matching learning characteristics of students
        with attributes of computer software,
        244–249
    placement of computers in the classroom,
        240–241
    scheduling of computer time, 241–242
    software selection by list, 249
Computer operator's license, 236–237
Computer proficiency in classroom
    color coding of software, 238–242

computer control of student access to
    programs, 239–240
computer instructions chart, 237–238
computer operator's license, 236–237
hunt and peck typing, 233
individual student folders, 239
notebook of computer use, 240
positions of fingers, 233–234
pseudo-keyboards, 234
touch typing, 233
using computer software to teach touch
    typing, 234–236
Computer use, teaching students basics of,
    236–238
    computer instructions chart, 237–238
    computer operator's license, 236–237
    steps to be taught, 236
Computer writing, 185–187
Computers for language instruction, 17–18
Concrete application, teaching, 120
Concrete-descriptive stage of written expression,
    182
Concrete-imaginative stage of written
    expression, 182
Concrete-representational-abstract (C-R-A)
    teaching sequence method, 120, 121
Consequences, managing, 84
Content instruction, specific, 213
Contingency contracting, 85–86
Continuous progress for gifted students, 52
Controlled materials practice, 205
Coordination procedure in writing, 190
Corrective feedback for multipass strategy, 205
Corrective spelling through morphographs,
    179–180
Correspondence, writing, 184
Correspondence courses for gifted students, 53
Correspondence training, for young children,
    44–45
Counting frames, 116
Cover-write methods, 178–179
C-R-A, *see* Concrete-representational-abstract
Creative arts therapy, to accomplish therapeutic
    goals, 89–90
    programs, list of, 90
Creative expression, 91
Cuisenaire rods, as mathematical tool, 111–112
Curriculum compacting, for gifted students, 52
Cursive handwriting, learning to use, 175

D

Daily living skills for young children and
    adolescents, 104

Data based gymnasium, 72–73
  instructional model, 73
Developmental Profile, 293
Developmental Test of Visual Perception, 288
Developmental visual perception, 288–289
  structural activities, 288–289
Developmentally based instruction for child
    with autism and other disorders of
    behavior and development, 40–41
Dialogue, writing, 184
Direct instruction
  corrective reading, 136–137
  reading, 137–138
Direct instruction, arithmetic, 112–114
Direct instruction methods for early childhood
    interventions, 24
Direct intervention techniques, utilizing, 15
Disabilities, peer-mediated interventions for
    young children with, 44
Diversity, teaching, 15–16
Division of Early Childhood (DEC) of Council
    for Exceptional Children, recommended
    practices for early intervention, 24–25
Drafting stage of writing, 191
DRAW strategy, 120
Dyslexia
  auditory, 134
  visual, 133–134

E

Early childhood interventions for child with
    special needs
  activity-based intervention, 25–26
  affection training, 45–46
  child relationship enhancement family
    therapy (CREFT), 35–37
  correspondence training, 44–45
  developmentally based instruction, 40–41
  enabling and empowering families, 34
  encouraging use of mastery behaviors in
    play, 42–43
  enhanced milieu language intervention, 39
  environmental organization, 30–31
  home service delivery paradigm, 34–35
  INREAL, 33
  interactional approach to working with
    parents and infants, 37–38
  language interaction intervention program,
    40
  literature review, 24–25
  milieu language intervention, 32–33
  Montessori method for early childhood, 28

  peer-mediated interventions for promoting
    social competence, 44
  project participation, 41–42
  self-management, 4344
  systemic approach to infant intervention,
    27–28
  systemic direct instructional methods, 28–30
  transactional intervention program (TRIP),
    38–39
  transdisciplinary play-based intervention
    (TPBI), 26–27
Easy reading, 150
Edmark reading method, 138–139
Education for All Handicapped Children Act
    (EHA), 212, 224, 225
Elaboration skills, teaching, 8–9
  model of for student, 9
  verbal elaboration, 9
Elliptical forms of conversation, accepting, 15
Embedding procedure in writing, 190
Emergent literacy, 168
Employers, orientation and training of, 216
Employment skills workshop, 218
Enabling and empowering families, 34
Encouraging use of mastery behaviors in play,
    42–43
Enhanced milieu language intervention for
    parent implementation, 39
Enrichment triad model for gifted student, 57
Environmental organization for promoting
    child development and functioning in
    classroom, 30–31
Error awareness in written expression, 182
Evaluation of multimedia software, 258–264
  MIM checklist, 260–264
Every child a winner, 68
Expansion and elaboration of child's language,
    33
Experiential education, 91
Expressive language, teaching, 282
Extinction techniques, 84
Extracurricular programs for gifted students, 53

F

Facilitative play, 2–3
  guidelines for implementing, 3
Family, orientation and training of, 216
Family support team, 164
FAST strategy, 121
Feed the Monster, 77
Fernald method, 139–140
Figure-ground activities, 288
  perception, 289

Find the Answer, 79
Fingers, positions of on keyboard, 233–234
Five step method for taking lecture notes, 206–207
Fluency in math, practicing, 121
Folders, student, 239
Free play, 8
Future problem solving program for gifted student, 60–61

G

Geography, 75–76
    Around the World, 75
    Community Match Race, 75–76
    How to Get to Africa, 75
    Let's Make Africa, 75
    Map Toss, 75
    Steal the Globe, 76
    Transportation, 76
Germs and the Toothbrush, 77–78
Gifted learners, *see* Methods for gifted
Gillingham and Stillman, approach to reading, 140–142
Glass analysis, 142–143
Grade-level material practice, 205
Grammatic closure, 280
Graphic organizer, modified, 203–204
Grid model for gifted learners, 56–57
Grocery Shopping, 76
Guidelines for implementation of CAI, 242–244

H

Halliwick method of swimming, 71
Handwriting
    for brain-injured child, 290
    clinical teaching of, 283
Handwriting, Spaulding method of, 170–171
Handwriting methods
    adaptation of simultaneous oral spelling, 175–176
    Johnson handwriting program, 174–175
    keyboarding skills, 176
    learning to use cursive handwriting, 175
    learning to use manuscript handwriting, 175
    left-handed writers' accommodations, 174
    manu-cursive, 177–178
    progressive approximation procedure, 176–177
Hearing impairments, *see* Methods for learners with hearing impairments
Hegge-Kirk-Kirk Remedial reading drills, 157–158

Herman method for reversing reading failure, 143–144
History, 77
    categories, 77
Home service delivery paradigm, 34–35
Homework, structuring, 207
Horn method, 178
How to Get to Africa, 75
Hunt and peck typing, 233
Hygiene, 77–78
    Germs and the Toothbrush, 77–78
Hygiene-related tests, 70
Hyperactive children, teaching method for, 289–292
Hypermedia for language instruction, 18–20
    analysis, 19
        client characteristic identification, 19
        instructional goal development, 19
        task analysis, 19–20
    design, 20
        evaluation instruments, 20
        instructional strategy and media selection, 20
        objectives, 20
    implementation, 20

I

I CAN achievement-based curriculum project, 67
i.t.a., *see* Individualized teaching alphabet
Illinois Test of Psycholinguistic Abilities, 277, *see also* ITPA remediation
Implementing local agreement, strategies for, 223
Incidental teaching of language, 5–6
    arranging environment, 5–6
    maintenance and generalization, 6–7
    preliminary assessment of student language skills, 5
    prompting and target response, 6
Inclass reactive language (INREAL) intervention for language-delayed and bilingual children, 33
Incomplete sentence exercises, 184
Individual education plan (IEP), 222–223
Individual student folders, 239
Individual written rehabilitation plan (IWRP), 222–223
Individualized Educational Programs (IEPs), 64
Individualized programming planning model (IPPM) for gifted student, 59
Individualized reading, 144–145

Individualized teaching of gifted in regular classroom, 54–55

Individuals with Disabilities Act (IDEA), 212, 224

Infants with visual impairments, cognitive and communicative development in, 102–103

Initial teaching alphabet (i.t.a.), 145–146

Instrumental enrichment (IE), 295–298

Integrated method of teaching composition, 187–188

Integrating writing strategy, 185

Integration of CAI, 244

Integrative education model (IEM) for gifted student, 54

Intellikeys, 233, 267

Interactional approach to working with parents and infants, 37–38

Interactive unit (IU), *see* Mathematics as communication

Interactive strategies of TRIP, 39

Interagency agreement development, vocational education model, 222–224

International baccalaureate for gifted student, 61–62

Internships, 217

Intervention steps for students with special needs, 4

Inventive spelling, 180–181

IPPM, *see* Individualized programming planning model

ITPA remediation, 277–280

IWRP, *see* Individual Written Rehabilitation Plan

J

Job development, 216–217, 220

Job site activities, 218

Job training and tryout model, 219–220

Johnson handwriting program, 174–175

Joysticks, 265

Just Enough to Know Better, 107

K

Keyboarding skills, 176

Keyboarding skills, teaching, 232–236
  hunt and peck typing, 233
  positions of fingers, 233–234
  pseudo keyboards, 234
  touch typing, 233
  using computer software to teach touch typing, 234–236

Keyboards
  position of fingers on, 233–234
  pseudo-keyboards, 234

Keyword method, 198–199
  implementation of, 199
  and memory, 198–199

Knowing versus performing, area of mathematical activity, 117

Kumon Math, 121–122

Kurzweil Reading Machine (KRM), for students with visual impairments, 107–108

L

Laboratory method for mathematics, 114–115

Language, methods of
  enhancing nonsymbolic communication with severe disabilities, 16–17
  facilitative play, 2–3
  incidental teaching of language, 5–7
  integrating microcomputers into language instruction, 17–18
  parallel talk, 10–11
  peer-mediated language intervention, 3–5
  pragmatic language, 13–16
  sociodramatic script training, 7–8
  storytelling, 11–2
  teaching elaboration skills, 8–9
  teaching figurative language, 12–13
  technology, hypermedia for language intervention, 18–20
  "wh" questions, 9–10

Language arts, 76
  Word action board or mat, 76

Language experience method of reading, 146–147

Language interaction intervention program, 40

Language proficiency, and listening skills, 201

Laubach method of reading, 147–149

LCCE, *see* Life centered career education

Learning characteristics of students, matching, 244–249

Learning multipass strategy, 205

Learning strategies, 207–209
  seven-area model, 207

Learning to use cursive handwriting, 175

Learning to use manuscript handwriting, 175

Learning to write, 160–161

Lecture notes, five-step method for taking, 206–207

Left-handed writers' accommodations, 174

Leisure interventions, 91–92

Let's Make Africa, 75

Let's read, a linguistic approach, 149–150
Letters, reading, 141
Life centered career education (LCCE), 213–214
Life skills instruction
  Cronin, 214–216
  Falvey, 212–213
Lindamood-Bell learning processes, 130
Linguistic approach to reading, 149–150
Listening, as step for taking lecture notes, 206
Listening skills, 200–202
  instruction recommendations, 201
  intervention strategies for, 201
Local agreement
  implementing, 223
  writing, 223
Local community problem solving, for gifted
  students, 61
Logical classification are of mathematical
  activity, 117

M

Making words, 181
Manu-cursive, 177–178
Manual expression, 279
Manuscript handwriting, learning to use, 175
Map Toss, 75
MAPS, *see* McGill action planning system
Marketing principles for employment of people
  with disabilities, 220
Mastery behaviors in play, encouraging use of,
  42–43
Match the Meaning, 78
Matching learning characteristics of students
  with attributes of computer software,
  244–249
Math, 78
  Come and Go, 78
  Find the Answer, 79
  Maze, 79
  Numbers, 78–79
  Red Light, 79
Math-problem solving strategy, 123–124
  eight-step approach, 123
Mathematical memory, 117
Mathematics as communication: IU, 125-126
Mathematics methods
  Chisanbop, 110-111
  Cuisenaire rods, 111-112
  direct instruction, arithmetic, 112-114
  Kumon Math, 121-122
  laboratory model, 114-115
  mathematics as communication: IU, 125-126

MATHFACT, 122-123
  math-problem solving strategy, 123–124
  Montessori arithmetic, 116
  Piagetian mathematics, 116–118
  problem-solving and conceptual math
    development, 118
  Saxon mathematics, 124
  structural arithmetic, 119–120
  strategic math series approach, 120–121
  touch math, 124–125
Mathematics readiness for brain-injured child,
  274
MATHFACT, for students with learning
    disabilities, 122–123
  ten factors of, 122
Mavis Beacon Teaches Typing, 235
Maze, 79
McGill action planning system (MAPS),
  227–228
Measurement, as area of mathematical activity,
  117
Mediated learning experiences (MLE), 295, 296
Memory, 199
  and listening skills, 201
Mentorships, for gifted students, 52–53
Methods for brain-injured and hyperactive
  children, 289–292
Methods for gifted learners
  academic acceleration, 51–53
  academic competitions, 60
  autonomous learner model (ALM), 53–54
  enrichment triad/revolving door model, 57
  future problem solving program, 60–61
  grid model designed for gifted learners,
    56–57
  integrative education model (IEM), 54
  individualized programming planning
    model, 59
  individualized teaching of gifted in regular
    classroom, 54–55
  international baccalaureate, 61–62
  multiple talent approach (MTA), 58
  Purdue secondary model (PSM), for gifted
    student, 56
  Purdue three-stage enrichment model (PEM),
    for gifted learners, 55
  talent searches, 62
  talents unlimited (TU), 58
Methods for learners with hearing impairments,
  96–101
  American Sign Language (ASL), 98–99
  auditory-verbal method, 97
  cued speech, 98

Methods for learners with hearing impairments
      (continued)
   diagnostic early intervention program, 100
   Ling speech program, 99–100
   oralism, 97
   prelinguistic communication, 96–97
   SKI*HI program, 101
   total communication, 98
Methods for learners with visual impairments,
      101–108
   alternative modes of reading, 107–108
   braille, 105–107
   cognitive and communicative development
      in infancy and early childhood, 102–103
   daily living skills for young children and
      adolescents, 104
   orientation and mobility skills, 103–104
   social competence skills for young children
      and adolescents, 104–105
Microcomputers, integrating into language
      instruction, 17–18
   embedding computerized activities within
      language program, 17
   focus of intervention, 17
   individualization, 18
   role of student and educator, 18
   software for, 18
   stimuli, responses and reinforcements, 18
   theoretical considerations, 17–18
Microelectric devices, use of in biofeedback,
      92–93
Milieu language intervention, 32–33
Modality blocking, for students with dyslexia,
      150–151
Modeling appropriate language, 33
Modified graphic organizer, 203–204
Modified self-questioning training, 202–203
Montessori method
   for early childhood, 28
   Montessori arithmetic, 116
   Montessori reading, 151–152
More easy reading, 150
Morphographs, corrective spelling through,
      179–180
Motivating interactivity in multimedia (MIM),
      checklist, 260–264
Motor activities training program (MATP), 72
Motor skill, for brain-injured child, 292
Multimedia software, evaluation of, 258–259,
      260–264
Multipass strategy, 204–205
   instructional procedure, 205
   substrategy goals, 204–205

Multiple talent approach (MTA), to teach
      thinking skills, 58
Muppet learning keys, 233, 267

N

Negative reinforcers, 84
Nemeth code, 106
Neurological impress method of unison
      reading, 152–153
Neurological organization, 292–294
New games, 68–70
   tournament, 70
Nombres en Couleurs, 111
Noncompetitive games, 91
Nondisabled peers, preparation of for language
      intervention, 4
Nonsymbolic communication in individual
      with severe disabilities, enhancing, 16–17
   communicative interventions, 17
   description of, 16–17
Nonverbal skills, clinical teaching of, 284
Notebook
   of computer use, 240
   Spaulding method of, 170–171
Number, as area of mathematical activity, 117
Numbers, 78–79
Nutrition, 77
   Animal, Vegetable, Mineral, 77
   Feed the Monster, 77
   Smiley Face Food, 77
   Vitamin Toss, 77

O

Oral language growth, 11
Oral spelling, simultaneous, 175–176
Ordered writing, 184
Organic reading, 153–154
Organizing, as step for taking lecture notes, 206
Orientation and mobility skills, 103–104
Orientation and training of employers, youth
      and family, 216
Orton and Gillingham, reading, 298–299

P

Paget's paradigm, components of, 35
Parallel talk, 10–11
   description of, 11
   to stimulate language use, 33
Paraphrasing, 184
Parent Behavior Progression, for assessment of
      parent behavior, 38

Parent case management, 224–225
  description of model, 224
Partnerships with parents and significant
    others, 213
Patterns: The Primary Braille Reading Program,
    107
Peer tutors, physical education opportunity
    program for exceptional children
    (PEOPEL), 66–67
Peer-mediated interventions for promoting
    social competence in young children with
    disabilities, 44
Peer-mediated language intervention, 3–5
  considerations, 4–5
  description of, 4–5
  intervention steps for students with special
    needs, 4
  maintenance and generalization, 4–5
  preparation of nondisabled peers, 4
  student selection criteria, 4
PEM, *see* Purdue three-stage enrichment model
Perceptual processing, 287
Perceptual-motor activities, 74–80
  astronomy, 76
  community, 76
  geography, 75–76
  history, 77
  hygiene, 77–78
  language arts, 76
  math, 78
  nutrition, 77
  reading, 78
  spelling, 79
Perceptual-motor match, 286–288
  integrating activities, 287
  visual activities to enhance perception, 286
Personalized job development, 220
Phelps sentence guide, 188–189
Physical best and individuals with disabilities,
    74
Physical education programs, *see* Special physi-
    cal education programs
  achievement-based curriculum (ABC) and
    project I CAN, 67
  aquatics for individuals with disabilities,
    65–66
  body skills, motor development curriculum
    for children, 73
  data based gymnasium, 72–73
  every child a winner, 68
  Halliwick method of swimming, 71
  new games, 68–70
  peer tutors, 66–67

perceptual-motor activities, 74–80
  physical best and individuals with
    disabilities, 74
  physical management, 67–68
  PREP, 65
  project ACTIVE, 71
  project CREOLE, 70–71
  project explore, 73–74
  project transition, 70
  Special Olympics, 72
  sports, play, and active recreation for kids
    (SPARK), 68
Physical management, 67–68
Piagetian mathematics, 116–118
  levels of intellectual development, 117
PL-142, *see* The Education for All Handicapped
    Children Act
Placement of computers in the classroom,
    240–241
Planets, 76
Planning stage of writing, 191
Play, use of to encourage mastery behaviors in
    young child, 42–43
Play Interaction Measure for assessment of
    parent-child interaction, 38
Positions of fingers, 233–234
Positive affect, role of in learning, 41
Positive and corrective feedback for multi-pass
    strategy, 205
Posttest diagnostic assessment, 120–121
Pragmatic language, 13–16
  communicative intentions, 14
  intervention guidelines and strategies, 14–16
  presupposition, 14
  social organization discourse, 14
Prereading, 149
Precision teaching (PT), 294–295
PREP Implementation and Resource Guide, 65
Preschool recreation enrichment program
    (PREP), 65
Preschool and kindergarten, 164
Pretest diagnostic assessment, 120
Prewriting stage of writing, 191
Primary reading, 138
Problem solving program to increase creative
    thinking among gifted students, 60–61
  future problem solving competition, 60–61
  local community problem solving, 61
  scenario writing competition, 61
Problem-solving and conceptual math
    development, 118
Progressive approximation procedure, 176–177
Project ACTIVE, 71

Project transition, 70
Project participation, facilitating active learner participation, 41–42
Project explore, 73–74
Project CREOLE, 70–71
Prompting, 6
Proofreading guidelines for writing, 192
Prudential FITNESSGRAM, 74
Pseudo-keyboards, 234
PSM, *see* Purdue secondary model
Psychopathology and education of brain-injured child, 272–276
Public Law 101-476, 212, 224
Public Law 94-142, 212, 224, 225
Publishing written work, 193
Punishment techniques, 84
Purdue three-stage enrichment model (PEM), for gifted learners, 55
Purdue secondary model (PSM), for gifted student, 56

Q

Quadrille paper, 116
Questioning, as step for taking lecture notes, 206

R

Reading
  Alphabet Relay, 78
  alternative modes of, 107–108
  beginning, 137
  Body Alphabet, 78
  for brain-injured child, 290
  Match the Meaning, 78
  readiness for brain-injured child, 273
  Sentence Relay, 78
  Spaulding method of, 170–171
  and written expression, clinical teaching of, 282–283
  from words to sentences, 163
Reading methods
  ABDs of reading, 128–129
  auditory conceptual function, 129–130
  ball-stick-bird, 130–131
  basic language skills program, 131–132
  Carden method, 132–133
  clinical teaching, reading, 133–134
  Cloze procedure, 135–136
  ColorSounds, 136
  direct instruction, corrective reading, 136–137
  direct instruction, reading, 137–138

Edmark reading, 138–139
  Fernald method, 139–140
  Gillingham and Stillman, reading, 140–142
  Glass analysis, 142–143
  Herman method, 143–144
  individualized reading, 144–145
  initial teaching alphabet (i.t.a.), 145–146
  language experience, 146–147
  Laubach method, 147–149
  Let's Read, a linguistic approach, 149–150
  modality blocking, 150–151
  Montessori reading, 151–152
  neurological impress, 152–153
  organic reading, 153–154
  reading recovery, 154–155
  rebus reading, 155–157
  remedial reading drills, 157–158
  repeated reading, 158–159
  semantography (blissymbolics), 159–160
  Slingerland multi-sensory approach, 160–162
  structural reading, 162–164
  success for all, 164–165
  taped books/audio books, 165–166
  Traub systematic wholistic, 166–167
  Unifon, 167
  whole language method, 167–168
  words in color, 168–170
  writing road to reading, 170–172
Reading problems, auditory conceptual function as key to, 129–130
Reading recovery, for at-risk first-grade students, 154–155
Rebus reading, 155–157
Receptive language, training for, 282
Reciprocal teaching, 197–198
  steps for effective implementation, 198
  strategies that enhance text comprehension, 197–198
Recreation and leisure interventions, 91–92
  activities, 91–92
Red Light, 79
Regularity, teaching, 15–16
Reinforcement, schedules of, 84–85
Reluctant writers, strategies for, 183–185
Remedial reading drills, 157–158
Repeated reading technique, 158–159
Representational application, 120
Responsive interaction methods for early childhood interventions, 24
Reviewing and revising, as step for taking lecture notes, 206
Revising, step-by-step, 183
Revising stage of writing, 191
Revolving door model for gifted student, 57

S

Saxon mathematics, 124
Scenario writing competition, for gifted
    students, 61
Scheduling of computer time, 241–242
School to work model, bridges from, 216–217
Screen magnification systems, 266
Scribbling, 184
Script training, 7–8
Self-behavior management, 87–88
Self-determination, 226
    description of model, 226
Self-management, for young children, 43–44
Self-management program of SPARK, 68
Self-paced instruction, for gifted students, 52
Self-questioning training, modified, 202–203
Self-talk, 11
    technique to stimulate language use, 33
Semantic mapping, as prereading strategy,
    196–197
Semantography (blissymbolics), 159–160
Seminal methods, for developing other methods
    clinical teaching, 280–286
    developmental visual perception, 288–289
    instrumental enrichment, 295–298
    ITPA remediation, 277–280
    method for brain-injured and hyper-active
        children, 289–292
    neurological organization, 292–294
    Orton and Gillingham, reading, 298–299
    perceptual-motor match, 286–288
    precision teaching, 294–295
    psychopathology and education of brain
        injured child, 272–276
    TALK, 276–277
Sentence combining, 189–191
Sentence guide, Phelps, 188–189
Sentence reading, 163
Sentence Relay, 78
Simultaneous oral spelling, adaptation of,
    175–176
Size-up pass, objective of, 204–205
Skillstreaming, 82–83
    managing antecedent events, 84
    managing consequences, 84
    schedules of reinforcement, 84–85
Slam Dunk Spelling, 79
Slingerland multi-sensory approach to
    language arts, 160–162
Smiley Face Food, 77
Social competence, 88–89
    in young children, peer-mediated
        interventions for, 44

Social competence skills for young children and
    adolescents, 104–105
Social organization discourse, 14
Social relationships, emphasis on for child with
    behavior disorders, 41
Sociodramatic script training, 7–8
    developing groups for script training, 7–8
    free play, 8
    development of script, 7
    script training, 8
    structure environment, 7
Software, color coding, 238–242
Software, use of to teach touch typing, 234–236
Software evaluation
    applications evaluation, 249–258
    assistive technology, 259
    Braille access systems, 266–267
    evaluation of multimedia software, 258–259,
        260–264
    intellikeys, 267
    joysticks, 265
    muppet learning keys, 267
    screen magnification systems, 266
    software selection by list, 249
    speech recognition systems, 264–265
    speech synthesizer, 259, 264
    switching systems, 265
    touch screen, 265
    touch tablets, 266
Software for microcomputers, 17–18
Software organization, 238–242
    color coding of, 238–239
    computer control of student access to
        programs, 239–240
    computer methods for teachers, 240
    individual student folders, 239
    notebook of computer use, 240
    placement of computers in the classroom,
        240–241
    scheduling of computer time, 241–242
Software programs for Edmark reading
    method, 139
Software selection by list, 249
Sort-out pass, purpose of, 205
Space orientation area of mathematical activity,
    117
Spatial relationships, perception of, 289
Special Olympics, 72
Special needs, child with, *see* Early childhood
    interventions for child with special needs
Special education, definition of, 64
Speech recognition systems, 264–265
Speech synthesizers, 259, 264

Spelling
    clinical teaching of, 283
    corrective, 179–180
    Slam Dunk Spelling, 79
    Spaulding method of, 170–171
    Spelling Baseball, 79
    Spelling with a Twist, 79
Spelling Baseball, 79
Spelling methods
    corrective spelling through morphograms,
        179–180
    cover-write methods, 178–179
    Horn method, 178
    inventive spelling, 180–181
    making words, 181
    syllable approach, 179
Spelling problems, auditory conceptual
        function as key to, 129–130
Spelling with a Twist, 79
Sports, play, and active recreation for kids
        (SPARK), 68
Sports Partnership program, 72
SQ3R (survey, question, read, recite, review),
        209
Staff roles in CVTP, 218–219
Steal the Globe, 76
Step-by-step revising, 183
Story mapping, 12
Story reading, 141
Storytelling, 11–12
    description of, 11–12
    story mapping, 12
Strategic math series approach, 120–121
    C-R-A, 120, 121
    seven-phase instructional sequence, 120–121
Strategies for reluctant writers, 183–185
    activities, 184
Structural arithmetic, 119–120
Structural reading, 162–164
Structure environment for sociodramatic script
        training, 7
Student access to programs, computer control
        of, 239–240
Student language skills, preliminary assessment
        of, 5
Student selection criteria for peer-mediated
        language intervention, 4
Study guides, 207
    guidelines for developing, 207
Study skills strategy instruction
    advance organizers,199–200
    five step method for taking lecture notes,
        206–207

keyword method, 198–199
learning strategies, 207–209
listening skills, 200–202
modified graphic organizer, 203–204
modified self-questioning training, 202–203
multipass, 204–205
reciprocal teaching, 197–198
semantic mapping, 196–197
SQ3R, 209
study guides, 207
Subject-matter acceleration, for gifted students,
        52
Success for all method, 164–165
Survey pass, goal of, 204
Surveying, as step for taking lecture notes, 206
Switching systems, 265
Syllabic or logographic systems, 156
Syllable approach method, 179
Systemic approach to infant intervention, 27–28
Systemic direct instructional methods, 28–30

T

Talent searches to identify high achieving junior
        high school students, 62
Talents unlimited (TU), as practical application
        of MTA in school setting, 58
TALK, 276–277
Talking Fingers, software program, 235
Tape recorded material for person who is
        visually impaired, 108
Taped books/audio books, 165–166
Target response, 6
Teacher-directed social intervention strategies,
        44
Teachers, computer methods for, *see* Computer
        methods for teachers
Teaching figurative language, 12–13
    early work, 13
    extension, 13
    practice, 13
Technology, hypermedia for language
        intervention, 18
Telescoping, for gifted students, 52
The ColorSounds Monthly, 136
The Commonest Irregular Words, 150
The Education for All Handicapped Children
        Act (PL-142), 64
    definition of physical education, 65
The Slingerland Screening Tests for Identifying
        Children with Specific Language
        Disabilities, 160
The Word Building Book, 169

Theory of Knowledge course, 61
Therapeutic use of biofeedback, 92–93
Time on computer, scheduling, 241–242
Token economy, 86–87
Touch math, 124–125
Touch screen, 265
Touch tablets, 266
Touch typing, 233
    use of software to teach, 234–236
Tracing, 184
Transactional intervention program (TRIP), 38–39
Transdisciplinary play-based intervention (TPBI), 26–27
Transition methods, from school to work
    bridges from school to work model, 216–217
    career portfolios, 226–227
    ChoiceMaker, 225
    community transition team model, 220–222
    community vocational training program, 217–219
    interagency agreement development, vocational education model, 222–224
    job development, 220
    job training and tryout model, 219–220
    life centered career education (LCCE), 213–214
    life skills instruction, 212–213, 214–216
    McGill action planning system (MAPS), 227–228
    parent case management, 224–225
    self-determination, 226
Transportation, 76
Traub systematic wholistic method, 166–167
TRIP, *see* Transactional intervention program
Turn-taking strategies of TRIP, 38
Tutors for reading, 164
Type to Learn software program, 235
Typing, hunt and peck, 233

U

Undesirable behavior, managing, 41
Unified phonics method, *see* Writing road to reading
Unifon, 167
Using computer software to teach touch typing, 234–236

V

Verbal elaboration skills, teaching, 8–9
Verbal expression, 279

Verbal monitoring and reflecting, 33
Verbal rehearsal of learning strategy, 205
Visual approach to reading, 161
Visual closure, 280
Visual Dictation 2, 169
Visual dyslexia, 133–134
Visual impairments, *see* Methods for learners with visual impairments
Visual modality blocking, for students with dyslexia, 150–151
Visual orientation, 287
Visual perception, for understanding spoken messages, 278–279
Visual sequential memory, 280
Visual symbolic systems of reading, 155
Visual-motor coordination, 289
Visualization, 287
Visualizing and verbalizing program, 130
Vitamin Toss, 77
Vocabulary and language teaching, 138
Vocabulary instruction, 196
Vocational education model, interagency agreement development, 222–224
Vocational training program, community, 217–219

W

"Wh" questions, 9–10
    adult topic continuance questions, use of, 10
    description of, 10
Whole language method, 167–168
Word action board or mat, 76
Word processing, 193–194
Words in color, 168–170
Work, *see* Transition methods, from school to work
Writer's workshop, 192–193
    process approach to writing, 193
Writers, reluctant, strategies for, 183–185
Writing, computer, 185–187
Writing fluency, 192
Writing local agreement, strategies for, 223
Writing process, 191–192
Writing readiness for brain-injured child, 273–274
Writing road to reading, 170–172
Writing strategy, integrating, 185
Written composition methods
    clinical teaching, written expression, 181–183
    computer writing, 185–187
    integrated method of teaching composition, 187–188

Written composition methods *(continued)*
    integrating writing strategy, 185
    Phelps sentence guide, 188–189
    sentence combining, 189–191
    step-by-step revising, 183
    strategies for reluctant writers, 183–185
    writer's workshop, 192–193
    writing fluency, 192
    writing process, 191–192

Written expression methods
    handwriting methods, 174–178
    spelling methods, 178–181
    written composition methods, 181–193

Y

Youth, orientation and training of, 216, *see also*
    Transition methods, from school to work